REDEFINING POLITICS

People, resources and power

REDEFINING POLITICS

People, resources and power

ADRIAN LEFTWICH

METHUEN

London and New York

First published in 1983 by
Methuen & Co. Ltd
11 New Fetter Lane, London EC4P 4EE

Published in the USA by
Methuen & Co.
in association with Methuen, Inc.
733 Third Avenue, New York, NY 10017

Printed in Great Britain
by Richard Clay & Co.
The Chaucer Press, Bungay, Suffolk

British Library Cataloguing in Publication Data

Leftwich, Adrian
Redefining politics.
1. Political sociology
I. Title
306′.2   JA76

ISBN 0-416-73590-8
ISBN 0-416-73600-9 Pbk

Library of Congress Cataloging in Publication Data

Leftwich, Adrian.
Redefining politics.

Includes bibliographical references and index.
1. Political science. 2. Political sociology.
3. Power (Social sciences) I. Title.
JA74.L36 1983   306 .2   83-11372
ISBN 0-416-73590-8
ISBN 0-416-73600-9 (pbk.)

Contents

Acknowledgements

This book was conceived in the summer of 1978, but the bulk of the writing was done between January 1980 and July 1982. It was originally planned that it be written in collaboration with my colleague, David Skidmore. In the event, circumstances did not permit that, but I none the less owe him a considerable debt. All the main ideas, arguments and illustrations contained here were discussed with him, and those discussions helped to shape the structure of the book. He has read and commented on each chapter, sometimes more than once as they went through various drafts. At times he helped greatly by undertaking the laborious task of tracking down material which was difficult to find, and he invariably came up with something useful. He backed the whole enterprise from the start and guided me in relation to Latin America matters especially. The book grew out of our much longer cooperation in the Politics Department at the University of York, going back a decade. Over that period he and I have tried to introduce students to a view of politics which is historically deeper, geographically wider and anthropologically more comparative than the usual undergraduate diet. The fruit of those efforts, first tried this way then that in a variety of courses, is to some extent reflected in this book, and it is therefore right to acknowledge his wider contribution to it.

There is also something particularly rewarding to be able to acknowledge the help I have received from many former students, especially Jeremy Pickard, Andy Flockhart, David Goodhart and Philip Evans, who read parts of the manuscript in various drafts at different stages. They were relentless but always constructive in their criticisms and comments, ticking me off where the argument was weak, the evidence clogged or patchy and for lapses in style. They always gave the right kind of criticism at the right time, and showed a very shrewd sense of what was needed.

I should also like to thank Jannie Mead for encouragement at all stages, for making sure that I kept the central purpose in sight, and my feet on the ground. She provided invaluable help with some of the medical and medically-related material in particular. More generally, by asking difficult questions she always helped to sharpen the argument. Dick Funkhouser and Delsie Gandia provided a quiet place to work at *Paschall's Chance*, and in the course of many good discussions came up with the original idea for the main title.

Towards the end, when there was a great deal of checking and reading to be done, Dorothy Nott generously gave weeks of her time to go over the manuscript with the greatest of care, improving grammar, clarifying meaning and generally helping to get things done on time. It would have been a much more difficult and painful task without her help, and I am indebted to her for her skill and attention to detail.

A relay of Inter-Library Loan Librarians in the J. B. Morrell Library in the University of York unfailingly got me material with efficiency and patience. One could hope for no better service than that provided in particular by Margaret Lawty, Heather Blackburn, Anita Gowlett and Anthea Bracken.

An anonymous reader for the publisher made some very useful comments on an early synopsis and a few draft chapters, which helped to identify and overcome some of the problems of presenting such a wide range of material. At Methuen, first John Whitehead and then Nancy Marten edged this project along gently but firmly and were always helpful with responses to queries.

Audrey Freeborn typed the manuscript with precision and speed, between dispensing justice on the Bench of the York Magistrates' Court.

Without such help this book would never have appeared, though I alone remain responsible for its shortcomings.

Finally, I would like to thank Grant McIntyre for permission to reproduce Table 3.1 from Ivan Reid, *Social Class Differences in Britain* (London, Grant McIntyre, 2nd edn, 1981); the World Bank for permission to reproduce certain data from *World Tables, 1980* (Baltimore, Md, and London, The Johns Hopkins University Press, 1980); and Her Majesty's Stationery Office for permission to reproduce Table 7.1 from *Report No. 7* of the Royal Commission on the Distribution of Income and Wealth (London, HMSO, 1977).

Adrian Leftwich
August 1982

Map 1

Map 1 (continued)

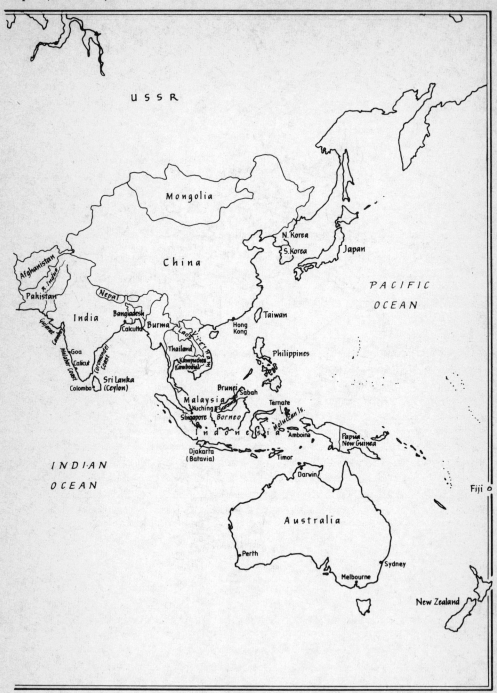

Introduction and background

It was the best of times, it was the worst of times, it was the age of foolishness, it was the epoch of incredulity, it was the season of Light, it was the season of Darkness, it was the spring of hope, it was the winter of despair, we had everything before us, we had nothing before us, we were all going direct to Heaven, we were all going direct the other way - in short, the period was so far like the present period, that some of its noisiest authorities insisted on its being received, for good or evil, in the superlative degree of comparison only.

Charles Dickens, *A Tale of Two Cities*[1]

I

Thus wrote Dickens, more than a century ago, to describe the condition of France and England during the uneasy years before the French Revolution of 1789. Great technological and social change has occurred since then, but it is still reasonable to argue that most societies in the modern world remain characterized by that tension between hope and crisis which Dickens captured so well.

It has been common practice over the centuries for princes, politicians and priests to hold out hope to us - on certain conditions. They often point backwards to a golden age (which seldom existed), and they point forward to the promise of a new one, if only people would work harder, tighten their belts, exercise restraint in their wage demands, pray more, do what they are told, or generally show respect for the wisdom of their elders and leaders, and the rightness of their policies. Promises of this kind may help to keep hope afloat in troubled times. But it is difficult to have much faith in them when even the most casual glance around the world shows how frequently our societies are punctuated by crisis after crisis, how little our leaders appear to understand about their origins, and how impotent or unserious they are in tackling their causes.

The forms which these crises take today are depressingly familiar. In the industrial societies they include inflation, unemployment, industrial conflict, the decay of inner cities, urban violence, ecological and nuclear hazards, and a series of killer epidemics - heart disease, cancers and death through accidents. In the Third World, the crises are often more stark. They include gross poverty, widespread malnutrition, the outbreak of massive famines, the growth of swollen shanty towns, sharp inequalities between rich and poor, and unequal trading relations with the industrial world. In the middle of all this, authoritarian civil and military governments often circulate in a vacuum of absolute poverty.[2]

Around the world, people are deeply concerned about these matters, though understandably the focus of their immediate concern tends to be on the problems of their own particular family, village or town. Next to wanting these problems to be eliminated, people seek desperately for an understanding of their causes. They want to know why these things happen and what can be done about them. Some people take refuge in fatalism ('these things are sent to try us'); others find religious explanations convincing and perhaps even reassuring (it is the wrath of the gods); or they attribute some of the problems to the accidents of nature, or to 'the government', or 'the unions', or the international recession, or the Russians or Japanese, or some distant theory, like 'monetarism'.

There may be elements of truth in bits of some of these views. But the central argument of this book is that all major social problems of this kind cannot be attributed to bad luck, natural causes or Acts of God. They can be traced to the *politics* of our societies, or the relations between them. Now 'politics' is usually misunderstood to refer to the activities of politicians, parties, parliaments and governments, and all the dreary bickering and bargaining associated with them. That is *not* what is meant here. Politics, as it will be defined in the next chapter, refers to a much wider and much more important range of activities, found in all human groups, institutions and societies. Whatever we do, or wherever we work, we are constantly engaged in politics. The purpose of this book is therefore to specify what these activities are, and why they are political. But because of the conventionally narrow usage of the term, that involves 'redefining politics'. The essence of the book, therefore, consists in elaborating that redefinition of politics, illustrating it with as many different examples as possible, and showing how the approach can be put to use in other contexts.

It would be naive in the extreme to believe that a book of this kind can have any direct impact on the resolution of the problems which occur in modern societies. But I hope that the broad introductory framework which is used here will enable readers to think about the politics and problems of their own societies and institutions in a different light. If this, in turn, enables them to act in ways which are appropriate for attacking the causes of those problems, so much the better.

II

But why is such a book necessary, and why an introductory book? After all, there is a constant flow of learned articles, journals and books that is almost overwhelming. There has been a massive expansion of knowledge in the social and natural sciences. Specialist research proliferates in almost every field, and it gets more specialized.

These facts highlight a central issue. The 'data explosion' and the advanced specialization which has occurred are themselves symptoms of a problem for which this book seeks to provide one kind of answer. For specialization is also fragmentation. And while great advances have been made within particular disciplines, this has not been matched by comparable attempts to integrate some of this progress into wider frameworks of understanding about our societies and their politics as a whole.

This specialization is nowhere more clearly revealed than in the division between the natural and social sciences. One result is that most people now think of and study the 'social' and 'natural' worlds as if they were utterly distinct. The imprint of this fragmentation has been stamped on almost every school syllabus and university degree course.

This specialization, even *within* the social sciences, would leave the founding fathers - like Adam Smith, Comte, Marx, Weber and Spencer - profoundly depressed. Their commitments were to develop understandings of societies as wholes, and to trace the principles and forms of their evolution and structure. However, a brief survey of some of the central preoccupations of the main disciplines within the social sciences will indicate just how far removed they have become from those concerns.

Broadly speaking, 'the economy', the 'social system', and the 'political system' are usually conceived of as if they were more or less autonomous spheres of activity in human societies. That is certainly how they are usually studied, and this is reflected in the conventionally rigorous separation of the disciplines of Economics, Sociology and Politics (or Political Science, or Government), and their main concerns.

For instance, Economics is mainly concerned with how choices are allegedly made in the allocation of scarce resources in societies, or institutions within them. Economists have developed some very sophisticated mathematical techniques for measuring things, like the costs and benefits of different actions on 'the economy', or on firms and institutions within it. But their often highly abstract models of 'the economy' generally assume that it is a field of activity which can be more or less isolated for both analysis and treatment. Usually, therefore, the so-called 'non-economic' factors are viewed as 'external' to the workings of 'the economy' which remains very closely identified in much academic Economics with the competitive market economy and the ubiquitous forces of supply and demand.

Sociology, on the other hand, has come to be associated broadly with the study of 'social institutions' and 'social structure', which includes such groups as the family, sex-groups and classes. It is concerned in general with their interactions and with various theories about their origins, behaviours and forms. The changing attitudes and relations between such groups often form the core of discussion about social change. These considerations are supplemented by the analysis of customs, values, norms and ideologies, and their place in sustaining social structure or in promoting or reflecting social change.

Finally, the discipline of Politics is still today largely concerned with two main areas. The first is 'government', in a rather formal sense, and with associated constitutional issues and political processes, narrowly defined. These include political parties and movements, elections, rival policies, and the formal administrative processes of decision-making within the 'political system'. These concerns reveal one of the major antecedents of the discipline, which is constitutional history and law. The second is philosophy, and especially that branch of it called political philosophy. This accounts for the other main preoccupation of the discipline, the study of political theory, philosophy and ideology, often concerned with such matters as 'rights', 'freedom', 'justice', 'obligation', 'liberty' and 'power', but also with such concepts as 'class', 'élites', 'bureaucracy' and 'the state'. This is usually done through the study of the texts of major political theorists.

Such brief accounts do not, of course, do justice to these disciplines and their achievements to date. Moreover, there are areas where the concerns of the disciplines do overlap, and where some productive 'interdisciplinary' work takes place. Geographers, anthropologists and economic historians, especially, have also contributed important insights to the understanding of our own and other societies. None the less, it is true to say that the social sciences in general remain characterized by specialization and hence fragmentation.

The limitations of this become particularly clear when one considers concrete problems in modern societies, such as unemployment in the industrial societies on the one hand, and rural poverty in the Third World on the other. The harder you think about these issues, the more difficult it is to identify them as strictly economic, social or political in their causes or consequences. And the closer you get to analysing them, the more it becomes apparent that they cannot be explained satisfactorily from *within* any one of the disciplines mentioned above. In both instances, as will emerge more fully in later chapters, there are complicated relationships between, for example, the control, ownership and use of *economic* resources (like capital, factories or land), the distribution of *political* power and decision-making authority between various *social* groups (such as boards of directors, shareholders and unions; or between 'high caste' landlords and 'low caste' or 'untouchable' landless peasants, as in parts of rural India today, for instance).

In short, if one is concerned to explain the causes of such problems, it is essential to start by recognizing the relatedness of these kinds of factors in most problems which face human societies. But to undertake an analysis of these requires a framework which can identify what these factors are, and also provide a means of tracing the relations between them. Such a framework must therefore be interdisciplinary in character, and it cannot by definition arise from any one of the specialist disciplines within the social sciences as presently constituted. One reason for this book, therefore, is that it offers such an introductory framework of analysis – or a way of looking at things – before specialization begins.

III

There is a second reason why such a book is necessary.

The mass media today are major sources of information, impressions and opinions about the world. What we see and read is often dramatic. But in general the media contribute very little to our *understanding* of what they report. There is the obvious trivialization and personalization of what is loosely called 'politics' – 'Prime Minister attacks Opposition Leader', or 'President accused by Senate', or 'New Split in National Executive'. This sort of reporting reaches its peak at election times when the media mount football-like coverage of the events. Opinion is offered by former politicians (rather like former football players), by professional commentators (like their equivalents who live off football), and by various academic experts operating 'swingometers' or recalling some spectacular comparison from Grimsby at the turn of the century. Moralism and scoring of debating points, not analysis, pervade the electoral atmosphere and likewise the discussion of problems. Trying to trip up Cabinet Ministers or their opponents, by confronting them with statements they made in previous years, seems to be the dominant preoccupation of the commentators and interviewers. But what does one learn from all this about the causes of the central issues at stake, or their possible consequences?

In the heady rush for up-to-the-minute reporting, the media subject us to a ceaseless barrage of generally undifferentiated news items. Today, these include strikes and industrial disputes; details of national and international economic performances; wars and famines; pollution; the rise and fall of governments or *juntas*; 'political unrest', and so forth. But the fact of the matter is that the media rarely attempt to explore the deeper causes which underlie these happenings. So, they provide no real *explanation* for them. In general, they report these kinds of things almost as if they were apparently inexplicable, unconnected and random happenings which erupt without cause or context in the open plane of human societies, now here, now there.

It is central to the argument of this book that such events are neither random nor inexplicable. They *can* be explained if they are understood in terms of the *politics* of the societies in which they occur. But such a view in itself rests heavily here on a distinct notion of what politics is, a notion which is more inclusive, every-day and comparative than the conventional scope and meaning of the term as used in the discipline of Politics. Many students of politics, and most people in their daily lives, recognize this intuitively: that politics is much *more*, and much more *important* than the goings-on of politicians or parties or government. But the discipline of Politics has let them down in not clarifying how such intuitive understandings may be made analytically sharper and explanatorily effective. And that is also why it is necessary to redefine politics, so that people may use such a conception in conjunction with their own experiences to make sense of what they see around them, and to act upon that accordingly.

IV

The central task of this book may seem an ambitious one, and the general argument may at first appear unusual. For this reason, the contents are arranged in the following way.

Part One is concerned to outline the argument and illustrate it with examples from very different societies and problems. Thus, the first chapter redefines politics and shows why it is such a universal activity in human societies. The second, third and fourth chapters show the character of politics in unfamiliar societies: hunter-gatherers in the Kalahari; the now extinct empire of the Aztecs in Middle America, before the Spanish Conquest; and the Pastoral Maasai in East Africa. But politics is found also in institutions which are sometimes smaller than whole societies, and sometimes greater than them. So chapter 5 shows how the framework can be put to work in analysing the politics of villages, a typical university department and a large global institution; the World Bank. It is also central to the argument here that many of the problems which societies experience can be attributed to their politics, and that the approach of the book can help to explain these. Thus, chapter 6 looks at some such problems: the extraordinary 'cattle-killing' episode amongst the Xhosa people in South Africa in 1857; the development of the disease pellagra in Europe from the seventeenth century; and some famines in Africa and Asia in modern times.

Part Two is concerned with politics in contemporary societies. However, an understanding of their politics requires awareness of their historical relations with each other, for there are few societies today which have been unaffected by the expansion of Europe from the end of the fifteenth century, and the legacy of global relations that it has left us with. Chapter 7 provides that background. In the light of that, chapter 8 examines the politics of societies in the Third World. At this point in the argument it will be possible to turn back from the concern with unfamiliar societies and unusual problems to focus in chapters 9 and 10 on politics in Britain, as an example of an industrial society, using the same framework that has been applied throughout.

Part Three offers some conclusions which draw together the lessons from this redefinition of politics, and show what implications there might be for the discipline of Politics.

The book is aimed at two categories of readers. The first is an undergraduate audience, mainly in the social sciences and especially Politics, but I hope that it may interest others. The second category of readers is that much larger public who may be concerned with the kinds of issues mentioned in this Introduction and who seek a way of interpreting them. Because the scope is large and the examples both diverse and unusual, there is the danger of some oversimplification. At other times the argument and detail may be hard going, but I have tried to avoid jargon wherever possible and to strive for clarity. Moreover, because the central argument surfaces again and again in each chapter, there may be some repetition. I have tried to keep this to a minimum but have not wanted to eliminate it entirely, since these themes of the argument are what is really important.

PART ONE

CHAPTER ONE

Redefining politics: the argument

I

Most people feel that 'politics' has very little to do with them. It is a world which appears removed and distant from the activities through which they live their daily lives. Politicians are often regarded as people engaged in unpleasant squabbles for power, who manoeuvre and jockey for position and advantage, and they are viewed with a mixture of resigned contempt or humorous mistrust.

The way in which the media treat politics has helped to shape such a view and acts daily to confirm it. The discipline of Politics, moreover, serves to sustain this by one of its mainstream occupations. This is its focus on largely constitutional affairs, parties, voting, elections and the institutions of government, mainly in the so-called 'advanced' societies, or where there is a 'state'. Indeed, some specialists in the discipline argue that there are societies where there is simply no politics.[1]

The central thesis of this book is that such a focus is misguided, and is quite unhelpful in understanding the world and its problems. The argument here flows from a very different definition of politics from the conventional one. This first chapter therefore sets out to define what that is and to illustrate this redefinition in some preliminary ways.

So, what is politics?

II

Politics consists of all the activities of cooperation and conflict, within and between societies, whereby the human species goes about obtaining, using, producing and distributing resources in the course of the production and reproduction of its social and biological life. These activities are not isolated from other features of social life. They everywhere influence, and are influenced by, the distribution of power and decision-making, the systems of social organization, culture and ideology in a society, as well as its relations with the natural environment and other societies. Politics is therefore a defining characteristic of *all* human groups, and always has been.

Politics is found in families, groups of kin or 'tribes'; in villages, towns, regions, nation-states or associations of them; and, in the modern world, on a global basis. It occurs also in formal institutions, such as churches, factories, bureaucracies, universities and clubs, as well as political parties, trade unions, women's groups, chambers of commerce, parents' associations, *mafia* and armies, and in all the complex relations between them. It may also occur in informal organizations, such as bus queues, football crowds, people meeting for the first time on a camp site, or children inventing and playing games. The way people use and distribute resources - their politics - also helps to explain the problems which occur within or between societies, institutions or groups, whether it be unemployment, war, famine, disease, overcrowding or various forms of conflict.

The central point to emphasize at this stage is that the *politics* of societies - *not* their government, but it includes that - is at every level and in every sphere inextricably involved with how resources are used, produced, organized, distributed and redistributed, and by whom and with what consequences. 'Resources' here mean a very wide range of things. They include capital, land, income, labour and other natural resources like rivers and seas. But they also include things that are not always or immediately thought of in this context, such as time, education, status, influence, health and knowledge.

This definition suggests how the notion of politics will be used in this book. But it requires further elaboration.

III

We commonly tend to forget how closely intertwined are the 'natural' and 'social' worlds. It is important to remember that human beings are animals - primates - and are constantly engaged in activities which are at one and the same time natural *and* social, such as birth, marriage and death, and all that goes on before, during and after them. For instance, different systems of marriage can be usefully seen - at least in part - as the *social* means whereby societies organize their *natural*, that is their biological, reproduction. Moreover, everything which we use to sustain our individual and collective lives, that is our 'material culture' - food, energy sources, tools, clothing, dwellings, forms of transport and so forth - is derived from some part of the natural environment. Human beings have constantly been engaged in organizing and reorganizing the social use of these natural resources.

No society, whatever the character of its technology, is able to evacuate itself from this natural environment, or from the effects of its actions upon it. For example, if pastoralists overgraze their pastures, then their herds and they themselves will suffer consequences. Equally, if people in industrial societies pollute their rivers or seas or atmosphere, they may poison themselves or deprive themselves of necessary resources. Societies abuse their environment at their peril. It may seem as if industrial societies have been able to use their advanced technology to insulate themselves from this natural world. This is an illusion. A falter in the supply of their massive energy requirements, upon which such societies depend, would quickly bring about a collapse in the whole edifice of industrial urban life and would rapidly throw their agricultural systems into chaos.

.The starting-point, therefore, for the analysis of politics in societies must be this conception of the human species as animals, engaged in these simultaneously natural and social activities of production and reproduction. In the course of these, they adapt more or less successfully to their natural and social environments, and they innovate more or less effectively in relation to the problems and opportunities encountered in the process.

IV

How has this come about?

It is a pity that social scientists (with the important exception of some anthropologists) pay so little attention to the work of archaeologists.[2] For the emergence and history of politics is directly bound up with the evolution of the human species over the last 4 million years. There are still vast gaps in our knowledge. But recent interdisciplinary work on this incredibly complex question has shown more clearly than ever before that the long evolutionary history of the human species goes back, from the emergence of modern *homo sapiens sapiens*, about 50,000 years ago, through a series of prior *homo* species, to *homo habilis*, about 3 million years ago; and that the major evolutionary step, the emergence of *homo erectus*, occurred about one-and-a-half million years ago, almost certainly in East Africa. From there, our ancestors spread to the Middle East, Europe and Asia. And the first human migrants reached Australia by about 50,000 years ago, and the Americas, via the Bering Straits, about 30,000 or 40,000 years ago.

Then, from about 10,000 years ago, small groups of people first started to tend crops and domesticate animals in a number of different places - the 'neolithic revolution'. Resources - land, crops, water, animals, pasture and metals - came to be used and distributed in new ways. New forms of productive activity followed. Since then, the history of the species has been characterized by an astonishing variety of societies, and a growth in population from an estimated 10 million in 8000 BC to about 300 million at the time of Christ to the present figure of approximately 4000 million.

For nearly 2 million years, until the neolithic revolution, hunting and gathering in various forms and in an increasing variety of places characterized the life of the *homo* species, from *homo erectus* to *homo sapiens sapiens*, and continues today in a few parts of the world. During this long history, major technological innovations were achieved, for example in stone tool-kits, wooden spears, hand-axes and - crucially - in the use of fire. People made shelters, produced protective clothing and decorative ornaments, and began to build burial sites for their dead. Cooperation in the course of work enabled people to do new things, and to do old things in new ways, and hence helped to establish the central principles of social organization which, in turn, facilitated the hunting and gathering of food, and the sharing of it at a home base or camp, as well as other productive activities. People working in groups could fell trees and place them across streams or gullies as bridges; nets could be constructed and game could be flushed into them by organized hunting parties; rock traps in rivers and at the coast could be set up to catch fish. In the course of all this, language, music, art and ritual emerged.

How was this achieved?

There are many features which have progressively defined and distinguished human beings from other species in the course of our evolution, which help to explain this. These include our physiological and especially neurological constitution, the use of language, and the capacity for non-conditioned learning and problem solving. But most important for the present argument is the fact that the history of our *physical* evolution as a species has gone hand-in-hand with our *social* history. For human beings are only found living in societies, and this social character of our existence also helps to explain the achievements. It is as important as our biological evolution. Indeed, the two, the natural and social history of the species, are inseparable.

And the major organizing activity at the heart of this history of cooperation, conflict, innovation and adaptation in the use, production and distribution of resources has been, and still is, *politics*.

V

It was argued at the start of this chapter that these activities of cooperation and conflict always both influence and reflect the systems of power, social organization, culture and ideology in a society. It is necessary now to indicate what these are. However, it is important at the outset to stress that these 'systems' – as they will be called here for shorthand purposes only – are not separate elements of a society. They are overlapping activities, behaviours, relationships and outlooks which together compose the defining features of a society. Though every society is unique, and always has been, they all share these common and underlying structural features. What are they, and to what do they refer?

First and foremost, at the core of any society, and hence its politics, is a *system of production*. This is constituted by the manner in which it obtains, uses and produces resources, through *work*. Some societies have done this by hunting and gathering; others primarily by subsistence agriculture, or pastoralism. Some are involved in more or less commercialized agriculture and trade; others are mainly industrial producers; and yet others combine a variety of these activities. In each instance, this productive core of the society is characterized by a particular technology, and an associated division of labour.

Secondly, each society has a *system of distribution and redistribution*. This refers broadly to the principles and processes whereby the ownership and control of its major productive resources (land, animals, capital, tools, factories and so on) are distributed amongst the population. It also includes the way the products and rewards of work (such as food, shelter, income) are distributed and redistributed. Thus, for any given society it is important to establish carefully the pattern of ownership and control of resources, and how they are distributed. Evenly or unevenly? Is a surplus produced over and above what is needed? What happens to it? Is it stored for later consumption, or exchanged? And by whom? How much of what people produce do they keep for themselves? How much of its flows 'upwards' or 'outwards' as tribute, tax or tithes, and to whom? How much of that in turn is redistributed? That is, how much flows 'inwards' and 'downwards' to the community, and in what form? For instance, as roads, services, feasts, education, protection or insurance against lean times? And is this evenly distributed between groups and regions?

Thirdly, all societies have a structure or *system of power and decision-making* which directly determines how decisions are made, and by whom and why, especially about the above matters of production and distribution. There may be a number of decision-making groups, such as family heads, or age-sets, or village leaders, or chiefs, or elected representatives, or landlords or boards of directors, or officials, or wider gatherings of men and women. Do these decision-making circles overlap or conflict and over what and why? Is there wide consultation or are there strict lines of authority? Do some people have more power than others and, if so, why? Is there any correlation between birth and power? Or ownership, wealth and power? Or sex and power? Or achievement and power?

Fourthly, every society has a *system of a social organization*. This refers to many factors. It includes the typical composition of families; are they nuclear or extended, monogamous or polygamous, matriarchal or patriarchal? It also includes the organization of communities into lineages, clans, age-sets, 'tribes' or nations; the typical residential patterns, such as camps, hamlets, villages, estates, suburbs or towns, or a combination of them; it includes any major social divisions which may exist in the society, like castes or classes, or ethnic and cultural groups, and the relations between them; it refers to the patterns of inheritance whereby possessions and wealth are transmitted from one generation to the next; and it also includes the manner in which young and old are cared for, and the way the young are brought up and trained ('socialized') to become adult members of the society. The importance of social organization and structure for politics is considerable. In some societies, for instance, relations by blood or marriage, or membership of a particular clan, may have very important implications for an individual's position in the productive, distributive and power structures of the society. In others, membership of certain clubs, classes, organizations, or the school one attended, may be more important.

Fifthly, and very closely implicated in the above, every society has a *system of culture and ideology*, and sometimes more than one. This covers much more than simply its artistic activities and forms, or the status of its scientific knowledge, but includes them. 'Culture' in the present sense refers to a very wide network of standardized customs and regular behaviours found in all societies. These include its customs of courtship and marriage, its basic styles of dress, its food habits and taboos, its typical leisure activities, its principles and practices of hospitality, and much more. It is everywhere closely associated with ideology, which includes such things as religious beliefs and practices, myths, values, moral codes, general endorsement of certain ways of behaving, and broad outlooks in terms of which people interpret the world about them. The cultures of most societies have symbols, flags and other outward means whereby their members assert their own identity and distinguish themselves from others. It is of course true that there are some societies, 'plural societies', in which there may be more than one culture. This usually flows from the fact that previously separate societies, or people from them, have been brought together in a single common society, and that the previous cultural differences remain strong. In time, such differences may fade, as a common culture begins to emerge, or as one group adopts the culture of another. This has happened in the USA and some other societies which have been composed of immigrants from a variety of cultural backgrounds, though significant trace elements may of course remain. There may also be important cultural distinctions associated with different classes in a common society, like Britain, which arise out of the divisions of ownership, wealth and labour, and the accompanying differences in income, reward and opportunity. These differences may be expressed in terms of lifestyles, including dress, diet, social behaviours and leisure activities, as well as accents and outlooks. But whether there is a more or less common culture or not, all societies are rich in these features. They enable people within them, or parts of them, to conduct their affairs, since cultures and ideologies form part of that broadly common 'language' of shared behaviours and understandings which make interaction and communication possible within a society, or within segments of it in the case of 'plural' societies.

Finally, no society is static. All are in a constant process of change, sometimes fast, sometimes slow, if only in that their membership is constantly changing, from generation to generation. More significant, rich industrial societies were not always so, and will certainly not always be so. Poor rural societies were not always poor in the way they are today, and may not remain so. That is to say, all societies have a *history* and will always have one. 'History' here refers to a whole legacy of related technological capacities, social behaviours, institutions and ideological outlooks inherited from the past. These are sustained and changed by communities in the course of making and re-making their history through their politics, and this includes their relations with other societies.

VI

The great variety of societies which have existed is remarkable, and is worth indicating here briefly.

Some societies can trace a continuous history going back for a very substantial period - as in the case of China and Japan. By contrast, there are others - like modern Brazil, the USA and New Zealand - which have been established relatively recently, in the course of exploration, conquest and migration, and whose formation has often involved the destruction or incorporation of earlier societies found in those places.

Most of human history has been lived in hunting and gathering societies, some of which have lasted into modern times, and the politics of one of them will be examined in the next chapter. Where societies of herders (pastoral societies) have emerged from these hunting and gathering communities, they have usually been very mobile, moving with their herds between pasturing and watering points. Hence most of them, such as the Khoikhoi of Southern Africa, or the Karimojong and other pastoral peoples of East Africa, have had very loose forms of social organization and decentralized systems of power and decision-making, as will be discussed in chapter 4. A few pastoral societies have developed strong central institutions, complete with courts of advisers, retainers, soldiers and slaves. Perhaps the best-known example of this was the Mongol Empire of central Asia, which reached the height of its power in the early thirteen century under Chingis Khan.

Where more settled agricultural societies have emerged, all round the globe, they too have shown diversity. Some - like the Ibo, on the edge of the great equatorial forests of West Africa - were quite small in scale, and composed of autonomous but related village settlements, which moved from clearing to clearing in the course of their agricultural life. This method of cultivation has evolved widely throughout the world and is known as 'shifting cultivation' or 'slash and burn'.[3]

Other agricultural societies, too, have given rise to powerful and centralized states or even 'empires', such as those further north in Africa, in the western Sudanic belt, like the kingdoms of Ghana, Mali and Songhai, between the fifth and fifteenth centuries. They were also involved in long-distance commerce with the Mediterranean ports of North Africa and traded gold, ivory, ebony, feathers and slaves in return for salt, copper, dates and figs. These commercial empires sustained large cities of stone, a flourishing art in bronze, pottery and wood, and urban-based communities surrounding the kings and the courts. These cities were fed by the produce of outlying agricultural and pastoral societies over which they ruled.[4] Similar developments occurred in other settled agricultural societies - notably in Asia - where there were complex imperial systems, supporting emperors and their elaborate bureaucracies on the basis of intensive agrarian production at home and far-flung trade abroad, as was the case in China under successive regimes over the last 2000 years. The case of the Aztecs of Central America (now Mexico) will be discussed in chapter 3. More recently, in Europe, some societies which had once been primarily agricultural turned increasingly to seaborne commerce and came to derive a major portion of their living from it and associated activities, as in the case of the Netherlands in the seventeenth and eighteenth centuries.[5]

Today, there is a rich mosaic of societies which are involved in complex relations with each other, and the historical background to these relations will be examined later. There are some which are heavily industrial and urban, as in much of Western Europe. There are others which remain primarily agricultural and rural, as in most of sub-Saharan Africa and Asia. And there are those which combine a changing and variable mixture of agriculture, mining and emerging forms of manufacture and light industry, as in Taiwan, Rumania, Greece and Mexico - and the oil-producing societies of the Middle East.

VII

This variety of societies, arising in the first instance from the core characteristics of their productive systems, has been associated with considerable diversity in respect of the other 'systems' discussed above.

For instance, in so far as the distributive principles and patterns are concerned, there have been some in which important assets like land, water and occasionally factories have not been 'owned' by anyone, but have been controlled or managed by the people who use or work in them. In others, they have been owned by private individuals, companies or the state, or a combination of them. Different legal systems and customs regulate the use and the inheritance of such resources. Many societies have been characterized therefore by considerable equality between people. Others have been - and are - highly unequal as between social groups in terms of such things as access to resources, or income, welfare and rights. This inequality was the case in the classical Graeco-Roman world, in the slave societies of the Caribbean, in imperial China, Tsarist Russia, Dickens's England, and many others. It remains the case in modern Bolivia, El Salvador, Liberia, South Africa, Mauritius and the Philippines, where very small minorities own the bulk of wealth and receive most of the income.[6]

These differences in the productive and *especially* distributive characteristics of human societies have usually been associated with particular features in their systems of power and decision-making. It has in general been the case that the more uneven they have been in distributional terms, the more unequal they have been in terms of their patterns of power and decision-making authority. For instance, in hunting and gathering societies, as well as most pastoral societies, the relatively even distribution of their major resources (land, water, pastures and animals) between sections of the society has been closely associated with community control and management of them. On the other hand, often profound inequalities have been both sustained by and reflected in systems of power which have monopolized decision-making in the hands of the wealthy and have excluded the majority from effective participation in it. This has been the case in some pre-industrial empires (such as in China or Aztec society), in 'feudal' societies (such as in medieval Europe or pre-nineteenth-century Japan), in sharply divided class societies (such as in England in the eighteenth and nineteenth centuries), in societies composed of more or less closed castes (as in India), and in societies where major social divisions have existed between colour or 'racial' groups (as in the southern USA or South Africa).

Broad features of social organization have varied widely too. As mentioned above, the caste system in India has established groups between which it has been extremely rare and difficult for people to move, and it has been decisive in affecting the use, control and distribution of resources. In the industrial capitalist societies, the often sharp divisions between classes have both expressed and influenced their politics, and do so on an ever-increasing scale in many other parts of the world. At the heart of class distinctions are differences between social groups in terms of their ownership and control of resources, and their access to power and opportunity in the society.

Even where class divisions are strong, or emerging, there may none the less be a broadly common culture which all people share, as in Italy or Lesotho. But the social composition of some other societies - such as Trinidad, Belgium, Ireland, Uganda and Sri Lanka - has been marked by a 'plurality' of cultural, ethnic, religious or linguistic groups or regions, which have sometimes become locked in conflict with each other. Such conflict seldom arises *only* from the fact that there may inevitably be some suspicion and tension between peoples whose daily behaviours and customs differ. They arise more commonly from the often uneven distribution of resources, power, rewards and opportunities between such different communities in the same society. This too is of critical importance in shaping politics in such societies.

The diversity of the systems of culture and ideology in human societies is also remarkable, and may be illustrated with a few examples. Marriage is a central feature in the culture of all societies. More or less complicated rules influence who you can and cannot marry, and they regulate the rights and responsibilities of spouses to each other, their families and their kin. They also govern important aspects of resource distribution in and between families. In some societies, marriage is not simply a relationship between two individuals, but is a much more complex affair linking families, kin and even villages. Accordingly, it is common for marriages to be arranged, as in Pakistan and areas of Mediterranean Europe. Elsewhere, polygamy is the standard and preferred practice, as in many parts of Africa and the Islamic world. Polygamous marriages usually give rise to large families, which is not the case with polyandrous marriage (that is, one wife and a number of husbands). This can be very important in agricultural societies where family labour is important, and the more of it the better. In such societies, children contribute in many ways to the productive activities: they collect wood and carry water, they help with the livestock, and undertake many household chores - such as looking after their younger sisters and brothers - and they may provide valuable labour in the fields, especially at harvest times. Moreover, where there is no such thing as a 'national insurance' scheme, they provide the main form of security for parents in old age. All over the world, the general pattern of marriage has been for both polygamy *and* family size to decrease as new productive systems (often involving greater mechanization) have evolved, where the general levels of material welfare have increased, and where private insurance schemes or social security provisions for old age and ill-health are established by the community through the market or the state.[7] In short, patterns of marriage, as central aspects of culture, are not separable from the broader productive and distributive features of societies, and hence their politics.

Religious beliefs and practices are also central for culture and are significant politically. The variety of myths and stories which different societies have used to account for their origins and aspects of their histories testifies to the creative imaginations of human beings in their search for meaning and explanation. The Hurutshe (in Southern Africa) traditionally believed that all people (and their cattle) came from a hole in the ground, while the Maasai in East Africa claimed that God gave them their cattle by letting them down on a bark rope from the sky. The Aztecs believed in a vast assembly of gods, who controlled and influenced almost everything, above all the rising and setting of the sun. Aztec daily life was punctuated with various kinds of sacrifices to these gods. The G/wi hunter-gatherers of the Kalahari have a conception of two higher beings, N!adima (who is good and created the universe, though no one really knows why) and G//amama (who is evil). With the help of N!adima, as well as various medicines and dances, they believe they can frustrate the evil intentions of G//amama. Some Christians both believe and teach that the world and all living things were created by God in seven days, that Christ was the Son of God - born of a virgin - and will come again. While they pray to these divinities to guide and protect them in peace and war, many African peoples believe that the spirits of their ancestors (the 'shades') can be far more influential in the affairs of living people, for good or for bad. Even in apparently 'secular' societies in the industrial world, religious beliefs, practices and priests constitute a steady background to daily affairs. There are christenings of babies, marriages in church, the burial of the dead, blessings at the launching of ships. Armies go to war with chaplains, and religious remembrance ceremonies are held to commemorate those killed in battle. In recent years, millions of people have travelled long distances to see the Pope, even in some societies of Eastern Europe which are officially hostile to religion. In Moscow one may still see people (usually the more elderly) making the sign of the cross as they file past Lenin's tomb.

But the role of religious ideas has often had a more directly important place in politics. In many societies, notions similar to that of the 'divine right' of kings and queens have historically acted to sustain inequalities in the distribution of both resources and power. Right into contemporary times, princes, prime ministers and presidents have liked to be closely identified with the church, and especially its senior officials. In many societies, the top members of the religious hierarchy (the 'Lords Spiritual' in Britain for instance) are often enmeshed with 'the Establishment'. The converse is sometimes also true: in some of the predominantly Roman Catholic societies of the Third

World (in Latin America and the Philippines for instance) radical priests have joined forces with revolutionary groups, arguing that it is their Christian duty to help the poor and oppressed.

The broader ideologies of some societies encourage people to believe that it is good and proper to try to 'get ahead' and 'better themselves' in material or social terms, and hence promote highly competitive behaviours in business, sport and individual advancement. Very elaborate 'economic' theories and government policies are often built on the assumption that such behaviour is not only 'natural' and 'morally' right but also efficient, and that people respond best to incentives and rewards. In other societies, such aspirations and behaviours have been regarded with the deepest disapproval, and even contempt, for they are thought to foster aggression, conflict and inequality, and hence disrupt the well-being of the community.

There has, thus, been a great variety of ideologies and theories in human societies. Today many contrasting ones often compete directly with each other in the same society, from the Moonies to the Marxists. It is important to see all these as being *not* merely the selfish, simplistic or sophisticated babble of narrow, sectional interests - though some clearly are. Ideologies are very complicated.[8] They act in many ways. They provide a broad interpretative framework, or *way of looking at the world*, or particular aspects of it. Moreover, ideas and values which may at first sight appear to be purely 'moral' or 'ideological' guides to conduct and action in practice turn out to represent diverse proposals of different interests and groups as to how resources should be controlled, produced and distributed. Ideologies, in short, arise out of the politics of a society and usually have far-reaching implications for it.

It is tempting to explore any of these 'systems' illustrated above in isolation from each other. This is often what the specialist disciplines in the social sciences tend to do. But if one is concerned to analyse the *politics* of a society, this must be resisted. It is absolutely crucial that the *structure of the relations* between these features be kept at the centre of analysis. For instance, to separate the question of the use, production and distribution of *resources* from the question of the use and distribution of *power* is to empty politics of its real content. Likewise, as some of the brief examples above will have shown, the influence of the systems of social organization, culture and ideology on politics - and vice versa - can be far-reaching. The great variety in the politics of human societies has everywhere represented varying combinations of these underlying structural features.[9] To understand the politics of a society, therefore, always requires a firm grasp of the relations between its past and its present, between internal and external factors, between its history and its structure.

VIII

Those who argue that there are some societies in which there is no politics suggest that it is an activity found only in 'quite complicated societies'.[10] Such as view rests of course on a much narrower conception of politics than the one being used here. Ultimately the difference of approach comes down to different definitions, but the justification for the present definition is that it helps to make sense of a wide variety of comparable activities which may be identified in all human societies. Moreover, my claim here is that politics is an activity found within and between even smaller groups and institutions in societies, from families to factories. It would be as well to offer some preliminary examples to illustrate this.

There is politics in the family in all societies, for all families obtain, use, produce and distribute resources such as food, income, space, time and labour. It is both a fascinating and legitimate topic of political enquiry to try to find out how this is done within individual families, or generally in a society, or comparatively between them. For instance, in some families decisions have to be made between, say, going on holiday or redecorating the kitchen. How is this done, and what influences the outcome? Elsewhere family labour needs to be organized for many different purposes - perhaps to clean the house or the car or to mow the lawn; or to prepare fields for sowing, or weeding, or harvesting the crops. Alternatively, how is food obtained and distributed? In many societies, including our own, there is evidence to show that the distribution of the food within the family may sometimes be uneven: males may get the better quality and larger quantity of food, or dishes they prefer. Why? There may be disputes over the use of family income, such as for 'housekeeping' money or pocket money. In polygamous families, in many parts of Africa, for instance, tensions may arise amongst wives, or between them and their husband, over unequal treatment, or treatment which is inappropriate to their respective statuses - perhaps with regard to the placing of their huts, or their plots or domestic property. All this is politics. An understanding of any particular instance will require a careful analysis of the relations between the *internal* systems of power, social organization, culture and ideology of the particular family, which will of course be strongly influenced by the wider general patterns of politics in the society.[11]

Consider some other examples. Anyone who works in an institution or organization - whether explicitly 'political' in the conventional sense or whether a factory, school or bureaucracy - will immediately recognize that many of its cooperative activities and disputes are fundamentally concerned with how resources should be used, and by whom and for what purposes. That's politics. The same is true of discussions in local tennis clubs or bowls clubs as to whether savings or loans should be spent on building more courts or greens, or on a new clubhouse. In villages and local communities there is a vast range of activities which require the organization of cooperation through politics. In many agricultural societies in Asia, Africa and Latin America there are communal labour arrangements whereby people help each other to clear land, plant crops and harvest them. Everywhere, people formulate and present plays, dances and festivals; they invent games and the rules for playing them; they build more or less complex structures, such as bridges, irrigation systems or dams; they establish and enact various rituals and ceremonial activities. There may be local (or wider national) disputes about the distribution of resources in a community or society - as between playgrounds, crèches or car-parks, or housing and defence, or wages and investment. Conflicts may emerge concerning differential access of individuals, groups or regions to various opportunities and services - like jobs, education or health care.

All these activities require the organization of human and other resources and hence involve politics. There can be no such activities within human groups without politics. One can also point to a few issues and disputes involving some unusual resources - or ones not often thought about as such - which help to illustrate this further. Differences of opinion between, say, commercial and religious groups about the proper use of *time* (for instance in respect of Sunday Observance) are often conceived of as if they were *only* moral debates (which of course they partly are). But they are more than that. They have direct implications for the possible use of time and labour as resources, and hence are clearly political.

The same is true for arguments about contraception and abortion. They entail complex questions of morality; but the issue of family size, and hence family planning, in all societies is intimately bound up with the question of resource use, production and distribution, as the earlier discussion about the importance of children's labour in some societies will have suggested. In the light of this, it is not hard to see why family planning programmes have not always been successful in some Third World societies where they could adversely affect domestic production or security in old age. On the other hand, in other societies (or some parts of the Third World) where the main means of subsistence are wages, there is clearly an advantage in keeping the number of dependants relatively low, and hence reducing family size. Here family planning programmes have been far more effective. This question is also inextricably bound up with wider issues that have been raised by the women's movement in the last twenty years. There are few societies in the world in which women enjoy the same rights and opportunities as men.[12] The women's movement has been a major force in drawing attention to these facts and to campaigning for appropriate changes. Amongst the demands that they have made has been the right to control their own bodies and fertility, and hence their insistence on the right to contraception and, if necessary, abortion. This has brought such movements into direct conflict with powerful institutions such as the Roman Catholic and other Churches which in their structures of power and social organization are dominated by males. Though there are other 'moral' issues involved, the fact of male domination of such institutions has made the progress of such movements much more difficult.

Another related issue is that of the dispute between the transnational milk companies and the proponents of breast-feeding.[13] At one level, the argument is of course a specialist one, about nutrition. But it has very profound implications for the question of infant malnutrition, disease and mortality. It is also an argument about the use of resources (human milk and formulated cows' milk), and about the costs to both families and societies alike of buying and importing the latter. It is thus not simply a 'scientific' matter, but is profoundly political in a number of ways, involving such related issues as the problems of working mothers, the provision of facilities for them (and hence the commitment of other resources) and the role of the transnational corporations in promoting the uses and abuses of certain kinds of resources.

Imposed changes in the productive, distributive and power structures of societies have frequently occurred in the course of the establishment of colonial rule. In many parts of Africa, for instance, people were encouraged by colonial authorities to alter the way they used and produced resources, to turn from subsistence agriculture to growing cash crops. They were often also required to pay taxes, and hence compelled to take wage employment on farms, plantations or mines, perhaps far away from their villages. Sometimes they were forced to sell their cattle to pay their taxes, or to reduce the number of cattle they owned (cattle culling). Such changes as these have often had pronounced effects on the politics of their villages: sometimes there has been a dramatic reduction in male labour availability, thereby placing enormous burdens on the women and old people. The reduction in the number of cattle, moreover, has acted to disrupt both productive *and* social relationships, for cattle have played an important part in agriculture (for manure and traction) and in marriage (as in bride-price). This occurred in Zimbabwe in the first half of the present century, for instance.

Faced with such disruptions of their politics - colonization, loss of land, threat to their existence and ways of life - people everywhere have fought back. Across the world, from the Americas to New Zealand, indigenous people have been involved in openly anti-colonial conflicts throughout the history of European expansion from the fifteenth century. But where such resistance has failed, or hope has faded, people have often retreated into religious or mystical movements which have reflected their political plight. Such movements have often served, ideologically, to accommodate people and to some extent make their despair more tolerable. Movements of this kind included the 'Ghost dances' of Indians on the US plains in the second half of the nineteenth century, the 'Ethiopian' churches in Southern Africa in the first half of the present century, 'Rastafarianism' in Jamaica, the 'Lumpa' church of Alice Lenshina in Zambia in the 1950s and 1960s, the 'Hau Hau' movement amongst New Zealand Maoris in the 1860s, and the 'cargo cults' of Melanesia from the middle of the nineteenth century onwards. Such movements - the 'religions of the oppressed' as they have been called - differed widely in their forms and particulars. Some have been passive, withdrawn and inward-looking, others have been associated with attacks on the perceived agents of their oppression, in the belief that they must overturn the world. Many have mixed traditional beliefs and practices with bits and pieces of Christianity, or have developed entirely new ideologies and customs. The important thing to note here is that they have all arisen out of usually quite sudden and often far-reaching changes for the worse in the political circumstances of the people, and the despair associated with this. They have often also given rise to further conflict with secular or religious authorities trying to control them or stamp them out.[14]

Violent conflicts over the use and distribution of resources have occurred in the politics of most societies where people have had their livelihood threatened, for instance where they are deprived of land or jobs. These are the seeds of revolutionary politics, though many of these movements never get beyond the stage of protest, riot or rebellion. One such movement, associated with the mysterious name of 'Captain Swing', occurred in the eastern and southern counties of England in 1830, when groups of rural poor erupted in an angry rebellion of machine-breaking and haystack-burning to protest against unemployment and low wages. Similar outbreaks, and harsh counter-measures to contain them, have been occurring in parts of rural Spain recently.[15] Of course, not all rural people react in these ways: some do nothing; others may slowly move from place to place, perhaps ending up in the urban slums; others may try to emigrate.

The same is true of people whose livelihood is threatened in urban contexts, or who are poor and disadvantaged. The fear of losing their jobs to machines led some skilled workers in small workshops in the cloth industry in the Midlands, Lancashire and Yorkshire to smash machines in the second decade of the nineteenth century - the Luddite movement. In the 1960s in the USA, the 'long hot summers' of urban violence were directly associated with widespread deprivation amongst mainly black inhabitants of the inner-city ghettoes. The conditions which gave rise to these occurrences included real poverty, unemployment, the lack of facilities and a wide sense of grievance that access to the good things of life (which people saw about them) was impossible. In the late 1970s and early 1980s, similar violence has been seen in British cities.

Finally, it is important to use the present notion of politics to help recognize what is *really* going on in the course of so-called 'industrial disputes'. They are highly political, and inevitably so. Few can ever be satisfactorily explained by the alleged greed, laziness or incompetence of either workers or managers. These disputes represent conflicts about the proper or fair use and distribution of resources within an enterprise, whether these be new machines which may deprive people of jobs (for instance in the printing industry), investment, facilities or wages. At times, such particular disputes may merge with wider ideological differences about the distribution of power, control and ownership of factories or firms, and the social inequalities between managers and workers which flow from them. Such disputes have occurred in both 'capitalist' and 'communist' (or 'state capitalist') societies. For instance, the emergence of the Solidarity trade union movement in Poland in the early 1980s reflected the demand of Polish workers to participate more directly in the decision-making processes of their enterprises, with far-reaching implications for the wider politics of the society, in productive and distributional terms, affecting both resource use *and* power.

I X

The purpose of these various examples has been to illustrate and underline the central thesis of the book: if one wishes to make sense of a wide range of different kinds of societies, and the enormous number of issues, problems and conflicts which arise within and between them, the conception of politics used here will provide a firm starting-point. In conclusion, then, there are three strands of the argument to stress.

First, politics is central to the life of the human species, and always has been. It is found in all societies, institutions and groups, and is hence much wider and more important than its usual identification with 'government' and associated activities. Therefore, when administrators and politicians, for instance, ask us to 'keep politics out' of things like sport (or vice versa), or not to 'mix' politics with religion or industrial relations or 'race' relations, what they are *actually* asking is that we do not *participate* in politics, that is in decisions about the use and distribution of resources in relation to affairs that are often very important in our lives. They are not really seeking to promote, defend or even isolate politics, they are seeking to *suppress* it.

Secondly, if we are to understand politics, we should pay *less* attention to the narrow *institutional* context of bosses, chiefs, chairpersons, vice-chancellors, parties and parliaments, and *more* attention to the wider context of the relations of the 'systems' discussed earlier. This is *not* to say that institutional detail is unimportant: there may be circumstances, which will emerge later, when a great deal does need to be known about such detail. But it is *less* important, in the first instance, than a clear grasp of the relations of these 'systems' of production, distribution, power, social organization, culture and ideology.

Thirdly, the way to go about doing this in a preliminary fashion for any society or institution is to ask the following set of related questions about it:

What resources are being obtained, used, produced, argued about or mobilized? For what purposes are they being used, by whom and why?

How are they currently distributed and redistributed, and according to what principles and methods?

How are decisions taken about such matters, by whom and according to what procedures and rules? That is, what is the structure of power, how is it distributed, and why?

What is the social organization associated with this? For instance, is it composed of sharply defined and unequal groups, which are hierarchically arranged in relation to both the distribution of resources and power? In a society this may consist of kings, princes, barons, knights, priests, commoners and slaves. Or, more broadly, estates, castes, classes or 'racial' groups. In institutional terms, in a hospital for example, what are the relations between administrators, consultants, registrars, deputy registrars, junior doctors, nurses, patients and porters? Or, in a factory, what are the relations between shareholders, managers, clerical staff, foremen, workers and apprentices, and how does each group stand in relation to the control and distribution of resources and power? Alternatively, are the relations of social groups more egalitarian and informal, for instance within and between clans, villages and camps in some societies, or between the members of many voluntary associations in other societies?

Finally, in what ways do culture and ideology both reflect and influence all this? Even the smallest institutions have their own 'cultures', their regular ways of doing things, and also ideologies which encourage certain kinds of behaviours and frown on others. What are these? How are they sustained?

All the activities of cooperation and conflict which constitute politics flow through and around the relations of these features in all groups, institutions and societies, sometimes formally and sometimes informally. Moreover, all the major social problems faced by them, and their achievements, can be traced to these relations - their politics.

This then is the definition of politics which will be used throughout this book. It forms the foundation on which the structure of the argument is built. Each of the following chapters will serve to illustrate the usefulness of this conception when trying to understand the characteristics and problems of some unfamiliar and familiar societies and institutions, starting with the !Kung San of the Kalahari desert.

CHAPTER TWO

Sharing and equality in the Kalahari: the politics of the !Kung San

I

Most of human history has been lived in 'hunting and gathering' or 'foraging' societies. It has been estimated that this way of life has accounted for more than 90 per cent of the history of the human species. The rest of that history has been lived mainly in agricultural societies, while industrial societies are very recent indeed and account for a mere fraction of our history.[1] It is therefore not surprising that the hunting and gathering way of life has been described as 'the most successful and persistent adaptation man has ever achieved'.[2]

Before the neolithic revolution, some 10,000 years ago, when people first began to cultivate crops and domesticate animals, everybody lived in foraging societies. These have varied in their environmental context from arctic conditions to deserts. Only a relatively few foraging societies have lasted into modern times, and some have been studied in detail. They include such groups as the Guayaki in the Amazon basin, the Eskimos of northern Canada, the Mbuti pygmies of the Ituri forests of Zaire, the Birhors of north-east India, and the Aboriginals of Australia.

Such societies have conventionally been bracketed in the archaeological category of the Late Stone Age (and before). However, to regard such societies only as odd fossils which have by some chance survived into the modern age is simply mistaken. Precisely because such societies endured for so long it is important to consider whether we may learn anything from the principles according to which they organized the production and reproduction of their social life and material culture. This chapter is thus concerned to illustrate the framework sketched in the previous chapter by analysing one such foraging society, and to suggest some implications and lessons which this may have for modern societies.

II

The earliest societies in Southern Africa were foraging societies. Referred to once as Bushmen, the people who formed these societies have in recent years come to be called the San. Societies of San prevailed throughout Southern Africa long before pastoral and then agricultural societies were formed there

over the last 2000 years. The account which follows here sets out to describe
and analyse one such society, living on the northern edge of the Kalahari desert,
which is today divided between Botswana and Namibia (see Map 2). The
foragers of this area are known as the !Kung, and the particular groups which
will be the focus of attention here are the !Kung of the Dobe area and some of
their immediate neighbours, such as the !Kung of Nyae Nyae.[3]

Archaeological evidence suggests continuity in foraging societies in this area
for 11,000 years at the very least, and probably for a great deal longer. It was
only in the late nineteenth century that the San of this area came into contact
with iron-using peoples, such as the Tswana, who made seasonal hunting trips
into the Kalahari from the east. Despite some small changes resulting from this
outside contact, the way of life of the San remained largely unchanged. In the
last thirty years, however, the impact of the outside world has begun to have
more dramatic and destructive effects. But that is a different issue. At this
point, what we need to concentrate upon is the way in which the society of the
!Kung San worked prior to the very recent impact upon it of the outside world.

III

The northern Kalahari is a flat sandy area, covered by savannah-like grasses,
scrub and bush. It is not a particularly severe desert though the rainfall is both
meagre and highly variable. Annual rainfall is rarely more than 15 inches and

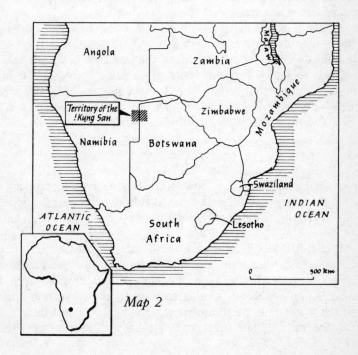

Map 2

drought is quite common. The rain falls in the heat of the summer months (from October to May), and it varies in intensity from place to place and year to year. It creates quite large pans, which are temporary shallow ponds. The winter months are dry. Apart from short periods during the summer rains, there is very little surface water. The focal points of human activity in this dry region are therefore around the permanent and semi-permanent water holes and the food resources on the territory in their vicinity. These form the coordinates of !Kung societies, though in summer - when the rains fall - people are able to spread out further afield.

This generally arid environment none the less supports a remarkably rich variety of animal and plant life. It is this which forms the subsistence base of !Kung society. There are more than 250 species of animals in the region, and the !Kung know them all and use many of them. The major sources of their animal food include such game as eland, kudu, duiker and wildebeest, as well as porcupines, ant-eaters, spring-hares and warthogs. There are also guinea-fowl, ostriches, and migrating geese and ducks. Then there are the slower animals such as tortoises, along with some snakes and insects like locusts. Honey is a rare but much sought-after delicacy.

But it is the plant life of the area which forms the central core of !Kung food intake, and also provides for other needs - for shelters, firewood, implements and so on. The !Kung know and can name over 200 plant species including roots and bulbs, nuts, fruit and berries. The most commonly eaten include the nutritious mongongo fruit and its nuts, as well as wild oranges and sour plums, tsin beans and tsama melons.

All other items in the material culture of the !Kung - like cloths, cloaks, aprons, bags, utensils, musical instruments and weapons - have to be derived from the animals killed, or adapted from the available raw materials. These include ostrich shells for carrying water, the sinews from larger animals for bow-strings, and gum from certain trees to help glue the bone arrow-heads to shafts. It has only been very recently in their history that iron has been used in making some of these things, or substituting for them.

I V

How, then, has the politics of the !Kung organized the production and reproduction of their social life and material culture in these conditions? What has enabled a society of this kind to endure so long without endemic internal crises?

In the 1960s the Dobe !Kung were estimated to be about 460 in number. They were associated with some ten water holes over an area of roughly 3000 square miles or more. In the past, the numbers might have been higher. Because the !Kung are always visiting each other, the population attached to any particular water hole has been characterized by a considerable degree of fluctuation and change, but not completely so. At times - for instance in conditions of sustained drought – a number of groups may gather at one water hole. This was the case with the !Kung of Nyae Nyae, who were about 570 in number in the early 1950s, associated with sixteen water holes over some 5400 square miles.

These populations are organized into related 'bands', or 'camps', which usually vary in size from about ten to thirty people, but sometimes congregate together in considerably larger numbers for short periods. Each camp is identified with a core group of relatives – usually brothers and sisters, their spouses and children. These groups are regarded collectively as the 'owners' of the water hole. Around each water hole is an area of land, called the *n!ore*, which contains the food resources and other water supplies of the camp. Beyond the *n!ore*, in turn, lies an area of land which is shared with other camps, but the boundaries between this and the *n!ores* are not always clear.

!Kung society is organized around what has usually been called a 'subsistence' way of life. They produce what is needed for the community. They do not produce a surplus over and above what they need, nor do they produce for storage or exchange or trade, and they do not accumulate possessions. In thinking about the structure of !Kung society, it is important to understand how their systems of production, distribution, power and decision-making, social organization, culture and ideology are all geared to sustain this way of life, and how effectively and closely these systems are integrated with each other through their politics.

The core of the productive system of !Kung society is the hunting of game and the gathering of available seasonal foods and slow-moving animals. The division of labour associated with this is straightforward. Men hunt and also do some gathering, while women do most of the gathering. Boys assist their elders with some hunting and so learn the craft. Small children of both sexes help the women to collect the plants, berries, fruits, nuts and roots which form the bulk of !Kung food – about 70 per cent of it by weight. Except in rare circumstances, they do not exhaust all the plant food resources of a particular camp area, but move on before that happens. The G/wi San of the central Kalahari area actually believe that to kill or gather more than they need would be to anger the creator, N!adima.[4]

The technology associated with these activities is simple but effective, and light in weight. Some groups use dogs to assist in hunting. Men use long sticks to probe the underground burrows of hares, as well as clubs, spears, snares for trapping animals, and bows and poison-tipped arrows. Digging sticks, bags for carrying gathered foods, shoulder nets for equipment and baby-carriers for the women are the main items used in gathering activities. In the late winter and early spring the !Kung sometimes set fire to the dry bush. When the rains come this stimulates the growth of new green vegetation and hence attracts the game to the area.

The !Kung are highly knowledgeable about their environment, and have to be. They constantly gather and monitor intelligence about the movement of game. They interpret the tracks which have been sighted to help assess the possible direction which animals will take in relation to available grazing resources and rainfall patterns. Men will discuss these matters at great length in the camp. The women know the location and condition of the many seasonal plant food resources in their area, and they teach their young about all this when they take them out to gather with them. All this knowledge is essential for such a society, and it represents one key aspect of their science.

In providing for their subsistence, the !Kung distribute themselves rationally over their territory. This is in part influenced by the seasonal variation of different kinds of food resources in the area, and it also influences their flexible cycles of migration. This leads to patterns of convergence and dispersion of groups. From a productive point of view it helps also to ensure a balanced distribution of people in relation to resources. But it further serves - as will shortly emerge more fully - certain important social functions. Rainfall is a key factor in this process amongst both the Dobe and Nyae Nyae !Kung. In the dry seasons, largish groups may congregate around the permanent water holes, and then disperse over 'their' territory to gather the plentiful mongongo nuts, melons and other abundant foods in the wet season.

Much hunting and gathering is collaborative, and it is generally done in groups. Like the 'picnic' gathering expeditions of the Eskimos in the short Arctic berry season, the !Kung women usually go out to gather in groups, often carrying their youngest babies on their shoulders. Older children assist with gathering while playing. The nature of the hunt - especially of larger game - requires cooperation. In the open ecological conditions of the Kalahari, and given the character of !Kung technology, this is necessary in tracking, chasing and killing the animals, and in lugging the carcass or cuts of meat back into the camp. Great cooperative skills have been developed in hunting. Men signal to each other while they silently close in on the kill and take aim with their bows and arrows, which are accurate over not much more than twenty-five yards. For smaller game they may hunt singly or in pairs.

The principles and practices of the !Kung distributive and redistributive systems both reflect and sustain this cooperation in production. These practices also ensure an even use of the resources of the area both within and between camps. There are two broad considerations here: the distribution of productive resources of the land (like water, plants and animals) *between* the camps, and the distribution of the product of hunting and gathering *within* the camps.

As noted earlier, each camp is associated with a particular water hole and its *n!ore*, though at times there may be more than one band found near a particular hole. Other camps (or people from them who are not visitors or relatives) must seek permission to use water or gather foods on a neighbouring *n!ore*. If they do not, conflict might break out. As one !Kung man explained to an anthropologist: 'so long as you eat together it is all right. Or if they come to you first (and seek permission) it is all right too. It's when they eat alone and you come along and later find them there, that's when the fight starts.'[5] As far as the Dobe and Nyae Nyae !Kung are concerned, animals are not the private possession of any camp, and may be tracked and hunted across a neighbouring *n!ore*. Further south, amongst the !Ko San of Botswana, access to territory seems to have been more sharply curtailed. This may well be because the conditions there are somewhat more harsh and dry. It may in general also be the case amongst foraging societies that, where conditions are more severe, the sense of territoriality is that much stronger, though the camps or bands may be further apart, and the evidence from Australia seems to confirm this.[6]

V

In analysing !Kung society, and particularly its distributive and redistributive processes, it is important *not* to think of each band or camp as an isolated society in itself. That would be to miss the central point. Rather, one must think of the related groups as composing a *society of camps*. A lattice of kin and friends spreads out through the camps, amongst the shifting population within and between each. This ensures that in times of hardship people have access to resources and to assistance through their relatives and friends. Constant visiting between camps, as will emerge shortly in a different context, establishes and cements these alliances and relationships.

Within any camp the principles of radical egalitarianism prevail in practice. Food - especially meat - is shared within the camp amongst all, including visitors who may help with hunting and gathering. Those who infringe the norms of sharing are regarded as anti-social and this can be a source of anger and conflict. The cuts of meat are distributed according to certain rules of allocation by the 'owner of the arrow' which killed the animal. But in this respect too there seems to be a conscious effort to blur 'ownership' of the arrow and to redistribute even the prestige that is associated with a kill. No one wants to risk the allegation of being stingy or inept in the distribution of meat. In communities of this kind survival has in large measure depended on group coherence and peace, and hence on cooperation, not on competition. And this is most effectively maintained by collaborative productive work and egalitarianism in distribution. In passing, it is worth noting that this principle of sharing has been taken to an interesting extreme amongst the Guayaki foragers of the Paraguayan forests. There, men do not eat *any* of the meat from game which they have personally downed. They give it to their friends and their families. No one thus feeds himself, and 'each Guayaki adult male spends his life hunting for others because they spend their lives hunting for him'.[7]

People make their own domestic and hunting equipment which is their own property, but will often borrow things from each other as necessary. Such equipment does not add up to very much and is light in total weight - not being much more than 20 lbs - for it has all to be carried when they move from camp to camp, or when they go visiting.

But the distributive and redistributive principles of sharing are very strong indeed and are sustained by a variety of other customs and behaviour. The !Kung are, for instance, constantly giving presents to each other, and these presents circulate between individuals and camps. They provide the opportunity for bringing people together and they create and sustain long-term bonds between the people of the camps. This helps to underpin the principles of equality and mutual access to the subsistence resources of the various *n!ores*. When a group of anthropologists gave the women of one camp a present of necklaces made up of West African cowrie shells (bought in New York!), they found a year later that all the necklaces had been broken down into individual shells and had been redistributed as gifts in ones and twos to other people throughout the Nyae Nyae area.[8] !Kung also give each other presents which consist of daily items of equipment and clothing, or simple decorative ornaments, like headbands or eggshell beads. 'The worst thing is not giving gifts', said one man. 'If people do not like each other but one gives a gift and the other must accept, this brings peace between them. We give to one another always. We give what we have. This is the way we live together.'[9]

Together, these practices of sharing and gift-giving act to strengthen the distributive processes and maintain egalitarianism and cooperation in the productive and social life of the society.

VI

The social organization and culture of the !Kung is deeply enmeshed in these productive and distributive activities, and both reflect and support them. The fact that the !Kung have evolved such intricate systems of social organization has contributed decisively to the endurance and harmony of their society. In analysing their systems of social organization and associated culture, it is sensible to think in terms of three broad levels of organization: the family, the camp, and the widest grouping of all, the very loose but none the less crucial framework of relations between camps.

It is best to think of 'camps' *not* as geographical locations but as related groups of families. It would be almost unthinkable for a couple (or individuals) to live in a camp where they had no relatives. Thus most camp members have *at least* a parent or a brother or a sister or a child or a spouse in the same camp. But the nucleus of each family is the core of husband and wife - or wives, since the !Kung practise polygamy, though this is not very common.

When a young couple marry, they first live in the camp of the bride's parents for anything between three and ten years, where the bridegroom does 'bride service' for his new parents-in-law. That is, he hunts for them and hence helps to prove himself as a suitable husband for their daughter. Thereafter, he and his wife and their offspring will usually return to the camp of his parents - that is, to his own *n!ore* - though they may also stay at the camp of the bride's parents. In either case the now extended family will live close to each other in the camp where they have settled, though they will of course be visiting the other camps often. The two generations of parents and newly-marrieds may well be extended further still by the presence of grandparents, for it is regarded as the duty of the young to look after the old and to ensure that they have food. There will also usually be brothers and sisters, married and unmarried, in the camp. Often, when people marry and go to live in another camp, they take a brother or sister with them. And in due course, when the couple have children, a further generation is added to the extended family in the camp.

In the culture and social organization of !Kung society, marriage is therefore a crucial factor in helping to establish and maintain links between camps. It is possible that people may marry someone from their own camp, provided they are not related. But, in general, the marital preferences and patterns have in fact operated so as to establish unions between more distant rather than less distant partners. This has had the very useful effect of distributing relatives and other kin over a wide area in other camps and places. In turn this has opened access to the resources of other camps, not only in times of hardship, and has helped to provide a rudimentary but important sense of involvement in groups other than that of the immediate camp. Amongst the G/wi San of central Botswana, this means that a person 'can trace some sort of kinship with practically every other G/wi with whom he is likely to come into contact'.[10]

Camps are thus composed of groups of families who have found that they can get on well with each other. A camp smaller than about ten people would barely be viable. But the composition of each is in a constant state of flux. At times, camps break down into smaller groups in the wet season, as noted earlier, and there are times when a number of camps may congregate together, perhaps in the dry season at a large and permanent water hole, when there may be as many as 200 people together. These gatherings provide opportunities for old contacts to be renewed, or for new ones to be made. Marriages might be arranged and an intense social life is enjoyed. This might involve trance-dancing, religious ceremonies, the exchange of gifts and bringing people up to date with news. But such large camps cannot last for too long. People may begin to get on each other's nerves through living so close to each other in numbers which, by their standards, are so large. Also, the food resources of the area would begin to be eaten out, and so people would have to work harder and harder by foraging further and further afield. So, in due course, the larger camps split up - perhaps after a month or so. People return to their water holes, or go off visiting, or spread out in smaller groups to collect spring foods when the early rains have come.

As will have been apparent, visiting is very important amongst the !Kung and is a central aspect of their culture. It contributes decisively to the social organization and also to the processes which provide for the production and reproduction of social life and material culture. People walk long distances to exchange gifts, to visit their relatives, to seek new company, to alleviate or avoid tensions, to carry news and so on. In the course of this constant ebb and flow of people within and between camps, new relations are forged and marriage possibilities are opened up. Sometimes, people may visit another camp for longer and longer periods and, finally, remain there. Entirely new camps may be formed as a result of two broad processes. On the one hand, if population growth within a camp were to reach a point where its resource base became strained, a few families might peel off. Some might join other camps, where resources permitted it. Others might in time gradually come to form the core of a new camp. But this would only happen if they could lay legitimate claim to a water hole, or a share in one, and where their existence as a camp came to be recognized and acknowledged by the neighbouring camps. Alternatively, two or more camps which suffered a dramatic decline in population might amalgamate, or fusion may occur where the separate identities of two camps had become increasingly blurred.

Ties between individuals and families in various camps appear in general to be the only bonds which have established and maintained wider inter-camp relationships. There are no formal institutions which link camps. However, among the G/wi San, to the south, there seem to have been very informal and temporary 'alliances' between camps. Thus a camp may have an alliance (or a series of alliances) with other camps, and they with others in turn.

The way in which the culture of the !Kung both reflects and sustains their systems of production and social organization can be illustrated in other ways. I have already referred to their patterns of marriage and residence, visiting, their concern to 'eat together' and to share, their giving of gifts, and aspects of the upbringing of the young. Children are cared for and looked after with great concern and affection. In the camp, people play with them and watch out for them, teaching them to do things. Thus the whole community is closely involved in their upbringing and know them well from birth.

For women, it is clearly important that they space the births of their babies, for the babies have to be carried by the mothers until they can walk, and even then there is still a fair amount of carrying to be done on gathering or visiting expeditions. A complex combination of low fertility, long lactation periods, natural death and - unusually, and only if necessary - infanticide has enabled !Kung women to space their children by three or four years.

VII

In all these ways the culture of the society acts to shape and control behaviour. The !Kung rarely 'work' more than three days in a week to provide for their needs. The rest of the time is devoted to talking and discussion, to games, to visiting and to playing their various musical instruments. The control of behaviour is thus *social* control, expressed in and through their culture and values. For the !Kung have no police forces, no standing armies nor law-enforcement agencies. Nor do they have councils or priests or officials. But there is leadership. This is usually associated with a man who has special personal qualities, such as being a good hunter or a good talker, or who argues well and whose opinions are well thought of. But such a person does not occupy any office, nor does he have any formal standing. Indeed such a person would go out of his way to be modest in behaviour and would in no way appear conspicuous in terms of possessions or privileges.

Thus, with the exception of this element of leadership, the system of power and decision-making in !Kung society is vested in the community and distributed by active participation throughout it. It is not a separate or institutionalized sphere of activity. The collective ownership of resources, the cooperative character of production, and the egalitarian nature of distribution are associated with a highly decentralized and what might be called a democratic distribution of power. Decision-making within or between families or camps is closely bound up with productive and distributive activities. There are thus no such categories as owners and workers, or leaders and followers. There are no chiefs and subordinates, there are no classes or castes, or princes and commoners. There are only *Zhu/twasi*, or 'genuine people'.[11]

But even amongst 'genuine people' there is conflict. It may arise from improper distribution of meat or inadequate gift exchanges. It may be provoked by accusations of laziness or stinginess, or it may be caused by jealousy and marital disputes. Conflict may occur between families - and hence parts of camps - over distributive issues, or behaviour, or unfulfilled obligations. Anti-social behaviour which, for instance, disturbed hunting activities or consistently created friction within a camp would give rise to tension and conflict. But wherever possible, the !Kung try to avoid the escalation of disputes into fights. 'Fighting is dangerous,' they say, 'someone might get killed.'[12] Where conflict does break out, other people in the camp rush to try to control it, for an argument which erupted into serious fighting could create a feud which might rip through the camp and destroy it, with wider implications for other camps as well.

There are various levels of conflict which the !Kung recognize. These range from arguing, shouting, the exchange of insults through to homicide. Though people in a camp will try to placate and control things when tempers are raised, disputes sometimes get out of hand and people do get killed. However, it is very rare indeed that fighting has occurred between camps. A comparative analysis of killing in various societies has shown just how effectively the !Kung have managed and controlled conflict when compared with modern industrial societies and the extraordinary amount of violence and blood-letting that goes on within, and especially between, them.[13]

It will be clear from all this that the social ideology of the !Kung is best described as one of relentless egalitarianism. They frown on behaviour which is immodest and boastful and they do not like to be seen to stand out from the community. They have very effective social means for putting down anyone who is arrogant, or who behaves in a mean or selfish way. To be thought of as being any of these things, or to be accused of behaving in such ways, is deeply humiliating to them. All this therefore helps to sustain their society, to avoid dangerous inequalities and to maintain the peace within and between !Kung camps.

In summary, it is important to recognize that the politics of this society can be found in all these activities. As a society they live in ecological balance with their environment. They have evolved a system of production which provides for the needs of all members of the community. Their systems of distribution and redistribution have been characterized by sharing and equality, and their system of power and decision-making has been democratic. Associated with this they have evolved systems of social organization, culture and ideology which sustain their productive life, by establishing and maintaining a network of relations within and between the camps. In short, by almost any standard, these societies have worked extraordinarily well. This illustrates the point that it is not simply the level of technology or the quantity of resources which determine the welfare of a society, but the way it organizes the use, production and distribution of the available resources through its politics.

VIII

Before looking at some of the lessons which societies of this kind may suggest for us, it is necessary first to record the fact that few such societies exist any longer. Wherever they have, for instance, lost control of access to the environment which has sustained them, they have been thrown into crisis. The balance between their productive, distributive and social relations has been ruptured, and this has brought about their collapse and disappearance. Or where the populations of foraging societies expanded beyond the capacity of the natural resources to support them, they have disintegrated or they have taken to cultivation and the domestication of animals. In the course of time various agricultural societies have emerged and have in turn encroached on the territory of other foragers. Foraging societies have either died out, adapted or been killed off. Or people from them have been assimilated in various ways into new and different societies which have almost everywhere replaced them.

In Africa foraging societies have not generally been organized for war, and hence they have not been organized for defence. Relative to the military capabilities of herding, agricultural, commercial and industrial societies, they have been very vulnerable indeed. Although they have been able to mount effective guerrilla resistance campaigns, in the end they have gone under.

For example, on the Kenya-Uganda border, the Ik - the Mountain People - have been confined to only a limited part of their former traditional yearly beat. Excluded from their major hunting territory - which was declared a game reserve - Ik society has been radically altered in both social and moral terms. In conditions of almost permanent hunger, they appear to have abandoned their cooperative and communal relations of production and distribution, and have become highly individualistic, solitary and greedy. Scratching a bare living in the mountains, they were found to be selfish and brutal towards young and old alike. Clearly their society was in an advanced state of disintegration.[14]

Not all foraging societies have disintegrated in that fashion. In the Amazon jungle, groups have retreated from contact with the Brazilian authorities and have attacked officials and workers engaged in building roads through their territories. But where contact has occurred, disease has often decimated such societies and they have perished.

In Southern Africa, long before the advent of European colonialism in the seventeenth century, some groups of foragers took slowly to pastoralism, while others moved out of the path of emerging pastoral societies. Later still, immigrant cultivators - who raised crops and tended cattle - spread southwards from Central and East Africa, edging out the foragers, though often living for long periods in more or less comfortable relations with them. But San societies in Southern Africa have not, in the end, survived the cumulative effects of these migrations, nor the final blows imposed by expansionist settler colonialism.

Thus the San of the Kalahari are amongst the few groups of people who retained the foraging way of life, though it is not likely that this will last for much longer. External forces now penetrate to the core of such areas as Dobe and Nyae Nyae, and suck them into a wider world of very different relationships. These are matters to be pursued in later chapters. For the present it is necessary to stand back from the detail and to explore some wider implications.

IX

Societies of this kind have, in general, only been of interest to anthropologists, to whom we owe a great deal for their careful and detailed studies. To most other people they have seemed, at best, quaint and exotic, and at worst, barely human. Nor have they seemed of significance in any other way. Such a view is extremely short-sighted. For all social scientists can learn a great deal of value by examining the central characteristics of such societies. And anyone who is interested in politics - as defined earlier - cannot fail to derive some important lessons by analysing the central principles according to which such societies have organized their productive and social life.

It is of course not possible to generalize about all foraging societies on the basis of the !Kung San. Interesting and important variations have everywhere been found. Some, living closer to coasts and rivers, have developed local technologies which have enabled them to exploit the resources of their environments - by using tidal traps and fishing spears, for instance. Their seasonal movements have often been between the coastal regions (in winter) and further inland (in summer).[15] In yet different ecological contexts - like jungles - some have developed net-hunting techniques. Elsewhere, where populations have been more substantial overall and resources relatively more limited, relations between camps of hunters and gatherers have been more edgy, and stricter rules have governed access to each other's territory. And not all the foraging societies which have been studied have revealed the same degree of friendliness and happiness which all who have worked with the !Kung report. So it is important to bear in mind the variety of societies of this type.

However, having said that, it is none the less the case that around the world there has been a remarkable consistency in the underlying structural features of such societies, with few exceptions. Comparable functional requirements appear to have been met through variations on the same structural themes. It seems almost as if societies of hunters and gatherers (and some have hunted more than gathered, and vice versa) all over the world evolved and systematically applied those principles which not only ensured their survival but also made for a remarkable 'quality of life'. In concluding this chapter, it is worth exploring some of these principles and asking whether there may be any lessons for us in the modern world.

The first point to make is that societies of this kind have not been characterized by an existence which was 'nasty, brutish and short'.[16] As shown here in relation to the !Kung, social relations have been marked by friendliness, a commitment to peaceful ways of doing things, and a concern to avoid or damp down violence and conflict. Such societies, moreover, have rarely waged war on each other, nor have they conquered other peoples. The title of one book about the !Kung seeks to emphasize these features of their life by calling them *The Harmless People*.[17] Detailed medical studies of the !Kung are few and far between. However, the evidence which has been collected suggests that they are, in general, healthy. They are vulnerable, of course, to attacks by wild animals - an 'occupational hazard' of the hunting and gathering way of life. Viruses, bacteria and internal parasites are major threats to health and life amongst the !Kung, while some of the major causes of death in modern societies - cardiovascular diseases and cancer - are virtually non-existent.[18] But there can be little doubt that the general levels of health in such societies have been far better than that of the broad mass of people in the crowded urban slums of, say, nineteenth-century English cities, or twentieth-century Calcutta. Members of societies such as that of the !Kung have usually had plenty to eat, and they have enjoyed more leisure time than do most people in the industrial world. And a real achievement of their politics has unquestionably been to ensure that the needs of all people were satisfied, and that competitive activities which could lead to conflict have been kept to a minimum. In general, they have been at pains not to deplete their natural environment upon which their existence has depended, nor have they polluted or scarred it.

Secondly, they have usually distributed their populations rationally in relation to the available resources, and vice versa. In the establishment of reciprocal relations within and between camps they have ensured a more or less balanced access to the resources which make life possible. Gross imbalances or inequalities between groups in these societies of camps have therefore been avoided. And they have recognized that such inequalities could create dangerous tensions and conflicts which might destroy them.

Thirdly, of the greatest importance, is the fact that, given the character of their technology, science and productive life, they seem to have solved for themselves what is perhaps the central problem for any society, the question of distribution and redistribution. Moreover, they have recognized that such processes cannot be left to the automatic workings of 'the economy', but require the careful integration of the productive and social life of the community. For the question of distribution is fundamentally a social question, and hence central to the politics of a society. It seems clear that if a society is to avoid serious conflict, tension and disruption - arising for instance from inequality and deprivation - then its systems of production, distribution, social organization and power must be effectively related and integrated. That is to say, these systems need to be organized so that they contribute to the coherence and solidarity of the society and not to the emergence of pressures and forces which can threaten its disintegration. For where the politics of distribution, for instance, generates inequalities at the heart of a society, it also contributes directly to dissension and conflict. And where the system of social organization further acts to entrench these inequalities, or where an ideology fans such inequalities into competitive behaviours, then the system of power will tend to coerce or suppress the disputes and disturbances which arise around such unequal patterns of distribution. And this in turn only acts to aggravate further the dissatisfaction and conflict.

In the organization of their society, the !Kung have shown how to avoid this. Their systems of production, distribution and power have been mutually reinforcing, not contradictory. Their systems of social organization, culture and ideology have supported this. In turn and together they emphasize in practice the necessarily *interdependent* principles of cooperation, sharing, equality and participation. While it may be premature in the argument of the book to suggest comparisons with modern societies, there are stark and obvious ways in which this general pattern contrasts with many societies today, in both the industrial and Third worlds. Often we see societies where there is private concentration or public centralization of resources, where systems of production stress competition for individual success and wealth rather than public satisfaction of needs, where systems of uneven distribution of resources result in great poverty for some and enormous power and control for others, and where all this is supposed to cohere in a democratic culture, sustained by an ideology which advertises human equality. It is hardly surprising that it rarely does.

The commitment to equality and sharing, and the hostility to competition and conflict, pervade all aspects of !Kung society. Thus, in assessing the principal lessons of such societies as these, it is clear that equality has not simply been regarded as a desirable state of affairs, as something which it would be nice to have if it could be arranged. Rather it has been recognized as an *essential* and necessary condition of peaceful social existence. The associated practices of cooperation and an intensely 'democratic' way of life in turn seem to be what have sustained those conditions of equality.

Now it could be said that, since such societies as these have been so small in scale and so simple in their technology, we can derive few lessons from them. There are at least two important responses to this view. First, the fact of the matter is that all societies, by their very nature as societies, have and must have systems of production, distribution, social organization, power, culture and ideology. No society will survive or prosper (except at the cost of *other* societies) unless these systems are integrated in such a way that they contribute to the well-being of the community. To that extent, the principles which have ensured the welfare of societies such as the !Kung are very relevant indeed for all other societies, whatever the character of their technology and their size. Secondly, it ought surely to be the case that so-called 'modern' societies should be more than able to provide for the needs of their members, especially given the enormous developments in food production, technology and science. If they do not, then it is hardly likely to be the case that this is due to faults or limitations in their technological or productive capacities. Rather, we must look at the way in which these productive activities, and their products, are organized and distributed; that is, we must look to the *politics* of the society for an explanation.

This is the point where a comparison with foraging societies can become instructive. For one need only ask of contemporary societies whether they meet the needs of all their people and, if not, why not? How successfully have societies in the post-neolithic world evolved systems of distribution, social organization and popular control which are comparable and appropriate to the advances they have made in their productive systems? Do societies in the modern world provide equally for the welfare of their members? Do the distributive arrangements promote balance and equity as necessary components of welfare, or do they promote conflict?

These are the kinds of questions which will be asked time and again through this book. For such issues are central to the politics of all human societies, and the relations between them: that is, how communities go about using, producing and distributing resources, for instance with regard to land, food, housing, jobs, income and welfare.

The purpose of this chapter has been to put the framework of analysis to work in a preliminary way and to illustrate its usefulness by answering these questions for the !Kung. What emerges clearly here is that the manner in which the 'systems' referred to in the previous chapter are related to each other through the politics of a society will decisively shape its general condition and the problems it faces.

This approach now needs to be illustrated more fully in the context of other societies and different problems before seeing how it can be used to explain the characteristics of politics in modern societies. The next chapter does so by exploring the structure and politics of the extraordinary Aztec 'empire' in the fifteenth century, on the eve of the Spanish conquest of the New World.

CHAPTER THREE

Predatory politics: the Aztecs

I

The world of the Aztecs could hardly have been more different from that of the
!Kung San. However, in turning to analyse the remarkable politics of this non-
industrial society of Middle America, the same approach which has been
outlined and illustrated in previous chapters will be applied here to help reveal
the nature of the contrast and also to underline and extend the general
argument.

When, in 1519, the Spanish *conquistadores* under Hernán Cortés
commenced their expedition inland from Vera Cruz on the Gulf of Mexico to
locate the capital of the Aztecs, they simply had no idea of what they would find.
Nothing in their experience could have prepared them for it. After struggling
up the rugged mountains which form the central highlands of Mexico, they
finally reached the city, Tenochtitlán (see Map 3). What they saw before them
left them stunned. Cupped in the great Valley of Mexico was a lake, and
anchored in the lake was a city:

And when we saw all those cities and villages in the lake, and other great

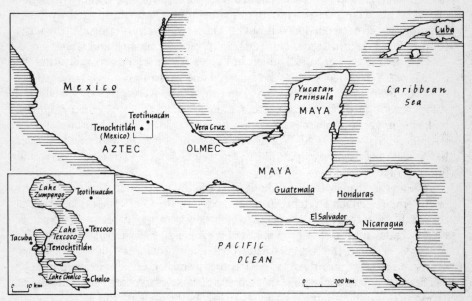

Map 3

towns on dry land, and that straight and level causeway leading to Mexico, we were astonished. Those great towns and buildings rising from the water, all made of stone, seemed like an enchanted vision . . . . Indeed some of our soldiers asked if it was not a dream . . . . It was all so wonderful that I do not know how to describe this first glimpse of things never heard of, seen or dreamed before.[1]

What the Spanish were encountering was the last of a number of large and complex societies which had risen and fallen in Middle America from early in the first millennium BC - that is from 1000 years before Christ.

The great upland Valley of Mexico covers an area of about 3000 square miles, and its population in 1519 was probably no less than two million. The city of Tenochtitlán itself covered an area of some 2500 acres (or 4 square miles) and those who saw it reported that there were at least 6000 houses in it. Population estimates for the city vary from 200,000 to half a million. Even the lowest figure indicates an urban population which was well in excess of the major cities of Europe at the start of the sixteenth century.

The houses and their floating allotments - the *chinampas* - plus the fields and villages round the shore of the major lake, Lake Texcoco, were connected by canals and causeways via open plazas, broad streets and market places to the central core of the city. This was dominated by the main pyramid-shaped temple and by the palace of the ruler and the residences of the rich. It was a city of astonishing proportions and complex internal structure. There were no draught animals and hence no wheeled transport in Mexico.[2] Everywhere food and produce were carried into the city by people, or transported by boats around the lake. Aqueducts brought clean water from outside the city. Craftsmen worked in stone, obsidian, cloth, mosaics of shell and stone, wood, cold-hammered copper, gold, silver and clay. An enormous market attracted 20-25,000 buyers and sellers who bartered and exchanged an amazing variety of goods from throughout Middle America. There were precious metals and stones, exotic feathers, clothes, shoes, skins, foodstuffs, dyes, pottery, knives, builders' materials, tobacco and pipes. Spanish soldiers who had been in the trading centres of the Old World - in Constantinople, in Rome and all over Italy - had never seen a market like it, 'so well laid out, so large, so orderly and full of people'.[3]

Though the Spaniards did not know it at the time, Tenochtitlán was the heart of an 'empire' which stretched from the coast of the Gulf of Mexico across to the Pacific, and from the dry plains which flow north to modern Arizona and California down to the steamy jungles of what is today Guatemala. This empire consisted of some thirty-eight major 'tributary provinces' plus the villages, towns and cities within them, as well as many smaller vassal states and towns.[4]

The total population within this empire may well have been substantially in excess of 11 million, and perhaps as many as 25 million. But it was not an ordered empire in the conventional sense of the term, ruled by administrators and governors, or patrolled and garrisoned by armies of occupation. Tenochtitlán was a predatory city-state which both controlled its empire and sustained itself through a combination of intensive local agriculture in the Valley of Mexico, through trade, the extraction of a massive volume of tribute, and terror.

Although Aztec society and culture was in some respects a gentle one, which prized music and poetry and flowers, it was none the less premissed on war - and human sacrifice. Each year, thousands of people - mainly those captured in war - were sacrificed to the gods. When the Spaniards were shown inside the great temple in Tenochtitlán, which gleamed white on the outside, they found the walls inside to be caked with blood. The stench was overwhelming. The priests' clothing and hair were matted with gore from the task of knifing open the chests of the victims and wrenching out the still-beating hearts which were then held up and burned as an offering to the gods.

What system of production sustained this city and its growing population? What systems of distribution and social organization both established and reflected the steeply hierarchical structure of power which was dominated by a powerful king-emperor and his court, in close association with an influential priesthood? How might one explain the extraordinary pattern of predation by which the Aztecs relentlessly squeezed tribute from the subordinate peoples in their empire? What contribution did this make to the availability of resources in the society, and how were they redistributed and used within it? Wherein lies the explanation for the obsession with slaughter and human sacrifice? What ideology both provoked and fuelled these practices?

To answer these questions it is necessary to return to the framework outlined before. There is no need to repeat it in detail here. However, it might be useful to reiterate the central starting-points of the approach. Their importance in relation to the development and character of Aztec society will quickly become apparent.

The central features of the politics of any society are shaped by two broad and related sets of factors. On the one hand, there are the constraints and possibilities offered by its natural environment and also by its relations with neighbouring and more distant societies with which it may be in contact. On the other hand, given its population size and technological capacities, the condition of a society is decisively shaped by the way it goes about exploiting this environment in the course of the production and reproduction of both its social life and material culture. That is, by the way in which it obtains, uses, produces and distributes resources.

To understand the structure of Aztec society in relation to these matters it is necessary to understand something of its history. And to understand that history is to locate the rise of the Aztecs fairly and squarely in the ecological and demographic context of Middle America. One introductory qualification is necessary here. Just as the deep history of the !Kung is obscure, so too are many aspects of the history and structure of Aztec society. None the less, it is possible to use the evidence gathered and presented by scholars in various disciplines - from Archaeology to Demography - to offer an account, which must be speculative in places, of the politics of the Aztec empire, thus stressing, in passing, the importance of an interdisciplinary approach in work of this kind.

II

The first immigrants to the New World crossed into Alaska from Siberia about 30,000 years ago at least. Slowly, small groups fanned out towards the south. By 14,000 BC, if not before, they were living in Middle America, and by 9000 BC they had reached the very tip of the continent.[5] In both North and South America, the archaeological record reveals that societies of foragers lived by exploiting diverse ecological environments in different ways. Those near the coasts, for instance, relied more on seafoods, while those further inland hunted game. All of them gathered plant foodstuffs on a seasonal basis, like the !Kung. It is likely that for very long periods such societies lived in isolation from each other, as is shown by the incredible diversity of pre-Conquest languages in the region. In Mexico alone there are today more than 200 indigenous languages, most of which are mutually unintelligible, and in many areas even neighbouring villages are not able to communicate with each other in their own language.

Everywhere, extensive herds of game - such as horses, bison, oxen, camels, elephants, antelopes, pigs and giant rodents - were in abundance, and evidence of these has been found near the Valley of Mexico.[6] Conditions for hunting were good and appropriate technologies were developed from place to place. Human populations grew slowly but steadily. This in turn put pressure on the herds; so much so that many of these species became extinct, and so communities came to rely increasingly on vegetable foods.

Throughout Middle and South America from 6000 BC at different times, in different places, at different speeds and in different combinations, such communities began slowly to domesticate plants and animals to secure their food resources. The plants included the more familiar ones of maize, squashes, potatoes, amaranth, beans and chili peppers, while the animals which they raised included llamas and alpacas (especially in the Andes) as well as dogs, guinea pigs, water fowl and turkeys. The process was everywhere a slow and patchy one. It varied from place to place and it occurred side by side with the continuation of foraging societies. And everywhere amongst the early agriculturalists there remained a continued but decreasing reliance on hunting and gathering which went on in the first fully settled agricultural societies that began to emerge in a few places from about 2500 BC.

The emergence of these early agricultural societies was associated with yet further population increases, as has happened almost everywhere. This is because agricultural production and settlement remove some of the constraints which the constant mobility of hunting and gathering imposes on population size. Also, agricultural production and storage techniques provide generally larger and more dependable food supplies which can support expanding populations.[7] But this in turn placed further pressures in due course on the land resources available.

As people change the way they use and produce resources, so too they change their politics, where they live and how they live. The new pressures on land compelled people to open up and use new areas for cultivation and to develop new techniques for doing so. In devising new farming systems, some groups evolved simple irrigation methods which enabled them to use additional land. Then, as people began to settle more permanently, the structure of their social organization shifted from one based on bands and camps to village-based societies and, ultimately, to city states.

This process has been aptly described as a cycle involving successive 'intensifications' of production, followed by 'depletions' of resources, which have in turn provoked either crisis and collapse, or technological innovation, or a combination of both.[8] This was beginning to happen in a number of areas in the Americas in the course of the 7000 years before the time of Christ, notably in Middle America.

A fine reconstruction of this kind of process has been suggested by archaeologists working in the Tehuacán Valley, south of the Valley of Mexico. There, a small population of foragers in the period from 7000 BC had grown to one of perhaps 1500 people by 800 BC, living in groups of related villages concentrated in valley bottoms. With the opening-up of new lands by simple irrigation, people came to rely more and more on agriculture, and population increase was rapid. By the time of Christ it may have been about 4-5000, and it had reached some 100,000 on the eve of the Spanish conquest. As these changes occurred in the Valley, the archaeological record reveals the results. The diet of the people had shifted from one of primarily meat-eating (from hunting) to one involving greater reliance on mainly gathered plants, with produce from agriculture beginning to emerge from 1500 BC as the major source of food. By the time of Christ, agriculture had become the dominant productive activity, and was assisted by irrigation methods. New plants from outside the Valley - like guavas and peanuts - were being planted, indicating connections with other areas. And in the 1000 years before the Spanish set foot on American soil, there is abundant evidence of a large city with defensive fortifications; administrative, ceremonial and religious specialization; trade, and a hierarchical structure of power, wealth and prestige - reflecting a social organization of different class and status groups in the society.[9]

But such processes of 'intensification' of production, in any society, may be fatally flawed. Unless they are skilfully managed through the politics of a society they may lead to ecological depletion or social crisis, or both. What this requires, in practice, is that the procedures of intensification be accompanied by appropriate practices of conservation. It also requires appropriate innovations and adaptations in the systems of distribution, redistribution, power and decision-making, culture and ideology. This was a central problem in and between the many societies of Middle America, and it remains a problem for societies of the modern world. For just as productive intensifications (in agriculture, for instance) have often been responses to the depletion of resources, or to increases or redistribution of populations, such new methods of production may in time stimulate yet further population expansion or lead to further pressure on resources, for instance in the form of increased energy or raw materials requirements. This may in time create additional problems. These may be temporarily alleviated by yet further intensification of exploitation, either by the application of new technology (irrigation or tools, for instance) or by the intensive use of labour, or a combination of both. Whatever method is used, the social organization and structure of power necessary to mobilize and organize such activities have usually been hierarchical and strict, while the internal distribution of resources in the society has usually become or remained very uneven. Or, such problems may be temporarily solved by expansionist politics involving the seizure of additional resources and perhaps involving the domination and incorporation by one society of others. But this also can lead in time to edgy and unstable arrangements which promote resentment and hostility amongst dominated people. Finally, a combination of ecological disruption or depletion, impoverishment, internal civil unrest and external attack or revolt by rival or dominated groups may combine in a crisis which ultimately brings the structure of a society to the point of collapse. As disintegration occurs, formerly dominated groups break loose and the old centres of power subside. A period of less centralized autonomy may follow for such groups, before a new centre of power begins to emerge.

In the long history that preceded the emergence of the Aztec empire, such processes as these were occurring throughout Middle America. From 2000 BC 'human societies have grown and declined in continuous pulsations, first widening their scope, then retreating again, in continuous tension between expansion and decay'.[10] Until 600 BC the Olmecs influenced Middle America from their centres on the lowland Gulf coast where an extensive, shifting 'slash and burn' pattern of cultivation slowly seems to have eroded the ecological basis of their societies. They were followed, before the time of Christ, by the rise of the settlement of Teotihuacán, in the Valley of Mexico. There, between AD 400 and 700, relying on intensive and irrigated agriculture, Teotihuacán reached an astonishing urban peak, with a population of perhaps 100,000 people, dominating the Valley and spreading its influence and power throughout Middle America by a combination of trade, tribute, conquest and colonization.[11] But by the eighth century AD, Teotihuacán was in decline, and by AD 750 only some eight thousand people seem to have lived in its silent ruins. At the same time, in the region of the Gulf, there had arisen the civilization associated with the Mayas, which reached its peak between AD 300 and 900, only to collapse thereafter with staggering speed. Once again the centre of gravity shifted back to the uplands, to the Valley of Mexico, where the Toltecs, based on Tula, came to dominate until the middle of the thirteenth

century, developing a powerful military capacity and also increasing the rate
and scope of human sacrifice. But as their grip on the region loosened, perhaps
triggered or hastened by a prolonged period of severe drought, new forces
emerged in the Valley and conflict erupted as groups began to compete for a
secure place in the favourable agricultural lands.

It is against such a background as this that one needs to understand the rise
and characteristic features of Aztec society and its empire from the twelfth
century AD. But before examining this there are a number of important points
to draw together here.

III

First, many features of Aztec society were based on those which had been
developed earlier in Middle America. They did not start from scratch - no
societies do - but borrowed, elaborated and intensified many of these features in
their systems of agricultural production, in their systems of power and control
over other peoples, and in their civil and religious institutions.

Secondly, given the technological capacities of the major societies that had
preceded the Aztecs in Middle America, little of what they had attained in the
way of production and urban development could have been achieved without
the massive deployment and intensive organization of human labour. For
example, in Teotihuacán there were more than 100 temples and pyramids in
the city, some of which were enormous. These would have required a sustained
concentration of human resources to build. And they contrasted sharply with
the windowless compounds in which the urban poor - who no doubt helped to
build them - lived.

Thirdly, those areas which were agriculturally attractive, like the Valley of
Mexico, inevitably acted as magnets for populations. It follows that as groups
moved into such areas, they competed for a secure hold on the resources of land
and water, and such competition provoked conflict and warfare. Only those
who were able to defend their territory could survive, and this acted to reward
military organization and capacity, as the Toltecs had demonstrated - but only
in the medium run. Militarism in turn promoted expansion and this brought its
own results in terms of additional resources which helped to build and sustain
the centres of power, and those who dominated them. But at the same time it
engendered fear and opposition in conquered or subordinate groups which were
a major source of vulnerability in such empires of conquest and tribute.

Finally, the evidence around them of such a history, plus their own
experience of ecological depletion, climatic uncertainty, scarcity, conflict and
destruction, must have given rise to a conception of a world inhabited by
civilizations which continually rose and fell, a world 'created and consumed in
recurrent cataclysms'.[12] Under such conditions, people in Middle America (and
indeed elsewhere in the world right through to modern times) have regularly
sought theological explanations for their plight. They have likewise also

developed an extraordinary variety of religious practices, as we would call them, which they believed would assist in staving off disaster.

Some of these wider implications will be taken up later in this chapter and in subsequent chapters. For the moment, having sketched the broad historical and ecological context, it is necessary to look now in further detail at the development and structure of Aztec society and its politics.

I V

The Valley of Mexico lies at a height of some 7000 feet. Because it is surrounded by mountains it is more usefully thought of as a basin, for it has no natural outlets. These features acted in pre-Spanish times to trap rainfall in the Valley and created a linked system of five shallow lakes. Rain falls only in the summer months from June to September, but it is not heavy, and droughts are not uncommon. The overall climate is temperate and, compared with the rough mountainous environment in which it lies, the Valley - like others in the area - was very attractive for agricultural purposes.

The Aztecs, or the Tenochas or Mexica as they were known, had migrated in the direction of central Mexico from the north-west in the course of the twelfth and thirteenth centuries. But in such an insecure and conflict-ridden world they did not cease their migration until they had established a firm foothold in the Valley. They first settled round the western shores of Lake Texcoco at the end of the thirteenth century. There they began to expand and secure their society, in the wake of the disintegrating Toltec power, especially after 1345 when they settled on the marshy island on which they were to build the city of Tenochtitlán. Over the following 150 years, the Aztecs 'through adroit political and military manoeuvring, emerged as the last native empire of Mesoamerica'.[13] It is on this transformation of the politics of Aztec society - from a loose and relatively egalitarian organization of clans into a highly structured predatory empire - that attention now turns. In doing so, it is important to emphasize again a major theme of the book. Namely, that changes in the way people obtain, use, produce and distribute resources also involve changes in the character of their social organization, their systems of power and decision-making and crucial aspects of their culture and ideology.

Before this transformation, the structure of Aztec society was probably in many respects not unlike that of other groups in the region. They hunted and gathered what they could. But they also stopped, for a year or a decade or more, in the course of their long and slow migration, to plant and harvest crops. Their systems of production, social organization and power were closely integrated with each other through the loose assemblage of clans which made up the society. Clans were composed of groups of families. Each clan was essentially a land-holding and land-regulating unit, managing its own internal affairs. Land was not privately owned by individuals or families but was held collectively by the clans which allocated it to their members for their use.

As with many other primarily subsistence agricultural societies in the Americas and elsewhere, different kinds of cooperative working groups within the clans were organized and institutionalized in order to pool and distribute labour. This was especially useful and important for the heavy tasks of preparing the fields for cultivation and in harvesting. Aspects of these collaborative working groups remain today in many parts of rural Latin America. Thus, the productive system of the Aztecs rested on the collaborative cultivation of crops - notably maize - on lands which were collectively controlled by the clans.

There is no reason to believe that in the early days they produced much surplus for upward distribution to support a full-time administrative, aristocratic or priestly élite, though it is important to note that the seeds of such a group were there and were later to grow. The local autonomy of each clan was, initially, probably too strong for that, nor was such an apparatus necessary. The regulation of clan land and other affairs was governed by what one might loosely call a clan council, composed of men of prestige, ability, bravery or astuteness. In turn, the regulation of affairs between clans (and relations with other societies) was governed by an inter-clan council, whose members were drawn from the clan councils. It seems likely that some of the sources of leadership and kingship in later Aztec society lay in these institutions, both at clan and inter-clan level. For under conditions of defensive and then offensive militarism, certain officers within such institutions could rapidly accumulate considerable power. Likewise, the collaborative organization of agricultural work within and between clans could provide the basis for the effective mobilizing of peasant soldiers for war, and also for coordinating people in intensive labour tasks, such as building temples or irrigation systems.

It would also appear that it was in the course of their migration to the Valley of Mexico that the influence of religious leaders began to grow. One account of their journey records that they were led and guided by four 'priest rulers', suggesting something of the dual nature of power that was to emerge so decisively later.[14] 'Religious' explanation - which may refer, for instance, to the alleged intervention by a god or gods - is often the residual category of explanation which all societies (modern and historical) use for natural disasters and social crises which seem inexplicable. As suggested earlier, therefore, it is not surprising that in the circumstances of climatic uncertainty, threat and conflict which prevailed in the region, people turned not only to religious explanations but also to religious activities. These were undertaken on their behalf by emerging specialists in religious affairs and ceremonial, to try to ensure the benign and positive intervention of the gods in their favour.

V

In the Valley of Mexico there had not developed any integrating system of social or political organization which could distribute resources peacefully and evenly amongst the many groups who laid claim to them. This meant, as it had under the regime of the Toltecs and before them in Teotihuacán, that conflict was inevitable. Effective militarism became a necessary condition of survival, and expansion was a consequence of victory. The capacity to develop useful alliances and to conduct winning campaigns was therefore a key to Aztec success, but not the only key. The central features of the processes which brought about the transformation of Aztec society into a predatory imperial power were a series of cumulative developments in the politics of that society. These involved the intensification of production, an uneven pattern of distribution, a tightening and upward concentration of power, and the expansion and elaboration of social organization, culture and ideology. In the course of these developments, the relative significance of clan organization was diminished. The shape of the society came to be fashioned by the emergence of a class structure, topped by an exceedingly powerful ruler, surrounded and supported by a property-owning aristocracy of civil and military élites, and an influential priesthood.

Considering first the system of production, a number of changes stand out. The intensification of agricultural production is perhaps one of the most important. This was achieved by a variety of methods. The hillsides close to the lake were terraced, and the run-off water used to irrigate them. Other kinds of water control systems were introduced, marshy ground was drained, and the famous *chinampas* – the floating allotments in the lake – were extended and widely used for cultivation. Such produce as was generated by all this activity was used by the Aztecs to obtain in exchange some of the materials they needed to build the city, which consumed considerable amounts of stone and wood.

It is also important to recognize that, as population grew, increasing amounts of food were needed to feed the people – especially the many officials, urban craftsmen and other workers who were not directly involved in agricultural production. For this reason it makes sense to regard the politics of predatory militarism which was associated with the rise of the Aztec empire as having become an integral part of its system of production, and vice versa. The tribute which flowed back into Tenochtitlán thus contributed crucially both to its survival and its growth. While much of this tribute was creamed off to support the ruler and his court, or to reward the military, some of it seems also to have been redistributed to key sections of the population. So, to some extent, they too benefited from the successes of conquest. It has been estimated that, by the early sixteenth century, some 52,000 tons of food were carried into the city each year on the backs of staggering porters, as well as 123,000 cotton garments, 33,680 bundles of feathers and a vast assortment of other precious items from the length and breadth of the Middle American empire which the Aztecs had come to dominate.[15]

But not everything which flowed into Tenochtitlán was tribute. In the course of their long campaigns, alliances were forged and settlements negotiated. This enabled the Aztecs to link up with complex and far-flung trading networks which brought additional goods to the capital and its markets. Goods such as these - from tribute or trade - not only contributed to the sustenance of the population. They also provided the raw materials for skilled craftsmen to work into finished goods, which were in turn exported and traded throughout Middle America. Such specialization was an important feature of the Aztec system of production, as were the *pochteca*, the merchants, who traded the goods throughout the region and acted also as spies for the civil and military establishment. The Aztec rulers and the military encouraged and protected such trade. In return, they benefited from it. This further consolidated both their position as an emerging ruling class and their close relationship with the merchants.

The division of labour associated with this intensification and diversification of production came to differ radically from the previous egalitarian clan-based organization of agricultural work. A considerable amount of labour was required to establish Tenochtitlán. Temples had to be built, the city had to be kept clean, aqueducts had to be maintained, land cleared and an enormous volume of goods transported. This all involved the organization and deployment of far more labour than could be generated from within the clans by a labour tax alone. There were also other methods.

First, it is clear that much of this additional labour came from groups which had been conquered in war. Some of it (especially beyond Tenochtitlán) was in the form of contract labour, provided by conquered peoples under negotiated settlements. Much of it, too, was in the form of slave labour, derived from those captured in battle. For although a large number of such captives was sacrificed - as will emerge later - many of them could have contributed decisively to the expanding labour requirements of Tenochtitlán and elsewhere in the empire.

Secondly, there were internal sources of slaves within Aztec society. Enslavement came to be a punishment for certain crimes or infringements of social norms, especially of a religious kind. Slavery was also a consequence of periods of famine, which were not infrequent in the area. For maize, the staple crop, is easily decimated by adverse weather conditions, especially inadequate rainfall. The people of Middle America lived with that danger constantly in their consciousness. And famines, like recessions, impoverish the poor. One such period of prolonged famine occurred, for instance, in the middle of the fifteenth century, when first locusts, then floods, then droughts and a succession of poor harvests left people starving in the Valley. Under these circumstances, the inability of the ruler to provide for all the people compelled some families to sell youngsters into slavery, receiving perhaps 400 cobs of maize for a girl and 500 for a boy. Alternatively, families who were badly in debt were forced to sell one or two of their children. Moreover, there was a substantial section of the slave population who were voluntary slaves. These were people who had become either landless or impoverished and who had no alternative but to offer themselves as slaves if they were to stay alive.

Finally, there is evidence to show that a class of landless (but non-slave) labour had developed by the fifteenth century. They no doubt contributed to the building and maintenance of the city, as well as to the agricultural and other labour needs of the larger private and state lands which had emerged.

In all these ways, therefore, a substantial pool of free and unfree landless had developed within the structure of Aztec society.[16]

VI

Such changes as these in the system of production did not occur without related changes in the systems of power, distribution and social organization. Indeed, in considering these it is crucial to recognize how closely all these changes were linked to each other in the politics of Aztec society. For it is clear that the intensification of production both generated and reflected an intensification of power and resources at the top of the society. The ecological and demographic conditions of scarcity and the ensuing competition for limited resources which had provoked these processes have already been explored, but the central implications must be underlined here.

In most societies any sustained period of intense warfare or threat of it (as opposed to occasional raiding, for instance) usually acts to precipitate power at the top, in a convergence of civil, military and productive purposes. When peace returns it is usual (though not inevitable) for certain kinds of emergency powers and procedures to be dismantled or to be suspended. In the case of the Aztecs, however, it is important to remember that for more than 200 years they were continually engaged in conflict and war. And, even when they had secured their position in the Valley of Mexico, they had to defend it and continue to ensure that tribute and the necessary resources flowed in to support Tenochtitlán and the two other city-states (Texcoco and Tacuba) which formed the core of the empire in a tight Triple Alliance. It is hardly surprising that, in these circumstances, the loose assemblage of clans crystallized into a hierarchical and military state.

While evidence of the micro-politics of the processes involved barely exists, the institutions around which this crystallization occurred were there from early on. It seems therefore probable that the ruler - or King or Emperor - emerged from a strengthened inter-clan council. And from the time of Acampichtli (1367) the emperorship remained within one family. By the fifteenth century, the ruler was advised by a small inner council of four, usually his relatives, from whom his successor was chosen. Backing this up was a wider council, which had probably been based originally in the inter-clan council which had formerly linked the clans. But in the course of the intensification of productive and military activities - especially from the 1420s, from the time of Itzcoatl and Moctezuma I - the trend seems to have been decisively away from any earlier concern there might have been to ensure representation from the clans. What appears to have supplanted this was the emergence of an hereditary nobility, itself internally ranked, from which members of this council (and other officials and administrative bodies) came to be drawn by nomination and appointment from above. Below and beyond this there had emerged a yet wider pool of lesser nobles, who had contributed in significant ways in war or perhaps trade, and who had been rewarded by the ruler with grants of land, status and jobs. It seems, too, that this group tended in time to become hereditary, passing both its land and status from father to son, and marrying strategically within (or, where possible, above) itself.[17] Apart from the higher echelons surrounding the ruler, the upper class as a whole does not seem to have become an entirely closed caste. Individuals who had distinguished themselves in war and other activities of importance to the society seem to have filtered into it regularly in the course of Aztec expansion.

And it was largely in the course of this expansion that the tiers of this nobility had emerged. It would not be far-fetched to assume that, in these conditions, the manoeuvring and jockeying for position and influence were fierce. Many appointments were made and these were filled by people who were drawn from, or promoted into, various levels of the nobility. Officials were appointed to manage the granaries, for instance; tax-gatherers were sent to various parts of the empire to supervise the systematic flow of tribute; judicial officers and magistrates regulated the affairs of the city and the markets; and many minor officials administered the increasingly complex organization of the city and empire.

Above all, there were military matters. The closeness of the relations between the civil and military leaders acted to forge enormous power within the administration. This was backed up - as will be discussed shortly - by the insistent urgings, advice, murmurings and directions of a numerous priesthood, itself organized in a complex hierarchy of responsibilities and attachments to the vast pantheon of gods who dominated the hopes and fears of the Aztecs.

Such centralization of power and decision-making was at one and the same time the cause, condition and consequence of the politics of intensified production, predatory expansion and the uneven distribution of resources. The effect was thus to eclipse the previous significance and egalitarianism of the clans as the central organizing institutions of Aztec society. The clans still retained some control over the regulation and distribution of land (or some of it) at the wide base of the rural society, and in parts of the city as well. But new sources of wealth - *independent* of clan control - flowed to the ruler and his bureaucracy. It was this which cemented their power and formed the basis for their emergence as a ruling class. For the resources which flowed in from conquest and tribute were steered largely in their direction, partly to support the military effort, partly to provide for the temples and their priests, partly to be deployed in buying allies and securing friends within and outside the Valley, partly to sustain an increasingly sumptuous social and ceremonial life, and partly to reward and enrich their own position.

The uneven distribution of resources within a society may not be the inevitable consequence of intensification of production, the upward

concentration of power or even conquest – provided a commitment to a policy
of equality through redistribution influences the regulation of affairs. But, in the
case of the Aztecs, such procedures and principles did not apply. In the course
of their military campaigns substantial new areas of land came under Aztec
control. This formed the basis of an emerging system of private land-ownership
in the Valley and beyond it, which existed side by side with the clan-regulated
lands. And it was this new land which came into the possession of the civil and
military leadership.[18] Other land acquired in this way was kept by the Aztec
state, as one might now justly call it, for the support of palaces, temples and
their staff. It was worked by the various categories of free and unfree labour
described above. The general flow of resources inwards to the heart of the
Aztec empire from tribute and trade was thus supplemented by this internal
generation of such additional resources, and also by taxation in labour and kind
from the ordinary people.

The cumulative effect of these changes was therefore to bring about a
massive shift in the politics of distribution. The more or less simple but
egalitarian arrangements of clan organization of Aztec society in the early days
declined. By the sixteenth century the pattern was one of profound inequality,
associated with the almost god-like supremacy of the ruler, surrounded by an
elaborate, wealthy and powerful ruling class, constituted by a web of civil,
military and religious élites. Such élites, and especially the emperor, were
supposed in theory to redistribute at least some of their wealth downwards –
especially in times of hardship – and to provide protection, services and peace.
There is no doubt that in certain respects they did so, but there are also
indications that some expressions of resentment and opposition to this state of
affairs had been provoked within and *certainly* beyond Tenochtitlán. For the
central fact is that this pattern of distribution was an integral part of the politics
of predation and inequality that was itself a shaky basis for the long-term
survival and welfare of the society.

The major elements of social institutions and organization which influenced
the politics of Aztec society have been indicated in the above analysis. The
central principle of social organization which had emerged was that of class,
replacing clan. This influenced social institutions in most spheres of life but can
best be illustrated by the patterns of residence, education and marriage.

The homes and estates of the upper classes were both substantial and
beautiful, and they were attended by servants and slaves. Ordinary people lived
in small houses, or reed-and-mud shacks, and tilled their small plots of clan land
or worked in the city. Complex and detailed sumptuary laws governed the kind
of ornaments and clothing – like shoes for instance – which different classes in
the community could or could not wear, thereby giving visual expression to the
differences in rank, status, power and wealth between them.

While all levels of Aztec society were concerned to provide appropriate
education for their young, there were special schools for the children of the
upper classes. These provided intensive education in civic, military and religious

matters, and trained them for official positions within the administration of the state and empire. There were also special schools for male and female priests, while smaller, less specialized schools - perhaps organized through the residual power of the clans in the various sectors of the city and its surroundings - were available for other children. While in this, as in other spheres of the society, there was some room for upward mobility, the general effect of such institutions was to underline the class and status differences within the community.

It is generally thought that in the early days the Aztecs had been monogamous in marriage, which may only have been permitted between clans, not within them. However, in the course of their migration to the Valley and during their expansion within and beyond it, polygamy had become common. But it was concentrated - even extreme - amongst the upper classes, whose wealth and power made it possible. It was also a means of establishing and maintaining good diplomatic relations with neighbouring groups and thereby consolidating this power. Polygamous marriage of this kind is not uncommon in societies organized so whole-heartedly for war, where male offspring are important as warriors. It is equally common for polygamy and concubinage to be found in a variety of forms at the more wealthy and powerful apex of a society, where it may occur in combination with the widespread seizure of women from enemies. This seems to have developed amongst the upper strata of Aztec society at the same time as the previous norms dictating marriage between clans declined in importance amongst the broader mass of people.

VII

It is tempting to explore other features of the culture and ideology of Aztec politics in isolation from all this. But it would be both misleading and false. For present purposes, as suggested in chapter 1, the important and interesting aspect of *any* culture or ideology is the character of its relationship with the other central features in the politics of the society. The changing systems of production, power, distribution and social organization in Aztec society can only be understood when seen in relation to each other - and traced historically in the ecological and demographic circumstances of Middle America. So too must the complex texture of their culture and ideology be seen as forming an intimate part of their unique response to this set of conditions.

There are many aspects of Aztec culture which were remarkable, not least of which was their material culture - their buildings, art, clothing, pottery and sculpture. But perhaps the central and most pervasive feature of Aztec culture was the role of religion and religious practices. These were so closely bound up with the production, reproduction and insurance of their social life and material culture, as they saw it, that they were in practice inseparable.

To grasp its significance one need only remember the world in which they lived. It was hardly a secure one. As far as one can tell they themselves experienced it as intensely vulnerable, threatened by natural disasters, in danger of attack by rivals, and its future in doubt. Other worlds had risen and collapsed, so they feared theirs was bound to follow that course, as was every living thing within it. Such beliefs - rooted in their experience and the history around them - were reflected in the way they accounted for all this, in their ideology. And these beliefs were expressed in the 'religious' actions they took to try to avert catastrophe.

Simply stated - although the theology and social theory of the Aztecs were astonishingly complex - they regarded their fate as being in the hands of the gods, of which there were hundreds. There were gods of creation, of fire, of fertility, of the planets, of death. And there were gods for each of the crops, plants and animals they used, and for a wide range of activities such as hunting, planting, harvesting, marriage, birth and death. Broadly speaking, they seem to have lived in a state of acute anxiety that, if they did not perform the appropriate rituals in honour of these gods, the rains would not fall, the maize would not grow, the women would not be fruitful and - worst of all - the sun would not rise and their world would be invaded by the forces of darkness which would plunge them into the terrifying blackness and death of permanent night.

To avert such dangers and to ensure the benevolent intervention of the gods, they had to enact regular ceremonies and rituals. Some were undertaken daily by individuals or families, and some collectively on public occasions. Others were the duty of priests who were responsible for making and interpreting complicated astronomical and calendrical calculations which dictated the time and form of the larger ceremonies. And it is important to remember how closely associated, institutionally and socially, were the priests with the military and landed élites surrounding the emperor.

Dominating their hierarchy of gods were, appropriately, the god of rain, Tlaloc, and the great warrior god of the Sun, Huizilopochtli. Such gods as these, especially the latter, waged war on their behalf against the forces of darkness that might engulf them. These gods, the priests insisted and the people seem to have believed, had to be continually fed on blood from human hearts, and hence humans had to be sacrificed.

There was nothing new about human sacrifice in the Americas. What was new was the intensification and elaboration of this practice into such an important feature of Aztec politics. There is little dispute about this or about its extent in Middle America. It has been estimated that, in the fifteenth century, some 250,000 people (or 1 per cent of the population) were sacrificed each year at the many temples throughout the domains of the Triple Alliance. On a conservative estimate, the number for Tenochtitlán alone was about 15,000 people a year. And one authority reckons that at least 14,000 people - and perhaps as many as 20,000 - were sacrificed in a single four-day stretch at the dedication of the temple of Huizilopochtli in 1487.[19]

The main sources for this stream of sacrificial victims were the captives taken in the endless wars which the Aztecs waged. Under the conditions of scarcity and threat of hunger which prevailed in the area there would have been little point in making long-term prisoners out of these captives, for this would have only meant more mouths to feed. They may have served as useful labour for a time, which is not an uncommon fate for prisoners of war. But after that they were sacrificed in the manner described earlier.

But what happened to the bodies, once the hearts had been ripped out and offered to the gods? The evidence, which has been recently re-assessed and analysed, points powerfully in one direction. They were eaten, having been first cooked in a stew seasoned with tomatoes, peppers and salt:

> Most of the sacrifices involved tearing out the heart, offering it to the sun and, with some blood, also the idols. The corpse then was tumbled down the steps of the pyramid, where elderly attendants cut off the arms, legs and head. While the head went onto the local skull rack, at least three of the limbs were normally the property of the captor, who formally retained ownership of the victim. He then hosted a feast at his quarters, of which the central dish was a stew of tomatoes, peppers, and the limbs of the victim. The torso of the victim, in Tenochtitlán at least, went to the royal zoo to feed carnivorous mammals, birds and snakes.[20]

Though we may be horrified by this, it is rather more important to try to understand it. The first point that needs to be emphasized is that any serious and widespread ritual practice of this kind - or any other social policy in a society, however gruesome, cruel or bizarre - is usually a response to some perceived problem in the material and social life of that society. Whether it is an effective (or even 'worthy') response to the problem is an important but entirely separate matter. Societies, or those taking decisions in them, often make incredible mistakes. But the problems which societies face always flow from the way in which the major systems are related to each other through their politics, or from their relations with the natural environment or other societies, or a combination of all these factors.

Secondly, the 'solution' adopted in any instance will usually be rooted in some idea, belief, theory or practice which is already present in the society, but which gets seized on and, sooner or later, elaborated into a new technology, institution or policy.

Thirdly, there is nothing new about human sacrifice. Even the most 'civilized' people, when hungry, have been known to eat other people, though it is unusual to admit it and often the evidence about it is suppressed. Finally, respect for the life and limbs of enemies usually evaporates in time of warfare. In the course of conflict societies have bombed, gassed, burned and incinerated their enemies with little indication of guilt or anxiety.

Now the central problem which faced the Aztecs - as it had faced other societies in Middle America before them - was a profound pressure on resources, especially food resources and notably animal protein. It is therefore not hard to see how, in these circumstances, and under conditions of persistent warfare, a system of institutionalized cannibalism grew up around the previously minor - but long-standing - practice of human sacrifice, and hence came to merge with the religious ceremonies associated with it. In short, this practice was presided over and legitimized by the influential priesthood. And it is plausible to regard it as having become 'a state-sponsored system geared to the production and redistribution of animal protein in the form of human flesh'.[21]

It should not be surprising that, given the structure of Aztec society as explored above, the politics of cannibalism seems to have prohibited the eating of human flesh by ordinary members of the society (though they no doubt did so when they could), and that these scarce resources were distributed mainly to the upper and military classes. As Harner notes 'the rules for Aztec cannibalism were probably forged under the extreme conditions of scarce food situations. Not surprisingly, the ruling class made the rules.'[22]

VIII

Before examining some of the wider implications of the politics of Aztec society it is necessary here briefly to record its fate. Although it may seem as if this empire was both secure and strong, it was not. Its strength was in its spread, and its spread was its fragility. And this is the case in the politics of most empires. At the core was a city that was dependent on a regular flow of tribute and trade to sustain it. Any serious disruption to that flow would have been catastrophic, and may have been one element in the mixture of factors that had brought about the collapse of previous empires in the region. The Aztecs knew this only too well. An uneasy but constantly serviced system of alliances and the display of overwhelming force acted to keep the tributary provinces and the local populace under control. But that was no basis for harmony or stability in the long run. Because the Aztecs provided so little in return for their predation and their relentless extraction of tribute, it is hardly surprising that the outlying provinces felt little loyalty to them and sought any chance to break away. The arrival of the Spanish gave them just such an opportunity, and the Spanish were quick to take advantage of this. In alliance with the Spaniards, these outlying peoples turned with ferocity and vengeance on the Aztecs. With such local help and the technical advantage of their cannons and their horses, the small band of Spaniards quickly overcame the resistance at Tenochtitlán, though not without the usual mixture of viciousness and treachery that occurs in the course of all wars. Yet the central point to stress is that, without the soldiers, supplies and intelligence provided by the local communities who chafed under the domination of the Aztecs, the conquest would not have taken place.

By the middle of 1521 the city was in ruins. It was later systematically destroyed. In a couple of years, the last of the major pre-Columbian empires of Middle America had ceased to exist.

IX

The societies of Middle America have mainly been of interest to archaeologists and historians alone. Without their careful work we would be so much the poorer. But, as argued in relation to the !Kung, it is of the greatest importance for anyone interested in the politics of the modern world to pay greater attention to such societies, and not merely to shrug them off as old history. Without wishing to labour the point, such 'history' is the richest and only laboratory we have for the accumulation of comparative evidence and understanding about the politics of human societies. Historians may find too little detail in this account, and some social scientists may find it too dense. The correct balance between evidence and argument is not always easy to strike. But social scientists, especially, simply cannot afford to disregard such historical concerns if they are going to say anything to anyone at all about any of the problems and politics of the modern world. The need for interdisciplinary collaboration in such work may seem obvious, but given the state of relations between the disciplines today, the point needs to be stressed.[23]

There are therefore some features in the history and politics of the Aztec empire which are unnervingly familiar to anyone who is prepared to look for parallels in the modern world. In concluding this chapter, it is worth trying to stand back from the immediate detail and to suggest what some of these might be.

First, it is clear that when societies (or groups within them) try to collar scarce resources for themselves, this almost always promotes conflict within or between them. The history of Aztec imperialism has shown that the subordination of other societies may bring short-term benefits to the dominant. But the politics of imperial predation can only bring about catastrophe and collapse in the long run. A society which comes to depend on force or fraud to sustain and enrich itself always generates resistance within those which it dominates or cheats. This is not to be moralistic, but a point of fact. The parallels between the pre-Columbian history of Middle America and more recent European history are, in this respect, remarkable.

It is, secondly, interesting to note how often the benefits of such conquest and expansion are unevenly distributed within the dominant society. The upper classes of Aztec society elaborated a complex ideology - a theory to them - and enacted it through a social policy which they claimed (and no doubt believed) was in the national interest. But was it? It required the sacrifice by (and indeed of) others, but in point of fact yielded substantially more benefits to the dominant classes than to anyone else. This, too, is a familiar feature of many European, African and Asian societies, past and present. And it is worth noting that the uneven distribution of food resources in respect of both quantity and quality is something which is still found in many 'advanced' industrial societies today, including Britain, and is even more extreme in the Third World, as will emerge in greater detail later.[24]

Thirdly, the analysis of Aztec politics raises many other uncomfortably modern issues. It is, of course, true that in general we tend not to sacrifice other human beings, nor do we eat them. But how many lives have been sacrificed, one might ask, in the pursuit of increased output or production targets in factories and fields? And how many people have lost their lives in the course of twentieth-century wars which have almost all turned on disputes about securing resources of one kind or another, or gaining access to them? And why? Can this not be avoided? Do we not know how? To take the analogy one step further, can we rest easily with the proposition that the modern world is *less* militarized than the world of Middle America, and less likely to be plunged into darkness? Have we simply no idea - nationally or globally - how we may evolve systems of social and political organization which could produce and distribute resources so as to avoid conflict? And if not, why not?

In summary, the problems which faced the Aztecs do not seem greatly dissimilar to those which face many societies today. Hence, by pointing to these parallels it is possible to see also that many of the solutions adopted in the context of Middle America seem remarkably similar, and the results not much more and not much less effective, than those adopted today. For it can certainly be argued that on a regional, national and global level we have not had much success. We also seem to be obsessively concerned with the intensification of production, with little thought for distributive considerations, conservation or social consequences. We encourage and escalate competition, we heighten conflict, we centralize and concentrate decision-making power, and we often seem to increase inequalities.

In a period (the early 1980s) when unemployment is on a massive scale in the industrial societies, can it be said with any confidence that we use and distribute the valuable human resources of our societies in intelligent and productive ways? And is it not possible that these things are related? Is it not fair to say that we seem either unable or unwilling to learn from all the history that has gone before, and which the present example of the Aztecs so graphically illustrates?

X

This discussion suggests, therefore, some important conclusions which underline those already argued in relation to the !Kung San. It is clearly important for all societies to ensure an even balance of populations in relation to resources. But this is not simply a question of population, but also of production and distribution, and hence politics. When a given set of such population-resource relations begins to change, appropriate innovations are required. But such innovations in the productive system of a society must be accompanied by equally appropriate innovations in its distributive and redistributive arrangements, and in its systems of decision-making, power and social organization. And if the politics in or between societies cannot ensure that such a related set of changes is associated with a more or less even distribution of resources and power, then they are headed for crisis.

A major problem in the politics of what is loosely called 'development' in the modern world is concerned with this central issue. It is something to be explored more fully in later chapters.

CHAPTER FOUR

Cattle, kraals and pastures: the politics of the Pastoral Maasai

I

A major feature of the long 'neolithic revolution' was not only the addition of crop-growing to the range of agrarian productive activities undertaken by human societies, but also the herding of livestock. Since that time and right into the present, many different societies have combined different forms of hunting and gathering, agriculture and herding.[1] Some, more recently, have not grown crops at all, but have been primarily herders, hunters and gatherers. Whatever the particular patterns of their productive systems, the adoption of herding has had important implications for the politics of these societies, adding new factors to their activities of cooperation and conflict. One such pastoral society is that of the Maasai of East Africa, who grow no crops. This chapter sets out to show how the framework of enquiry adopted in the book can also help to illuminate their distinctive politics. But, first, there are some wider points to make about nomadic pastoral societies in general.

II

Nomadic pastoral societies organize their productive life around the exploitation of the herbage resources of rangelands by domesticated flocks or herds of herbivorous animals, managed by human groups.[2] 'Pastoralism' refers to the husbandry of animals, from which pastoralists directly or indirectly derive their subsistence. This includes milk, blood, meat, skins, hair, wool and items of food or equipment which they obtain in exchange from non-pastoral peoples. 'Nomadism' refers to the pattern of movement, of people and stock, which is usually seasonal, whereby pastoralists distribute themselves and their herds around more or less regular and known territorial beats. Such societies thus combine the use of a variety of resources, which include land, water, vegetation, and domesticated herbivores. 'It is indeed a "chain" whose links cannot arbitrarily be separated: man depends on the animal which itself depends on the plant, which in turn depends on climatic factors' such as water and soil.[3]

Nomadic pastoralism as a distinctive way of life seems to have emerged some 3000 years ago, long after the domestication of animals which goes back 10,000 years. It has existed for longest in the Middle East, which has been one of the main areas where pastoralism has flourished, and from where it has spread.

Historically, other major pastoral areas range from the Mediterranean to the Indus valley, and in the Caucasus, through Europe, in the great steppes of Northern Europe and Northern Russia to Siberia as far as the Chuckchi peninsula, in Central and South Asia, and in North, East and Southern Africa.[4]

The areas in which nomadic pastoralism has developed have generally been arid or semi-arid, sparsely populated, and too dry, high or steep for agriculture to be viable. Cultivation in such areas would generally be difficult or very unreliable without irrigation, and this would involve an intensive use of labour and capital. Pastoral nomadism has therefore been 'ecologically adjusted at a particular technological level to the utilization of marginal resources'.[5] It is not therefore simply the domestication of stock but very specialized forms of the domestication and use of animal and other resources which define the central characteristics of these societies, as will become clear when looking more closely at the Maasai.

Nomadic pastoral societies display certain broadly common features in their systems of pastoral production, most obviously their dependence on the use of animals to exploit marginal resources. Their survival depends on their herds. Generally, they have done little to improve the rangelands or water supplies, but have usually been concerned to ensure the conservation of pastures against destructive over-grazing, both by distributing groups of people and their herds between local herding areas, and by movement within them. While stock is usually owned by the constituent families of herding groups, all herders who are members of such communities have equal rights of access to their communal pastures and watering points. But conflict between groups may break out if trespassing occurs. Their systems of decision-making and power have tended to be decentralized and dispersed, based on the local groups of herders, though chiefdoms are not uncommon, and the 'state' in the Mongol 'empire' under Chingis Khan, at the end of the twelfth century, was both powerful and complex.

The social organization and culture of these societies reveal other broadly similar features, especially in the relative autonomy and fluidity of the local herding groups, and the absence of fixed social hierarchies within or between them.[6] This can be attributed largely to the necessity of regular movement of stock and people between pastures, which is something that does not favour the development of either rigid social relations between groups or the centralization of power. Moreover, it has been common for animals to pass between families in the course of establishing marriage bonds and other social relationships. Such movements of stock and people establish wider social connections which can be very important. It is quite common for substantial inequalities in herd size to build up over time between families within particular herding groups. This enables such families (or, more commonly, their heads) to spread their network of kin, friends and other relations through marriage or patronage, for instance, and this gives such people considerable status. Yet inequalities of this kind - which may rise and then fall over time within the groups - have not tended to become institutionalized. Rather, they have generally been held in check by powerful ideologies of equality, at least amongst the herders, and by effective redistributive practices and obligations to help the needy, which operate especially amongst kin, clansmen, age-sets, 'hordes', tribal sections, or other subdivisions of the wider society.

Yet it is important to stress that within these characteristics which define pastoral nomadism, there has been enormous variety. In most forms and particulars, the structure and politics of specific pastoral societies which have been found in the vast area stretching from the south-west Atlantic seaboard of Africa to Mongolia, have been unique and distinctive. They have differed in respect of the territory and climatic zones they have inhabited within the general category of arid and semi-arid areas. This has had implications for the kind of animals they have herded, their pasture practices, and the form and scope of their seasonal movements. They have herded reindeer, sheep, yaks, goats, cattle, donkeys and camels, or various combinations of some of them. Some pastoralists have been 'pure', having almost nothing to do with agricultural production or produce. Others have sometimes grown a few significant staple crops, and yet others have depended on exchanges with producers of such crops to provide them with dietary supplements or luxuries.

Within the scope of the broad principles sketched above, remarkable variations in social organization have been evolved, borrowed, adapted and combined by pastoral peoples over substantial periods of time. Most of these seem to have proved compatible with the requirements and limitations which a pastoral way of life imposes. In general terms their cultural forms, ideologies and views of the world have reflected their necessarily intense preoccupation with pastoralism, and have in turn influenced this. Yet the degree to which this has been the case has varied from the almost obsessional to the disinterested. The Nuer of the southern Sudan, for instance, never cease - it would seem - to talk about their cattle, to praise them, to sing songs about them and even give each other names which are based on the shape and colour of their favourite beasts.[7] Other pastoralists are far less emotional about their herds, but take no less of a direct and practical interest in them and their welfare.

This background to the account of the Pastoral Maasai is necessary for two reasons. First, it is important to place the politics of the Maasai within the context of this rich tradition of pastoral nomadism. As a way of life, it is associated with the names of some of the better-known societies, such as the Kazaks and Mongols of Central and East Asia; the Kurds and Baluchis of the Near East; the Tuaregs and Bedouin of North Africa and Arabia; and the Somali, Turkana, Karimojong and Samburu of East Africa. Secondly, such societies have often been regarded by settled peoples, Europeans and more latterly colonial administrators and independent governments, as being wild, unruly and apparently structureless. They have been viewed as inconvenient and difficult to 'govern', moving around at random, often refusing to barter their stock or, later, to reduce the size of their herds and increase their quality, and being especially obstinate about not wanting to 'settle down'. Yet what an analysis of Maasai politics reveals – as it does for almost any society of pastoral nomads – is the detailed and intricate web of social processes and relationships whereby they have gone about using, producing and distributing pastoral resources in the course of the production and reproduction of their social and biological lives. But what it also indicates is how vulnerable such societies have been, both to natural disasters such as droughts and diseases which have decimated their herds, *and* to social changes brought about, for instance, by incursions on their territory or confinement to reduced areas of it. For, since the sixteenth century, and more dramatically within the twentieth century, pastoral societies have been both on the defensive and decline as innovations in the military technology, amongst other things, of settled peoples have tipped the balance against the advantages of mobility formerly enjoyed by pastoralists.[8] I turn now to the Pastoral Maasai.

III

Down the eastern side of Africa a great two-pronged fault runs deep in the surface of the earth. This is the Rift Valley. At its widest point, the Valley is some 70 miles across at the rim, while its floor ranges from 20 to 40 miles in width. The eastern arm of the Rift slices southwards through the 300-mile-wide domed Highlands of Kenya, ranging from 3000 to 6000 feet, and merges with the elevated northern plains of Tanzania. This is the area inhabited by the Pastoral Maasai.[9] Historically, their distribution spread from near Mt Elgon in North-west Kenya to south of Arusha in modern Tanzania, though this has been considerably curtailed in recent times (see Map 4).

The specific local climate and ecology of this large expanse of Maasai territory varies widely, the east being drier than the west, for instance, and the topography varying from rolling table-land high up to flat scrub low down in the Valley. This area supports a great variety of grasses, some of them good and some not. Examples of the sleekest cattle in Africa may be seen in the better areas, especially after good rains have fallen and the pasture is lush. Generally, however, the rainfall is seasonal, torrential and extremely unreliable, which makes much (though not all) of Maasailand 'essentially marginal to agricultural development'.[10]

It is not clear when the Maasai evolved as a distinct society, nor exactly when they came to inhabit this area, nor precisely where they came from. But pastoralism has a long and complex history in North-east and East Africa, going back deep into the first millennium BC. It is a history characterized by diffusions, innovations and adaptations of stock and herding techniques, as well as the migrations and mergings of people. The Maasai are inextricably part of that history.[11] But there is interesting evidence which suggests that they may have developed their distinctive features a long time ago, perhaps a thousand years back. One important characteristic of the Pastoral Maasai is that some 80

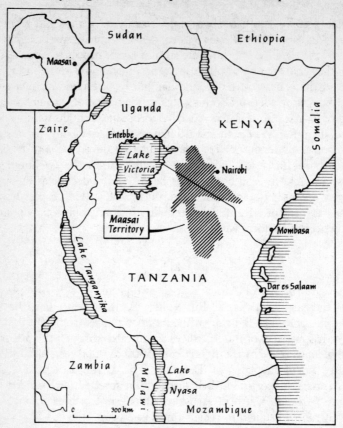

Map 4

per cent of their annual diet has traditionally consisted of milk products from their herds, sometimes mixed with blood. They do not each much meat, and have a profound disdain for agricultural produce (and agriculturalists). In most human communities, such a diet could well lead to very high levels of blood cholesterol and consequent coronary disease. But the Maasai have been found able to assimilate the high animal fat levels in their diet without such effects, owing to the presence of 'unique biological characteristics'.[12] For such characteristics to become genetically established within a large population would take at least a thousand years and, if this evidence is correct, it suggests a long history, at least of that kind of diet which is so unique amongst East African pastoralists. Moreover, a Chinese account from the ninth century AD refers to a people in East Africa who 'do not eat any grains but only meat. They often stick a needle into the veins of the cattle and draw blood which they drink raw, mixed with milk.'[13] In their own account of their history, the Maasai tell of a migration from the north, and it is clear from other evidence that they had come to inhabit some of their present domains by the seventeenth century, for sure, and possibly two centuries earlier.

Today, there are roughly a quarter of a million Pastoral Maasai, some two-thirds of whom live in Kenya and the rest in Tanzania. They are divided into a number of autonomous sections, 'tribes', which have their own names and territories. The two main ones are the Kisonko of Tanzania and the Purko of Kenya. Territory is regarded as belonging to the 'tribe', and it is in turn divided into smaller areas, called 'localities', each of which may be about 200-300 square miles in size. Each locality is inhabited by about 600-700 persons, on average, who live in some fifteen to twenty semi-nomadic 'kraal camps'. Each 'kraal camp' is composed of perhaps eight families, some fifty to eighty people, who have found that they get on well with each other and hence choose to live together and herd their stock together. In any one kraal camp there may be between 400 and 700 head of cattle, plus sheep and goats. These networks of kraal camps constitute the focal points of herding activity. And the politics of the Maasai may thus be identified in the processes of cooperation and conflict whereby they organize the use, production and distribution of the resources of people, pasture and animals within and between the kraal camps, 'localities' and the 'tribes' which compose the major territorial and social components of Maasai society.

IV

The productive core of the society consists of the herding and accumulation of cattle - the East African humped Zebu - as well as sheep and goats. They use donkeys to help them in their work, for instance in more recent times to transport water. The Maasai grow no crops and only a minor portion of their diet is derived from agricultural produce. For young warriors, especially, the eating of such foods is frowned upon. They do not depend on hunting, but live in a necessarily complex tension with the abundant game of the area, deriving both pleasure and assistance from the behaviour of the animals. Of course they hunt and kill predators which attack their herds, and they also recognize that the plains game competes with their cattle for dry season grazing, and that some game are carriers of disease which affects their herds. Yet they regard elephants, for instance, as useful for making paths and enlarging water holes. When they kill wild animals the Maasai are able to use the skins, horns, hair and other items for shields, bags, decorations and so forth. But this is secondary to their herding preoccupations. In the past, Maasai herders were shrewd about obtaining good bulls for their herds, getting them in exchange from other pastoral people, or through raiding.

The bulk of their diet is derived from the milk of their cows, prepared in various ways, sometimes fresh, sometimes fermented, and sometimes mixed with the blood of steers. They rarely slaughter their cattle simply to eat the meat. But they do kill cattle, usually bullocks, for ceremonies and rituals, such as marriages, births, circumcisions, age-set initiations and so on. Since such events are fairly regular, it is reasonable to assume that their intake of meat from this source is also regular, but slight. Thus their herds and flocks also provide them with leather for clothes, thongs, blankets, and other items of equipment, as well as fat for rubbing on their bodies to protect them from the sun. Cattle also constitute the single most important form of legal tender for transactions between people, like bride-wealth, blood-price, inheritance and so forth. Given this importance of cattle in both nutritional and social terms, it will be clear that they have needed large herds to sustain themselves and hence have worked actively to accumulate them. It is also therefore understandable that they have not taken kindly to attempts in the modern era to reduce the size of their herds.

The nomadic movements of kraal camps vary in both distance and frequency, depending on the particular ecologies of the different localities. For instance, in the drier eastern territory of Maasailand they may move twice a year (or more in especially dry times or areas), whereas in the wetter west they move less often. Choice of places where they settle depends on a careful assessment of the water supplies, the information they gather about stock diseases in the area, and of course the condition of the pastures. In general, the pattern is for camps to congregate at the more permanent water holes in the dry season and then to disperse in the wet season to locate new pastures. Once a kraal camp has been established, the people move their herds around the pastures in its vicinity by day, and bring them back to the kraal at night.

Most herding is done by young boys, supervised and instructed by the elder men of the camp, and watched over by the young warriors, while most milking is done by the women and girls. Usually the families who compose the kraal camps herd their cattle together, but not always. And it is important to recognize that the control and use of individual family herds is firmly under the authority of the family, and especially the male head of the family. Thus a mixture of family decision-making over the use of family herds on the one hand, and cooperative herding practices of the kraal camp as a group on the other, defines the organizational character of these activities.

Traditionally, there could be no such thing as landless and hence unemployed Maasai. As mentioned earlier, land is regarded as 'tribal' territory and, within that, the localities provide communal pasture for the constituent camps. This distributive principle of communal ownership of a vital pastoral resource is clearly central to the politics of Maasai nomadic pastoralism. It facilitates the flexible movement of people and stock in the locality, which private ownership or control of pasture would prevent. For it allows *all* Massai access to the resources which make life and prosperity possible.

Average family herd size seems to have been about sixty-five to eighty-five head of cattle in the early 1960s, though wealthy families might have had hundreds of head and poor families might have had very few. The more cattle possessed by a family, the fewer sheep and goats they would have had. But such differences in cattle fortunes fluctuate and change over time. They are influenced by both natural and social factors, such as disease and rainfall, as well as herding decisions, and the size, structure and distribution of families. While control over the family herd is vested in the male head of the family, wives and sons may be allocated certain head of cattle to look after in their own right. People know all their animals very well indeed, and can recognize them immediately.

V

There is no central 'government', nor concentration of power, within Maasai society, nor are there 'chiefs' or 'headmen' at the level of 'tribe', locality or kraal camp. So how do Maasi politics regulate the activities of cooperation and conflict which are involved in their use and distribution of pastoral resources? The answer to this question lies in understanding some of the central features of the social organization of the society through which the systems of power and decision-making are dispersed. These in turn reflect the requirements of nomadic pastoralism and appear to have served them well.

Within each kraal camp the family heads (elders) discuss herding strategies, deciding, for instance, which boys should pasture the cattle and where, though some people may graze their herds on their own if they wish to do so. Cooperation is promoted by the spirit of friendship between the families in the camp. People understand that you gain respect, wisdom and affection by living congenially with others, and they prefer to do so rather than to squabble or fight. There are no formal procedures for settling disputes within the camp. However, the 'most respected' elders (in the camp and more widely) will have influence in the interpretation of correct behaviour according to Maasai customs and values. People recognize how disruptive conflict within a camp may be, and how it can sour good companionship, which they value highly. But if it occurs, families may break away to start a new camp, join others or even move to a different locality.

The affairs of each local group are much more important for the politics of the society as a whole. It is here - at this level - that the relations between camps (and between localities within the 'tribe') are regulated by the elders. To appreciate how this is achieved it is necessary to describe one of the major institutions of Maasai social organization, the age-set system.

Between the ages of about fourteen and eighteen all males become members of an 'age-set', to which they belong for life. Women identify with the age-set of the warriors with whom they danced as young girls. The period of recruitment into the age-set lasts for about seven to eight years, so that members of the set may vary somewhat in age. Then the recruitment period is closed, and the age-set is formally and ceremonially initiated and constituted. This is followed by another period of some six to eight years in which no age-set is initiated in the tribe, so that there are clear distinctions between the sets. The age-sets are established on a tribe-wide basis, but their importance is greatest at the level of the locality, where local members of any particular age-set live. This local 'branch' of the age-set therefore experiences solidarity from acting throughout its life as a group in certain matters.

Each age-set passes through a series of age-grades, or phases of life, from Junior Warriors to Senior Warriors to Junior Elders to Senior Elders to retired and even 'ancient' Elders. Each grade carries with it certain duties, rights, responsibilities and obligations for the age-set as it passes through them in the course of its life. For instance, an age-set which has just been initiated into the first grade, the Junior Warrior grade, is expected to live for a while in a special warrior village in the locality. Junior Warriors spend their time learning about the resources of the locality, amongst other things. During this period their knowledge of the grazing value of many different grasses is increased from the time they were herdboys. They get to know the territory of the locality, and, in doing so, they begin to learn the relevant components of the science of herding as understood in their society. They also carry out socially useful jobs (like keeping an eye on the young herdboys); they enforce rulings from the Elders; they fight for and defend local territory and herds, if necessary; they hunt down predators, and they begin to develop that sense of corporate solidarity which they will have for life as an age-set.

In time, when they graduate to Senior Warrior status (a formal ceremony, as are other such major graduations through the grades), they usually return to their own kraal camps, may marry and start the process of learning to be Elders, while still carrying out their duties as warriors which may involve fighting and raiding. They become Elders when, in due course, they graduate out of Senior Warrior status. They then begin (initially as Junior Elders) to assume responsibilities for watching over the affairs of the locality. They participate (at first mainly by listening) in the discussions of the Senior Elders, who have to handle the important matters which affect the welfare of all camps in the locality. And it is at this level, that of the locality, where the duties of the age-set when it enters the grade of Senior Elders become most important. For this is the level where most cooperative activities (like ceremonies or defence) or disputes (for instance over pasture or raiding) occur, and hence need to be organized or settled.[14]

The members of the sets form strong bonds amongst themselves, and have their own spokesmen. As age-sets they regulate their own internal affairs, except where the issue or problem is one which has implications for the wider society. Such issues as these, and many others, are then discussed and resolved by the 'council' of Elders of the locality, composed of the Junior and Senior Elders' age-sets. It is not so much a formal 'council' but a gathering of members of those age-sets for the specific purpose of discussing and sorting out a problem. The spokesman for the Elders' age-set summons the other Elders when such an issue arises. The kind of problem which they have to deal with varies from time to time, season to season, and place to place, and issues also arise from relations between Maasai and other societies. Examples of problems which crop up include disputes between camps; breaches of customary rules and proper behaviour; the encroachment of their pastures by others; problems to do with cattle-sickness or dry-season grazing or watering; attacks on their herds by predators or other people; how, in modern times, to respond to national government policy; whether and when to burn the grass to stimulate the growth of new pastures; conflict over rights and duties between age-sets; accusations of sorcery; requests for help from other groups. In short, they concern all the major activities of cooperation and conflict, of politics, which occur in the use, production and distribution of pastoral resources in Maasailand, within and between localities.

The frequency of such gatherings also varies, depending on the urgency of the issue and the season. They may be once a month or less. Discussions are introduced by the spokesman. Then everyone has the chance to have his say and people listen attentively to each other, always standing up when speaking. The meeting may last a few hours or a few days, depending on the issue, the number of people who attend (it may a hundred or more) and the number of people who wish to speak. The role of the spokesman at this level (and also within age-set discussions) is essentially that of a 'chairman'. His duty is to preside, to promote fair discussion, to have the case put fairly and openly, and to try to ensure that, by patient discussion and argument, a consensus is reached. Decision-making is therefore 'highly democratic and usually long'.[15] The spokesman is not a 'chief' or 'headman': he has no power or privileges, but he has status and enjoys respect, and is regarded as someone who is able to put a case clearly and well.

Disputes between members of different localities are usually dealt with by the local council of Elders of the defendant, though fighting may occur between localities if this procedure breaks down. Fighting may also erupt between tribes within the society, though this seems to have been rare. There is no council of Elders at the level of the 'tribe', but common tribal affairs (for instance an age-set ceremony) are discussed by *ad hoc* meetings of representatives from local councils. But the key point to stress is that the politics of Maasai society are concentrated mainly in and around the affairs of the localities. They are concerned with local disputes, infringements of the peace or proper behaviour, pastoral and ceremonial matters. The centre of gravity of political life is thus closely identified with the pastoral activities of each locality.

It will be clear, therefore, that the age-set system acts to structure the relations between groups in the social organization of Maasai society by establishing relations of authority, respect, status, rights and responsibilities. It also serves to distribute power between age-sets, and it provides a context for decision-making about key aspects of their productive and distributive activities. For all intents and purposes it seems to have worked effectively. While women are not included in the age-sets (except indirectly as indicated above) and hence not in these judicial and decision-making matters, they have a very firm grip on the affairs of their own homes. Just as men may be said to 'own', or rather control, the herds, their wives 'own' their homes and they control the affairs of the domestic economy, looking after the calves, milking the cows and other activities. They have rights and responsibilities which may not be ignored or infringed by their husbands, or any other males in the kraal camps.

In addition to these aspects of the social organization of Maasai society through which their politics are expressed, there are other non-territorial groups to which all Maasai belong. For instance there are (now) seven major clans (in turn divided into sub-clans and lineages). These clans in Maasai society are best thought of as broad categories of people with whom one feels associated in a special way, and on whom one may call for assistance in some circumstances, for example in paying off debts, and in relation to whom certain loyalties and ways of behaving are due. Each clan has its own name, like Laiser, Lukamai and Makesan. Membership of these clans is not acquired by 'joining' them. One is born into the clan of one's father, and both men and women remain in them for life.

Ideally, Maasai men do not marry women of their own clan, or women of their mother's clan, or even women of their wife's or wives' clans. But in practice, this degree of clan exogamy (or marrying outside a close clan) does not always prevail. Yet the clans are not especially important in the politics of Maasai society, since they neither control nor influence in any major way the use or distribution of pastoral or other resources, and they have no effective authority over their members. Certainly they do not have the significance of the age-sets. Yet the fact that it is not considered wise for members of a kraal camp to be composed of close relatives or members of the same clan or sub-clan does help to distribute people of the same clan widely over the localities within the 'tribe', and even beyond it.

Overall, then, while there are no formal or institutional bonds which link the whole society together, these looser kinds of relations - such as the clans to which everyone belongs - their common lifestyles and beliefs, and their particular form of pastoralism, enable all Maasai to recognize each other and to identify as Maasai.

VI

The culture and ideology of the Pastoral Maasai reflect and sustain their politics. In all this, cattle are central. Marriage, for instance, which is polygamous, is only properly formalized and established when the bridegroom gives some head of cattle (usually four) to his bride's father. Likewise, the compensation paid as a result of blood being spilled, say in a fight or a feud which may develop out of one, was traditionally in cattle. And the education of the young in the science of pastoralism which characterizes the ideology of the Maasai is clearly also of the greatest importance in maintaining their way of life, and is hence an integral part of their politics. It distinguishes them from other pastoral peoples in East Africa, and they regard themselves as superior to them, and certainly to those who grow crops and hunt. One version of Maasai history and mythology tells how God gave them their cattle by letting them down on a bark rope from the sky.[16] Since then they have been pastoralists, and 'pure' ones at that. They could, if they wanted to, grow crops. Many other pastoral people in the area - like the Jie and the Turkana, for instance - do so.[17] But the Maasai choose not to do so. This illustrates how such a preference, rooted in their ideology, and which in turn requires a detailed historical explanation, has religious significance for them, and influences the politics of their society.

VII

It would be wrong to suggest that the history and politics of Maasai society reveal a picture of unqualified bucolic bliss. They do not. Given their fairly arid habitat and the nomadic requirements of pastoralism, life is not easy. Problems face them daily. Rainfall is unreliable. Pastures cannot be guaranteed. Cattle get sick. Maasai have enemies. Raiding and war occur. Herders, or groups of herders, make mistakes about their pastoral practices. Their herds suffer. People get hungry. They are vulnerable to the effects of particularly savage droughts, as are their herds to epizootics which may decimate them. These things may edge the societies close to the margin of collapse. Yet the politics of Maasai society has enabled them to respond to quite severe fluctuations in natural conditions. The Maasai have a kind of 'insurance' system which is made up of a series of risk-averting strategies forming part of their productive social life.[18] The owner of a large herd, for instance, may redistribute some of the cattle which are surplus to the needs of his immediate family. They may be loaned for long periods to kinsmen or age-set colleagues or clansmen, and may be recalled in times of need. The borrower may perhaps keep a specified number of the offspring. The 'loan' is herded in a different place (for example another locality) and this is a form of insurance against local disasters. But the practice also serves to share resources with others who may be in need. It helps to institutionalize the egalitarian ideology within Maasai society. At the same time, it is highly functional from the point of view of distributing vital resources widely (both in the geographical and social senses) so that some may survive in the event of drought, disease or attack in one place but not another. It has been estimated that some 30 to 40 per cent of Maasai cattle are distributed in this way.

More locally than this, herders keep a close watch on the condition of the pasture and water supplies, and they receive regular intelligence about cattle disease in their area. By prudent management of their herds they can move them to good pastures and away from contact with disease. If they have to move out of their locality, they seek permission from other localities to use their resources. In all this, the important principles governing reciprocal assistance, and the existence of kin, clansmen and age-set colleagues in neighbouring localities (or further afield) are crucial. 'In an environment where uncertainty is often localized, individuals would face extinction if they were not part of a wider network.'[19]

VIII

This brief account of Maasai pastoralism has illustrated how inextricably their politics are bound up with the way they use, produce and distribute pastoral resources, and vice versa. It has shown how their systems of social organization, power and decision-making, culture and ideology both influence and are influenced by this. And it is possible to conclude that the conventional image of these people (and other pastoralists) as either anarchic or wildly aggressive, or both, is incorrect. On the contrary, given the level of their technology and science, their politics have combined these 'systems' in a remarkable manner to ensure a substantial degree of peace (which they value) within their society, and a balance within it and their environment. But, when threatened, they have fought.

But once this internally organized balance between people, animals and the environment is seriously disturbed, in a manner with which their insurance systems cannot cope, then the successful operation of nomadic pastoralism is in jeopardy. For the *related* processes of individual *and* social survival require the maintenance of certain conditions. Pastoralists use resources extensively, not intensively. To be able to do this they must have access to those resources, especially land, and they must be able to move freely around it. Once that access and mobility is cramped, the complex web of social and natural factors which their politics combine in the production and reproduction of their lives, is torn apart.

In the twentieth century this has begun to happen to the Maasai. The prospects for the future are not particularly good. The origin of these changes has been mainly external to Maasai society, and the causes have been more social than natural in character, though they have often been expressed as both in occurrence and consequence. In the 1890s, for example, the inadvertent introduction by Europeans of rinderpest amongst their cattle and smallpox amongst the people, combined with a particularly sustained drought, virtually eliminated Maasai herds and perhaps half the human population. More recently, national boundaries have been drawn between Kenya and Tanzania, thereby officially slicing Maasailand in half, with implications for the structure, mobility and relations of groups, though Maasai have not always paid too much attention to these frontiers. More seriously, encroachment on their land and dispossession of some of it - in Kenya for example, during and after the colonial period - has had grave effects. Some 10,000 square miles of Maasai territory, over which they once freely moved, has been turned into gameparks. This has deprived some Maasai of dry-season grazing, thereby affecting the condition of their herds and hence human nutrition and health. Population pressures have served to exacerbate the problems under these conditions, and rangelands have deteriorated too in consequence.[20]

The effects of all this have been uneven and patchy throughout Maasailand. But where they have been most acute they have meant that the nomadic pastoralism of the Maasai has ceased to be viable. The internal balance of their productive and social systems has been disrupted beyond the point of recovery in certain areas. Some Maasai have begun to cultivate crops to supplement food supplies. Others have become involved in the livestock trade, while yet others have been drawn into casual wage-labour to make ends meet. All these things have acted further to corrode the principles and structure of the society. There are areas of despair, apathy and an increase in drunkenness.[21]

That this is 'change' is not in doubt. Whether it is 'development', or whether it can lead to 'development' is another question. What would 'development' involve in these circumstances, and what would the politics of that be?

For the moment, the final point here is a relatively straightforward one. The problems which occur in societies are sometimes natural in cause and internal in origin, as in the case of the Maasai. I shall illustrate the point later in respect of other societies. But not all problems are of that kind. What has been happening to the Maasai shows how external social factors have played a major part in disrupting the politics of this society by creating ruptures in the relations between its systems of production, distribution, power, social organization, culture and ideology. The greater the disruption, the graver the problems, the more stark the symptoms, and the harder it becomes to restore balance, or to reconstitute it as part of a new or wider society. This is what often happens in the meeting of different societies, or groups of people, with different histories, different forms of social organization, differential access to power, and with radically contrasting cultures and ideologies. Sometimes they cooperate over the control, use and distribution of resources, and sometimes they fight. Thus - at a wider level of analysis - this underlines yet again what is meant by politics. I shall explore the politics of such encounters shortly. Before doing so, it will be helpful to indicate some of the other contexts and problems for which the approach can be useful.

CHAPTER FIVE

From village to World Bank: politics in departments and institutions

I

Politics occurs not only in whole societies, but in parts of them and in the course of relations between them. These parts may be villages or towns or regions. Or they may be major institutions - whether 'political' in the conventional sense, or commercial, educational or religious. All are involved in the use, production and distribution of various resources, and hence are political institutions. With appropriate adjustments, therefore, the framework of analysis adopted in this book can be used to explore their politics. To show how this may be done, the present chapter looks at the politics of villages, a typical university department, and a large international organization, the World Bank.

II

The vast majority of people in Asia, Africa and some of Latin America live in rural areas. Most of them live in villages, where their lives are bound up with agricultural production. While this is no longer generally the case in Europe or North America, there are none the less large and important areas in Southern Europe and the islands of the Mediterranean region where it is so. Rural life has nowhere ever been either easy or idyllic. Relations between villages and urban centres have always been complex. In times of rapid change, village societies may find their ways of life severely disrupted without much compensation in the form of 'development'. Life may actually get harder for some, for example if change in the distribution of land adversely affects their ability to produce enough food to support themselves. These are the typical conditions under which many of the problems which face rural communities have begun to emerge. Some people start to drift into part-time wage-labour, if there is work to be had; others migrate to towns, perhaps keeping some loose connections with their rural roots, commuting back when they can; some get into debt; while others sink into what are perhaps the most hopeless circumstances of all, those of rural unemployment or underemployment in conditions of landlessness or near-landlessness. Some of these problems and their causes in Third World societies will be examined in a later chapter. For the present my purpose is to stress and illustrate the profoundly *political* character of these occurrences, in both cause and consequence. And to do so, it is worth starting nearer home, in the rural mountain villages of Portugal and Cyprus.

For centuries, communities in these villages have been engaged in very localized subsistence agricultural production. They have used rural technologies and techniques which have hardly changed for a thousand years or more. Contact with the wider society has been slim and, until recently, the influence of outside forces and developments on the productive practices of the villages has not been very strong. While different kinds of governments, or colonial authorities, have come and gone, perhaps extracting different kinds of taxes or contributing some improvements in administration, communications or health in the society at large, life in these more remote places has generally gone on without much change.

In villages such as these, it has often been the case that people have worked very small and sometimes considerably fragmented land-holdings. As population has risen, so the fragmentation of these resources has increased too. In some areas of the Pitsilia region in the Troodos mountains of Cyprus, for instance, people (often women in this case) have to travel some 25 miles each week, on donkey or on foot, to tend and water their crops. This is because their small parcels of land are so fragmented and dispersed.[1]

In the same region, certain rural resources - like arable land and trees - are often very scarce indeed. Such scarcity, combined with the patterns of inheritance which operate within the culture, have sometimes resulted in a one-acre field, for instance, being jointly owned by ten people or more. Apricot or olive trees may be owned separately from the land on which they stand, and have sometimes had as many as fifty-eight joint owners. In such parts of both Cyprus and Portugal, even today, people usually irrigate their lands from communal village tanks or ponds, which the communities have built themselves and which they maintain. But access to this crucial rural resource of water is often a very complex matter, bound up with history and inheritance, negotiations and deals. In the dry summer months, people may have very strictly defined rights of access to one or two hours' water for their land every few days, or even less. Serious disputes may arise over alleged or actual infringements of these rights, as they can also arise over boundary disputes between owners of unenclosed and unfenced lands.[2]

The politics of such matters, rooted in the use of certain important resources, and concerned with the productive and distributive practices of the communities, both reflect and influence long-standing features of the social organization and culture of village society. So too do questions of marriage within and between villages, and the associated issue of property transfers which accompany marriage, for instance from parents to children, and from bridegroom to bride, or vice versa.

All these matters are the stuff of local politics, as are relations with neighbouring villages. The forms which cooperation may take within the village - for instance in the water-regulating organizations in rural Cyprus, called 'irrigation divisions' or 'irrigation associations' - and the contours of social life along which conflict may flow, are simply inexplicable without understanding how these communities have gone about using and distributing resources in the course of agricultural production.

In recent years, of course, many external factors have impinged on the local politics of rural communities and village societies all over the world, and hence have changed them. Some of these changes have been of immense benefit to the welfare of the people. For instance, in both Cyprus and Portugal improved roads and communications have penetrated into the villages, and various facilities and services have flowed along them. In some parts fresh water has been piped in, and electricity connections have been made. New forms of fuel (for instance, bottled gas) have become available for cooking and heating, thus eliminating many hardships, such as the daily search for firewood, and thus also reducing some of the pressure on the forests. Boreholes have been sunk, and new tanks or ponds built. A variety of new resources and technologies - like commercial fertilizers and plastic pipes for irrigation - have been introduced as these local societies have been drawn into wider networks of production and exchange.

Not all the effects of this have been uniformly beneficial, however. In some areas dramatic changes have occurred in the character of productive activities and in the structure and politics of village societies. The shift to commercial production for the market, and away from primarily subsistence food production to various cash crops (like eucalyptus plantations in parts of Portugal, for instance), has of course been made *possible* by the innovations, but it has also been made *necessary*, because all the above services, facilities and goods have to be paid for. And changes in the way people use resources also involve changes in their politics, and hence changes in their relations with each other. Thus, some previous subsistence farmers have become local entrepreneurs, controlling larger acreages of land, accumulating capital and hiring labour. They have done well out of the changes. Others, who may have lost or been compelled to sell land in the course of land-consolidation projects, or whose small plots have no longer been able to support them and pay for services, may have emigrated, temporarily or permanently. Others have become rural wage-labourers, where there are jobs. In general, it is the young who move or who can move. The older people find it difficult, or do not wish to.

The social structure and organization of the communities has also begun to shift. Even certain aspects of marriage seem to have been affected. For instance, early in the present century in Cyprus it was customary for parents to provide their *sons* with a house at marriage. But it is now increasingly the case that they must instead provide their *daughters* with one. An explanation which has been offered for this change is that in the past there were more men than women available at the age of marriage, but now there are more women than men. So parents need to provide their daughters with houses as an effective means of facilitating their marriage, for an unmarried daughter is a source of some concern, if not shame, for a family. As older villagers told one researcher: 'It's this way: men have got fewer. Once men were cheap, but then they got more expensive.'[3] And a major reason for the decreasing availability of men is their migration not only from the villages to the towns, but from Cyprus to places abroad, though of course the effects of this vary from village to village.

In short, old resources have come to be used in new ways, and new resources have come on the scene, with implications for the politics of village societies, that is for the relations of production, distribution, power, social organization and culture. The important thing to note, however, is that the processes of politics which I am concerned to emphasize are illustrated here from another angle. Conflict and cooperation at the local level now turn on how the variety of resources (both old and new) are used, in both different and new ways by individuals and groups, with far-reaching consequences for all.

What is true for the emerging new relations *within* such villages is equally true for the relations between them and wider - perhaps national - institutions in the society. These include companies, cooperatives, governments, 'development' agencies and, of course, political parties - all of which command or influence the use of other resources. In the course of these interactions, as villages have come to be incorporated into the wider society and its institutions, control over the use of resources has begun to move out of their hands into the power of private companies or the government. And the people know it. Once, they were poor, more or less autonomous, closely-knit, but largely self-sufficient communities. Although it was effective to provide for their livelihood, their simple technology left them vulnerable to the vicissitudes of nature. Now, such communities have in many cases become more or less dependent, rather more internally divided than before, and not always or equally enjoying a greatly enhanced livelihood. Moreover, as their dependence has increased, their vulnerability - especially to *social* forces beyond their control - has also increased.[4]

This point of course echoes one already touched on in relation to the Maasai. It concerns the relations between local societies and their politics on the one hand, and the regional or national society and its politics, on the other hand. Such relations are often intensely complex, and never easy to trace. But they are of the greatest importance. They lie at the heart of many disputes and deals between local communities, institutions and regions, and the national centres of power and resources, whether private or public. Such deals or disputes very much affect the fate of local communities in the villages of the modern world, especially when so much power and so many resources are concentrated beyond their effective influence or control.

The long-term effects of this are often reflected in unequal material and social conditions which prevail amongst different social groups, or regions. For there are few societies in the world today which do not have some social groups or regions which, relative to others, are poor, less healthy, in decline, starved of resources or have little 'development' effort directed to them. This often lumpy and uneven distribution of welfare and 'development' can be found world-wide, whether you look in Brazil, Britain or Bangladesh. There are many reasons for it. These include such natural factors as climate, location and topography, which do not make the 'development' of such regions easy or cheap. Other factors - which might account for the decline of once prosperous regions, for example - may stem from changes in the demand for their resources, and hence are social in character. Within such areas, the fate of different social groups may vary as the fortunes of the region decline. Over time, these differences may accumulate and even harden, thus distributing life chances and prospects even more unequally, with little chance of correcting the balance.

The point, however, serves to illustrate a major strand of the argument. The condition of such regions and social groups cannot simply be attributed to 'nature'. Still less can it be explained with reference only to the allegedly impersonal forces of the market. Purposive actions and counter-actions by national groups and institutions with power which directly influences the use and, especially, the distribution of resources have always been a major factor. Such factors decisively affect village societies, influencing their 'development', or lack of it, and indeed their 'underdevelopment'. Viewed in yet wider terms, these processes have come to influence relations between societies at an international level.[5] In all this, politics is central.

III

Formal institutions are also social entities. In the industrial societies they may typically be factories, banks, corporations, local governments, schools or churches. There are also countless voluntary, charitable, recreational, 'political', commercial and promotional organizations which rise and fall, merge and separate, expand and contract. In the Third World, most people are engaged in rural and agricultural activities. So the kinds of institutions there also include informal village working groups, cultivation committees, organizations for maintaining irrigation systems or looking after herds, agricultural cooperatives and rural credit associations, as well as official and international 'development' agencies.

Now it is of course true that such institutions are not themselves small-scale 'societies', as villages are, in the sense described in chapter 1. They do not reproduce themselves socially *and* biologically! But their members *do* regularly seek to maintain such institutions socially, that is to perpetuate them. Indeed, they often try to expand their scope and their influence. Certainly, they all use resources. Some are engaged in producing other resources, and all are engaged in distributing or redistributing resources. Their activities are therefore political, both in respect of their internal working processes and also in respect of their relations with other institutions. They are legitimate subjects for political analysis, and the present framework can help to reveal the characteristics of their politics. Two examples will help to illustrate this: the first is concerned with the politics of what might be a typical academic department in a university or college; the second is the politics of the World Bank.

IV

All college or university departments are different, and each is unique. But one can learn a great deal about any particular one by asking and trying to answer the kinds of questions outlined in chapter 1. The twin major objectives of most departments are to teach and to undertake research. Teaching is usually geared to producing graduates and post-graduates, and research has as its aim the advancement of knowledge, whether pure or applied. Typically, the resources which a given department uses in seeking to attain these objectives are made up of various kinds, derived from a variety of sources. First, the department will have a number of staff, academic and other. The staff will themselves have particular specialist skills, experience and knowledge - a highly valuable set of resources which are deployed in teaching and in research. The spread of such specialisms may be wide or narrow. The department may have a tradition of interest and commitment in a few particular areas of the discipline. In History, it might be European history; in Politics it might be comparative government or political theory or methodology; in Economics it might be international trade or development economics, and so forth. Or, in the course of regularly reviewing its central objectives (if it does so), the department may strive to obtain or retain a balance between the main established areas of the discipline with which it is primarily concerned.

Secondly, students are another major resource. They may be undergraduates or graduates at various stages of their degree courses. A department may seek to increase the number of students it has (within limits established by the university or college), which may in turn be specified by national bodies, like the University Grants Committee. It may seek to attract certain kinds of students - mature students or students from certain kinds of schools, for instance - and it may vary the kind of conditional offers it makes to candidates for admission to the department so as to increase 'quality' or 'quantity', or both.

In addition to these major resources, the department will have a grant, allocated by the finance or planning committee of the institution. Also, the department (or individual members within it) may have some independent research funding for their work from an outside body - perhaps in industry, or a private foundation, or one of the research councils established by the government. Other resources include teaching and research space, in the form of lecture and seminar rooms, offices, laboratories and so forth. Time is yet another resource, and a department may be constrained by the university (or other departments) as to how much of the students' time it may use in its teaching, and how it uses the facilities it shares with other departments - such as lecture halls and seminar rooms.

As well as 'producing' graduates and post-graduates, the department may also be producing research results, publications and policy recommendations on a wide variety of issues. Some of these may provide an additional source of direct income to it, though this is rather rare. All these items comprise the kinds of resources which it uses and produces.

Now the politics of a department is constituted by the way it uses and distributes these resources to produce its graduates and its research findings. To establish the main features of the politics of the department it is important to be able to identify the patterns of cooperation and conflict, and the division of labour involved in the pursuit of its goals. The following questions help one to do this.

What are its procedures and principles for attracting and admitting both undergraduate and post-graduate students? Does it do more teaching than research? Or do some staff do more of one than the other? What is the ratio of undergraduates to post-graduates, and are the students distributed evenly between the courses taught within the department? How are individual staff-student ratios established? Do junior staff do more teaching and senior staff more administration, or is this balanced out or compensated in some way? Are these issues ones which cause conflict?

How are decisions taken about all these matters? Are the objectives of the department carefully discussed and mapped out by the staff, and are resources allocated accordingly? Or are procedures more *ad hoc*? What is the distribution of power within the department, for instance between the Head, Readers, Senior Lecturers, Lecturers, other staff and students? Are the procedures for decision-taking governed by university-wide regulations which specify the principles and rules in great detail, or are there only general guidelines? Are there sub-committees for special matters - like examinations and admissions - and do they have power? Does membership of these committees rotate? Do students attend and vote at departmental meetings? If so, how many are present and do they participate in discussion on all matters? How is the allocation of the departmental grant divided between support for staff research, funding for travel to conferences, departmental equipment and stationery, payment and entertainment of visiting speakers and so forth? Does the Head of the department decide this alone, and if so, why? Or, is the grant discussed at departmental meetings and a budget for the year drawn up by the staff as a whole? How does the department decide, in the light of its objectives, to teach various courses? Are individual members of staff appointed to teach particular courses, or in particular areas? How are they appointed, and by whom? And what factors influence the decisions about areas to be filled by new staff? How much freedom do staff have in defining the content and methods of courses which they teach? How free are students to choose courses, and what criteria govern this? Are proposals for new courses put before the whole department for discussion, comment and approval, or are teachers entirely free to teach what they wish, within the broad terms of their appointment? How far may they drift away from this in the course of time?

The composition and social organization of the department will both influence and reflect its politics. The ratio of senior to junior staff may be a significant factor, as may be the ratio of tenured to contract staff, and full-time to part-time ones. How do these ratios affect the exercise of power, for instance over long-term planning in the department? Are the relations between the various categories of staff very formal? Do they have distinctive rights, duties and responsibilities? Do they mix socially, and do staff and students get together on a regular basis, or are there more or less formal occasions when this happens? Within the department what is the status of any distinct groups of staff with specialist interests? How, if at all, are such groups organized, formally or informally? Are there established 'teaching syndicates' of such members, or are such groupings more fluid and undefined? Do they form organized factions within the department and do they seek to expand their areas of teaching specialisms, commitments and courses? Do they lay claim to a greater share of the departmental resources, whether in terms of the grant, time, new staff appointments or graduate students?

The 'academic culture' and ideology of the department will also be shaped by its politics and will help to sustain it. By 'academic culture' I mean such things as its commitment to certain components of the discipline, to certain ways of teaching and examining, and to other related practices of academic life. For example, a department may be very 'traditional' in what it teaches, how it teaches and the methods of assessment which it uses, relying mainly on lectures, seminars, tutorials, laboratory practicals, essays and three-hour unseen examinations. Such 'traditionalism', as some would define it, may be explained by the history of the department, especially in the domination of its affairs by older members who are not sympathetic to innovations in the discipline, or to new practices in teaching methods or examining. Everyone in the department may be quite happy with these customs, accepting the principles which underlie them and sharing the objectives they seek to achieve. On the other hand, as change in the composition and social organization of the department occurs, this may be reflected in a shift in its age-structure, or in the balance of experience, background and specialist teaching interests and wider ideology of new staff. Long-running disputes about such matters may result. Changes may be proposed, for instance in the kind, content and structure of courses taught in the department, perhaps urging more emphasis in some areas than in others, and recommending new methods of teaching and assessment. Student demands and pressures may be a factor in this. Such proposals as these represent divergent 'academic ideologies', involving different views about the way in which departmental resources should be used. This has direct implications for the politics of the department, and it may reflect wider ideologies and outlooks as well.

The way in which these kinds of factors work against and with each other in the processes of cooperation and conflict in the department's work all constitute its politics. But like any other institution or society, it does not operate in isolation. It is subject to a variety of external sources of influence and pressure. It is, after all, only part of a wider institution, the university or college, and there are many pressures which bear upon it.[6] Many of its activities will be governed by rules and regulations which apply throughout the university and will have to be obeyed. Other departments may have claims on student time and on facilities. 'Treaties' with such departments, for example in respect of joint degrees, will have to be negotiated and adhered to. More widely, government policy affecting universities and colleges may have direct effects upon the morale, direction and size of the department, as the public expenditure 'cuts' in the early 1980s in the UK have illustrated. In so far as professional or vocational courses are concerned - as in social work and medicine - other external bodies, far beyond the university, may have to validate and monitor its teaching programme. In all these respects the department is not autonomous.

No department (within a university or any other institution) is static. It undergoes change, for some of the above reasons as well as others. New staff may be appointed with new interests and commitments. Their influence on the direction of the department may come to be felt in time. A reduction in the number of students or of staff, or in the size of its grant, may occur. This may compel the department to review its teaching programme - for instance the range and kind of courses it offers - and perhaps may involve it in developing relations and alliances with other departments which otherwise it would not have done. Alternatively, an increase in student numbers may place grave strain on teaching and other facilities, compelling the department to review its priorities and practices, perhaps devoting more time to undergraduate teaching, or less time to research, or involving changes in the organization and methods of its teaching. In all these respects, changes in the use and distribution of resources - staff, students, courses, time, books, rooms, laboratories, grant, etc. - will involve changes in relations between people in the department, and are hence profoundly political.

All too often such issues are regarded as simply 'personal', in the crudest terms - and sometimes they are. Not all people get on with each other. Hence it is often difficult from the middle of a department to stand back and assess its politics in the terms suggested here. Yet it is important to try to do so, for the politics of institutions are not explicable simply in terms of their personalities and characters. The politics, therefore, of a typical academic department can also only really be grasped when the control, use, production and distribution of its resources are analysed through the relations of its particular systems of power and decision-making, social organization, culture and ideology. For instance, in those departments where most decisions about the use of resources - whether time or jobs or money or syllabus - are characterized by open discussion and the following of clear and established procedures, the politics (and atmosphere) are quite different from those where manipulative or authoritarian procedures prevail. More complicated still, where there are groups of staff with commitments to radically contrasting academic cultures and ideologies, *and* where there is little open discussion, the politics of the department can become extremely unstable, riddled with intrigue and internal warfare. The differences between such departments lie not *only* in the personalities concerned, but in the 'systemic' components of its make-up as an institution, that is its politics.

It might be thought that the politics of such a small-scale institution in a university (or anywhere else) is relatively easy to analyse. It is not. Even in a small institution relevant facts are not always easy to discover. Moreover, the distribution of power, or the perhaps fluid shape of social organization, and the hidden assumptions which may underlie customs and ideologies are not immediately obvious to the observer, even (or especially) to the participant-observer. The same is true for all the activities of cooperation and conflict which flow through and around the department. But this is not to say that such understanding cannot be achieved. This point only serves to underline a major feature of all social science: it is not easy.[7]

And if one expands the focus and scale of analysis - say to the whole university or factory or company or bureaucracy - the complex relations which need to be examined and the amount of evidence involved also expand. In the case of a whole university, for example, the volume, range and origin of resources involved are greater; the number of interacting groups and departments increases; the variety of claims and counter-claims on the resources multiplies; the structure of decision-making and the distribution of power are more elaborate; the social organization is necessarily more dense; there may be a wider spread of more or less distinctive academic cultures and ideologies, for instance, between Engineering and Drama departments. Such complexity inevitably tempts one to concentrate on certain limited or specific aspects of the workings of the institution - perhaps its committee structure, or teaching programme, or planning of academic expansion, or the facts of institutional income and expenditure, and so forth. Knowledge of such detail is of course both necessary and important. The point, however, is that such detailed but fragmented data will not, in themselves, yield an understanding of the *politics* of the institution. Only an analysis of the relations between these and the other features referred to above will do so.

V

The second example of an institution whose activities may be analysed in terms of the present approach is the World Bank. It is a very large and extremely powerful institution, whose operations have far-reaching implications for the politics of other societies and institutions on a global basis. Although there are a number of histories and general descriptions of the Bank and its work, as well as some critical accounts of it, there is no detailed analysis of its politics, as understood here.[8] This is in large part due to the fact that the Bank regards much of the information which it collects and uses as confidential – as is common in many large institutions. Access to this material is very limited indeed. Information about the daily flow of meetings and details of negotiations is almost impossible to get, even for citizens of countries whose governments borrow money from the Bank, and which they, the citizens, will in fact have to repay in due course. While official Bank publications available to the general public are of great value in providing facts and figures about international 'development' issues, they are not intended to explain the internal processes whereby the Bank allocates resources in the course of its 'development' work. But enough information is known to be able to ask some central questions about the Bank and so help to illuminate the kinds of factors which must influence its politics.

The World Bank (The International Bank for Reconstruction and Development), along with the International Monetary Fund (IMF), commenced operations in 1946 after the Bretton Woods Conference, which met to establish new international financial institutions parallel to the United Nations. Its main objective was to obtain and distribute the large amounts of capital which it was recognized would be necessary for post-war reconstruction and development, mainly in Europe at first. It also sought to help 'developing' countries increase their productivity. Since then, the Bank has moved away from 'reconstruction' to become the most important agency involved in 'development', especially in the Third World, where most of its activities are concentrated.[9]

Whatever one may think about the objectives, design and effects of its work, there can be little doubt that the Bank has had a major influence on the 'development' strategies of many societies, and on thinking about 'development' in many quarters.[10] And if nothing else about its activities were political in the present sense, this fact alone – its influence on the theory and practice of 'development' – would make it profoundly political. But there is more to it than that.

What are the main resources of the Bank and where do they come from? The Bank is actually owned by the (currently) 139 governments which have joined it. Each government contributes a certain amount to the subscription capital of the Bank, roughly in accordance with its economic strength. Not more than about 10 per cent of this is actually paid in, the bulk remaining as a guarantee of Bank borrowings. These borrowings – the major source of funds for its lending operations – are raised on the capital markets of the world on standard commercial terms. Other financial resources come from the profits which the Bank makes on its loans and from the flow of repayments to it from the governments which borrow from it. In addition to these capital resources, the Bank has a large professional staff, of about 2500 in 1980. Many have a training in economics or accountancy, or have experience in banking, or in agriculture, transportation, irrigation, engineering or other specialist areas in which it undertakes 'development' projects. These skills are a very valuable part of its overall resources.

The main activity of the Bank is to lend money to governments in the Third World for 'development' projects and programmes in their societies, in such sectors as agriculture and rural development, power, transportation, development finance corporations, water supply and sewerage, and education.[11]

Broadly speaking, the way the Bank goes about its lending is as follows: possible projects are identified by Bank staff or other institutions, like the Food and Agriculture Organization (FAO) or the United Nations Development Programme (UNDP), or by the government of a particular country. There then follows a more or less intensive period of project preparation, during which data is collected, the main elements of the project mapped out and various feasibility studies undertaken. Bank involvement in this may only be slight. Then the project is 'appraised' by Bank staff in the light of the general economic conditions of the country. The technical, institutional, economic and financial aspects of the project are carefully assessed. In the appraisal, Bank staff are concerned to analyse the capacity of the project to increase productivity so that it may more than pay for itself over a given number of years.

In the course of both preparation and appraisal, the details and components are worked out, usually in close conjunction with officials of the relevant government. For example, the Bank may lend for an integrated rural development project which aims to increase the agricultural productivity of a poor region in a particular society. The project may seek to improve the irrigation system, crop yields, the availability of fertilizers and other 'inputs', as well as marketing, transport, communication and extension services. It might also provide small components for health care, education and other 'social' investments. In appraising the project, the Bank staff try to assess how much increase in productivity there will be over a given number of years as a result of the investment of capital, and hence what flow of benefits there would be to the 'target' population of the region - and to the society more generally, for example in increased export earnings or reduced import costs, say of food. Using various techniques of cost-benefit analysis, they try to estimate whether the investment in all these things would generate a sufficient return on the capital to justify the loan, and hence assist in its repayment. The Bank will generally only lend for projects or programmes which will increase productivity and hence provide a rate of return above a given amount. Once appraisal has been completed, there follows a period of negotiation with the borrower government about the terms and conditions of the loan. And once these negotiations are finalized, the loan agreement is signed, usually in Washington. Thereafter, Bank staff take a continuing interest in the project, though its implementation is the responsibility of the government concerned. Bank staff visit it regularly to 'supervise' the work and evaluate its effects.[12]

Loans are repaid over twenty years on average, at an appropriate rate of interest to cover the Bank's own borrowings. Some loans, through the Bank's 'soft loan' affiliate, the International Development Association (IDA), are extremely generous, carrying almost no interest at all. But they are generally only granted to governments in the poorest societies, and they do not comprise the bulk of the Bank's loans. However, the funds for lending through IDA have to be regularly replenished mainly by member governments, and, if the large contributors decline to do so, this aspect of Bank operations may collapse. It would be important and interesting to know what considerations act to influence member governments (especially the rich ones) in their decision whether or not to contribute to IDA.

Now, just as with any other institution, the politics of the World Bank are bound up in the way it obtains, uses and distributes resources. And these politics are greatly influenced by the distribution of power in the Bank, and by its decision-making structure, the social organization of the institution, and by the culture and ideology of banking and a particular view on 'development' which both guide and express its principal activities.

The major way in which the Bank uses and distributes its resources is in lending them. Therefore the really important questions concern how this is done. How does it lend, to whom, under what conditions and for what purposes? What factors influence both general policy and particular decisions in these matters? For instance, what are the relations between the Bank and those *from* whom it borrows? Do the latter exercise any direct or indirect influence on the way it uses resources, for example in the character and kind of projects which it undertakes, or the conditions attached to loans or the countries to which it lends, or the amounts available for loans to particular countries? If there is such influence, how is it achieved? Moreover, how do the member governments control the activities of the Bank through their representatives on its Board of Governors? They have voting strengths in proportion to their contributions to the Bank's subscription capital – and the main contributors are the USA, and United Kingdom, France, West Germany and Japan. Is there any sense in which they exercise their power and cast their votes to promote their own (national and sometimes joint) interests? If so, could such goals ever conflict with the particular objectives of 'development' to which the Bank is committed? Or, is there unanimity on both ends and means? For instance, would support for textile industry projects in Asia be welcomed by British members of the Board of Governors?

And what of the internal politics of the Bank? The day-to-day operations of the Bank are supervised by the President and the Executive Directors, who are appointed and elected by the Governors. In this way, the influence of the member governments, and especially the Big Five, is expressed at the apex of power and decision-making of the Bank. Formally, the President and the Executive Directors have to scrutinize and approve each project and loan proposal. But there are clearly far too many for them to do this in great detail. Thus the *de facto* power of departments in the Bank is quite considerable in the way they identify and formulate projects. This is also true for other committees, below the level of the Executive Directors, such as the Loan Committee which looks carefully at all proposals. But there are many departments in the Bank. Some are regional ones (like South Asia, West Africa, Latin America and the Caribbean) and are concerned with identifying and developing projects for countries in their areas. Some departments are functional, or sectoral, like Education, Tourism, Population, Agriculture and Rural Development. And some are both functional and regional. Others have research, advisory, monitoring or evaluation functions - like the Development Policy Department, or the Projects Advisory Staff, or the Operations and Evaluation Department, and so forth. All these departments and their personnel are ranked in lines of hierarchy and are structured in relationships with each other. This, in general terms, may be regarded as the social organization of the Bank, corresponding in this instance to the broad division of labour within it.

Again, as in most institutions, different departments and groups in the Bank may pursue or promote different goals and approaches, within the broad framework of Bank objectives, policy and outlook, and may even strive to change these. Each department will stake claims on Bank resources for its work. How much conflict is there between departments and divisions over the use and distribution of Bank resources, and how are these resolved? Do the regional project departments, for instance, compete with each other to identify, appraise and reach agreement on more projects in 'their' region than in others? Or are regions expected to lend a given amount over a given period, and how is this amount arrived at? If this is the case, what happens if they do not achieve their lending targets, or project targets? And what are the implications of such policy for the kind and quality of projects they help to devise? On what does promotion or transfer inside the Bank depend? And how are new ideas and approaches assimilated from research into the identification and design of projects?

When it comes to what one may refer to as the 'culture' and 'ideology' of the Bank, many interesting issues arise. It is most important to remember that the World Bank is a bank, *not* the Red Cross. It therefore has certain banking customs which define its culture, so to speak, and which decisively influence and reflect its politics. It does not give money away. It lends it on carefully worked out terms, like any other bank. Not unreasonably, it insists on getting it back. There are, moreover, fairly standard operating procedures which it follows, referred to earlier, through the various stages of the 'project cycle', of identification, preparation, appraisal, negotiation and agreement. These are designed to ensure sound projects which will generate a return on capital.

Many Bank staff view a return on capital as being synonomous with 'development', the prime engine of which is 'growth' in their view. The extremely energetic staff are thus the bearers of this culture, that is of the way the Bank sees things and does things, and they communicate it to those with whom they come into contact in the course of their work around the world - especially to officials of the governments which borrow from it. There is also a training division in the Bank, the Economic Development Institute, which runs courses on how to appraise, manage and evaluate projects, which many officials from Third World countries find very valuable indeed. In this and other ways, the Bank spreads knowledge about its principles and techniques of operation, and also wins friends, influences people and gains customers.

It would be both simplistic and incorrect to suggest that there is a single, inflexible ideology which dominates the activities of the World Bank and which could be described in a few sentences. There are many currents of opinion and theory about 'development' and the role of the Bank in it. Some staff will say that they see the Bank as a 'capital transfer institution', while others will emphasize its role in 'institution building'. Some will argue that 'growth' must precede redistributional activities within societies, while others will point to evidence which suggests that it may *not* be possible to 'grow first and redistribute later'.[13] But it would be interesting to know how wide the range and spread of such views are inside the Bank, and how vigorous the debate actually is. How wide can it be in *any* institution (or society for that matter) without its disintegrating through conflict?

In practice, however, it appears clear that despite some differences of opinion and approach, the Bank is committed to the notion that 'development' and the elimination of poverty flow primarily from increased 'growth', and that stimulating private enterprise is the best way to achieve this. In so far as there is a dominant ideology in the Bank, for which its staff would advance both theoretical justification and empirical evidence, it is that. Yet it is fair to say that the Bank has lent to officially 'socialist' governments, including Algeria, the People's Democratic Republic of Laos, Romania, Tanzania, Yugoslavia and Vietnam, though these do not constitute anything more than a fraction of Bank lendings.[14] And there is nothing, in principle, to prevent other 'socialist' governments joining the Bank and borrowing from it, except of course that their ideologies about 'growth' and 'development' may in many fundamental respects be incompatible with those of the Bank.

But it would be fascinating to know how, in practice and if at all, such outlooks inside the Bank and amongst its management committees influence decisions about lending, and especially the conditions which it attaches to loans. What happens in the course of negotiations? Is the Bank able to influence the policy of national governments and, if so, how? How free is the Bank to consider radically alternative policies aimed at reducing poverty or promoting 'development'? For example, in recent years the Bank has been committed to helping the 'poorest of the poor', especially in rural areas. How has this policy been translated into action? Have the benefits of loans it has been making to governments actually reached the poor? Is it too soon to say? Is there any sense in which such goals may be incompatible with the central objectives of the Bank, to ensure a sound return on capital? The Bank claims to be non-political, in the conventional sense, and hence proceeds with great caution in certain areas, for instance in land reform or other aspects of the redistribution of wealth.[15] But would or could it respond if it were clearly established that 'development' (or even 'growth') on the scale needed in the next twenty years can simply not take place in the conditions of gross inequality which prevail in so many societies in the Third World? Would it be able to include redistributional conditions amongst the other conditions which it already imposes on borrowers? And what would be the reactions of borrowing governments? Or those of other member governments on and through their representatives on the Board of Governors? How would the money markets of the world respond? Would such a shift in outlook and policy affect the flow of resources to the Bank?

Because the World Bank maintains such secrecy about its internal workings and also about its relations with both member governments and borrowers, it is *usually* impossible to answer these kinds of questions in detail. Even its appraisal reports and loan agreements are strictly confidential. Those scholars who, on occasions, have had access to interesting and important material, and who have then sought to publish the findings of their research, have had considerable pressure brought to bear on them not to do so, especially if critical, as in the celebrated case of Teresa Hayter.[16] Occasionally, however, *something* happens which suddenly opens a window on the real politics in and around the Bank. One such incident occurred in 1981.

In the summer of that year, after a long period of gestation, a proposal was put forward by the Bank to establish an energy affiliate which would promote the exploration and development of energy sources (such as coal, gas and oil) by Third World governments.[17] If successful, this would have enabled societies in the Third World to reduce their energy imports and hence ease the often crushing burdens on their balance of payments. Such proposals are of course examined closely by the Bank's Board of Governors, composed of the representatives of its members, amongst which the USA as the major stockholder is dominant. The Governors are in close touch with their governments. This particular energy proposal of the Bank had been given preliminary approval by the Carter administration. But when it came to get final approval, Carter had been defeated in the USA Presidential election and a new administration was in office. The Reagan administration turned it down, and hence killed it. Their reasons for doing so were quite clear. They said that

the scheme would hamper US coal exports by subsidizing foreign mines and could diminish the role - and profits - of private oil firms. If state oil firms in developing countries could obtain World Bank risk capital normally provided by private firms, the Treasury argued, they would have 'little incentive to turn to private foreign companies to share in the profits'.[18]

This reaction by the USA was part of a wider campaign to alter Bank policy, according to an Under Secretary of the US Treasury, Beryl Sprinkel. There was too much of a tendency, he said, 'to encourage socialism, rigged prices and the kinds of economic systems abroad that are inconsistent with our own outlook on the world'.[19] By early 1982, to drive home its point, and to encourage direct private lending and investment in Third World countries, the USA had sliced back its lending to the 'soft loan' affiliate of the Bank, the IDA, by some 26 per cent. Mr Sprinkel once more said that the USA wanted the World Bank to impose tougher conditions on Third World borrowers, and said that they might even have to 'submit to some form of economic management from outside, even if it proves, as it has done in the past, politically destructive'. This would have the effect of compelling borrowers to submit to the 'magic of the marketplace' as President Reagan calls it.[20]

One consequence of this new policy was the resignation of a senior Bank official, Mr Mahbub ul Haq, who said: 'I happen to believe that this amounts to condemning poor people to absolute, intolerable poverty, because they are at best on the fringe of the marketplace, more often outside it altogether.'[21]

Anyone who has met or worked with Bank staff in Washington or around the world will no doubt gape at Mr Sprinkel's claim that the Bank promotes what he calls 'socialism'. Its policy towards Chile, between 1970 and 1973, hardly bears this out, as a later chapter will show; nor does a recent (1982) World Bank *Country Program Paper* on Nicaragua, which was 'leaked' from Washington. This document apparently recommends that, in conjunction with the IMF, the Bank should *not* lend to Nicaragua on a significant scale, if at all, unless and until that country makes a fundamental shift in policy so as to permit the private sector once again to play a major role in the politics of Nicaraguan development.[22] If this recommendation becomes 'official' policy, so to speak, it will influence other banks and financial agencies and hence make it very difficult for Nicaragua to raise funds on the international money markets.

What this and the energy affiliate episode helps to underline is that the World Bank, like any other institution, is not a 'neutral' technical agency. It is not simply 'an international cooperative development institution, dedicated to assisting member governments to meet the economic and social needs of their people'.[23] It is a *political* institution, for what is at issue - always - is the manner in which the Bank defines and promotes 'development'. It obtains, uses and distributes very substantial sums of money and expertise. This gives it considerable power. In these activities it has a profound effect upon the politics of societies around the world, as does the IMF. In turn, it affects their access to and use of resources, and this influence penetrates to the remotest villages, such as those discussed earlier. I have seen the direct and visible effects in the dry zone of Sri Lanka, in the high mountain villages of Cyprus and in and around Iban longhouses in Sarawak. And the particular way the Bank goes about using and distributing resources - that is, its politics - is shaped by the structure and distribution of power within and around it, and by the interests and ideologies, in or outside it, of those who are able to influence or control it. In particular this means the major stockholders, and especially the USA, as well as those who lend to the Bank. Thus, whether one agrees or not with Bank policy on these or any other matters, it is simply silly for it to claim, as it regularly does, that it is 'non-political'. It is not. No institution can be.

It would therefore be of the greatest interest to be able to analyse the politics of the Bank in much greater detail. But the secrecy of the institution (*and* its member governments) makes this impossible. This world's largest 'development' institution simply refuses to allow the world to learn about its politics. What possible justification can there be for that, one wonders?

VI

This chapter has shown that the definition of politics outlined in the first chapter can be extended to the analysis of the activities of cooperation and conflict in entities other than whole societies, such as villages or institutions. It has shown, in passing, how important institutional detail can be. But not on its own. It is necessary always to go beyond institutional analysis to see how the systems of power and decision-making, social organization, culture and ideology both influence and reflect the use or changed use of resources in the politics of villages or institutions, or in the relations between them.

It will also be clear that the conception of politics used in this book requires an approach which is sometimes referred to as 'interdisciplinary'. What does this mean? Why is it necessary? How can it be illustrated? These questions are examined in the next chapter.

CHAPTER SIX

The politics of despair, dustbowls, disease and devastation

I

This chapter sets out to show why the conception of politics used here requires an interdisciplinary approach, and to illustrate what this means in practice. The general argument is that if we are to understand the historical or contemporary politics of human societies, and especially the problems which occur within them, it is necessary to draw on the work of many disciplines both within and beyond the social sciences. The claim here is that the kind of framework used in this book provides a useful way of doing that in a preliminary fashion. Three central themes run through the argument.

First, and most generally, I am concerned to emphasize a point made in chapter 1 and illustrated in the subsequent discussion of the !Kung, Aztecs and Maasai. There it was stressed that, in their politics, human societies are constantly engaged in activities which are simultaneously social (through human action) and natural. For everywhere, human societies are *part* of particular ecologies, not separated from them. This means that they are both affected by nature and also act upon it. The term 'nature' encompasses a vast range of things, but the obvious examples include climate, land, vegetation, animals, air, sea, rivers and an enormous number of other biological, biochemical and physical processes which affect our health and welfare. Thus, in analysing the politics of societies we need to be constantly aware of the continuity of relations between the social and natural worlds. However, these worlds tend in practice to be studied by different disciplines. There is therefore a case for trying to break down some of the often strict divisions between the natural and social sciences which can often obstruct our understanding. For, as one writer has observed, 'the world extends across disciplines, continents and centuries. Nothing in nature is quite so separate as two mounds of expertise.'[1]

Secondly, this chapter will show that the reality of these social-natural relations can be most clearly exposed by looking at examples of particular *problems* which erupt in human societies. In their origins, conditions and consequences, few such problems involve factors which are either *purely* natural or social. Rather, the *social* dimensions of such problems are often decisive, even where the immediate (or 'trigger') factors may be natural, such as drought or infectious disease. Conversely, problems which are often thought of as 'natural' (the outbreak of epidemics, for instance) may often be triggered by social factors, as will emerge later.

It is of course true that some problems are more social than natural. But their explanation can seldom be satisfactorily achieved in terms of any one discipline *within* the social sciences - and this again underlines the need for inter-disciplinary work between them.

I am all too aware that discussion of these issues can draw one deep into the area of the philosophy and methodology of the social sciences.[2] It is an intellectual minefield, dotted with booby-traps, diversions and dead-ends. Some people who enter it never seem to emerge alive. And those who do are often in such a state of shock that they never seem able to say anything again about any concrete problems or politics of the world. I do not propose to enter it here, but think it is more useful to state why an interdisciplinary approach is needed, what is meant by it for present purposes, and to illustrate this with appropriate examples. Before proceeding to do that, there are some introductory points to make.

II

The term 'discipline' means, simply, a field of study. Now disciplines have not arrived fully formed in the world of scholarship. Like all other aspects of life, they evolve and change over time in the course of interaction with their environment, and with each other, and in response to problems occurring both in the disciplines and in their ultimate point of reference, the real world. But disciplines, it is important to remember, are constituted largely by conventions, and they are sustained by the communities of scholars who work within them. In general, disciplines are distinguished from each other by the typical kinds of problems with which they concern themselves, and by the typical kinds of questions which they ask about such problems. Each discipline is thus defined in general by its broad method of enquiry, that is by its analytical or theoretical framework (or competing frameworks), and by its typical operational procedures.[3]

But it is even more important to recognize that different disciplines do not correspond with, or match, in any one-to-one form, *separate* 'bits' of social or natural life. For instance, to talk of 'the economy' or the 'political system' may be necessary (for shorthand, if nothing else) to refer to some set of relations or activities. But it is none the less a *selective abstraction* from a wider set of relations, of the kind referred to earlier. Few people seriously dispute this. Yet because we have become so used to talking of 'the economy' or 'the political system', for example, it sometimes seems as if they assume an autonomous and independent character. This acts to reinforce the autonomy and separation of the disciplines of Economics, or Political Science - or Sociology, and other disciplines within the social sciences. The same is generally true in the natural sciences, where the closer one approaches the 'real thing' - the structure and functioning of the insect or animal or human body or swamp or forest or climate - the less and less possible it becomes to maintain sharp distinctions between, say, Chemistry or Biology or Physics, or branches of them.

Thus, the only way in which disciplines can maintain their purity or exclusivity is through a process of *selection and abstraction* - away from the complex interactions of the real world. And this is precisely what disciplines involve and what particular scholars working within them do in practice. They select in terms of the different problems they define, the different questions they ask, the different 'facts' they identify and use, the different theories and purposes which shape their explanations, and the different 'levels' of detail or generality at which they work.[4]

This process of selection and abstraction occurs most obviously in the laboratory, where scientists isolate particular relations for investigation, and hold others constant - or leave them out. It happens in a comparable way in the historical and social sciences, where scholars select a particular set or sequence of happenings to investigate. And the kinds of sequences they choose to explore are, in general, influenced by the prevailing concerns of their disciplines, or branches or 'schools' within them. That being said, it is necessary to note that it is not uncommon for the *same* event or events, or even the *same* 'fact', to be examined from different angles by different scholars working in different disciplines. Indeed, they may even be examined and re-examined by different scholars from the same discipline, using different analytical or theoretical frameworks - and so on.

Now there can be no doubt that this process of research by selection and specialization has been extremely fruitful, and will continue to be so. It has yielded very important knowledge and understanding. And as such work has developed, so too have the disciplines expanded. In some respects they have - in both the social and natural sciences - edged closer to each other, and have begun to converge on common territory and common problems.[5] But there are two points which must none the less be stressed. First, it remains in general the case that disciplinary specialization has necessarily meant fragmentation. Secondly - and crucially for the argument here - the fact of the matter is that there are few *problems* which arise in the real world (whether they be pollution or unemployment or famine or war or social conflict or epidemics) which present themselves for analysis in neatly packaged disciplinary terms. Hence they are not easily consigned to a particular discipline - or even part of one - for explanation. And this is precisely the reason why interdisciplinary work becomes necessary, especially if one is concerned to analyse specific real world problems. But how can this be done, and what is 'interdisciplinarity'?

III

It is important to start by saying that interdisciplinary work is neither straight-forward nor without problems.[6] There are difficulties, for instance, in combining evidence from different disciplines in inderdisciplinary explanations. But it is necessary to insist that, especially if one is starting with actual problems which occur in the real world, it should be done and can be done with far less fuss than much of the cautionary literature on methodology would suggest. Indeed, it is often the parochialism of the disciplinarians themselves, rather than the exclusivity of their disciplines or the allegedly incompatible richness of their respective findings, which stands in the way of more and better interdisciplinary work. That being said, the main points to be made about interdisciplinarity are these.

First, and most generally, all interdisciplinary approaches will be prompted in the first instance by the kinds of problems which are identified for analysis, the way they are specified and the nature of the questions being asked about them. The character of the problem will usually be such that its explanation cannot be 'contained' within the boundaries of the conventional concerns of any one discipline. Such problems, by their very nature, can only be explained in interdisciplinary terms.

Secondly, therefore, there are and will be many versions and forms of 'inter-disciplinarity', which vary in scope and depth. For this reason, and others, there can be no such thing as a single new 'synthetic' discipline called 'Interdiscipline' or 'Unidiscipline'.[7] While it may be possible to elaborate certain *very* broad general principles about social and/or natural processes in the world, they are - as yet - *far* too broad to be of much analytical value in practice. Productive interdisciplinary work - which may, in time, contribute to a clarification and tighter formulation of such principles - starts at a much lower level, but at a level which is above that usually found in the specialist concerns of particular disciplines. Thus, in interdisciplinary work, selection is *also* both necessary and inevitable, for you have to start somewhere, with some problem or set of questions. And, in tackling these, each *particular* interdisciplinary account will therefore involve a *particular* 'coalition' of organized 'facts' and explanations from a more or less wide range of disciplines.

However, thirdly, any such explanatory 'coalition' does not stand of its own accord, nor is it merely 'a broad-minded accumulation of complementary perspectives' on a particular problem.[8] What is decisive in making any particular interdisciplinary account hang together is the set of organizing principles which are expressed in the framework of enquiry being used. And it is this which helps to identify potentially relevant contributions from different disciplines, and which acts to integrate them in the account. In trying to explain a particular problem, or the character of the society in which it occurs, it is the framework of enquiry - or the analytical or theoretical framework - which in the first instance directs us where to look and what to look for, and which provides a set of starting-points for the explanation of what one finds. For both in mono-disciplinary and interdisciplinary work, the 'facts' *never* speak for themselves.

I V

What then shapes the general framework of enquiry used in this book, and how does this influence the kind of interdisciplinary approach being used?

It is necessary to return to the conception of politics, as defined before. The kinds of activities included in this notion of politics clearly extend far beyond the traditional analytical concerns and empirical range of the discipline of Politics as conventionally taught in educational institutions or discussed in the media. It was argued earlier that politics in all human societies is bound up with all the activities of cooperation and conflict which are involved in resource use and distribution. Such activities have occurred in an enormous variety of ecological conditions, historical contexts and social circumstances. Everywhere they both influence and are influenced by central features of social organization, power and culture.

It is this conception which shapes the broad framework of enquiry used here. More to the point, in analysing the politics of particular societies by exploring the relations between these systems and contexts, I have necessarily had to turn to the rich contributions of scholars in many different disciplines, outside Politics, both within and beyond the historical and social sciences. For example, the chapter on the !Kung drew heavily on the fascinating work of anthropologists who have used a variety of methods to accumulate and interpret data about them. Most notable amongst their methods are those of participant observation and measurement. But their field observations and assessments have in turn been enriched by very important contributions from other disciplines - such as Archaeology, Linguistics, Human Biology, Physical Anthropology, Demography and History, to mention but a few. Each of these disciplines, using its own methods of enquiry and procedures, has been able to offer insights into some aspects of the history and structure of !Kung society. Each has also provided useful comparative understanding.

Archaeological research, for instance, has yielded important information about the type and continuity of tools and weapons used, and about food consumed. Linguists have carefully examined the differences and connections between the various San languages and have been able to suggest important ideas about the degree of isolation or contact between people who spoke them. It is possible to use such linguistic evidence (for instance in the form of 'loan words') to help establish which groups and societies have been in contact with each other on a wider scale in Southern Africa. Human biologists and physical anthropologists, meanwhile, have used techniques of genetic analysis - of blood for instance - to help trace relations between San and other peoples. Demographers and medical scientists have observed child-rearing customs of !Kung women and have been able to relate these to some of the population patterns of the society. Historians, using documentary sources as well as 'oral' histories, have helped to reveal aspects of the recent history of the San and their relations with other societies in the area.[9]

In these and other respects different disciplines have used the past to help explain the present. But the opposite can *also* be the case. Some archaeologists today are trying to use the present to help explain the past. For instance, by examining the politics (as the term is used here) of surviving hunter-gatherer (or herding or agricultural) societies, they are trying to reconstruct the way in which past societies - using similar tools and technologies which have been found - may have worked.[10]

Such diverse information about the !Kung from various disciplines is of course fascinating in its own right. But when organized by the present kind of framework, it enables one to offer an account of the structure and politics of !Kung society in a manner which the disciplines within the social sciences - and certainly Politics - would simply not have permitted. The same is true for the brief accounts offered of the politics of the Aztecs and the Maasai. Likewise, a full discussion of the politics of village societies in Cyprus or Portugal - or anywhere else for that matter - would require a careful exploration of yet other kinds of disciplines concerning their specific geographical, ecological and climatic conditions; their systems of agricultural production and resource distribution; their systems of family and village social organization and decision-making, and their cultures and their ideologies. Problems which might be encountered in such analysis would in turn steer one to yet other disciplines.

There is an important point to emphasize here. The politics of societies, institutions and problems explored in this book are generally not dealt with in courses in Politics. Indeed some of the activities discussed are seldom even considered to be 'political'. This is a great pity. It can of course be explained by the pretty widespread parochialism and Euro-centricity of the historical and social sciences generally. But, in so far as 'mainstream' Politics is concerned in the universities and colleges, that is probably less important than the fact that the conception of politics within the discipline of Politics is rather limited. This is reflected and expressed in its traditional focus on narrowly political institutions (like 'government') and narrowly political theory (both normative - to do with freedom, rights, justice and democracy - and analytical). And it is this rather narrow conception of politics which precludes consideration of a far wider range of societies, events, relationships and problems. Conversely, the conception of politics used here is precisely what has permitted an exploration of the politics of a wider range of unfamiliar societies and institutions.

But the claim goes further than this. As indicated before, I am concerned to *expand* the range of processes, issues, occurrences and problems which can and should be legitimately considered as 'political'. How then, can the framework help to explain particular instances of these in the politics of human societies? In the rest of this chapter I refer to some unusual examples which both illustrate this conception of politics further and also underline the need for different kinds of interdisciplinary 'coalitions' in the explanation of each.

V

The first example serves to show how the politics of human societies are not constituted only by the way they use and distribute resources, but how these activities may be powerfully influenced by the culture and ideology of the society in the course of its relations with other societies.

In what are today the Eastern Cape and Transkei regions of South Africa there was, before the expansion of the Dutch (and later British) colonial society from the end of the eighteenth century, a number of small chiefdoms of Nguni-speaking peoples, referrred to loosely as the Xhosa. Though the chiefs tried from time to time to establish regular forms of defensive cooperation amongst the chiefdoms - especially as colonial expansion increased - they did not build lasting alliances which might have constituted the basis of wider societies. In any event, there had been no prior need for that. These Xhosa societies engaged in both the cultivation of crops and the herding of cattle and other animals. They grew various types of grain, pumpkins, calabashes, melons, beans and other root crops - tended mainly by the women. Men herded cattle which also played an important part in the social and ritual life of the societies, for instance as bride-wealth (or *lobola*) at marriage, and also in ceremonies to do with puberty, sickness and death. They also hunted and gathered to supplement diet and provide for items of equipment.

In the course of the first half of the nineteenth century, and especially after 1820, as the Cape Colony (by then under British rule) expanded, the whole structure of these Xhosa societies came under severe pressure. This resulted from a combination of population expansion in conditions of decreasing land, brought about primarily by military defeat in the course of conflict over territory with the colonial government and the white settlers. In 1856 there arose a prophetess, called Nongquase, who declared that she had seen a vision. The central message of her teaching was that people should destroy all their grain and kill all their cattle. Such sacrifice would bring back their dead heroes and ancestors, would fill their kraals with grain and cattle, and would sweep the whites into the sea in a great wind.

These prophecies (which were supported by others) implied very precise and very drastic action. There was some dispute and difference of opinion amongst the chiefs and subordinate family heads as to what they should do. Prophetesses were not dismissed lightly in Xhosa society, so should they do as they were bidden? Despite the conflict and difference of opinion, many chiefs and sub-chiefs called on their people to do what had been prescribed. So, between October and February 1856-7, grain was destroyed and thousands of head of cattle were slaughtered, perhaps as many as 200,000. The results were disastrous. As many as 20,000 people died from starvation, and many thousands more left their homes to find food and work. None of the predictions came true.[11] The whole 'cattle-killing' episode was a staggering tragedy in the history of the Xhosa societies, leaving them only more vulnerable to further penetration and conquest by an expanding colonial society.

What does one make of this incident? Does one say it was collective madness? Do we say it shows the typical irrationality of 'simple' people? Do we say that it shows the profoundly dangerous influence which religion or magic can have on the politics of a society? Any of these judgements is of course possible, but not at all useful. For none explains what happened, and why. None gets to the root of the causes which combined in this fashion in the politics of Xhosa society at a particular time and in particular circumstances. Such judgements also imply that comparable events do not happen in the politics of modern societies. This is hardly the case.

But if you start to ask questions about the systems of production, distribution, social organization, decision-making, power, culture and ideology of Xhosa society, things become a bit clearer. For here was a set of societies which depended crucially on access to land in order to produce and reproduce by cultivation and herding. As pressure on their politics mounted, that is as the particular character of their interaction with another society impinged directly on their capacity to produce and reproduce their social life, they experienced direct material and social crises. Being unsuccessful in holding off the encroachment of the colonial society by military means, they must have experienced despair. But 'despair' does not explain why the Xhosa reacted as they did. This requires some understanding of the social organization, culture and ideology of the society. That is to say, it is especially important to appreciate the place of prophetesses, respect for their visions and interpretations, and the belief in the effectiveness of sacrifice and the intervention in the affairs of humans by the 'shades', the dead ancestors. But even then, such beliefs had to be translated into action. And action of the kind which they took was possible only because the chiefs (or some of them) instructed their people to do as they were bidden, since chiefs had that kind of power and authority, though it was not lightly or unanimously exercised in this case.

Events of this sort are not unique. They have occurred around the world in the course of the recent history of colonial encounters of one kind or another, or where societies have experienced problems which they are not able to resolve.[12] But what this particular instance also illustrates so clearly is that occurrences of this kind are the product of the politics of a society. They are best understood when seen as the outcome of complex interactions over time of the kinds of systems described, and that these interactions can be dramatically influenced by relations with other societies. Moreover, an analysis of the politics of the 'cattle-killing' episode requires one to look beyond the confines of Politics, to Anthropology, History, Social Psychology and the Sociology of Religion, for instance, in order to compose an explanatory account of what happened, and why. It is also important not to think that such events are confined to allegedly 'primitive' people. In *all* societies, politics serves to integrate ideology and action. In every instance this occurs in a particular set of material circumstances, a pattern of social organization and a structure of power. At times the politics of societies are influenced by external factors, at other times internal crises play a major role. It could be argued that in the industrial societies today the 'ideological' influences of what may loosely be referred to as 'religion' or 'magic' seem pretty slim, for we are, after all, living in very 'rational' and 'scientific' times. But that all depends on what you mean by 'magic' or 'science'. For there have been some pretty strange and powerful beliefs and ideologies in modern times - sometimes referred to as 'scientific' by their exponents - which have had very profound effects on policy and practice, with results that have been as catastrophic for their societies - and others - as Nongquase's vision was for the Xhosa.

VI

Many problems which occur in societies are the direct outcome of the way in which their politics act to combine social *and* natural factors. This can be dramatically illustrated in the next example, drawn from the modern history of the United States. It is the story of the Dust Bowl.[13] This will again show that an understanding of the politics of this problem requires an interdisciplinary approach, constituted in this instance by a different 'coalition' of interdisciplinary contributions from that of the previous example.

The Southern Plains of the United States cover a vast area of some 100 million acres, and include parts of the States of Kansas, Oklahoma, Texas, New Mexico and Colorado. The climate of the region can be harsh, with bitterly cold winters and ferociously hot and dry summers. It is an area which on average receives little more than 20 inches of rain a year. Moreover, every twenty years or so, it has been visited by savage and sustained drought. Until the present century, the plains were covered by a tight and tough matting of grasses, which held the soil in place and which had sustained a rich life of wild flora and fauna. And until settlers spread to the Plains, especially in the middle years of the nineteenth century, they had been the domain of the vast herds of buffalo, and the home of the nomadic Indian societies who lived off them.

In the early 1930s drought returned to the Plains. But something new occurred which had never happened before. Enormous 'black blizzards' of sand and dust - or 'sand blows' or 'dusters' as they were called - rolled across the Plains. These blizzards sometimes blacked out the sun for weeks. In 1935 in Kansas, you could not see clear sky for some six weeks on end after February. Millions and millions of tons of top soil were being blown away. When surface winds combined with high altitude winds, the soil was whipped up high into the sky and carried as far afield as Boston, New York and Washington, as occurred in May 1934. Some twelve million tons of dust and sand fell on Chicago that month.[14] Photographs of the 'sand blows' in the countryside and towns of the Plains show walls of dust, like solid banks of thick fog, rolling across the land. Respiratory infections and what became known as 'dust pneumonia' spread across the Plains, and people died from the effects. Calves and cattle suffered, too, as did game and all living things. What had once been the vast expanse of grasslands had been transformed in some places into deserts, with dirt and dust being blown against houses, fences and barns, leaving the land unworkable and, in a manner of speaking, dead, rippled with sand dunes. Some 10 million acres lost at least 5 inches of top soil, and another 13.5 million lost 2½ inches of top soil. About 408 tons of soil were blown away per acre, on average.[15] From the heart of the crisis area there was soon a steady flow of immigrants, people streaming in their thousands to find work or food elsewhere, notably in California.[16] Between 1935 and 1937 some 34 per cent of the population from the worst affected counties left the area, abandoning homes and property, and leaving their land to sun and wind and sand. Both the events and the place where the epicentre of this drama occurred on those Southern Plains became known as the Dust Bowl. What had happened, and why?

The story is a long and complex one. But the main elements of what happened are clear. As Americans moved West in the course of the nineteenth century, and especially after 1860, they came to settle on the Southern Plains. Having systematically eliminated the buffalo (perhaps some 20 million of them), and having elbowed the Indians aside and onto reservations in the course of a series of bitter wars, the early settlers first used the land for ranching.[17] Thereafter came farmers, 'homesteaders', who staked out and settled the land and sought to make good on it. But over the next fifty years or more, the small farmers were overshadowed (and often bought out) by land speculators and by both resident and absentee large land-holders and commercial farming on a massive scale.[18]

By the early years of the twentieth century, the Southern Plains were being systematically ploughed and planted with grains which did particularly well there, and parts of the area continued to be intensively grazed by cattle. At first, cultivation had been undertaken by the homesteaders on a small scale by slow and traditional methods. But then, especially after 1910 - and particularly when the domestic and international demand for American grain rocketed during and immediately after the First World War - the whole process was speeded up and became much more capital intensive. Machines were used to break up the soil, tear up the grasses, sow the seeds, reap the grain, bale it and convey it to the granaries. This was 'sod-busting' on an enormous scale. So that by 1935 some 33 million acres (or one-third) of what came to be called the Dust Bowl area 'lay naked, ungrassed and vulnerable to the wind'.[19] Machines, tractors and combine-harvesters ploughed, planted and reaped the land between 1910 and 1930 as had never happened before. As farming became more intensive, it also became more expensive. This squeezed further the smaller farmers, as finance companies, investors and larger farm enterprises moved in. Many of the smaller farmers became employees or tenant farmers, while some of the larger farms - factory farms as they came to be known - grew to be as big as 54 square miles or 34,500 acres.[20]

Yet what drove all the parties - small farmers, factory farming, the people in the agricultural machinery and agricultural produce businesses, and the investors back East - was not only their wish to have their own farm or business, or to be free, or to share in the opportunities which the 'frontier' opened up. What drove them to rip up the plains was the ideology, or 'economic culture', as Worster calls it, of which they were a part and to which they contributed. This 'economic culture', or the system of production and its associated social organization, was both fuelled by the profit-seeking and expansionary ideology of American society and was reflected in it. But 'the culture they had brought to the plains . . . was ecologically the most unadaptive ever devised. This was the message written in the darkened skies, shifting dunes and defeated faces.'[21] For, by recklessly ploughing out the grasses and vegetation of the Plains, and by not giving serious attention to conservation as well as production, they had rendered their most valuable resource - the soil - vulnerable to drastic erosion by drought and wind when it came, as indeed it did in the 1930s.

The Dust Bowl was not an Act of God. Nor was it a visitation by the forces of Nature. Rather, the way people combined their use of natural, social and technological resources - that is, in the particular expression of the politics of commercial agriculture on the Southern Plains - *created* the Dust Bowl, and the appalling tragedy for both people and nature which it represented.

This example illustrates graphically the conception of politics used throughout the book. It again shows how such problems are the *product* of the politics of human society, and it demonstrates the continuity of relations between the social and natural worlds. Moreover, an understanding of the causes and conditions of the Dust Bowl as a case study in politics requires one to draw on contributions from the natural sciences and also the social and historical sciences in such areas as the climate, ecology, land use, agricultural practices, economic and social history, technology, culture, ideology and government of the United States.

VII

While the Dust Bowl represents a particularly acute example of the way in which human societies can create their own problems through their politics, it is by no means unique or exceptional. Such things are occurring all the time, and it is worth remembering the earlier discussion of Marvin Harris's notion of 'intensifications' and 'depletions', and that the Aztec city of Teotihuacán was surrounded by a circle of eroded land.[22] In their use, production and distribution of resources, societies are constantly engaged in interaction with the natural world. Where the politics of these relations are mismanaged, there are profound consequences for the health and welfare of the people.

During the course of the present century these processes have been dramatically speeded up as technological developments have been intensively and extensively applied to an increasing range of productive activities, on a world scale. One need be no 'eco-freak' to recognize that this is the case.[23] Ecologists, for instance, point with concern to the destruction of various kinds of forests on a global basis, which can have very dangerous consequences for the oxygen supply of the planet. The pace at which this is happening in the Brazilian

Amazon Basin, in the Sahara-Sahel region of West Africa, the lower ranges of
the Himalayas, in East-Central Mexico, in Indonesia and in Soviet Siberia
provides cause for alarm.[24] Not only are there worrying implications for the
oxygen supply, but some of the immediate consequences in the societies of the
Third World can be identified in the spread of the deserts, the loss of valuable
top-soils and in flooding.[25] In each instance, the particular combination of
factors in the politics of the society which has brought this about differs, and
each requires careful analysis. In Brazil large areas of forest are being cleared
and some of it used for rural colonization schemes. But even more substantial
tracts of jungle have been sold off to local and foreign companies for highly
profitable forms of exploration, mining and ranching. In Nepal, on the other
hand, the forests are being eroded by the poor whose poverty - and that of their
country - prevents them from getting or using any other forms of fuel.[26] But
whatever the particular mix of local factors which combine to produce these
interactions of the social and natural worlds, it is to the *politics* of the societies
that we need to look for explanations and, in the long run, solutions.

Nor are the problems of this kind confined to rural areas of the world. Our
cities, where industrial production and associated ways of urban life are concentrated, have been the focal points of dangerous and damaging pollution,
resulting from the way we have gone about using and producing resources. The
London 'smogs' - the most ferocious of which in 1952 killed some 4000
Londoners in five days - were the result of fog combining with the intensive
burning of coal and fuel-oil in domestic and industrial contexts. In Los Angeles,
a major 'smog' culprit turned out to be the very high levels of emission of
hydrocarbons from cars, buses and trucks.[27] And there are many other
instances of chemical pollution of air, rivers and seas from the way in
which modern industrial societies, in both West and East, use and produce
resources.

The emerging debate about the question of nuclear energy is a further
illustration of the point. Nuclear power may become the major source of energy
in the course of the next fifty years. There can be no doubt that *unless* we are
able to apply the most rigorous controls, the possibilities of very long-term and
fatal levels of pollution on an enormous scale are considerable. Some people
argue that such controls are impossible on a global basis. But there are two
points to stress. First, wherever one may stand on the question of nuclear
energy, it is a good example of how, in the use and production of resources,
human societies are engaged in a complex set of interactions with their environment, with far-reaching implications for their well-being. Secondly, precisely
because so many different interests, ideologies and resources are involved in the
debate, the whole subject is intensely political. But one of the features of the
debate so far is that it is not yet an open or fully public one, because so much
secrecy surrounds many of the facts about the experience of nuclear energy to
date.[28] And this raises again the 'democratic' issue referred to earlier, and to
which I return in later chapters.

VIII

In their politics, human societies do not only act in the above ways to affect their natural environments, and hence their welfare as societies. The way we use, produce and distribute resources can also have *direct* effects on the health of communities, or sections of them. That is, the social conditions and social organizations associated with the way we organize production have been, and remain, central factors in the spread of many diseases and aspects of ill-health. The case of pellagra is a good example to illustrate the point, since people in Europe are not at all familiar with it, though they once were.

'Pellagra is a nutritional disease associated with an inadequate intake of niacin', which is one of the vital B vitamins.[29] The term 'pellagra' comes from the Italian, which means 'dry skin', for the disease causes severe irritation of the skin (dermatitis), as well as diarrhoea and dementia (insanity) and a slow, painful death. The effects of the sun seem to exaggerate it and hence it may be seasonal, occurring during or after long summers, but not exclusively so.

The disease seems to have first appeared in Spain, in the seventeenth century, but was first written about medically in the middle of the eighteenth century by Dr Gaspar Casal. Since then it has been commonly found wherever people - especially poor rural people - live off a staple diet of maize and little else.

Now maize does have niacin in it, but it is in a 'bound' form, which is not readily 'available' for human consumption. Maize was introduced to Europe in the sixteenth century by the Spanish after their conquests in Latin America, where it has been widely eaten and used as a staple, for instance in the form of *tortilla*, for a very long time indeed. But there has been little evidence of pellagra in Latin America: why? In part because the diet of the pre-Columbian societies was also composed of other items, like chillies, squashes, beans and other vegetables which all contain niacin - as do milk, eggs, liver, meat and other cereals. Moreover, the people of the area soaked their maize in lime-water and heated it for some eighteen hours, and this appears to have had the effect of 'releasing' the bound niacin, thereby making it available for consumption when the maize was eaten. This particular cooking technique was *not* transferred to Europe at the same time as the maize - which raises in passing a wider general point about the problems of the *partial* transfer of technological or cultural items from one society to another.

Maize spread widely as a crop through Spain and from there to other parts of Europe - to Italy, Hungary, Yugoslavia and France. It was easy to grow, filling as a food, and cheap. Rulers, princes and landlords encouraged its production, thereby boosting their tax, tithe and income yields, and at the same time providing cheap food for the poor. But where landlessness increased (and hence rural poverty), as in Italy and France in the eighteenth and nineteenth centuries, various kinds of tenant-farming and share-cropping also spread. Under these conditions where people did not own or control their land, they were not free to grow what they wanted, and hence were not able to obtain a balanced diet. Nor could they keep animals and poultry to provide themselves with meat and dairy produce. Many were compelled to grow maize for the landlord. General conditions of rural poverty hence increased the reliance on maize as the staple. This was especially true where people were encouraged or compelled to grow cash-crops, or were landless or share-croppers, or were drawn into rural wage-labour. This has happened also in the Southern United States and Egypt, at the end of the nineteenth century, and in large areas of Southern Africa and India in the present century, where it continues today.

Wherever this reliance on maize as a staple diet has taken root, pellagra - the 'plague of corn' - has followed. There were some people - like Théophile Roussel in France and Giovanni Batista Marzari in Italy in the nineteenth century - who suggested that maize and pellagra were connected, but they did not know how or why, and few people were particularly interested in finding either cure or prevention for it. There were other ideas about its causes as well. It was attributed at various times and in various places to contagion from sheep, to 'bad air', hereditary disease, insects, bad (usually foreign and imported) maize, and sewage. A Federal Commission in the USA in 1913-16 found that it had no connection with diet or nutrition! And it was only a team of community health workers, led by Dr Joseph Goldberger, who started work in 1914, that finally established that:[30]

> Pellagra was not only a disease of the poor and those who lived off corn, but it was a deficiency disease which developed because certain groups of people were unable to raise or purchase those items of diet which would maintain them in health.

Goldberger and his team did not know that the immediate cause of the disease was the niacin deficiency, but they did establish that it could be prevented. It was to be another fifteen years before niacin was identified by scientists as the specific vitamin which was deficient in the maize diet. But the key point to note in all this is that 'endemic vitamin deficiencies, such as that which caused pellagra, have occurred only when men have been fed an unnatural diet not of their own choice'.[31] And the main category of people who have been affected by pellagra has been the poor, and especially the rural poor. It has never affected wealthy people who could provide themselves with a balanced diet, either by growing the food or buying it.

There are more familiar examples of how social organization and distributional factors may promote ill-health and the spread of disease. In the nineteenth century the industrial revolution brought an enormous concentration of people into the cities of Victorian Britain. The social, residential and sanitary circumstances of the slums which resulted were directly associated with the new organization of production in the factory system and the uneven distribution of resources amongst the population. They established the conditions under which diseases took hold and spread. Scarlet fever, measles, whooping cough, diptheria, typhoid, tuberculosis, smallpox and cholera were both rife and fatal.[32] And it is precisely these kinds of infectious (often water-borne), parasitic and respiratory diseases which currently characterize the disease patterns in the societies of the Third World, especially the cities.[33]

In the industrial societies today the fatal 'epidemics' include heart disease, cancers, bronchitis and accidents. The social conditions under which these have achieved epidemic proportions can be traced directly to our systems of production and the cultures they promote, in terms of lifestyles and consumption patterns. These include unbalanced diets, smoking, stress, lack of exercise, high-speed motoring, and exposure to technological dangers at home and at work. Moreover, it has recently been argued that the increasingly high levels of unemployment contribute to the mortality rates in a number of ways.[34]

Of great importance to the present argument is the fact that, in general, what people die from differs from class to class. That is, the *distribution* of the causes of death is remarkably uneven. In England and Wales, for example, one finds the incidence of death from lung cancers, bronchitis and accidents (excluding road accidents) to be far higher amongst males in the skilled, semi-skilled and unskilled occupational categories than amongst males in the professional and managerial categories. Moreover, the rate of chronic and acute sickness is much greater amongst semi-skilled men, in middle age, than amongst equivalent managerial and professional groups.[35]

The central purpose of these examples has been to illustrate and further underline some of the major themes of the book and the chapter. Social conditions, in both broad and very specific terms, have played a major part in the occurrence, spread and distribution of fatal diseases in all the above instances. Such conditions are created by people. They flow from the way we use, produce and distribute resources and they directly influence and are influenced by the systems of power, social organization, culture and ideology associated with those activities. Such conditions, that is to say, are the result of our politics. Hence politics plays a major role in determining the kind and pattern of disease in societies (as it can, and must, in preventing it: 'medicine' alone will not). For this reason, the study of disease patterns (epidemiology), which is itself interdisciplinary in approach, cannot be separated from the study of politics. Likewise, an understanding of the politics of epidemics and other health problems in societies requires us to evolve interdisciplinary explanations that draw on the rich and detailed investigations of other disciplines, notably those which fall conventionally into the loose and large category of the medical sciences, but not only those.

IX

There are of course also many problems which face societies that flow directly from the impact of natural disasters – such as hurricanes, earthquakes, floods, storms and drought. But the capacity of societies (or those areas or groups especially badly hit) to recover from the effects of such disasters depends very much on the control and distribution of resources in the society, and the structure of power and social organization which can mobilize and redistribute them in the form of 'relief' or make them available in terms of access. Societies differ considerably in respect of the social procedures and institutions they have for handling these occurrences. But one thing is quite clear. Where societies are sharply divided in terms of rich and poor, it is consistently the case that those who suffer most from the effects of such onslaughts are the poor. They have neither the resources nor immediate access to them which can enable them to recover from the blows. Moreover, it is precisely such conditions of inequality - in terms of resources or power, or both - which can convert natural disasters into much more sustained and catastrophic social crises. Famine is a good example of this.

According to the *Revelation of St John the Divine* there were Four Horsemen of the Apocalypse. One of these agents of destruction was Famine. Now *some* famines are clearly the direct result of natural disasters, but not all. The great famine in the Sahelian zone of West Africa covered many countries, including Chad, Mali, Senegal, Upper Volta and Niger - and it is not yet over. During the worst years of the famine (1969-73) there was, in fact, a substantial *export* of agricultural products - cotton, peanuts, vegetables, meat and fish - from the region. Furthermore, many of the Sahelian countries produced sufficient food-grains to feed their people during the famine, but it did not reach them. The same had also been the case in one of the worst previous famines in the twentieth century, in Bengal in India in the 1940s. But in neither the Sahelian nor Indian cases did either the ownership and distribution of resources, or the social organization in the societies, allow the needy to receive food. Communities of small-scale agricultural producers, who had once been self-sufficient, now grew too little food to support themselves in an emergency. And the wider and older social obligations - of redistribution - of 'chiefs' and 'big men', no longer operated in the way they once had, because of changes in social structure and social relationships.

How all this had come about is complex. But the main elements of the story seem clear enough. During the colonial era (and in some cases even more so after Independence), Sahelian cultivators had in effect no alternative but to grow cash crops, like peanuts and cotton, because they had to pay money taxes which they could only raise by growing and selling such crops. This meant that they no longer had the time or labour to grow as much food as they had done in the past, and hence had to *buy* the additional foodstuffs they needed. They thus became dependent on the market and vulnerable to excessive price fluctuations. Intensive cultivation of such cash crops also exhausted the not particularly good soils. And local pastoralists, finding that grain too was now more scarce and hence expensive, increased the size of their herds so that they could sell more cattle and hence buy the grain they needed. This in turn put further strain on the environment and helped to spread the desert. If one then adds to this cumulative build-up of problems an increase in population and a tightening grip on the food markets by a small and powerful minority, one can see all too clearly why, when the drought came, the result was catastrophic, especially for the poor.

It would thus be folly to think of the Sahelian famine simply in terms of drought or population increase, or a decline in the availability of food, though these factors played a part. Likewise, in considering other modern famines - in Bengal in 1943, the Wollo famine in Ethiopia in 1973, and the East African famines in the early 1980s in Karamoja and Somalia - a much wider set of causes and conditions has to be grasped, which arise out of the historical and contemporary interactions in these societies of both natural *and* social factors. These include colonial conquest and penetration, which have caused major shifts in the patterns of production and distribution (such as land-ownership and land usage); warfare, arising for instance out of border disputes, or internal conflicts (as on the Ethiopian-Somalian border, or in Uganda), and hence giving rise to refugees; changes in social organization and ideology (such as the decline in the importance of redistributional practices and values by 'big men' or 'chiefs'); deterioration in soils and desertification; poor rainfalls; an increased dependence of an increasing number of people on uncertain employment, inadequate wages or fluctuating prices (of things they must buy or sell); and generally inadequate or non-existent institutions of social insurance to cope with the effects of all this.

All these natural and social factors combine through human action in the *politics* of famine.[36] And it is precisely for this reason that interdisciplinary approaches are needed to explain them.

X

The problems which have been used as examples in this chapter are rarely thought of as being 'political', but I have tried to show how *intensely* political they are in both cause and consequence. There are countless other examples which could be used to illustrate the need to expand our conception of politics to include issues which are conventionally left outside the scope of the discipline of Politics. These may be found in the Third World (such as landlessness, shanty towns and inter-communal violence), and in the industrial societies (unemployment, housing problems, pollution), some of which will be discussed in later chapters. In no way are any of these things peripheral to politics, but central to it, resulting from the use and allocation of resources in particular ways. Nor can they be considered simply 'technical' problems, left to the analysis of appropriate specialists (economists, agronomists, health workers or urban planners).

There is, of course, another very fundamental sense in which these things are all highly political. While it took Goldberger and later scientists to identify the broad social and nutritional causes of pellagra, it took political action to reduce its incidence. In Southern Africa today, the same is true: pellagra (and other deficiency diseases, like kwashiorkor) will only decline significantly when change occurs in the politics of those societies, when a different use and distribution of resources takes place so that people may have improved access to better land, or reliable income, and hence improved diets. Such political changes always encounter strenuous resistance from those who benefit from the prevailing arrangements. And the development of various social and political movements of people and ideas which are more commonly examined in the social and historical sciences need to be viewed against precisely this type of background, whether they be peasant uprisings, revolutions, coups, trade unions, and fascist, communist or even religious movements.[37]

Finally, this chapter has also sought to show why an interdisciplinary approach is needed in the analysis of politics and problems. And it has also been my concern to argue that the best starting-point for effective interdisciplinary work is *not* at the level of theoretical synthesis in some kind of abstract 'interdisciplinarity'. Rather, it is at the level of concrete problems occurring in the real world, past and present.

However, the argument has got a bit ahead of itself again, for many of the examples used in this chapter have been drawn from societies in the contemporary world. This has been necessary to illustrate the points about interdisciplinarity. But it is now appropriate to retrace the steps and sketch some of the historical background to the politics of such societies in the modern world. The next chapter is devoted to doing just that.

PART TWO

CHAPTER SEVEN

The politics of European expansion, conquest and control

The sun was fierce, the land seemed to glisten and drip with steam. Here and there grayish-whitish specks showed up clustered inside the white surf, with a flag flying above them . . . . We pounded along, stopped, landed soldiers; went on, landed custom-house clerks to levy toll in what looked like a God-forsaken wilderness, with a tin shed and flagpole lost in it . . . . Once, I remember, we came across a man-of-war anchored off the coast. There wasn't even a shed there, and she was shelling the bush. It appears that the French had one of their wars going on thereabouts . . . . In the empty immensity of earth, sky, and water, there she was, incomprehensible, firing into a continent.

Joseph Conrad, *The Heart of Darkness*

I

In this memorable passage, Conrad captures fictionally some of the bizarre moments which accompanied European expansion into the wider world. What could a British company have been doing, at the end of the nineteenth century, extracting taxes from people in West Africa? Why was a French warship anchored off that steaming coast, pounding it with shells?

One may ask these kinds of questions of other places and other times (see Map 1). For instance, what was the Portuguese Viceroy, Francisco de Almeida, doing at the tip of the African continent in 1510, and what circumstances explain the short burst of conflict with the indigenous inhabitants there which ended in his death? Why, as mentioned in an earlier chapter, was Cortés in the Caribbean, and was his search for the Aztec capital in 1519 part of a wider purpose? Why were 160 Dutchmen massacred in Western Ceram in the Moluccan islands in 1651, and why - in return - did the Dutch forcibly transfer some 12,000 people from their island villages to Amboina, and why did they also cut down all 'unauthorized' plantations of cloves? Why were English gentlemen, like Warren Hastings, Lord Cornwallis and Arthur Wellesley (later the Duke of Wellington) fighting and bargaining with Indian states and their rulers in the second half of the eighteenth century, and attempting to establish a central government administration? What was the American Commodore, Perry, doing on the coast of Japan in 1853, and why did he insist that the

Japanese open their doors to American trade, and threaten trouble if they did not? How was it that European, Russian and American merchants, backed by their governments and the force of their arms, were able to carve out settlements and concessions round the coast of China in the second half of the nineteenth century and to proclaim 'extra-territorial' rights over these places in order to run their own affairs by their own methods on Chinese soil? Why was the British General Gordon killed in fighting the troops of al Mahdi, Muhammad Ahmad, a Sudanese religious leader in Khartoum in 1885? And why, in the years after 1945, were the French, British, Portuguese, Dutch and, latterly, the Americans involved in bitter wars, for example in Indonesia, Indo-China, Algeria, Malaysia, Kenya, Cyprus, Angola, Mozambique and Vietnam?

This chapter will sketch some of the background to these extraordinary and often violent incidents which formed part of European expansion from the fifteenth century to the present time. In doing so, it will concentrate on four main aspects of this enormous occurrence in human history.

First, it will try to give some idea of the extent and scale of European expansion, conquest and control which has brought about what one author has appropriately called 'the creation of the world'.[1] Secondly, it will illustrate with the use of a detailed example how the politics of this process has penetrated slowly but steadily into even the most remote parts of the world. Thirdly, it will indicate broadly the kinds of changes which occurred in the politics of European societies behind this outwards thrust, and partly in consequence of it, using England as the main example. Finally, I shall bring the story up to date by discussing briefly the activities and role of the multinational or transnational corporations, and point to some of the consequences of all this, today, especially for the societies of the Third World.

A topic as large as this can only be sketched in the broadest of strokes. But I hope that this will whet the appetite of those unfamiliar with these events to explore in greater detail those aspects of world politics, past and present, which interest them. I also believe that the general conception of politics adopted in this book can help to explain some of the major characteristics and consequences of these processes.

A major claim here is that the politics of modern Third World and industrial societies cannot be understood unless seen against this emergence of world politics. Throughout, the central argument will be that the politics of these processes has involved a vast transformation of the way in which resources have been obtained, used, produced and distributed on an unprecedented scale, both globally and within individual societies. That is the essence of what is meant by 'world politics'.

The societies which have been discussed before - such as the !Kung, the Aztecs and the Pastoral Maasai - all existed for most of their history in *relative* isolation, though of course they were at times in more or less direct contact with other societies. This is also true for other societies in the Americas, Africa and Asia before and after the sixteenth century. And this was the case in large areas of Europe. But from the sixteenth century until the present time, this isolation has systematically diminished. Sometimes the pace has been slow, sometimes fast. But it has been persistent. In place of the relative isolation of human societies, there has emerged a complex web of connections which increasingly bind them together into a variety of relations of cooperation and conflict. The uneven and unequal patterns of these form the nub of inter-national relations, to use the conventional term, and they impinge more or less directly and critically on the domestic politics of *all* societies.

Such concerns are sometimes thought to be boringly 'historical', having little to do with the immediate cut and thrust of modern domestic and international politics - whether these be wars, revolutions, diplomatic incidents, hi-jacking, oil or food crises. But such a view, for students of politics, is short-sighted to say the least. For the contemporary politics of *all* societies are bound up with the history and present character of these emerging global relations. And 'history' is nothing but a shorthand term for the changing character of politics within and between societies. That is to say, the real stuff of 'history' consists of a variety of changing ways in which the human species has obtained, used, produced and distributed resources over time in and between different societies. History, in this sense, is the politics of change, and all politics have a history. Since I believe that nothing can be more central for understanding the politics of the modern world, this chapter sets out to provide an introduction to that background.

II

Before European societies began to establish this world-wide lattice of relations through their seaborne empires of commerce, conquest and colonialism, there had indeed been other empires, outside Europe. But they had largely been regional ones. European expansion co-existed with many non-European empires, and clashed violently with some of them around the world in the course of competition for the control and use of resources and people, and in the struggle for the hegemony of ideas.[2]

For instance, long before the time of Christ, empires such as those of the Hittites, Assyrians, Egyptians and Greeks exercised powerful influence over the people and resources of the Eastern Mediterranean, the Middle East and further afield. The Roman Empire, at its peak in the first century AD, stretched from northern Britain to the Persian Gulf. In Middle and South America, as we have seen, the empires of the Mayas, Incas and Aztecs controlled diverse peoples and resources through both trade and conquest. The Sudanic empires of West Africa appropriated goods, people and services from the societies they dominated, and were linked by long, looping trade networks with North Africa, the Mediterranean and the Middle East. There, in the Middle East, the whirlwind rise of the Islamic Arab empires in the course of the seventh and eighth centuries spread their conquests across the whole of North Africa as far as the Iberian peninsula in the west, where they dominated Spain and Portugal, and east to the Indus. On the other side of the Mediterranean, the influence of the Mongols - who had originated in Central Asia and who had fought and conquered from Albania to China - had been at its peak in the thirteenth century, but then the empire began to break up. It was in this context that there arose the powerful empire of the Ottoman Turks, reaching its peak in the seventeenth century. The Turks penetrated far into Eastern and South-east Europe, dominated the Eastern Mediterranean, controlled important parts of the Middle East, and thereby cut off Mediterranean Europeans from the land routes to and from Asia. In Asia the Islamic Moghul empire pressed down deep into India, while in the south of the sub-continent the Hindu Vijayanagar empire consolidated its position and prevailed from the fifteenth century. Further east and south the supremacy of the Ming dynasty in China, from the fourteenth century to the seventeenth century, followed a succession of empires there whose influence radiated widely in East and South-east Asia. At times Ming power spread down the South China Sea as far as the islands of Indonesia, while Chinese ships sailed westwards into the Indian Ocean and into the world of the Arabs.[3]

So, very much prior to the expansion of Europe there had been states and empires such as these which had traded in, conquered and controlled substantial areas. But, relative to the expanse of the world, they were more or less local or regional in scope and scale. And they had more or less exclusive histories, largely disconnected in time or place from each other, as were the histories of the societies and local empires of Europe prior to the sixteenth century. But the 'discovery' of the Americas and the opening-up of the sea route round the Cape to the East Indies by Europeans at the end of the fifteenth century initiated nothing less than an entirely new epoch in the politics of the whole human species. Looking back on these events at the end of the eighteenth century, Adam Smith considered them to have been the two greatest occurrences in recorded history:[4]

> By uniting, in some measure, the most distant parts of the world, by enabling them to relieve one another's wants, to increase one another's enjoyment, and to encourage one another's industry, their general tendency would seem to be beneficial.

But even Adam Smith, despite his enthusiasm for the commercial possibilities which this opening up of the world created, was already aware that the costs and benefits did not seem to be evenly or equally distributed. 'To the natives, however, both of the East and West Indies, all the commercial benefits which can have resulted from those events have been sunk and lost in the dreadful misfortunes which they have occasioned.'[6]

Equally important were the observations of Marx and Engels, after 1850, about a different feature of this process. The developments which followed the discovery of the Americas and the rounding of the Cape, they argued, included the opening up of the Indian and Chinese markets, the colonization of the New World, trade with the colonies which were established there, a massive increase in the means of exchange, and in the volume and flow of commodities generally. All this, they said, gave to commerce and industry in Europe 'an impulse never known before . . . . Modern industry has established a *world* market.'[7]

But the central point to grasp in all this, Marx and Engels were at pains to emphasize, was that 'It produced *world history* for the first time . . . thus destroying the former natural exclusiveness of separate nations', and hence the *relative* autonomy and regional focus of their *particular* histories.[8] This was the *really* significant implication for the politics of the modern world which followed from the establishment of the European seaborne empires. In the five centuries that have passed since then, the shape of world politics as we know it has emerged. We live in and with its legacy today. Though it continues to change its form and its particulars, this central *fact* of 'world politics' affects the politics of every modern society around the globe, something which the empires and states of the pre-sixteenth-century world never did.

III

What were the politics of European expansion? Why did it occur, where and when did it spread from, and how was it achieved?[9]

There can be little doubt that there were two related central purposes of the so-called 'voyages of discovery' of the fifteenth century which were undertaken primarily by Iberian (and Italian) explorers on behalf of the Crowns of Portugal and Spain. The first was the objective of gaining *direct* access to the rich resources of the East Indies - notably spices, but much else besides - which were believed to be fabulous. Closely associated with this, certainly for the Portuguese, was the determination to reach the source of the gold (and slaves), somewhere in West Africa, which had filtered through to Southern Europe across the Mediterranean via the Muslim societies and their merchants throughout the Middle Ages.[10] These twin objectives were related to each other. Islam blocked access to these valuable resources through the Middle East and North Africa. So the Europeans would have to either defeat Islam or 'get behind its back' to gain direct access to the resources, or both. This Christian hostility to Islam was in turn fuelled by the long history of Muslim domination of the Iberian peninsula from the eighth century. From the early thirteenth century the Iberian Christians had been engaged in reconquering Portugal and Spain from the Islamic Caliphates who ruled them, and finally succeeded in doing so in 1492. The momentum of this conflict carried the Iberians onwards, and merged with directly material interests which drew them outwards to the Indies and West Africa. Moreover, if contact could be made with the Christian Kingdom of Prester John - believed to be somewhere in 'the Indies', but in fact an isolated Christian Coptic community located in Ethiopia - and an alliance struck up with him against the Muslim powers, so much the better on all counts.[11]

These were the main strands which combined in the early politics of European expansion. One can recognize in all this some familiar elements from world politics today. Both East and West in the modern era seek direct and secure access to many resources they need in other parts of the world (like oil, or wheat, or vital raw materials). And both East and West, often in competition for such resources - or at least determined that the other side will not control or monopolize them - seek allies and agreements which will facilitate this. And just as Christianity and Islam both proclaimed their ideologies and implicit ways of ordering society to be not only the Truth but intrinsically better than each other, so too do modern powers, like the USA and the USSR, advertise their respective ideologies, and attempt to spread them. And ideologies, as discussed earlier, are not simply sets of ideas *in abstract*, which people hold and wish others to hold. The important thing about ideologies is that they always arise from, and entail very practical implications for, the use, control and organization of both resources and people. And it is in this sense too that the 'material' and 'ideal' interests and objectives of the Iberians (and later powers) converged in the early politics of European expansion.

European/Mediterranean contact with Asia, though slight, stretched back to Greek times, when Alexander the Great had penetrated as far as the Indus, overland. But there seems to have been a decay in geographical knowledge in the later years of the Roman Empire, so that only fragments of knowledge about Asia existed in the Middle Ages. Indirect contact via the Middle East, however, ensured that some goods and a little information filtered through to the Levantine and Italian ports, where they spread west and north. Some Christian pilgrims to the Holy Land between the sixth and ninth centuries, followed later by the Crusaders of the eleventh and twelfth centuries, may have procured more information and stories about the lands and peoples further East. But the hegemony of Islam in the Eastern Mediterranean had made *direct* contact with the East impossible, except for a short period when the Mongols controlled the land routes.

It was during this time, in the thirteenth century, that various expeditions to the East were mounted. The Genoese bank of Vivaldi maintained trading posts on the Gujerat and Malabar coasts of India, while descriptions of India by such travellers as Marco Polo, Oderic of Pordenone, Andrew of Perugia and others told of vast bazaars and great wealth in pearls, cottons, peppers, ginger, parrots and elephants. The belief in the fabulous wealth of the East, thought to be there for the trading if not the taking, was thus based on a few central facts derived from such contacts and information.

But these were massively embellished and grossly distorted by the incredible tales which were pedalled in the popular but entirely fictitious accounts of Eastern Kingdoms (including that of Prester John) and their riches. Perhaps the most fantastic (and totally false) was the account by Sir John Mandeville (whose real identity is still not known for sure) in his *Travels*. It was widely translated into European languages in the fourteenth and fifteenth centuries. In this he declared, for instance, of Africa (called 'Moritania') that 'In that country be folk that have one foot and they go so blue (in the cold) that it is marvelous. And the foot is so large that it shadoweth all the body against the sun when they would lie them to rest.' A forged letter, claiming to have come from Prester John himself (but probably written by an archbishop from Mainz), described his kingdom which was said to have seventy kings as tributaries; honey flowed in the land which was without poison, frogs, scorpions or serpents. Moreover, in one part of the kingdom there flowed the Indus, in which were to be found 'emeralds, sapphires, carbuncles, topazes, chrysolites, onyxes, beryls, sardonyxes, and many other precious stones . . . . For gold, silver, precious stones, animals of every kind and the number of our people, we believe there is no equal under heaven.' Mandeville's *Travels* embellished all this, and he added that he had seen it all 'with mine eyes and mickle more than I have told you. For my fellows and I were dwelling with him in his court a long time.'[12]

As for the New World to the west, across the Atlantic, Europeans knew nothing, although Vikings reached North America from Iceland in the early Middle Ages. Indeed, when Columbus reached the Bahamas and then went on to Cuba and modern Haiti, he believed that he was off the east coast of Asia, for which he was looking.[13]

These then were some of the material and ideological spurs which prompted the voyages of discovery and conquest which commenced in the fifteenth century. Strategically located at the most southwesterly point of Europe, at the corner where the Atlantic and the Mediterranean meet, the Iberians were well placed to initiate this outward movement and had good reason to do so. A long history of association with the sea had provided marine experience and skills which facilitated this. While Spain was still engaged in its struggle to expel the Moors from the country, the Portuguese (who had done so by the middle of the thirteenth century) took the lead. In this, they were authorized and urged by the Pope to

> attack, conquer and subdue Saracans, pagans and other unbelievers who were inimical to Christ; to capture their goods and their territories; to reduce their persons to perpetual slavery, and to transfer their lands and properties to the King of Portugal and his successors.[14]

It was in this spirit that the Portuguese Crown encouraged and supervised the explorations. In the subsequent centuries, the thousands of soldiers, sailors, settlers and officials who turned the wheels of empire did very much as the Pope had urged.

From 1419 Portuguese navigators, enthusiastically directed by Prince Henry, nosed their way down the unknown coast of West Africa, past Madeira, the Azores and the Cape Verde Islands, reaching modern Sierra Leone by 1460. Ghana - the Gold Coast - was reached by 1480, and coastal forts set up to attract the gold traffic to the coast and away from the overland routes. Gold and slaves flooded back to the Portuguese Crown, and profits from these resources helped to finance further explorations to the Congo, Angola and beyond. In 1488 Bartholmeu Dias reached and rounded the Cape of Good Hope, and sailed some distance up the coast of South-east Africa before turning back. Eleven years later, in May 1498, Vasco da Gama (who actually carried a letter on him to Prester John) arrived at Calicut on the south-west coast of India declaring that he had come in search of 'spices and Christians'.

Thereafter, Portuguese penetration into the rest of Asia was swift. But it was not without opposition, and it was punctuated by fierce conflict with local traders and their fleets as the Portuguese sought to control and monopolize the wealth of the seaborne trade of the area. They proceeded to carve out a vast commercial empire. In due course it stretched back to Mozambique on the East African coast, Angola on the other side of the continent, and across the Atlantic to Brazil. Having established a land base at Goa on the west coast of India, they moved on to the Moluccas (the spice islands) in 1511, and thence to Indonesia and the islands, South-east Asia, China (gaining a trading post at Macao in 1557) and Japan. For the next sixty years the Portuguese dominated European trade with Asia, and much of the intra-Asian seaborne trade too, extracting the most valued resources of the East for Europe. These included 'pepper from Malabar and Indonesia; mace and nutmeg from Banda; cloves from Ternate, Tidore and Amboina; cinnamon from Ceylon; gold, silks and porcelain from China; silver from Japan; horses from Persia and Arabia; cotton textiles from Cambay and Coromondel'.[15]

Portuguese penetration into Asia initiated direct Western dominance in the area for the next 400 years, until the rise of modern nationalist movements in the twentieth century brought formal empires to an end after 1945. For once the riches from the East reached Europe and found their way onto the markets of the Netherlands, England and France, there was nothing that would stop merchants from those societies seeking to reach the same sources of wealth in the East. Thus, conflict between the Europeans and Asians was bitter and brutal, as was the conflict between the European powers in their struggle for mastery of the Asian trade, for coastal strongholds, forts and factories.

If the sixteenth century can be said to have belonged to the Portuguese in Asia, the seventeenth and eighteenth centuries may be said to have been those of the Dutch and the British. During the eighteenth century British control of India proceeded apace and was complete by the second half of the nineteenth century. In the course of that period Britain gained a stranglehold on the vast Indian market, especially for the cotton goods that were pumped out of Lancashire in enormous quantities from the end of the eighteenth century, while the English market was protected against competition from Indian exports. The politics of protection in England was the reverse side of the politics of destruction in India under the East India Company, and latterly formal British rule.

While the British consolidated from India - spreading on to Burma, Sri Lanka (Ceylon) and Malaya - the Dutch secured their position in Indonesia, from Batavia (Djakarta) in the nineteenth century. Here they imposed a system of compulsory commercial crop production on the inhabitants - the Cultivation (or Culture) System - which produced an enormous volume of the valued and profitable resources of sugar, tea, spices, tobacco and, later, rubber.[16] The French tightened their hold on Indo-China. The Russians' interests and activities on the Eastern steppes and also in China and Japan increased. A virtual free-for-all developed amongst the British, French, Italians, Germans, Russians and Americans (amongst others) to compel China to open up for trade, and to gain concesssions or special relations with her.

One of the key elements in the trade with China was opium, for which there was a demand in that society but which was forbidden by an Imperial Chinese decree. The opium trade with China, and the associated piracy and privateering which accompanied it, went back to the early eighteenth century, when the Portuguese stumbled on the possibilities of selling it in China. But other European powers, especially Britain, followed. With the full knowledge and implicit backing of the British government and parliament, the opium trade was extended on a massive scale in the nineteenth century. It was entirely illegal in China; but the profits from the trade were a major source of revenue, first to the East India Company and then to the Treasury of the Imperial Indian government. In 1833, opium grown within the domains of the East India Company accounted for some 50 per cent of British exports to China, despite Chinese efforts to stop the illegal trade, for they well knew the effects of the drug. The volume of opium exported from India rose from about 10,000 chests in 1829-30, to 51,000 chests in 1849-50, to 105,000 chests in 1897-80 (the high point). The highest revenue in sterling received by the Imperial Indian government from the opium trade was over £7 million in 1871.[17]

Consistent attempts were made to persuade the Chinese to legalize the drug and hence allow its open importation. But the Chinese would not, and this led to a series of bloody conflicts, the Opium Wars, in the nineteenth century. A former American President, John Quincy Adams, was to justify these wars in 1842 in the following terms:[18]

> The moral obligation of commercial intercourses between nations is founded entirely, exclusively upon the Christian precept to love your neighbour as yourself . . . . But China, not being a Christian nation . . . admits no obligation to hold commercial intercourse with others . . . . It is time this enormous outrage upon the rights of human nature [i.e. China's refusal to legalize the drug and the trade] . . . should cease.

The USA, coming at Asia from the East across the Pacific, sought and forced bunkering and trading concessions from Japan, as did other nations from Europe. The Japanese were able to prevent this going further, following the Meiji Restoration in 1868, and began to industrialize with astonishing speed and so avoided being subordinated - as other Asian societies had been - to European and North American powers.[19]

Behind all this, around the coasts of Africa, the European powers - notably the Portuguese, British, Dutch and French - remained confined largely to the coasts, with the important exception of the Cape, which I shall discuss shortly. The West African slave trade to the Americas and the Caribbean, which resulted from this, was the largest forced migration in human history. The sheer enormity and brutality of the Atlantic slave trade generated huge profits for the slavers. It involved at least 4 million people and perhaps as many as 25 million being shipped in appalling misery across the 'Middle Passage', during which sometimes as many as 20 per cent of the people perished on board.[20]

Penetration into the heart of Africa really only began after 1880, with the 'Scramble for Africa'. During the course of this, European powers - mainly the French and the British, but also the Belgians and Germans - claimed ridiculously large empires for themselves (the Belgian Congo was 1 million square miles in extent, for instance). All these empires had entirely arbitrary boundaries, with little regard for, or understanding of, the variety of societies incorporated in any one colony, or split between two or more.[21]

By the time the Portuguese had begun their consolidation in Asia in the early sixteenth century, the Spanish were already well on the way to completing the conquest and control of Mexico, Peru and the major islands of the Caribbean. In the fifty years after 1492, when Columbus had sailed to the New World, vast areas of mainland South America were colonized by Spain. The great empires of the Aztecs in Mexico and the Incas in Peru were rapidly destroyed.

'I came to get gold, not to till the soil, like a peasant', said Cortés.[22] The colonial rulers of New Spain (Mexico) were true to Cortés. Enormous amounts of gold and silver flowed back to Spain through the control-point at Vera Cruz. By the 1590s the Spanish Crown relied for a quarter of its revenue on the treasure of 'the Indies'. It has been estimated that by 1660 some 18,000 tons of silver and 200 tons of gold objects had reached Europe. In total, between 1503 and 1660 some £257.5 million of bullion reached Spain, or an average of £4 million each year. It has been suggested that smuggling probably added 50 per cent more to the total estimate.[23]

The effects of the Spanish conquest - in terms of colonization, forced labour, the expropriation of huge tracts of land for settlers and their cattle, the resulting famines, and waves of epidemics, such as smallpox and measles - were to create a 'demographic catastrophe' amongst the Indian population in Spanish America.[24] In New Spain (Mexico) the pre-Conquest population had been about 25 million; by 1532 it had fallen to 17 million; by 1548 it had fallen to 6.3 million; and by 1580 it was not more than 1.9 million.[25] One graph drawn of the relative decrease in the Indian population and the relative increase in the number of livestock shows a directly inverse relationship; as livestock increased in the central Mexican region between 1550 and 1610, population decreased. The vast herds of cattle, sheep, mules, horses and goats had a highly destructive effect on Indian agriculture. The Spanish conquest was characterized by 'savagery', writes one author, involving

> famines; heavy taxes; the greed for immediate gain which did not scruple at overloading the natives with hard and unaccustomed labour, even impossible tasks, while stinting them regularly in their food; the imposition of similar labour in particular upon women and children; the separation of families; the transference of plain-dwellers to the mountains.[26]

Similar catastrophes occurred elsewhere in South America and the Caribbean in the course of the establishment there of Spanish colonies. By 1700 the Spanish empire in the Americas stretched from what is today New Mexico to the River Plate in modern Argentina. Further penetration into Bolivia, Chile and beyond followed, as did wave upon wave of settlers from Europe, as well as African slaves who were concentrated mainly in the tropical and semi-tropical coastal lowlands of Central and South America, and the islands of Cuba and Santo Domingo.

Even after most of Spanish America became independent during the nineteenth century, the patterns of inequality between settlers, Indians and slaves which were laid down during the formation of these colonies remained. They are expressed in some of the modern problems of those societies. These patterns varied in their forms and particulars, but they were shaped in each instance by the politics of the conquest in each place, and its aftermath. That is, they were shaped by the particular way in which resources and people were used, distributed and differentially incorporated in the structure of the various societies there, first for the profit of the Spanish Crown, then for the profit of the local élites and, later, international investment from Europe and North America. This was what defined the politics of conquest and colonialism in the New World - in the mines, on the plantations and on the vast *latifundios*.[27]

Spain was not without competition, especially in the Caribbean. The English, Dutch and French were there too, fighting with each other and Spain for the possession of the islands. This was partly the politics of sheer piracy and privateering. But the various West India Companies, and the governments which backed them with fleets and soldiers, also knew that there were valuable resources to be won or lost for the home societies, and control of the islands soon proved highly profitable in slave-based production of cotton, tobacco and then - above all - sugar.[28]

A series of Papal Bulls in the fifteenth century, culminating in the Treaty of Tordesillas in 1494, had divided the world for exploration and colonization between the Spanish in the West and the Portuguese in the East. The rough line drawn down the middle of the Atlantic (or so it was thought) in fact included the bulging enormity of Brazil on the eastern, that is Portuguese, side of the line, and hence the Portuguese presence there. From the sixteenth century, vast resources of land in Brazil were allotted by the Portuguese Crown to the captaincies (*capitanias*). The early focal points of Portuguese colonial activity were in the North-east, round Pernambuco and Bahia, where the politics of colonial production combined settlers, slaves and land in highly profitable sugar and tobacco plantations. With the discovery of gold further south, inland from modern Rio de Janeiro, in Minas Gerais, at the end of the seventeenth century, a further wave of slaves from Angola and the West African coast arrived, as did more settlers from Portugal and elsewhere in Brazil. One effect of this switch to the South was to leave the North-east, to this day, barren and impoverished, underdeveloped.[29] Much of the gold was shipped back to Portugal in the eighteenth century, where the Crown received 20 per cent of all that was mined. But much of that in turn flowed north to Germany, the Netherlands and, especially, to England in return for woollen texiles which were in demand in both Portugal and Brazil. This inflow of gold to England, in return for English manufactures for Portugal and Brazil, gave an impetus to London as the bullion market of the world.[30]

This brief account of some of the characteristics and consequences of European expansion, and its extent, would be incomplete without reference to the other colonies of European settlement outside Latin America. These included Australia and New Zealand from the end of the eighteenth century, South Africa (first by the Dutch, and then the British after 1806), Rhodesia and Kenya in the twentieth century, and French Algeria after 1830.

But unquestionably the most important area of European colonization and settlement was in North America. In the seventeenth century, the English, Dutch and French all had small and tentative colonies there. But it was from the small group of English colonies, established in the seventeenth century, that the future United States of America was to emerge. The broad politics of American history is well enough known, but the central elements are worth mentioning because of the profound effect which the emergence of the USA has had on the rest of the world.

In the South there emerged the politics of cotton and the plantations, including rice, tobacco and sugar, based on slave labour. By far the greatest volume of raw cotton produced there found its way to the English mills where it was woven into cloths and textiles. This in turn accounted for the overwhelming bulk of British exports, and constituted the 'leading sector' of industrialization in England.[31] The politics of the South were built around the core of this system of production, and were expressed in the patterns of social organization, culture and ideology of 'The World the Slaveholders Made'.[32] Long after the abolition of slavery in 1865, many of the features of this social order, laid down in the plantation days, have remained, influencing the character of relations between white and black in large areas of the South.

By contrast, the North-east of America came to be the centre of commercial and shipping activity and, in the nineteenth century, the explosion of manufacturing industry. The politics of the North were, accordingly, different. The conflict of these systems - in terms of their interests and ideologies - between

North and South ultimately erupted in the Civil War of the 1860s, precipitated by the attack on Southern slavery by the Federal Government.[33]

Meanwhile, the population of the USA had grown from fewer than 300,000 in 1701 to some 5 million in 1800, and 40 million in 1870, including 4 million slaves or (by then) freed slaves. During the second half of the nineteenth century railways were punched across the continent to California, sucking settlers and capital behind them from back East and from Europe. The settlers who came to America were drawn largely from Ireland, Britain, Germany, Scandinavia, Eastern Europe, Russia and Italy. More than 100,000 Chinese labourers were taken to San Francisco by the 1860s. And a very substantial volume of the capital was accounted for by British investment in America, which constituted some 30 per cent of all British foreign investment, the bulk of the rest going to Latin America, Europe and India.[34]

From California, the Americans struck out further into the Pacific (for instance, Hawaii) and beyond (the Philippines), coming at China and Japan from the East. Thus, just as the essential features of modern America were finally laid down by the end of the nineteenth century, so too this move into Asia via the Pacific by the USA seems finally to have locked together the global system of politics which the hesitant voyages of the Portuguese down the West African coast had begun, four centuries earlier. Moreover, a new power had emerged whose influence on the politics of the twentieth century has been dramatic.

I V

The politics of this transformation involved the discovery and capture by Europe of new resources of land, minerals, commodities, crops, markets and people – and their use and exploitation on a scale hitherto unknown. Spices, gold, diamonds, minerals, sugar, cotton, tobacco, rubber, copra, coffee and other raw or precious materials (most recently oil) flowed back to Europe, and later to the USA and Japan. Manufactured goods, capital and technology (like railway and mining systems) were shipped out to facilitate and speed up this process. People in diverse and previously isolated societies were drawn into new relationships with each other, with Europe and, later, with North America, Russia and Japan. Millions of African slaves were bought or captured, and shipped across the Atlantic to the New World via the horrors of the Middle Passage: millions died before reaching there. Europeans, attracted by the opportunities which were opening up, or fleeing poverty and oppression in Europe, migrated to North and South America and Australia; indentured labour from India was transported to East Africa, Mauritius, South Africa and some of the societies of the Caribbean, such as Trinidad and Guyana. Tamils from South India were drafted to work on the tea plantations of Ceylon (now Sri Lanka); Chinese labourers were sent to the South African gold mines and the West Coast of the USA. Over the whole period world population increased dramatically, from about 545 million in 1650, to 728 million in 1750, to 906 million in 1800, to 1608 million by 1900.[35] Today the global figure stands at more than 4000 million, that is 4 billion, people.[36]

The politics of this *global* pattern of organizing and using such resources - human and all others besides - has brought into being new systems of production, power, social organization, culture and ideology in Europe and abroad. Together they have combined to establish the foundations of the uneven patterns of distribution which characterize the modern global system. Some of the effects this had in Europe will be discussed later. But it is worth indicating broadly here the way these new productive and social relations were expressed in the structure of the formal empires and especially the constitution of the colonial societies formed within them.

It is important to stress that in every instance the character of the colonial societies which emerged was unique. Only careful analysis can bring out their precise features. The same applies to the transformations - slow and fast, then and now - which occurred outside and after formal colonialism ceased. Even within the same empires (say of Britain, France, Portugal or Spain) the patterns varied sharply from colony to colony. French Algeria was different from Indo-China and Chad; Nigeria was different from Jamaica and Malaya; Mozambique was different from Brazil; what is now Costa Rica was different from Chile. However, the variables involved which were combined in these diverse ways through the politics of penetration, control or colonization, were everywhere the same: ecological conditions, the character of the productive activities and labour arrangements, the patterns of resource distribution, the nature of the pre-colonial societies themselves, the structure of colonial administration and social organization, the systems of culture and ideology. These variables should be familiar from what has been argued before about all societies. In each case, what organized their relationships was politics.

For example, ecological and climatic conditions were generally decisive in influencing whether Europeans in any number actually settled in an area or not. In general, the tropics did not attract significant numbers of Europeans as settlers, though traders, planters, missionaries and officials came and went, and some stayed.[37] The temperate zones attracted the bulk of the settlers. Ecological conditions in the broadest sense also influenced the kind of agricultural production which was developed in the various colonies and corners of empire. For instance, consider the contrast between Malaya (rubber), Uganda and Kenya (coffee, cotton and mixed farming) and the *pampas* of Argentina (beef and grain). Ecological conditions, however, nowhere prevented the exploitation of mineral resources, wherever they were found and wherever available technology could dig them out. But when the mines were exhausted or the demand for their products dropped (as with nitrates in Chile), they become barren and deserted.

Secondly, the character of the productive activities undertaken by imperial powers, companies or settlers - or all of them - often had a decisive influence on the demographic patterns and politics of the wider society. For instance, mining cores (diamonds and gold in South Africa, copper in Zambia, nitrates in Chile) attracted small but dense concentrations of people (and many expatriate miners) to them. The presence of such concentrations of people in turn stimulated urban developments around the mines and these required agricultural produce and railway systems to feed them and to transport goods to and from the coasts. The slave plantations, on the other hand (such as in the Caribbean and Brazil), were surprisingly self-sufficient and less dense in terms of population, almost constituting small-scale societies in themselves, whose oppressive internal politics have received detailed scholarly attention. Elsewhere, settler farms and ranches gobbled up huge tracts of land, as in Argentina, Brazil, the USA, Southern Africa and the White Highlands of Kenya, alienating the territory of indigenous societies, sometimes by force of occupation, sometimes by ridiculous 'treaties' at absurd prices.[38]

Thirdly, the labour arrangements associated in different ways with these central productive activities in the colonial societies were a major factor in their politics. When indigenous people could not or would not be drawn voluntarily into working as wage-labourers on mines or farms or plantations, the general solution everywhere involved forced labour, slavery or indentured labour (or a combination of them). The plantations of the Caribbean, Brazil and the US South exemplify the slave solution (though indentured white labour from England had initially been used in the West Indies and the US South), but the patterns and results varied in each case.[39] The forced labour solution is illustrated classically in New Spain (Mexico) where the *encomienda* system involved individual Spanish colonists having the Indians of a whole district 'commended' to them. The colonist (*encomendero*) could and did obtain tribute and labour from them, and in return was supposed to protect them and teach the Gospel. This system was phased out and the more direct *repartimiento* (or *mita* in Peru) system replaced it. This required the headmen of every Indian village to provide a specified number of men to work for a given period each year - on public works, church buildings and silver mining, as well as estate labour, porterage, cloth and sugar production. On the other hand, where local people were induced to work in various colonial enterprises - for instance by being required to pay poll taxes or tolls in labour, kind or cash - formal slavery and forced labour were less common. This was the general, though not universal, pattern in much of Africa and Asia, though there were varying degrees of coercion and compulsion there too, and was most common everywhere in the nineteenth century after the abolition of slavery which occurred at different times and places.

Yet it would be simplistic to believe that the abolition of slavery brought slavery to an end. It certainly did not in Angola, for instance, though it had been abolished there in 1875. And one of the most gruesome episodes in African colonial history was that of the Congo Free State (subsequently the Belgian Congo and now Zaire). The Congo Free State was the personal property of King Leopold II of Belgium who was said to have 'possessed the Congo just as Rockefeller possessed Standard Oil'. In a twenty-year period from 1891 to 1908 a breathtaking pillage took place for wild rubber and ivory, by forcing Congolese to collect the rubber on pain of death, mutilation or destruction of their villages. Africans were shot or had their hands cut off if they did not collect sufficient quantities. One official of the Congo Free State described to a British consular official how he went about collecting the rubber:

> His method of procedure was to arrive in canoes at a village, the inhabitants of which invariably bolted on their arrival; the soldiers were then landed and commenced looting, taking all the chickens, grain etc., out of the houses; after this they attacked the natives until able to seize their women; these women were kept as hostages until the Chief of the district brought in the required number of kilogrammes of rubber. The rubber having been brought, the women were sold back to their owners [sic] for a couple of goats, and so he continued from village to village until the requisite amount of rubber had been collected.

The effects on the society and population of the Congo can be imagined. The vortex of internal violence, resistance and warfare which this unleashed, and the disruption of the productive life of the communities, were enormous. No one knows for sure how many people died in the course of this, both from the direct effects of the pillage and also from disease introduced from without by Europeans, though one writer at the time put the figure in millions.[40] It would be incorrect to suggest that the Congo Free State was typical of what happened elsewhere or everywhere in Africa in the nineteenth century. It was not. But it was also not unique; there were other excesses. What it represents is the most extreme end of a spectrum of coercion which was used by colonial authorities to generate labour supplies or services for a great variety of enterprises from Cape Agulhas to Algeria from the seventeenth to the twentieth centuries.

Fourthly, the politics of colonial and semi-colonial societies were influenced by the character and size of the indigenous society, or societies. Although this varied from place to place there was everywhere resistance to European penetration and control. The hunter-gatherer San and the pastoral Khoikhoi at the Cape in the seventeenth and eighteenth centuries resisted fiercely, as did the Red Indians on the Plains in the USA in the nineteenth century. The Indian 'Mutiny' of 1857, the Boxer Rebellion in China in the closing years of the nineteenth century ('Cherish the dynasty, exterminate the foreigner'), the Matabele and Shona Revolt in Southern Rhodesia in 1896-7, and the Hut Tax War in Sierra Leone in 1898 were all expressions of resistance. Despite such resistance, societies of hunter-gatherers were pushed aside or destroyed or their descendants incorporated in more or less menial positions in the emerging colonial societies. The sheer mobility of pastoralists - in Eastern Russia or East Africa - made them somewhat more elusive and difficult to control. But as pointed out earlier in relation to the Maasai, where the territory of pastoral societies has been encroached upon, or split up, they have found it difficult to continue as before.

The more complex settled agricultural societies, especially in Asia but also in many parts of Africa, were generally larger in scale and more concentrated in population terms. Though often brought under formal colonial rule, many have retained the rich cores of their culture to the present time, but these are being modified, as change spreads out from urban to rural areas. None the less, all were more or less transformed politically in the colonial period, or the process was begun, as resources and people were combined and used in new and different ways, and as their autonomy was overriden by colonial authority.

Finally, the kind of administrative arrangements used in the government of the colonial society, and the distribution of power within it, also helped to shape the contours along which political life flowed. Where chartered companies ran things, or where settlers were given or took large blocks of land and power, the administrative pattern (as in the *encomienda* system) was usually very arbitrary and lacking in any substantial local participation. This was different from the arrangements prevailing in India, under the bureaucratic grid of the India Civil Service, after 1850. This in turn contrasted with the practice of 'indirect rule' adopted widely in West and East Africa by the British (but not by the French). Here, traditional authorities (chiefs and headmen) were used to assist in the extraction of taxes and labour supplies and the administration of colonial law, leaving the chiefs to some extent responsible for regulating a parallel system of traditional customs and law, but decreasingly so as time went by. Everywhere, from the end of the nineteenth century especially, the new systems of production, distribution, administration and educational policies stimulated the emergence of new social groups amongst the indigenous societies. These groups included junior administrative officials, teachers, merchants, lawyers and trade unionists. Their interests in gaining access to the resources of power and wealth in the society often brought them into direct conflict with both traditional and colonial authorities. And from these groups there emerged the early nationalist leaders of the twentieth century. These leaders spearheaded movements which were to result in the granting of constitutional independence after 1945.[41]

There were other features, but these are some of the main variables which were combined in different ways in the politics of all colonial societies. These aspects of the use and distribution of human and other resources formed the central structure of cooperative and conflicting relationships between people, and influenced the new forms of social organization, culture and ideology in the colonial societies. Relations between social groups, arising from their differential incorporation in such new societies, generated overlapping and cumulative conflicts between cultures, colours and classes. These relations in turn served to promote ideologies amongst the dominant colonial community - whether officials or settlers - which sustained the systems of production and the universally uneven distribution of their benefits. In passing, it is worth noting here that if one looks for the origins of modern racist ideas and attitudes one will be hard pressed to find them in Europe. Their origins were almost entirely abroad, first in the epoch of African slavery (especially in the Americas), and then in other colonial situations. There, such ideas were forged and elaborated into exclusivist and often hostile ideologies towards people of different cultures and colours. This occurred in the course of the establishment of relations of domination and subordination which shaped social organization and which grew up around the broad division of resources, labour and rewards in the productive core of the societies. Ideas, attitudes and also ugly terms of abuse - like 'wog', 'coolie', 'chinkie', 'coon', 'sambo', and a more recent white Rhodesian speciality, 'munt' - germinated in the colonial encounters, and date largely from the eighteenth and nineteenth centuries. They came to be steadily recycled back to Europe. There, in the course of time, they were more or less effectively seeded and institutionalized in the prevailing images, conceptions, idioms, stories, vocabularies and songs of the metropolitan cultures. And they can still be found there today, reinforced or modified by subsequent developments.[42]

It is important in any instance to see how these variables were related to each other in the politics of each colony and other areas of European penetration, and not to treat them as autonomous factors. To illustrate this in a little more detail the next section looks at one example of the politics of penetration, control and colonization: what happened at the tip of the African continent between the seventeenth and twentieth centuries.

V

Most people have a broad idea of what *apartheid* in South Africa means. It is associated with the systematic and institutionalized exclusion of black South Africans (including the coloured and Asian communities) from equal or shared access to resources and power in the society. An understanding of how this has come about requires some appreciation of the history of South Africa, from the middle of the seventeenth century when the Dutch East India Company (the DEIC) established a refreshment station at the Cape for its fleets travelling to and from the East Indies. Thus, some of the major roots of modern South African politics lie in the expansion of Europe described above.

It is a long and complex story, and there is a good deal of literature on it.[43] But the central theme which helps to explain the politics of this history can be stated simply, and then illustrated. At each stage of the process, as European settlers penetrated deeper and deeper inland, from the Cape to the Northern Transvaal, the politics were about how different groups sought to defend or gain control of the use and distribution of resources - such as cattle, land, labour, diamonds, gold, jobs, capital, education and opportunities. In the course of this process of penetration, control and colonization, the indigenous societies were conquered and their independence undermined, though never without resistance which was often very bloody. As the autonomy of these indigenous societies disintegrated, they came to be incorporated in the new colonial societies which were established in the Cape, Orange Free State, Natal and Transvaal, and which ultimately were drawn together into the Union (now Republic) of South Africa in 1910. The incorporation of these people was never on equal terms but always as subordinates - as labourers on farms, sugar plantations, in mines and factories.

The major groups involved in these politics were the San hunter-gatherers, and the nomadic pastoralist Khoikhoi, mainly of the Cape; the many different societies of the Bantu-speaking Nguni and Sotho people (like the Xhosa and Zulu on the one hand, and the Sotho and Tswana on the other), who were farmers of mixed crops and cattle and who worked with iron; there were imported slaves (mainly from Madagascar and the East Coast of Africa, but also from India and Ceylon, Java, Ternate and Malabar, for instance); there were European settlers (at first largely Dutch and German, under the auspices of the DEIC, then British after the Crown took over the Cape in 1806, and then a variety of Western and Eastern European settlers from the end of the nineteenth century); and indentured labourers who were brought from India to Natal to work on the sugar plantations.

The politics of the first phase of European penetration in the seventeenth and eighteenth centuries involved the transfer of control over the two key resources of land and cattle from the Cape Khoikhoi to the DEIC and settlers. The contrast between the situation in 1652, when the refreshment station was established, and the end of the eighteenth century, when the British first took over, dramatizes the point. The Dutch had no intention of establishing a colony, merely a place from which to provide passing fleets with fresh water, meat and vegetables. So their initial presence consisted of about 100 people and a ramshackle fort, located somewhat precariously at the tip of the continent. They controlled almost no land to speak of, and during the first decade their stocks of cattle and sheep sometimes plummeted to a mere handful. By contrast, the Khoikhoi societies stretched in a great arc round the Cape from the north-west to the east, where they merged in the region of the Fish river with the southward-moving Nguni societies. Interspersed amongst them all were small groups of hunter-gatherers, the San. Khoikhoi herds were very substantial and the journal of the first Dutch Commander of the Cape talks with great enthusiasm (and envy) about the size of these herds and the trading (and raiding) possibilities. The Khoikhoi moved freely with their herds, according to the seasons, some of them coming into Table Bay when the grass was lush after the winter rains.

By the end of the eighteenth century, however, the situation was totally transformed. The refreshment station had become a colony. Geographically it extended some 500 miles inland round the coast to the north-east and almost as far northwards. The population of settlers and their families had risen to some 18,000 in number and there were also about 27,000 slaves. By 1793 the DEIC and colonists had, at least, 82,000 head of cattle and nearly half a million sheep.[44] By the middle of the eighteenth century, on the other hand, most Khoikhoi societies had already disintegrated, their numbers decimated in numerous wars and fights with the DEIC and settlers over land and cattle, and from a series of smallpox epidemics which ripped through their societies in the first half of the eighteenth century. Their herds were simply no longer large enough to support viable societies.

What explains the transformation? Some Khoikhoi reluctance to barter in the volume required and at the price offered by the Dutch led the Company to form their own herds. To facilitate this and to generate the fresh produce for the ships, they allowed the first settlers, the Free Burghers, to establish themselves before 1660. As the settlement grew, both geographically and socially, the vicious circle of escalating conflict began. The logic was relentless. Dutch requirements for cattle and produce led to their need for more land. That meant conflict with the Khoikhoi over pastures, which in turn resulted in the occupation of more land and the accumulation of more cattle by the DEIC and the settlers. This precipitated attacks by the Khoikhoi on Dutch herds, and hence more conflict, more land, more cattle, deeper penetration, more fighting, more decay of Khoikhoi societies and so on, and on. Not a single major Khoikhoi group in the Cape escaped being drawn into conflict with the DEIC and settlers, and many Khoikhoi groups turned on each other as their resources shrank and as the basis of their politics - access to land and cattle - was systematically eroded.

Behind this arc of settler expansion a new colonial society was being built, based in the Western Cape on the wine and grain farms and the commercial life of the port, and based inland on the thin but enormous spread of the pastoral economy of the trekboers. The labour to help run these farms came from two main sources in the seventeenth and eighteenth centuries: imported slaves, especially in the Western Cape, from the areas mentioned above, and impoverished Khoikhoi who sought work and food as their own societies crumbled. Though the pattern was at first fluid in some respects, the social organization associated with this distribution of resources and power confirmed mainly white settlers of largely European extraction in positions of control over resources and power, and also locked mainly dark Khoikhoi and slaves, of largely African and Asian extraction, in positions of subordination in the systems of production in both the Western Cape and the interior. Hence the politics of Cape colonialism served to fuse people of certain colours and cultures into certain classes, thereby laying down one of the enduring principles of *apartheid*, which must be seen less in terms of segregation and more in terms of relations of domination and subordination, directly affecting access to scarce resources.

From deep within the eighteenth century, cattle traders, hunters and trekkers from the Western Cape had been in contact with the Nguni societies of the Eastern Cape, like the Xhosa. The same cycle of 'trading and raiding' which had characterized DEIC and settler relations with the Western Cape Khoikhoi, soon commenced in the east, as it did in the north with Sotho groups.[45] Bitter frontier wars, escalating out of raids and counter-raids over land and cattle, punctuated the period into the second half of the nineteenth century in the Eastern Cape, as trekkers, farmers and other settlers from Europe after the 1820s added to the general pressure on the Nguni societies. By the 1870s, one historian of the period writes[46]

> The southern Nguni, alone among the Bantu-speaking peoples of South Africa, had had a full century of continuous contact with white people. They had suffered a series of defeats in which, time after time, their huts had been burnt, their cattle captured, their fields devastated. Successive blocks of land had been taken from them and turned into farms. Whole communities had been expelled from their homes and shunted about the country. The cattle-killing of 1857 had been a shattering blow to their moral fibre as well as their material welfare. Poverty was becoming endemic among the southern Nguni and the only way they had to alleviate it was by going out to work for white people.

What occurred in the Eastern Cape was repeated elsewhere in South Africa in the course of the nineteenth century as trekkers and other settlers established farms in what are today the provinces of the Orange Free State, Natal and Transvaal. Disputes over land and other resources, fear and mutual suspicion soon were fanned into local cycles of violence, which in turn escalated into full-scale battles and warfare. Settlers and European armies were not always victorious at first - as in the case of the defeat of the British army in Natal against the Zulus at Isandhlwana in 1879, which was regarded as the most severe reversal suffered by British troops since the Crimean War. But, sooner or later, subjugation followed in all the colonies or republics of South Africa and various forms of 'native administration' were imposed. Taxes - in cash, kind, cattle and labour - were extracted by levies on people, huts and marriages, and a variety of means were used to stimulate and regulate the flow of African labour.

With the discovery of diamonds in 1867, more settlers, fortune-hunters and others arrived in the Kimberley area. Fresh capital flowed in and railways crawled north from the coasts, bringing new machinery with them. The technological capacities of the nineteenth century facilitated the further defeat and control of the African chiefdoms. And around the minefields there grew up new patterns of social organization which built on the old principles derived from the Cape and the eastern frontier. There soon came to be a rigid division of industrial labour and rewards between the white owners of capital, white miners (including many immigrants from Cornwall, Lancashire and Scotland) and black workers. The associated controls on black workers on the diamond fields - pass laws and tightly regulated labour compounds - established patterns which were to be refined and developed on a large scale further north, round Johannesburg, when the gold-bearing reefs of the Witwatersrand were discovered and began to be mined from the 1880s.[47] These controls on labour -

supplemented by taxation and other pressures on rural communities – formed central elements in shaping the structure of modern *apartheid* and were extended into all urban contexts in the twentieth century. They acted decisively to lock black and other non-white labour into positions of subordination in the division of labour and distribution of rewards within the emerging system of industrial production.

If South Africa had become a distant and dusty place in the consciousness of Europe, especially England, the discovery and exploitation of diamonds and gold altered that. The mines became magnets which attracted a significant volume of capital, immigrants and new technology, which acted to involve South Africa deeply in the global system of production and distribution, especially at its imperial peak before the First World War. But the development of gold mining and associated industries not only extended the labour patterns of the diamond fields and attracted new material interests and settlers from Europe; it also provoked a complex clash of competing interests. This was not only the clash between Boer and Briton but also, on the gold-fields, between white miners and white owners, and between white and black miners. The conflict between Boers (who controlled the Transvaal and Orange Free State) and Britain (who controlled the Cape and Natal) finally erupted in the Boer War (or Gold War or English War, as it is variously called by different interests) in 1899. It resulted in British victory and then, in 1910, the establishment of formal independence for the Union of South Africa, within the Empire (later Commonwealth). Thereafter the future development of South Africa came increasingly to be in the hands of the small and mainly white population of European extraction.

But, by the end of the nineteenth century, the subjugation of the African societies was being completed, and direct control over them was being extended:[48]

> The African peoples of South Africa were being transformed from self-sufficient and autonomous chiefdoms into interlocking and dependent communities of peasants, living on attenuated tribal lands, and wage labourers, working in areas controlled by white people. Moreover, by the end of the nineteenth century the prototype of the typical black South African of the twentieth century had emerged: the African who was born and reared in a 'native Reserve' or 'Bantu Area', who spent the middle years of his life working intermittently for white employers in 'White Areas', and who, when he was no longer employable, was constrained by economic necessity or by law to return to his 'Reserve' and to stay there until he died.

With power over both the major resources and wealth of the country and also its machinery of government in white hands, the subordination of non-white South Africans continued in the twentieth century in ways that are well known. The land issue was settled between 1913 and 1936 when a series of Acts confined African landowning rights to a mere 13 per cent of the country, the

Reserves or Bantustans of today. The formal exclusion of Africans, Asians and Coloureds from a great variety of jobs; the very low farm, factory and mine wages; the meagre facilities in terms of education and health care in the twentieth century (by contrast with improving facilities for an increasing number of whites, especially after the Second World War); and hence the resulting unevenness in terms of life-chances and opportunities – all reflected accurately the politics of inequality resulting from white control over the use of private and public resources and their distribution. These politics of deprivation and subordination were to generate opposition from Africans which has today reached the edge of guerrilla warfare.

The social organization and the ideology of the dominant groups which had accompanied these processes varied to some extent regionally, reflecting different local politics. For instance, the Cape was traditionally less extreme than the Transvaal, and the Orange Free State more so than Natal. But in the course of the twentieth century, and especially after 1948, these differences were largely ironed out as national legislation and attitudes came to prevail amongst most whites – expressed in the philosophy and practice of *apartheid*.

Today even the most remote parts of South Africa or areas over which South Africa has exercised control (like Namibia) have been penetrated. Even the !Kung San, in the Kalahari, have been drawn into wage-labour on the South African gold mines. Other San have been recruited as trackers in the South African Army, operating along the Botswana-Namibia border (and further north on the Namibia-Angola border), checking for guerrilla incursions.[49] In this way the modern world of South African politics, expressing the new forms of conflict over who shall control the resources and people of South Africa, and how they shall be used, reaches right into the heart of these areas.

However, the purpose in pursuing these themes through to the present has not been to explore the politics of modern South Africa, characterized by severe inequalities in the distribution of power and resources. Rather, it has been to illustrate in some detail just how far-reaching the effects of European expansion from the sixteenth century have been. It would of course be absurd to hold the metropolitan Dutch or English wholly responsible for what occurred in South Africa. Indeed, part of the argument here has been to emphasize that, once *local* interests and objectives amongst settlers have become defined and established, the structure of colonial and post-colonial societies is very much the outcome of *local* variables, combined through local politics, though these have everywhere been influenced by external factors (such as imperial policy, capital, immigrants, trade and other foreign interests or requirements). As another of Joseph Conrad's characters observes in a different context, 'Only let the material interests once get a firm footing, and they are bound to impose the conditions on which they alone can continue to exist.'[50]

South Africa may seem an unusual case on the African continent in that it appears to be a very independent and rapidly industrializing society. But in fact it is highly vulnerable in a number of respects, resulting from its incorporation and position in the global system. It needs foreign capital and the fortunes of all its people are in no small way influenced by the world price of gold, for instance. Of course, what happened in South Africa was unique in most forms and particulars, though similarities may be found elsewhere in settler Africa, and further afield. But it is important to stress again that each colonial, semi-colonial or post-colonial situation is unique, combining the variables discussed earlier in different ways. But the current features of the former colonies, and indeed all societies of the world which have been penetrated, drawn into the structure of global politics and hence more or less transformed, are best understood and analysed against the background of these wider processes. In every instance, they have both accounted for their incorporation and influenced their subsequent development. The South African example has been used to illustrate the importance of local politics, but in the context of European penetration and its involvement in the global system.

VI

What was happening in Europe during this outward expansion and in the course of the establishment of new colonial societies around the world?

A detailed account of the long and complex politics of the transformation of Western Europe, led by England, from its agricultural and largely feudal origins in the Middle Ages, to its industrial and largely capitalist condition by the end of the nineteenth century, is beyond the scope and competence of this book. So is the equally important question as to *why* this transformation took place first in England and not, for example, in the societies which had gained initial advantages from exploration, conquest and control - Portugal and Spain.[51] But there are some general points to stress since the structure of modern world politics has been characterized by the dominance of Europe within it, at least until the more recent emergence of the USA, USSR and Japan in the twentieth century. There are two questions here: first, the character of this transformation in Europe; and secondly, the question of its relationship to the politics of expansion discussed above. England as the dominant society to the end of the nineteenth century provides the best example to use on both counts.

The central characteristics of the changes which occurred in England from the end of the Middle Ages are well enough known. A compact summary of these must include reference to the cumulative effects of the following factors. There was the growth of population, the relative scarcity of land (given available technology), and hence some of the early agricultural innovations (like new crops and experiments with fertilizers), the opening up of fresh land and the draining of marshes. There was a slow but steady growth of towns, the specialization of skills and increased trade both internally and with Europe, especially in wool and woollen materials. This in turn fostered the enclosure of common land, for instance to raise more sheep for the profitable wool trade, and the consequent exclusion of peasants from the land on which they had previously depended for subsistence ('when sheep ate men'). Parallel with this, there was the systematic growth of property rights and the consequent private ownership and control of vast acreages in relatively few hands, and the associated emergence of a merchant or 'bourgeois' class in the towns. These processes overlapped. There developed a rural and urban wage-labouring class and its correlate, urban and rural unemployment and pauperization. The prior structure of tightly bound personal bonds in the feudal relationship between lord and peasant came to be replaced by the looser, less secure and more impersonal bonds of a money economy and the fragility of the 'cash nexus', linking employer to worker.

The steady accumulation of capital by both merchants and rural landowners helped to promote the growth of various financial institutions and banks which in turn helped to attract, consolidate and distribute capital for investment in further agricultural developments, trade and shipping. From this – and the more general expansion of Europe abroad – there emerged the flurry of overseas trading companies, especially between 1500 and 1700 (such as the Merchant Adventurers' Company, the East India Company, the Levant Company, the Muscovy Company, the Russia Company, the South Sea Company, the Hudson's Bay Company and the Royal Africa Company, amongst many others).

Abroad, there followed the establishment of colonial plantations (especially in cotton, tobacco and sugar) and the expansion and monopolization of overseas trade, production, transport and markets (for instance through the Navigation Acts after 1651-60) with the help of the vastly increased size and strength of the British Navy. At home, there was a great surge of commodity and especially textile production from the end of the eighteenth century to supply these markets, following the overcoming of technical problems in the production processes (the 'spinning Jenny', the 'water frame', the 'mule'), plus the application and proliferation of steam power. All this promoted the burst of innovative, technical and industrial activity from the end of the eighteenth century, and was to find expression in the mechanization of agriculture and the mushrooming of the concentrated productivity of the factory system.

In close association with this was the further growth of cities and their densely packed slums, as well as the sumptuous town houses and country estates. There followed the sprawl of railway and other communication systems, at home and abroad, and also the emergence of the first industrial proletariat and the organizations of workers which grew out of it. The nineteenth century saw the rise to dominance of a class of industrial owners and entrepreneurs, closely linked with sections of the landed gentry and the finance houses, all having a powerful influence (if not always in the same direction) on government policy at home and abroad. The Manor had vanished, the Factory had arrived.

However, what is important to note for present purposes is the essentially *political* character of this transformation. The history of this long transition was its politics. It was argued in an earlier chapter that some of the major stimulants for change in the way people obtain, use, produce and distribute resources (in technological terms, for instance, or in the organization of labour, or in the direction and pattern of investment) are the *problems* and *opportunities* encountered in the course of the production and reproduction of social life, within local communities, institutions or more widely in societies. The transformation of English society illustrates this vividly.

There was no 'hidden hand' or divine force guiding the politics of English society. Nor were people planning their actions in the light of abstract theoretical or philosophical concerns. On the contrary, what one must focus on are the groups of strategically placed people, using their advantaged position within the structure of power and social organization to obtain, use, produce and distribute human and other resources in new and different ways. Theoretical justification and philosophical endorsement for such politics followed, but seldom preceded, such changes. In the course of their activities such groups had to overcome problems - agricultural, social, technical and institutional. It requires no conspiratorial view of history and politics to see that in the relentless pursuit of their interests and opportunities at home and abroad they were able to accumulate substantial control of both resources and power, which remains a central feature of British politics today. They were very successful indeed.

The politics of all this necessarily promoted new forms of conflict and cooperation between groups over the changing use and distribution of resources. There was close cooperation amongst rural landowners and bourgeoisie in the commercialization of agriculture. There was cooperation amongst the guilds, banks, joint-stock companies, owners of capital, chambers of commerce, cooperatives (both producer and consumer), as well as in the expanding political parties and labour organizations of the nineteenth century. In the course of this, different groups (merchants, bankers, industrialists, landowners, rural workers and the industrial proletariat) all evolved more or less distinctive subcultures and styles of life as well as ideologies which sought to promote or defend their interests under different circumstances (protectionism, free trade, Chartism, imperialism, the 'civilizing mission', socialism and so on).

There was also fierce conflict - between the emerging merchant classes and the Crown over fiscal policy and taxation; between landowners and dispossessed or unemployed rural poor; between industrialists and urban workers; and also with foreign competitors in Europe, in distant lands and on the high seas. Both domestically and abroad, the politics of the transition at each stage turned on the way different groups defined, promoted and defended their interests.

None of these activities occurred in a vacuum. The less centralized structure of power, the looser institutional arrangements and systems of social organization in England (by contrast with Portugal, Spain and France at any comparable point) facilitated the politics of this transformation, and were in turn reshaped by it. A material culture in which seafaring played on important part (as with the Dutch across the Channel) helped too, and in turn received a massive boost in the course of the transition. These processes were spurred on and consolidated in the eighteenth and nineteenth centuries by two linked developments. First, there was the redistribution of institutional control of power in England from Crown to Parliament after the Civil War of the seventeenth century. Secondly, there was a fundamental shift in the importance of resource use from countryside to town, from agriculture to commerce and industry, with far-reaching consequences for the full range of politics in the society.[52]

Thus the politics of the transition from feudalism to industrial capitalism at each stage involved new methods of obtaining, using, producing and distributing resources. It thereby established new relations of power and social organization between old and new groups of people (lords and peasants; town and country; landed gentry, urban merchants and industrialists; parliaments and Crowns; voters and parties; Europeans and non-Europeans, for instance). It generated a competitive and acquisitive culture, and it was sustained by an ideology which in general promoted individualism at home and both racial and cultural chauvinism abroad.[53] In short, the politics of the transition in England involved the total transformation of the 'systems' I have discussed earlier and their reconstitution in the structure of the new capitalist society which had emerged fully by the end of the nineteenth century.

VII

Would all this have occurred without the benefits which dominance in world politics brought to Europe, and especially and initially to England? Could the subsequent consolidation of formal empires and the yet deeper penetration (for instance by capital and railways) both within and outside their expanding empires have been achieved without the industrial and associated military capacity which European societies developed in the nineteenth century? And what were the effects of this in what has become the Third World? Could any of the societies there have developed their own technological and industrial capacities in due course, if the disruption of their politics and hence the domination of their resources and markets had not taken place?

To some extent all these questions can only be answered speculatively. We cannot know for sure what might have been, but as one author comments:[54]

> It is difficult to establish any direct connexion between wealth amassed in the plunder of India and other colonies and the capital which financed England's Industrial Revolution. It is even more difficult to believe that there is no link between the two.

Yet to raise any of these questions is to raise them all. It is also to suggest from another angle the progressive interconnectedness of the processes involved in the 'creation of the world'. When one considers the acquisition of bullion and loot, and accumulated profits from India, the slave trade and the plantations of the New World, and the exploitation of more or less protected markets and sources of raw materials, it is indeed difficult to believe that this did not contribute decisively to the timing, form and scope of industrialization. Some of the evidence about this is worth indicating, at least for Britain.

I have already pointed out the extent of the early flow of American gold and silver to Spain (and onwards to Amsterdam and London). It has also been reckoned that Drake's celebrated voyage on the *Golden Hind* produced booty of between £0.5 and £1.5 million, and that during the reign of Elizabeth I some £4.5 million worth of bullion flowed back to England. But it was in the eighteenth century that the major gains were made. The conquest of Bengal by Robert Clive and the East India Company after 1757 netted vast fortunes. As a result of the treaties which accompanied the conquest, Clive was reckoned to have made about £0.25 million personally, while something in the region of £4 million was received by the Company and its officials. Estimates of the volume of tribute which flowed back to England in the half century after the conquest vary. On one reckoning an *annual* drain of between £5 million and £15 million took place. Another estimate suggests a net value of between £100 million and £150 million over the first fifty years. What would that be worth today? Moreover, though I have not mentioned Ireland at all thus far, the conquest and control of Ireland from the time of Cromwell soon produced direct financial benefits for England. By the mid-eighteenth century an amount of some £750,000 *annually* was transferred from Ireland in rent to absentee English landlords.

From West Africa, across the Atlantic to the New World, the profits from the slave trade and the produce of the slave islands and plantations were enormous:[55]

> The triangular trade thereby gave a triple stimulus to British industry. The Negroes were purchased with British manufactures; transported to the plantations, they produced sugar, cotton, indigo, molasses and other tropical products, the processing of which created new industries in England; while the maintenance of the Negroes and their owners on the plantations provided another market for British industry, New England agriculture and the Newfoundland fisheries. By 1750 there was hardly a trading or manufacturing town in England which was not in some way connected with the triangular or direct colonial trade. The profits obtained provided one of the main streams of that accumulation of capital in England which financed the Industrial Revolution.

Once Britain had gained the *asiento* (the sole right to supply the Spanish colonies with slaves) in 1713, the trade in human beings boomed. According to one estimate the profit *per slave* in the eighteenth century was in the order of £25. Since as many as 3 million slaves may have been carried on British ships, a total profit on slaving alone in the century could have been as high as £75 million. Between 1783 and 1789 Liverpool slavers made a profit of £2.3 million on some 300,000 slaves shipped from Africa to the West Indies and beyond. Another reckoning suggests that the value to England of the produce of slave-labour from the West Indies in the decade 1770-80 was £40 million. The prosperity of such cities as Bristol and Liverpool, major centres of the slave-trading operations, was largely bound up with the slave trade, and profits from the transatlantic trade helped to finance a variety of associated industries in the Severn basin.[56]

Not all the profits from the Companies and colonies, from the trade in slaves, sugar and cotton goods were ploughed directly or immediately into industrial investment. Much was retained and reinvested in the slave trade or on other ventures abroad. Much also went into conspicuous consumption and fine buildings – town houses and country estates, for instance. But indirectly, its contribution to the industrial transformation of the society must have been steady. For example, it helped to develop the infrastructure (ports and shipping) which were later so vital in international trade. It also financed agricultural innovation and rural change which were a necessary condition of the industrial revolution.

The early penetration, conquest and colonization of important parts of the world, therefore, was partly cause, partly condition and partly consequence of the transformation of British politics. The process continued throughout the nineteenth century, and beyond. The industrial revolution brought Britain to dominance not only in Europe, not only within the confines of her colonies and possessions (which expanded rapidly in number, size and geographical distribution, especially after 1815 and again after 1870), but as the 'workshop of the world'. Three overlapping and cumulative features of this contributed further to the politics of British (and North European) growth: the control of markets, the opening up of investment opportunities abroad, and the gaining of access to sources of cheap raw materials. At the same time, the consequences of these activities in the wider world were steadily to draw distant societies into the global system of politics which first Britain and then the rest of North-west Europe, North America and Japan came to dominate; and to consolidate the international division of production and labour which remains today.

First, the markets which were captured, held and protected (as in India) had been a major factor in stimulating industrial development at home, especially in textiles. Once the products of industry were established as supreme on a global basis, the ideology and practice of Free Trade carried them further and further abroad, opening up yet more new markets – notably in South America. As the domestic use and production of resources shifted, the composition of exports shifted too, from textiles to heavier goods and raw materials, like machinery, ships, iron, steel and coal.

Secondly, where 'guns and sails', in Cipolla's phrase, had accomplished the early phases of conquest and control, the later extension and consolidation of Empire and the further penetration by capital of distant corners of the world were achieved through steam-power, railways and automated weapons like the maxim-gun – all products of the industrial revolution. Foreign investment became an important component in the development of nineteenth-century capitalism in Britain, and equally in France and Germany. Together with selling manufactured goods and gaining raw materials abroad, this further helped to stitch the world together and to confirm the international division of labour which has so centrally come to define global politics today.

National Income in Britain rose from £845 million in 1865-9 to £2120 million in 1910-13, while the accumulating balance of British capital abroad climbed from £46.1 million in 1820 to £489.8 million in 1865, to £1497.2 million in 1885, and to £3989.6 million in 1913. Despite a persistently negative balance of trade in the nineteenth century, the overall balance of payments was kept in surplus largely because of the steady return of interest and dividends from overseas investments. This increased from an *annual average* in the five-year period 1815-20 of £1.74 million, to an annual average in the five-year period 1881-5 of £64.76 million, to an annual average of £187.93 million in the three-year period 1911-13. To this must be added the other 'invisible' earnings from shipping, insurance and foreign trade and services.

During the nineteenth century as a whole, the average return on capital on foreign investment was about 5 per cent, but in some colonial and raw material investments it was at times as high as 10 per cent (for instance in South African gold and diamonds, Malayan tin and rubber, and Indian and Ceylonese tea). But the bulk of foreign investment between 1860 and 1913 inside the Empire was in Canada, the settler Dominions (including South Africa) and India. Outside the Empire it was in Europe (declining), the USA (steady) and Latin America (increasing).[57]

Thirdly, from the nineteenth century until the present, the wider world (both inside and outside the formal empires) came to be major sources of the raw materials for Britain and the rest of industrializing Europe. The range of these resources was very wide. They were grown, dug, picked, chopped, tapped and mined by cheap labour everywhere. They included foodstuffs, wool, wine, guano, copper, coffee, palm-oil, nitrates, rubber, tea, cotton, groundnuts, timber, jute, hides, tin, lead, tropical fruits and bauxite. They accounted for the bulk of British imports, and the patterns in both Germany and France came to be similar.[58]

Did European industrialization at home and its associated forms of expansion abroad - trade, investment and extraction of raw materials - have the effect of choking off the possibility of indigenous developments in the productive forces and technology in some societies of Africa, Asia and Latin America? Did it hold back - or worse, underdevelop - societies there? There are those who would argue that it did, and they would point, as Barratt Brown does, to the fact that 'the wealth per head of the present underdeveloped lands, not only in India, but in China, Latin America and Africa, was higher than in Europe in the seventeenth century and fell *pari passu* as wealth grew in capitalist Europe'. Some examples from the various continents will help to illustrate this.

In Africa, one can point to the bronze and iron technologies of West Africa, for example, and to the goldmining and manufacturing of leather goods; to the towns and trade networks which were both local and which also reached up to the Mediterranean. Some writers would argue that the specialization which was beginning to emerge in the politics of those societies might have provided the basis for further developments in the productive forces, had the effects of the slave trade - the disruption, the conflicts, the depopulation and the wars - not ravaged West Africa. Moreover, from the end of the nineteenth century and especially during the twentieth century, colonial administrations, companies and settlers in West, East and Southern Africa transformed the politics of many African societies. The re-direction of the use of local resources (land and labour) meant that they were not only constrained from innovating in their own ways, but also often that they became increasingly unable to feed themselves. Crowder observes:

> The cardinal principles of the colonial economic relationship were to stimulate the production and export of cash crops - palm produce, ground-nuts, cotton, rubber, cocoa, coffee and timber; to encourage the consumption and expand the importation of European manufactured goods; and, above all, to ensure that as much as possible the trade of the colony, both imports and exports, was conducted with the metropolitan country concerned.

The case of French Guinea is a good example. The initial phase of slavery was followed by a 'pillage' of local rubber. Then came the establishment of tropical fruit and coffee plantations and later bauxite mining. Not only did this drain valuable resources back to the metropolitan society, but it also required the regular mobilization of labour supplies and taxes which in turn debilitated the social organization of the communities and adversely affected their capacity for local food production. Elsewhere, in the groundnut-producing areas of the Gambia and Senegal for instance, people 'began to import rice and to endure annually what came to be known as "the hungry season" just before and during the cultivation of the groundnuts'. The same was true in East Africa, with respect to sisal, cotton and coffee. The layout of the railway and road systems 'represents a grid draining the exportable resources of the interior towards the coastal ports'.[59]

In Asia, one might point to the complex irrigation systems, for instance in the dry zone of Sri Lanka (Ceylon) and China. Could it not be argued that if these societies were capable of such feats of design, engineering and mobilization of labour - centuries before Western dominance - there is no reason to believe that they would not have regenerated and developed their productive capacities, especially since many were linked by seaborne trade with other parts of Asia, and even though their 'hydraulic civilizations' had collapsed before European penetration commenced?[60] Moreover, the wholesale 'plunder' of Bengal in the eighteenth century ('There had been nothing like it in history since the Spanish *conquistadores* looted the Aztec and Inca civilizations of America in the early sixteenth century'), and the subsequent destruction of the Indian textile industry in the course of the nineteenth century, must have

stunted whatever possibilities there may have been for autonomous development in the sub-continent. The results were to engender a 'terrible series of
famines in Bengal and Sind (after 1770), to cause the ruin of the Indian
handicraft industry and the great towns based upon it; and to create that over-
population of the land and that overpressure on the agricultural sector of the
economy which is India's tragedy today'. What happened in India was repeated
with more or less severity in Egypt, in South-east Asia, Malaya and in some
parts of sub-Saharan Africa.[61]

In South America, as already noted, there were the remarkable architectural
achievements of the Aztecs and Incas, long before many of the modern stone
cities of Western Europe were built. Would the cycles of 'intensification and
depletion' which seem to have characterized the politics of those societies have
been broken in due course and a more sustained process of development
inaugurated?

There are others who doubt whether such developments would have
occurred. Marx, for instance, was somewhat sceptical of the possibilities of
significant change in the politics of such societies, and especially Asian societies.
He regarded their structures of power and their systems of social organization
('Oriental despotism') as rigid, oppressive and stagnant, without any of the
dynamics for change within them which characterized feudal society in
England. For this reason, while being appalled at the oppression within
capitalist society in Europe and by what Europe was doing in India and China,
he seems reluctantly to have welcomed British imperialism in India for instance,
arguing that it had a 'double mission' to fulfil: to smash the old constraints in
Indian politics and to lay the 'material foundation of Western (capitalist) society
in Asia'.[62] Were he alive today to observe the effects, it is doubtful whether he
would still be optimistic about the outcome of that 'mission'.

There is no way in which one can be sure of what would have happened. Yet
a number of things seem quite clear. First, enormous benefits accrued to
Britain, Europe and the West in general in the course of the establishment of
world politics, that is, in the course of the establishment of the modern patterns
of obtaining, producing, distributing and exchanging resources. Secondly,
whatever prospects there may have been in at least some societies in Africa,
Asia and South America, the effects of European penetration and control were
gravely to disrupt their politics, and in some instances to destroy existing
societies entirely. The patterns of disruption and destruction were certainly not
the same everywhere. What happened in Middle America in the sixteenth and
seventeenth centuries was far more extreme than what happened in East Africa
in the twentieth century, for instance, as was what happened in South Africa.
And what happened in India was far more devastating than what occurred in
Ghana. The poverty of the peoples of most Caribbean islands today can be
traced directly to their creation as plantation societies, which generated
considerable wealth in tropical produce for Spanish, Dutch, British and French
societies.

But viewed globally, in overall terms, major costs have been borne by societies in what we today call the Third World. Whatever many of the inequalities in their politics may have been (and some were severe), most were *at least* self-sufficient in terms of food. Few are today, and most are in chronic debt. The world division of production and labour - raw materials from the Third World, manufactured and high-technology products from the West - has acted to lock these societies into disadvantaged positions within global politics, and has distorted their domestic politics. The terms of trade, whereby their raw materials exchange against manufactured goods, have got steadily worse in the years since the end of the Second World War. Their differential incorporation on such severely disadvantaged terms was intimately related in structure and timing to the emerging dominance of the West in world politics. The two processes went hand in hand. They continue today.

VIII

The foundations of modern world politics which constitute the context of politics in all societies today had been laid down by the start of the First World War in 1914. There have been subsequent shifts and spreads in the centres of gravity and influence since then, notably the emergence of the dominant position of the USA and the Soviet Union, and the growth of Japan as a major power. After the First World War this process continued, though the pace was uneven in time and space, and was interrupted first by the Great Depression of the 1930s and then by the Second World War. Thereafter, it speeded up again and goes on today.

After 1945 the tide of formal empire receded sharply around the world as societies in Asia, Africa and the Caribbean achieved their constitutional independence, as had happened in Latin America in the nineteenth century. But everywhere new forces replaced the formal empires. The seaborne empires of the early phase of European expansion were far greater in extent than anything which had gone before them. The subsequent phase of formal European colonization and imperialism had by 1914 brought 55 per cent of the world's surface and 34 per cent of the world's population under the control of a handful of societies - Britain, France, Germany and (in the east) Russia. But perhaps none of this could match the concentrated power of the modern successors of Company and Colony - the transnational (or multinational) corporations. This account of the emergence of modern politics would be incomplete without some discussion of the position of the transnationals in the structure of global politics today, and the implications of this for societies in the Third World.[63]

The rise to global power of the transnationals occurred simultaneously with the decline of empire. In the last forty years their growth has been spectacular, and many are today household names, not only in the industrial world but increasingly around the globe: Nestlés, Shell, Unilever, Goodyear, General Motors, Lonrho, General Foods, ITT, United Fruit, Booker McConnell, Alcoa,

ICI, Mobil, Sony, Toyota and Mitsubishi. The size, wealth and power of these corporations is astonishing. Some of them entirely overshadow many of the countries of the world. Comparing annual sales of certain corporations with the gross national product of various countries in 1973, Barnet and Müller found that 'General Motors is bigger than Iran, Venezuela and Turkey; and that Goodyear Tires is bigger than Saudi Arabia'.[64] This being the case, it takes little imagination to see how the corporations simply dwarf most of the societies of Central and South America, Africa and Asia where they operate.

The transnationals now control between one-quarter and one-third of *all* world production. 'The total sales of their foreign affiliates in 1976 were estimated at US $830 billion, which is about the same as the gross national product of all developing nations, excluding the oil-producing developing countries.'[65] The productive range of the corporations includes energy, raw materials, foodstuffs, minerals and many different manufactured goods from tennis shoes to electronic equipment. In addition to oil, a relatively few corporations dominate the production, processing and marketing of bauxite, copper, iron ore, nickel, zinc, tin, tobacco, bananas, coffee, sugar and tea. Their power, moreover, continues to accumulate, and *also* to concentrate. By 1985, according to one estimate, between 200 and 300 corporations will control 80 per cent of *all* productive assets outside the Communist World.[66]

The corporations are thus the modern heirs (and in some instances the direct descendants) of the Companies which brought back the plunder from India, the gold and copper from South Africa and Zambia, and the sugar, tobacco and cotton from the New World. With their headquarters in Japan, West Germany, France, the United Kingdom and especially North America, these corporations operate globally in obtaining, producing and distributing resources in almost every country of the world outside (but not excluding) the Communist bloc. They control, plant, reap, mine, ship, process, pack and market foods, minerals and raw materials in countless different societies. In their manufacturing activities they invest, employ, automate and advertise around the world. They shift capital, skills, machinery, goods, people and information from place to place and sector to sector. The power which derives from the control of these resources is formidable.

The power of the earlier seaborne Companies and empires rested not only on their 'guns and sails', but on their ability to seize and monopolize resources and markets, to coerce the labour of either indigenous people or imported slaves, and to exclude competitors, if necessary (and often) by force. The power of the subsequent empires rested more solidly on the formal control and direction of territories, resources and people by imperial governments, colonial administrations, armies, and settlers.

But the power of the modern transnationals derives from four main factors, whose *political* importance cannot be stressed enough. They have built up and control huge resources of finance capital, and have easy and direct access to more; they have a monopoly on much advanced technology and managerial skill, and they guard it very closely indeed; they have what is referred to as 'vertical integration', that is, the control of the linked processes of production, shipment, packaging and marketing - all within the same corporation, and hence reduce their dependence on other institutions or organizations; through advertising and other media they have a powerful influence on the cultures and ideology of all the societies in which they operate, shaping patterns of consumption, preferences and styles of life.[67]

The important thing to note about the role of the transnationals in the politics of the modern world is that their power is such that while they do not always *own* the resources (whether land or raw materials) of societies in which they operate, they control or decisively influence what is done with them, what is produced, how it is produced and its price; as well as what is consumed, and how it is consumed and its cost.

The content of processed food sold in supermarkets (and hence a major element in our diet) is a case in point. Many societies of the Third World have one or two major export crops or minerals: bananas and sugar in the Caribbean and Central America; copper in Zambia; tea and rubber in Sri Lanka. With the important exception, perhaps, of OPEC (the Organization of Petroleum Exporting Countries) they have little influence on the price they can set for their resources and very little to bargain with. Attempts by governments in these societies to increase the price of their natural resources, or to regulate the affairs of the corporations in obtaining or processing them, has led to swift retaliation by the transnationals. They can pull out, refuse to buy or ship, suspend or withdraw investment and even 'destabilize' the government concerned, as happened in Chile.[68] Given that the societies of the Third World have been drawn into these global patterns of production and distribution, and given their current dependence on the export of a few key items, they *have* to sell these raw materials and crops if they are to import the food and other equipment they require, at least for the moment. In the absence of internal sources of capital, technology, shipping and marketing, many societies of the Third World are simply stuck. The people who now live and work in and off the mines, plantations and factories dominated by the transnationals have little influence over the corporate decisions, perhaps taken thousands of miles away, which directly and immediately affect their lives. Some people say 'that's business': I say that's politics.

In many sectors of manufacturing industry in the Third World, the transnationals also play a major role. There may appear to be short-term advantages of this for the societies concerned. These include the inflow of investment, the training of personnel, the provision of jobs and the local production of various items (chemicals, tyres, electrical goods, car, motor bicycles and canned foods, for instance) which previously these societies had to import. But the central problem for the governments and people of these societies is that, as a result of this, the direction and control of resources in their societies, and what is produced, remains firmly in the hands of the foreign giants.[69]

There is little 'countervailing' power against the transnationals. There are usually very weak trade union movements, and as often as not their activities (if allowed) are severely curtailed by government policy - for instance in Bahrein, Thailand, the Philippines, Hong Kong, South Korea, Argentina, Nigeria and Zambia.[70] There is a relative paucity of local bureaucratic and accounting skills - which need to be very sophisticated to monitor the complex operations of the transnationals. There is also a lack of serious indigenous competition (in part the result of the effectiveness of the transnationals) and, as often as not, local patent rights are held by the corporations, thereby further elbowing local competition out of the way. It is sometimes also said that the locally employed managers and officials of the transnationals owe more allegiance, in the first instance, to the corporations than to their own society. Moreover, the often close relations between such personnel, government circles and the corporations, leave the broad mass of the people in these societies with even less protection and minimal influence over their life chances. In this latter respect, it could be argued, we are beginning to witness now the emergence of an international corporate class of owners and managers, united by similar interests, attachments, ideologies and behaviours, spreading across frontiers and continents. For all these reasons the short-term advantages are outweighed by the long-term loss of control and direction.

Finally, the extraction of very substantial profits by the corporations from their global operations in mines, plantations and factories has been going on systematically throughout the present century, and hence their size and power today, which has been built on the patterns laid down in the previous four centuries. It has been estimated that every year the corporations take out of the Third World about three times as much as they invest, and much of the new local investment comes from re-investment of local profit. Between 1960 and 1968, for instance, about one billion US dollars in new capital was being transferred to US subsidiaries in the Third World annually, while some US $2.5 billion was being withdrawn in income alone each year. Between 1971 and 1974 the flow to the USA averaged US $7.5 billion per year.[71]

How are such profits made? There are many aspects to this. A major one is that the corporations are able to exploit the prevailing low wage rates in those societies, which are far lower than in the industrial world. The absence of effective industrial or labour regulations (partly a consequence of weak trade unions and edgy governments) also means that workers there may put in cripplingly long hours (2800 hours per annum in South Korea, compared with about 1800 hours per annum in West Germany, for instance).[72] Conditions of work can be appalling, as can living arrangements on mines or plantations, as anyone who has seen the labour compounds on the South African goldmines, the 'line rooms' on the Sri Lankan tea estates and the tin-mining villages in Bolivia will testify. Workers who dislike this can be easily replaced. Moreover, many governments in the Third World have declared a variety of tax-holidays and tax-free zones, in order to attract investment, and this is a major advantage for the corporations. In these conditions the transnationals find it cheaper to produce manufactured goods in some Third World societies, especially the Middle Income or 'Newly Industrializing Countries' (the NICs), like Mexico, Brazil, Hong Kong, Singapore, South Korea and Taiwan. Many of the goods produced there (shoes, radios, television sets, textiles and other clothing) are shipped to the industrialized countries for sale in the large markets for such consumer goods there.[73] It is for these reasons that such 'export platforms', as they have been called, especially when located in insulated 'export zones', are said to contribute little to the wider 'development' of the host society.

In these respects the transnationals have both sustained and extended the uneven productive and distributive patterns of world politics which were described above. Some of the forms and particulars have changed: but the central principles remain the same. The control, use and production of most world resources, from the sixteenth century to the present, have increasingly come under the power of a narrow band of societies and a yet narrower band of corporate institutions within them. Moreover, the distribution of the benefits of these global operations remains firmly skewed in the direction of the industrial societies of the West, where the *internal* distribution of these benefits, as shall be seen later, also remains uneven. The cumulative effects of this in the post-war years have been to *increase* the gap between the rich and the poor countries.[74]

The merchants and early industrialists were able to operate in a relatively unregulated and loose institutional environment of power and social organization - and to transform it. So too, the modern transnationals operate in a largely unregulated and divided global structure of power and international organization. The international agencies (like the UN), which are supposed collectively to represent the societies of the world and to lay down procedures for governing the relations between them, are flimsy. The vast bulk of relations between societies - the politics of resource control and use - are effectively beyond their grasp. Few international laws constrain the transnationals, although some feeble 'codes of conduct' are recommended.

That some societies in the Third World (for example, Chile under Allende, Jamaica and Tanzania) have at various times tried to resist this, is hardly surprising. But what can they do? To whom or what do they appeal for assistance or, as they see it, justice? Appeals to the UN or other international institutions or negotiating conferences (like the United Nations Conference on Trade and Development, UNCTAD) expose the central fact that such institutions have neither control nor power over the transnationals. But this too is not surprising. For power in such international bodies is in the hands of representatives of governments (as is the World Bank, as shown in chapter 5). And the prevailing ideology in public policy in the industrial West is generally hostile to government intervention *or* public participation in the direction of how resources should be used, produced and distributed. Indeed, it is fair to say that most Western governments both encourage and support the foreign activities of their corporations. They seek actively to promote the diplomatic circumstances which favour the activities of the corporations. In many cases, relations between the corporations and governments in the West are very close.

IX

Modern politics in both global and domestic terms simply cannot be understood unless analysed against this background. The next three chapters will look at some aspects of the politics of particular Third World and industrial societies. But for the moment there are some points to make by way of conclusion.

It needs to be said that all Europeans did not in general set out consciously to destroy or underdevelop the world they had sought to 'discover' and whose riches and opportunities they prized. There were many groups and individuals in the course of this long and complex history who acted, by their own standards, with the best of motives. One can read of their lives and activities in the various accounts of travellers, missionaries and administrators who believed that they were bringing light and civilization to a dark world. There were others who cheated and robbed and killed for gain. The various Companies and colonial administrations not only coerced labour and drained valuable resources from the territories, but they also built roads, railways, dams and bridges. They mapped and measured, helped to eradicate certain diseases, dug wells, introduced new crops and improved animal breeds. They built schools and introduced Western scientific knowledge.

Is it possible to draw a balance sheet of empire? Were the costs to the societies of the wider world greater than the benefits? How does one calculate the moral economy of European expansion? Is it possible to make generalizations which hold for all places over the whole period? Did empire do more good than harm?

There are those who say that, for Africa, at least, it did. They argue that imperialism was one of 'the most powerful engines of cultural diffusion in the history of Africa; its credit balance outweighs its debit account'.[75] This is not a view I share, as the burden of this chapter and previous ones will indicate. Moreover, such a conclusion would be quite untenable for most of the Americas - the indigenous societies there were effectively destroyed. The transformations which have occurred since then, in building new societies, have involved the incorporation of refugees from those prior societies in often menial and inferior positions throughout the area. And it is difficult to believe that the millions of people who today live in rural poverty or in the slums of Latin American, African and Asian towns are in any sense better off than their ancestors were as a result of this 'cultural diffusion', though the potential *may* be there.

But the real point to make about technical and other innovations - brought about through diffusion - is that these things are in general neutral, in themselves. Their value and their contribution to a society depends on their *use*. For you can introduce medicines, food, new techniques and new kinds of crops, animals or knowledge along roads and railway lines. *Or* you can ferry guns, labour, troops and raw materials in and out of a society, and use these means of communication to subordinate people for the benefit of those who control the railways and the mines and the farms. And it is also in general true that the benefits of most such innovations have been confined to a very few people, and have been uneven in their distribution, both socially and geographically. Moreover, individual motives are not at issue here - who are we to judge, and how are we to calculate? But what is at issue here is the structural legacy of European expansion into the wider world and its impact on the politics of individual societies. And on this, there are clearer conclusions to draw.

First, the conventional definition of economics, used in one of the most popular textbooks on the subject, is:[76]

> the study of how people and society end up *choosing*, with or without the use of money, to employ *scarce* resources that could have alternative uses - to *produce* various commodities and *distribute* them for consumption, now or in the future, among various persons and groups in society. Economics analyses the costs and benefits of improving patterns of resource use.

There is no question that economists have developed highly skilled techniques of analysis and measurement. However, I have tried to suggest in this and earlier chapters that the way resources have *actually* come to be used, produced and distributed in particular societies and globally simply cannot be understood fully or historically in the terms of conventional economic analysis or conventional political (i.e. institutional) analysis. But the study of *politics*, as defined and used here, can help to achieve such an understanding. Moreover, I have tried to show that the politics of the modern world have *not* been shaped by the cheerful if sharp competitive bustle of free international trade, nor by the allegedly impartial and universally beneficial effects of the laws of supply and demand or comparative advantage. At each point, from the time the Portuguese came to dominate large areas of the Asian spice trade to the modern operations of the transnational corporations, the ways in which resources have been obtained, used, produced, distributed and exchanged have, at different times, been accompanied by varying mixtures of compulsion (of labour, for instance), of force (of arms), of expropriation (of land), of theft (of treasures and cattle), of monopolies over raw materials, of protected markets, and the accumulating concentration of global capital, production, technology and marketing in a few hands. This is the result of *politics*, not the 'invisible' hand of 'economic forces'. And the hands are clearly visible. Different groups at different times in different places (traders, slavers, settlers, plantation owners, mining and manufacturing and trading companies, financial institutions), backed by governments, navies and armies, have used all these methods around the world and against each other to establish the central patterns of modern world politics, and still do.

Secondly, it is perhaps one of the stranger illusions of our age that so many societies in the modern world - in the West, in the Communist bloc and in the South - declare themselves to be 'democratic' (though most of course mean very different things by that term). In fact, the actual degree of concentration of control over resources - whether people, land, capital, technology, food or jobs - suggests entirely the opposite. The same is true for decisions about the use of such resources which directly affect our life chances. This is a theme which will recur in later chapters.

Thirdly, the politics of many societies in the Third World have come to be identified with pervasive hunger and malnutrition, and with both absolute and relative poverty. Many have narrow and uncertain resource bases, and some are vulnerable through their desperate dependence on foreign aid, loans and food imports. Few have healthy balances of trade or payments and many have mounting debt. Most display gross and visible inequalities between a fraction of very rich and a mass of very poor people. These circumstances are either punctuated by frequent and sharp conflicts between rival colour groups, cultures and classes over what little there is, or what should be done about it, or they are frozen (but rarely eliminated) by the iron hand of military rule.

The historical and international background sketched above helps to explain the politics of *some* but not all of this. To see how such problems and conflicts are both extended and expressed in such societies it is necessary to look in greater detail at the particulars of their domestic politics. This is done in the next chapter.

CHAPTER EIGHT

Scarcity, inequality and imbalance: politics in Third World societies

I

Poverty, war, famine, revolution, swollen urban slums, military coups, rural landlessness and hunger: when people think about the Third World, or 'the South' as it has more recently been called, it is often that images of these things come to mind. They are familiar items today on television screens and in newspaper headlines in the industrial societies of Europe and North America, or 'the North'. The faces and distended bellies of starving children, pictures of terrified refugees clutching small bundles of possessions, and the cruel clatter of gunfire can be seen and heard in our media, side by side with advertisements for sunny holidays, new cars or washing machines, and a great variety of food and drink. These problems are associated with strange (and often changing) names of distant places in Asia (like Kampuchea, formerly Cambodia; Bangladesh, formerly East Pakistan, and before that part of India); in Africa (like Ethiopia, formerly Abyssinia; Uganda, Upper Volta and Lesotho); and in Latin America and the Caribbean (like El Salvador, Nicaragua, Chile and Haiti).

What are the causes of such problems? And why do they seem to be concentrated in the Third World? It is sometimes said that the problems of these societies are entirely of their own making, owing to varying combinations of hostile climatic conditions, the general 'primitiveness' or 'backwardness' of the people, their high rates of population growth, their immaturity, corruption or incompetence, their pervasive 'traditionalism' and so on. Moreover, a corollary of such a view is that the material prosperity and advantages of the rich (usually industrialized) societies of the North (including the few Southern exceptions of Japan, Australia and New Zealand, for instance) are the result of the thrusting energies, intelligence and application of the Northerners. In short, the argument runs, we live in a more or less divided world in which the respective fortunes and fates of North and South are largely unconnected and that, historically, each society is primarily responsible for its own condition.

The starting-point for the argument of this chapter is really rather different. The fact that politics in Third World societies is examined separately here does *not* mean that there is something different in principle about them, or that they constitute a distinctive species of society. They do not. The fundamental variables of their politics are the same as those in any other society, past or present, although the forms, degrees and combinations of these variables are particularly extreme in many of them. Thus the same general framework of analysis which has been used in previous chapters must be used here. By asking the same kinds of questions as have been asked before about other societies – about resources and their use and distribution, about their structures of power and decision-making, and about their systems of social organization, culture and ideology – the problems referred to above become explicable. For these problems are not random, unexpected or sudden eruptions in their affairs. They can be explained by, and are central to, their politics. To understand their politics is to understand their poverty, and vice versa. The same is true for their slums, wars, famines, coups, counter-coups and revolutions.

Before turning to look at these issues, there are some important historical points to establish by way of background.

II

In a famous passage, Marx once observed that people 'make their own history, but they do not make it just as they please; they do not make it under circumstances chosen by themselves, but under circumstances directly encountered, given and transmitted from the past'.[1] What is true for people in this general sense is true for societies as wholes. As the previous chapter showed, the domestic politics of Third World societies have been directly and decisively influenced by Western penetration over the last five centuries, and especially the last 150 years. It is of the utmost importance to recognize the impact of this legacy of external relations and to trace its various implications for their current politics and problems.

Despite this, it would be quite wrong to suggest that these societies in the past were all and always harmonious, without crisis, cruelty or conflict. An earlier chapter showed that this was certainly not the case in Aztec society at the time of the Spanish conquest, and there have been other ruthless regimes, based on concentrated military organization and power.

For example, in Southern Africa in the early nineteenth century, there arose the Zulu kingdom from amongst a number of small Nguni chiefdoms. The main architect of this kingdom was Shaka, who built on the military expansionism of his predecessor, Dingiswayo. The details are not important here except to say that it was an authoritarian and predatory military dictatorship, which shattered many established rights, customs and institutions of the Zulus and neighbouring societies. Subjects and captives were put to death on the flimsiest of grounds, as Shaka sought to eliminate any signs of opposition. Between about 1820 and 1825 the military expansion of the kingdom 'had repercussions from the Cape Colonial frontier to Lake Tanganyika' as the Zulu *impis* attacked, conquered and absorbed communities, devastated the countryside, seized cattle and burned grain.[2] Communities in the vicinity, fleeing from this onslaught, catapulted into others, creating further disruption and terror on a wide front. Whether the causes of the Zulu expansion lay more in population pressures or the wish to control the South-east African trade routes cannot be known for sure: there is not enough evidence. Shaka's downfall, in the end, was brought about by his assassination (by his half brothers). Such an end is not uncommon for military regimes or dictators, for what means are available to remove them, other than force and violence? Similar episodes may be found in the history of some other societies in the Third World, often leading to the emergence of the kinds of localized empires mentioned in the previous chapter.

Moreover, slavery was not an innovation of the European colonial era, though during that period it was extended and commercialized on a scale never seen before. Not only had slavery been a fact of life in the classical world of Greece and Rome, but it was found all round the Mediterranean basin, in ancient China, India, Egypt and throughout the Islamic world, as well as in both West and East Africa, and also South America. The capture, ownership and sale of other human beings has thus been found in quite a few societies which are today part of the Third World.[3]

So, not all the societies in Africa, Asia and Latin America were either egalitarian or democratic. In all parts of the world where settled agriculture has developed, there have been many instances of the emergence of steep hierarchies of power, wealth and status – often accompanied by sharp social divisions between groups in the society, as the chapter on the Aztecs also illustrated. In some parts of Asia, especially the dry zones, these hierarchies were often associated with the establishment and management of complex irrigation systems. Perhaps the most concrete expressions of social hierarchies may be seen in the monuments, dams, buildings, palaces, walls and temples found around the world. The great stone structures of the Incas and Aztecs, the Zimbabwe ruins, the pyramids of Egypt, the temples of India and other parts of Asia, the irrigation tanks and canals of Sri Lanka and the Great Wall of China, to mention a few, are unlikely to have been built without the massive deployment of labour, organized and controlled by ruling bureaucracies, castes, classes or aristocracies of one kind or another. Such regimes, in their wealth and power, enjoyed very high social status and esteem, often suffused with religious associations which gave them god-like authority. They were sustained by an upward flow of resources in the form of labour or tax or tribute. Around the world, different methods of doing this have been evolved, for no élite – then or now – could live such sumptuous lives, relative to the rest of their society, without the underlying population doing the work and generating sufficient surplus to support them. Often, élite control of local trade was an additional source of wealth and power. Social and political hierarchies have hence usually reflected and organized these unequal patterns of resource use and distribution in the politics of all societies.

For instance, the caste system in India reflects historically sharp divisions of labour, opportunity, rights and wealth.[4] In the East African kingdom of Bunyoro (in what is today Uganda) even the most important officials would kneel before the king, the Mukama, when approaching him. Tribute - in the form of crops, cattle, beer and even women - flowed upwards through a hierarchy of lesser chiefs to reach the Mukama. He, in turn, was expected to be a giver, not only of feasts and gifts but also of assistance in difficult times, and to organize protection. In all such societies, that two-way contract lies at the heart of 'feudal' politics.[5] But where that essential contract was strained or ruptured - often by rulers or their officials squeezing the people beyong their capacity or endurance - the typical result has been rebellion, a theme which runs, for example, through much of Chinese history. It can be found also in the folk tales and oral histories of many other societies where stories of 'bad' rulers and how they were overthrown are common.

Thus it is quite clear that none of the major regions of the Third World has been innocent, historically, of examples of fierce conflict, gross inequality and the lack of effective participation by people in decisions about the use and distribution of resources. These instances pre-dated direct colonial rule or the indirect forms of Western penetration, or had nothing to do with them. Hence it would be quite incorrect, also, to suggest that *all* the problems of all Third World societies can be laid at the door of European expansionism in the colonial era or transnational enterprises in the modern age. Many problems in some of these societies build on prior structures of inequality.

None the less, this is not to say that the politics of *all* societies in the Third World have been characterized by such relationships. Many thousands of human communities - some small in scale, some large; some composed of a few associated villages, some of many - lived for long periods in conditions of relative internal peace in their politics, though they experienced problems arising from natural conditions (such as drought, flood or disease, affecting them or their animals), and from conflict with their neighbours. Through their politics, societies of foragers, shifting cultivators, nomadic pastoralists and settled agricultural communities in all parts of the world established both efficient uses and relatively egalitarian distributions of resources, often in very difficult ecological circumstances.

They ensured this through a wide variety of democratic procedures, primarily involving a combination of group rights in resource use; checks and balances between sections of the community; and decentralized patterns of decision-making about such matters. Wherever this has occurred one may usually find a common structural theme at the heart of these politics. All the main social groups in such societies - tribal sections, villages, families, husbands, wives, men and women, for instance - enjoyed balanced, comparable and generally inalienable rights (though not always the *same* rights) of access, use and benefit in *some* aspect of community resources. For example, different hunting bands or villages or tribal sections had more or less equivalent rights of access to land, water and pasture - as illustrated earlier in respect of the !Kung and Maasai. The same has been true for societies of shifting cultivators, like the Iban of Borneo, now Sarawak in East Malaysia. Here, rights in land usage around the village (or longhouses) in which they live, accrued to families who marked out a particular area of jungle and cleared it for cultivation. This is not to say that there was never conflict at the margins between !Kung camps, Maasai kraals or localities, and Iban longhouses. There was; but the usual outcome of such disputes was to restore balanced rights and access, not the accumulation of territory.

Within such village or social units, similar principles of resource access and use applied to the component families. And within the families, in turn, it was common for both men and women to enjoy distinctive rights in domestic resource use and control. For instance, amongst shifting and other cultivators in many African and Asian societies, women did (and still do) much of the farming, and it was they who had rights to bring new land under cultivation. Similarly, in many African societies, women had important rights to land and the crops grown on it, and in some cases a distinction was drawn between the fields of men and women, and their crops.[6] Amongst the Maasai, as pointed out earlier, women enjoyed particularly strong rights of control over resource use and distribution in their homes. However, this is not to say that in all such societies the relations between men and women were equal or without assumptions or institutions involving relations of superiority and inferiority. They were not.

It is also important to see how such rights were sustained in practice by wider features of social organization and culture. For instance, marriage was not simply a relationship between two people but between two families, often from other villages. The maltreatment of a wife, or infringement of her rights, might involve sanctions by her family against the husband or his family, and hence possible tensions between villages, which the community would be concerned, if at all possible, to subdue. Alternatively, inheritance of both certain rights and property through both the male and the female lines helped to sustain balance in domestic politics.

Interestingly, these patterns of balance were often found even in those societies where there had emerged a powerful state, dominated by chiefs or rulers. Thus, people in the villages of the Third World societies (as individuals or groups) were not separated from, or deprived of, access to the resources which were needed by all to sustain life. Hence, in the histories (often oral) of these societies around the world, or in the accounts of early European travellers and the studies of colonial officials and anthropologists, one does not often encounter reports of landlessness, begging, rural impoverishment and helplessness brought about by *social* conditions.

In short, societies in the Third World, before the systematic penetration by the West, were extremely varied in their politics. But in most, at village level especially, there was substantial autonomy, self-sufficiency and balance between and within them. In many, of course, their lives were punctuated by periodic outbreaks of hunger or disease, brought about by natural catastrophes. And in some, extremely powerful and elaborate state structures emerged, dominated by kings, princes, chiefs, emperors and priests, who established more or less extensive local regimes or empires and who lived in relative splendour. And everywhere, there are examples of tyrants, oppression, exploitation and inequality.

There is still, today, great variety in the politics of Third World societies. But there are also *new* common themes. The local self-sufficiency and relative autonomy of village communities have now almost universally disappeared, or are doing so. Profound inequalities have opened up both within and between rural and urban areas, especially in the twentieth century. The problems of landlessness, poverty, slums and conflict referred to at the start of this chapter are now more generally the rule, not the exception. In the main, these are the symptoms of chronic imbalance. Previously balanced or equivalent rights of access in the use of local resources have been savagely disrupted. The commercialization of rural life has generally been accompanied by the development of systems of private ownership of the key resources, such as land. Control of such resources - the essential basis of rural power - has thus usually shifted from the community to individuals and companies, sometimes in the villages, sometimes to absentee landlords in the towns or abroad. Private, state or joint ownership of rich mineral deposits, and the mines which extract them, has brought great wealth to a few, relatively well-paid jobs to a tiny minority, and intermittently substantial revenues to the state, often maintained by a sprawling and relatively well-heeled bureaucracy.

Thus, urban inequalities run parallel to rural ones, often grow out of them, and reinforce them. The imbalances are striking: for instance, between the often breathtakingly rich minorities and the grindingly poor majorities; between town and country; between glistening military hardware and run-down or (more commonly) non-existent social services, like schools or clinics. And it is especially noticeable in the contrast between the often lush, irrigated plantations growing cash crops for export (fruits, vegetables, sugar, tea, coffee, tobacco, etc.), owned or run by transnational corporations or in association with the local élites, expatriate or native, on the one hand, and the landless or near-landless peasants on the other. These latter are hardly able to scratch a living from poor, dry soils and have to depend on badly paid and sometimes seasonal labouring jobs to buy food which is often imported at great cost to the society.

The purpose of this chapter is to use the framework of analysis adopted in the book to help explain these conditions and how they are sustained. In doing so, the relations between historical, external and internal factors must always be borne in mind, for together these have helped to shape the central characteristics of modern Third World politics.

These are big themes and complex issues. An introductory chapter of this kind can only touch on aspects of some of them. So, the rest of the chapter is concerned to do three main things. First, to introduce readers to some of the underlying characteristics of Third World societies in general; secondly, to illustrate these with reference to the politics of some particular societies; and, thirdly, to underline again the utility of the approach used in this book as a starting-point for the analysis of politics in all societies.

III

The term 'the Third World' has been used loosely over the last twenty years to refer to that large group of societies in Latin America, the Caribbean, Africa, some of the Middle East, much of Asia and Oceania which mostly have been (and in some very few remaining instances still are) under the colonial rule - in whole or in part - of mainly European powers. That is the general sense in which the term will be used in the present chapter. As a category it is not particularly satisfactory, but it is a great deal better than some of the earlier terms used, like 'primitive' and 'backward'. The 'Third' world was originally supposed to be differentiated as poor and non-aligned from the 'First' world of mainly Western 'capitalist' societies, and the 'Second' world of mainly Eastern European 'communist' societies. But such distinctions were never wholly valid and are even less so today. Thus, as used here, the term will exclude those poor societies of Southern Europe (notably in the Mediterranean basin) such as Yugoslavia, Cyprus, Greece, Spain and Portugal, though some of them have - or until recently did have - many of the characteristics of Third World societies in Africa, Asia and Latin America. One - Portugal, until the mid-1970s - not only shared some typical Third World features, but paradoxically retained a vast empire in Angola and Mozambique. The term will also *exclude* the oil-rich states of the Middle East, which are clearly exceptional for obvious reasons. In terms of their GNP *per capita*, for instance, the United Arab Emirates and Kuwait are now the richest societies in the world and have a surplus of capital, though in some other respects they are not unlike much of the Third World.

It is none the less important at the outset to stress the diversity of the many societies which are here classed as part of the Third World. This can be illustrated in countless ways. For example, one can (as the World Bank does) identify well over one hundred 'developing countries' (another shorthand term for these societies). They can in turn be divided into two further broad categories, according to their GNP *per capita*: the Middle Income societies (like Algeria, Jamaica, Peru and Thailand), and the Low Income societies (like Bangladesh, Kampuchea, Chad, Zaire and Haiti). Some other Third World societies - like China and Cuba for example - are said to be distinctive for many reasons, amongst which is their high degree of central planning. Another reason is that - unlike Chile or Kenya or the Philippines - they are not committed in their politics to the private ownership and use of resources or to the market as a means of distribution, but are opposed to this. Furthermore, within the societies of the Third World there is that group which is sometimes called the Newly Industrializing Countries (the NICs) such as Brazil, Mexico, Malaysia and South Korea, which have begun to develop significant industrial manufacturing sectors in the last twenty years.[7] However, they all retain at least *some* of the characteristics of other Third World societies, and are included for the purposes of the present discussion.

There are other features of diversity amongst these societies, for example with regard to their population sizes. Some have very large populations, such as China (now over 1000 million), India (about 700 million), Nigeria (about 83 million) and Mexico (about 68 million). These contrast with Botswana (775,000), Barbados (253,000) and Brunei (210,000). But population size on its own may not be specially significant, though both small or large populations under different circumstances can either hinder or enhance the fortunes of a society. Population size relative to land surface may be more important. And there are some very small societies which none the less have very densely packed populations. Thus the island of Mauritius in the Indian ocean has a small population of less than a million but a high density of 450 people per square kilometre, compared to Nigeria's density of 86 and China's density of 93 people per square kilometre. Bangladesh has a population of 87 million but a very high density of 564 people per square kilometre, compared to India's 192. (For comparison's sake, Britain and France, with roughly similar population sizes - 55 and 53 million respectively - have very different densities: 229 in Britain compared with 97 in France.)[8] But even this kind of data is not necessarily revealing, for populations are seldom to be found evenly spread over the land surfaces of their countries. The regional quality, usefulness or desirability of land may vary greatly within a country. One is thus likely to find people concentrated in the more sought-after areas. So, distributional factors are important, too, when considering populations in relation to land and other resources.

In this preliminary discussion of Third World diversity, it is clear that, even in terms of relatively conventional criteria - GNP *per capita*, degree of industrialization, role of government in 'economic' planning, population size and densities - there are great differences between these societies. This must always be borne in mind. But despite this, they all share some general characteristics apart from their geographical location and their past direct colonial or indirect associations with the West. What are they?

IV

With a few exceptions, most Third World societies (or significant parts of them) are within the tropics, between roughly thirty degrees north and south of the equator. The ecological conditions found in these regions vary from dense, rainy jungles to sparse, parched deserts. These are not the temperate zones of the world. In some areas the rainfall is sudden, torrential and violent, accompanied by typhoons, hurricanes and severe monsoons. Elsewhere, there are often very long periods - in some cases years - when almost no rain falls.[9] Some parts of these countries are mountainous and difficult to farm: others are flat. But, generally, the conditions are harsh, and they are not easy for human societies to shape and use productively.

Yet everywhere in these difficult circumstances different societies *have* historically achieved remarkable adaptations. Earlier chapters showed how the !Kung did so in the desert conditions of the Kalahari, and how the pastoral Maasai did so in the relatively marginal lands of East Africa. In the Valley of Mexico, as shown earlier, the Aztecs developed their agriculture with the help of the floating allotments, the *chinampas*, on which they grew food. In the dense jungles of the island of Borneo, Iban shifting cultivators evolved viable and self-sufficient agricultural systems. Elsewhere, in the high mountain areas, communities have made the land productive by hacking terraces from the steep slopes, as in the hill areas of Nepal or the Philippines. Complex irrigation systems transformed the dry zones of northern Sri Lanka - and elsewhere in Asia - into fertile rice-growing areas.

Thus, around the globe, ingenuity, energy, cooperation and innovative capacities - some of the most important distinguishing features of the human species - enabled communities to develop the viable productive basis of different kinds of societies, despite often difficult ecological conditions. These adaptations were both possible and effective largely because the local communities which composed these societies enjoyed substantial autonomy over their resources and decisions about their usage, and committed them, at least, to self-sufficiency in food production. They were, of course, vulnerable to assaults of nature, but none the less had the *social* means of re-starting and re-establishing their ways of life. However, they were even more vulnerable to the impact of political changes, brought about by various forms of Western penetration. And the problem here has been that many of those changes - in land tenure, commercialization of agriculture, emergence of wage-labour - were not only deeply disruptive of their politics, but generated some of the problems referred to earlier.

V

Most people in the Third World still live in the rural areas and work in agriculture. The average for all Third World societies is about 70 per cent, but this conceals important regional differences between and within the major areas. The average for sub-Saharan Africa is 83 per cent; for East Asia and the Pacific it is 70 per cent; for South Asia it is 87 per cent; for Latin America it is 40 per cent. Examples of the extremes are 96 per cent for Nepal and 22 per cent for Chile.[10] It might seem reasonable to assume that, with such a strong rural and agricultural concentration of people, most Third World societies should be able to feed all their people adequately, as they once usually did. But this is increasingly no longer the case. Many now import food, or receive food aid, often from the industrial societies. Globally, the USA is the largest net exporter of food-grains, for example, and Asia is the largest net importer. But from east to west in the Third World one finds large amounts of very scarce foreign currency being spent on food imports: in Bangladesh, India, Indonesia, Egypt, Chad, Guinea-Bissau, Botswana, many parts of the Caribbean, and Colombia, for example.

Yet there is a paradox. While many of these societies appear to have a food deficit, *very* few of even the poorest have inadequate food production. Many actually export agricultural produce and some even export food. Despite this, and perhaps in some cases even because of it (to be considered shortly), a central characteristic of many Third World societies is that substantial sections of their populations (both rural and urban) receive inadequate nutrition. The Food and Agriculture Organization (FAO) of the United Nations estimated in the mid-1970s that about 1.5 billion people were undernourished or malnourished. The problem affects children especially. The Fourth World Food Survey of the FAO in 1977 showed, for instance, that some 55 per cent of Indian children, 40 per cent of Cameroonian children and 32 per cent of Guayanese children suffered from severe or moderate malnutrition.[11] In Mexico, nearly 80 per cent of rural children are undernourished, while livestock (much of it raised for export to North America) consumes more grain than the entire rural population.[12] In Bangladesh, half the families consume less than the bare minimum of calories to sustain life properly, though there is sufficient grain to feed the entire population adequately. However, many of those who control the bulk of rice growing and distribution in the private sector find that they can get better prices for it by selling it through a flourishing black market across the border in India.[13] In Zaire (the former Belgian Congo), the intake of protein per capita is one of the lowest in the world, and most rural people are underfed. Once the country exported food, now some 20 per cent of the value of its imports is taken up by importing food items. In India, up to 40 per cent of the population is unable to get enough food for an adequate diet. Yet for most of the 1970s rice and wheat harvests enabled the government to maintain massive food stocks, closely guarded, and in 1978 the country actually exported a million tons of wheat.[14]

The *real* reason why people in the Third World go hungry is generally *not* that there is either globally or nationally a food shortage, or that the expansion of food production is impossible, or that there are too many people. Globally, food production has not only kept up with population growth but has surpassed it. World grain production in the 1970s was adequate to provide every person with more than 3000 calories and adequate protein, quite apart from other local foods like nuts, beans, root crops, fruits, vegetables, meat and fish. The additional food needed to feed the presently malnourished, if it could reach them, is in any event not especially great: in calorific terms it is equal to about 37 million tons of grain, which is one-fiftieth of global grain production and less than 10 per cent of grain fed to animals in the rich industrial societies. Global averages of course conceal national food deficiencies in some Third World societies. In many, there *is* enough food for all their members. In others, even without bringing new land under cultivation, food production could be tripled. On a global basis, less than half of the cultivable land is being farmed. The *Global 2000 Report*, commissioned by President Carter in 1977 (and 'disregarded' by President Reagan), predicted that while world population would increase by 50 per cent, world food production would increase by 90 per cent by the end of the twentieth century, yet the outlook for many of the world's poor will be no better.[15]

The real reason for world hunger, and especially Third World hunger, must hence be traced to politics, and especially to the *politics of distribution* of a variety of necessary resources. People go hungry either because they are denied access to the means of producing enough food for themselves (which may be land, agricultural inputs or credit, for instance) or because they cannot afford to buy it (since the price may be too high or their wages too low) or they are unemployed and hence especially vulnerable.

VI

Associated with these characteristics is a further aspect of the 'agrarian paradox' referred to earlier. It has been described most dramatically for Africa in the following terms:[16]

a continent unable to produce sufficient food to provide the majority of its citizens with even a barely minimal diet has been able to record sharp increases in its annual production of agricultural goods destined for external markets.

This is true for many parts of the Third World and is best illustrated by pointing to the reliance on perhaps one or two cash crops, which are grown for export and on which these societies depend for the bulk of their foreign earnings. These crops (coffee, cocoa, sugar, tea, cotton, rubber, tobacco, ground-nuts, etc.) account for anything between 50 and 80 per cent of their export earnings.[17] Some specific examples will help to anchor the point and underline one aspect of what is sometimes called 'dependency'.

More than 70 per cent of the export earnings of Argentina comes from agriculture and animal husbandry (meat, corn, wool and hides); in Bangladesh, jute and jute products account for 70 per cent of export earnings; in Burundi, over 90 per cent of earnings derive from the export of coffee, and in Chad 75 per cent comes from cotton exports; in Cuba, about 80 per cent of foreign revenue is accounted for by sugar exports, and in Colombia over 60 per cent comes from coffee. In Gambia, the main item is ground-nuts, in St Lucia it is bananas, in Ghana it is cocoa; in Kenya, tea and coffee are the major ones, and in Sri Lanka they are tea, rubber and coconut.[18]

This deep reliance on a few agricultural export crops usually started in the course of the colonial histories of these societies. Cash crops of these kinds were encouraged by the colonial authorities for three main purposes. First, because such commodities were wanted or needed in the metropolitan countries, cheaply; secondly, it was believed that the encouragement of cash cropping in the colonies would stimulate wider 'economic' development there; thirdly, the revenue which the local colonial governments would derive from this would help to make the colonies self-sufficient in terms of administrative costs and hence not be a drain on the metropolitan countries. This was particularly the case in colonial Africa and Asia. In Latin America and the Caribbean the *latifundio* estates and large plantations had their origins in the Iberian settlement of South America and the slave era. Once this process had begun, it was difficult for post-independence governments to alter the basic patterns in the productive systems. They had been orientated to external demands. Moreover, locally within the societies, powerful domestic social groups (small as they often were) had developed strong interests in maintaining these patterns of production, for their wealth and power were bound up with them and their association with governments was intimate. Hence, not many independent governments wished to alter the basic patterns, and in any event they often subscribed to the theories of 'economic development' inherited from the colonial powers and more recently elaborated in the West. Thus, these patterns of dependency continue today.

However, what is noticeable in many societies is that very often the 'success of export production has been achieved almost entirely at the expense of an economically impoverished peasant food-producing sector'.[19] Indeed, one study of the relationship between agricultural cash cropping and food production shows that productivity in *food* agriculture is generally lower in those societies where *export* agriculture plays a significant part in the productive system.[20] Moreover, it has generally been the case that export crops have been grown on large plantations or by bigger farmers – in Africa, in the twentieth century, these have been dominated by expatriate firms or by white settlers. These sectors of the productive systems, often concentrated in the better land areas, have also attracted the lion's share of investment and supporting infrastructure, like roads, storage facilities, marketing networks, research and various kinds of agricultural extension.

By contrast, the subsistence food-producing sector, usually undertaken by small peasant farmers, has been starved of investment. Seldom, for example, does one come across marketing or production boards in Africa which are directed at improving *food* production for local consumption. Moreover, in the last fifteen years, in many parts of the Third World, large transnational corporations have become deeply involved in growing vegetables, fruits and other luxury items for North American and European consumption, as well as raising livestock for the international market. One sees this in Mexico, other parts of Central America, the Sahel region of West Africa, Ethiopia, Malaysia and the Philippines.[21]

Not all the societies of the Third World rely so heavily on agricultural export items. Some are very dependent on the export earnings from minerals or crude petroleum (in the case of Ecuador, Venezuela, Nigeria and Indonesia). Societies which derive more than 50 per cent of their export earnings from one or two mineral resources include Bolivia (tin); Chile (until very recently, up to 60 per cent of its export earnings came from copper); Botswana (diamonds); Jamaica (alumina and bauxite); Zaire (cobalt and copper) and Zambia (copper).[22]

It is sometimes thought that societies in the Third World, therefore, have two productive systems: on the one hand, the 'modern' export-oriented and capital intensive plantation, cash-cropping or mining sector; and, on the other, the 'traditional', poor, small-scale peasant farming sector. There is some obvious plausibility in such a view of the 'dual' economy, as it is sometimes called. But the error is to assume that these sectors are isolated and unrelated to each other. This is not the case. For just as the global patterns of inequality between North and South are best explained by tracing the character of the relations *between* them, so too are the politics of many societies in the Third World best understood by seeing the relations between these sectors.

It has already been mentioned that the areas of export agriculture have attracted the bulk of investment and supporting services. The same has often been true for the allocation of resources to mining centres and their associated urban surroundings. The relative lack of resources for the development of food crops, the confinement of subsistence food production to poorer areas and more marginal lands, and the relative underdevelopment of these regions is thus not an isolated phenomenon. Similarly, from colonial days to the present, much of the labour that has worked the plantations and the mines has been both pushed and pulled out of the subsistence areas by taxation policies and the relative attraction of jobs, facilities and wages. In short, the *alleged* developmental benefits of 'modern' export sectors have regularly been achieved at the cost of the relative underdevelopment of the 'traditional' sector. The claim that, in time, the developmental benefits would 'trickle down' to the rest of the society has, in general, not yet been borne out.

VII

While this gives some idea of one aspect of 'dependency', there are others which are closely related. Two in particular must be noted.

First, primary commodities - both agricultural and mineral - have been subject in the last twenty-five years to considerable fluctuations in price on the world market. Some examples will help to illustrate the point.[23]

The annual average price of copper, in dollars per ton, was $678 in 1960, and had climbed to $1528 by 1966, but then sagged to $1081 in 1971, rose to $2058 in 1974, and fell again to about $1200 in 1977, and has continued to fluctuate - first up, then down - since then. It may easily be imagined how such fluctuations affect societies like Zambia, Zaire and Chile, which have depended heavily for export earnings on this single commodity. Between 1974 and 1975 alone, the value of imports which Zambia could buy fell by 45 per cent, and its

GNP fell by 15 per cent because of the plummeting price of copper.

The price of sugar, in dollars per ton, stood at $69 in 1960. It rose to $184 in 1963, had dropped to $46 in 1965, then rose to $160 in 1972, and up to a peak at $655 in 1974, but by 1978 was down to $172, though it rose again to $894 towards the end of 1980. Cocoa, coconut oil and other coconut produce, rubber and coffee have also fluctuated in similar ways, thus affecting the revenues of the Third World societies which depend crucially on the export earnings from these primary products. Such fluctuations make it very difficult indeed for governments to plan their development expenditure with any confidence in the medium or long term, since the prices shift - often between months - so quickly.

Secondly, the overall terms of trade of many primary products (with the important exception of oil and some minerals) against manufactured goods have in general been declining over the last twenty-five years.[24] This means that the volume of imported goods (especially manufactured goods, and particularly oil) which can be bought by a given volume of exports of primary commodities has been getting less and less. In other words, the price of imports has been getting higher and higher. The pattern varies as between Third World societies, but it is clear that the poorer societies (those with *per capita* GNPs of less than $800, mainly in Africa and Asia) have suffered most, with the purchasing power of their exports declining steadily since 1970.[25] Their plight in this respect was dramatized by former Prime Minister Manley of Jamaica when he pointed out that 21 tons of sugar could buy one tractor in 1965. However, by 1979, that same tractor cost the equivalent of 58 tons of sugar. Similar adverse terms of trade can be illustrated with respect to many other primary products: for example it took 3½ tons of Mozambican tea in 1975 to buy one truck, but by 1980 it required 33 tons.[26]

These problems do not affect all societies in the Third World equally, but the general patterns are common to many. During the 1970s, especially, they have become particularly acute for those societies which have had to continue to import oil to meet their energy requirements. The regular increases in the price of oil have meant that the costs of imported manufactured goods from the industrial societies have also shot up dramatically.

A further consequence of all this has been that many Third World societies have experienced persistent balance-of-payments crises. That is, they have simply not been able to pay for the goods which they must continue to import, like machinery, transport equipment, a variety of manufactured goods, as well as things such as fertilizers and food. This, in turn, has led to a further dimension of dependency which has undermined their capacity to direct their affairs independently - chronic debt. For, in order to cover their import bills, societies in the Third World have had to borrow heavily. The level of external debt of many Third World societies has simply rocketed in the last decade. Their total outstanding debt (*excluding* the oil-exporting countries) increased more than sixfold between 1970 and 1980, from US $48 billion to US $301 billion, and is still rising.[27] The amounts owed by some individual countries are very high. For example, in 1979/80 Bangladesh owed more than $3 billion, Brazil owed more than $35 billion, Egypt owed more than $11 billion, the Philippines owed $16 billion, and Indonesia more than $14 billion.[28]

Such debts have to be repaid. For some countries, the repayments of these loans have not all commenced, and so they have not yet felt the pinch, but they soon will. For those countries which are now paying back their loans (including interest on the borrowing) one way of indicating the burden they now carry is to express the annual amount of debt repayment as a percentage of the value of their exports. This figure – the so-called 'debt service ratio' – gives a good idea of how much of their earnings from exports goes directly out again in the form of debt repayments. More or less *one-quarter* of the export earnings of Burma, Sierra Leone, Guinea, Peru and Costa Rica went on debt repayment in 1979. More or less *one-third* of the export earnings of Argentina, Mauritania, Sudan, Bolivia and Brazil went on debt repayment in the same year, and a breath-taking *64 per cent* of Mexico's earnings went the same way.[29] Sometimes debts can be re-scheduled or even deferred; sometimes new borrowings can be obtained to cover outstanding debts, though this is usually easier for countries which have either good or stable export earnings prospects, *or* are politically or militarily important to the creditors.

But seldom can any of this be done without cost. And often the cost is not simply financial but may have direct influences on the politics of the society concerned, for those who lend money are in a position to impose conditions for the loan. The International Monetary Fund, the IMF, is especially well known for a broad pattern of conditions which include: reduction in welfare expenditure (for example eliminating or cutting food subsidies), devaluation of currency to boost exports, and the encouragement of private enterprise (both foreign and domestic) as against public ownership. Jamaica, Chile, Egypt and Tanzania have all experienced the insistence of such conditions, along with many other Third World societies. In recent years, however, much international lending to the Third World has come from private financial institutions in the West, not official ones. The terms and conditions of such loans are rarely made public, but it would be very surprising indeed if they differed much from the broad lines advocated by institutions like the IMF.

It can clearly be seen, therefore, how these various aspects of dependency give rise to and sustain each other, and how far-reaching are the implications of these external factors for the politics of Third World societies, especially as they affect their capacity to direct their own affairs. Moreover, as mentioned in the previous chapter, much of the manufacturing industry which has grown up in some Third World societies (notably the NICs) has been initiated by transnational corporations seeking the advantages of low-cost labour, favourable tax arrangements and the strict control of trade union activity. The products of many of these enterprises are generally made for export to richer markets, for only very small sections of Third World populations can afford to buy them.

VIII

These features in the productive systems of many Third World societies are accompanied by sharp inequalities in their distributional patterns, both regionally and socially. One of the most important divisions is between rural and urban areas. As one writer describes it:[30]

> The rural sector contains most of the poverty, and most of the low-cost sources of potential advance; but the urban sector contains most of the articulateness, organization and power. So the urban classes have been able to 'win' most of the rounds of the struggle with the countryside; but in doing so they have made the development process needlessly slow and unfair. Scarce land, which might grow millets and beansprouts for hungry villagers, instead produces a trickle of costly calories from meat and milk, which few except the urban rich (who have ample protein anyway) can afford. Scarce investment, instead of going into water-pumps to grow rice, is wasted on urban motorways. Scarce human skills design and administer, not clean village wells and agricultural extension services, but world boxing championships in showpiece stadia. Resource allocations, within the city and the village as well as between them, reflect urban priorities rather than equity or efficiency.

However, despite this 'urban bias', it should not be thought that all rural areas are deprived or poor, or that all people in those areas suffer accordingly. As indicated earlier, some sectors of the rural productive system have benefited greatly from the concentration of investment in them for export agriculture. But, side by side with this, the poverty and inequality can be seen in the naked figures for landlessness and near-landlessness. 'Near-landlessness' means having so little and usually such poor land that it cannot support a family, and it is often the last stage before total landlessness.

The data for Latin America are particularly stark. The general picture here is of a small number of more or less vast estates, a large number of small farms, and massive landlessness. For the region as a whole, something like the top 2 per cent of the farming population in 1973 controlled 47 per cent of the land. This is made up of mainly large estates, few in number, occupying anything from 37 per cent (in Argentina) to 82 per cent (in Chile and Peru) of the total farmed area. In Brazil, the large estates accounted for only 23 per cent of the *number* of farms, but occupied nearly 80 per cent of the farmed area. It is common, therefore, to find very high levels of landlessness and near-landlessness throughout Latin America. For example, in Bolivia, Brazil, El Salvador and Guatemala the figures for landless and near-landless households are all above 70 per cent of rural households, and some are nearer to 85 per cent.

The situation in Asia is not much better. In Bangladesh, Java (Indonesia), the Philippines and Sri Lanka, rural landlessness or near-landlessness is over 70 per cent. In India the top 22 per cent of landowners hold 76 per cent of the land, and landlessness has been increasing there over the last thirty years, as it has too in Bangladesh and the Philippines. For South Asia as a whole (Bangladesh, India and Pakistan) the absolute numbers of rural poor have been growing steadily over the last two decades.[31]

In Africa, such problems are generally not so extreme, or at least not yet. But in those areas where there was settler colonialism, the inequality in land distribution has been sharp. In Kenya, for instance, by 1953, some 4000 settlers owned the bulk of the good land in the so-called 'White Highlands' (over 7 million acres). In Southern Rhodesia, by 1969, Europeans controlled almost 49 million acres, or roughly half the land of the country, though they accounted for only 5 per cent of the population. Much of this was the best land of the colony, and close to the important railway lines. It is hardly surprising that in the bitter struggle for an independent and democratic Zimbabwe, the land question was central. Today, the problem of how to redistribute land back to African farmers without disrupting food production is a very complex issue. In Kenya, much of the Highlands was sold back to African farmers, but much of the basic inequality in distribution remains.[32]

With a majority of people living in the rural areas in most Third World societies, such levels of landlessness or near-landlessness are inevitably associated with severe rural poverty. The figures for overall income distribution confirm this. In Bolivia, El Salvador, Nicaragua (before the revolution), Brazil and Jamaica, the top 5 per cent of the population in the 1970s received between 30 and 42 per cent of income, while in none of these countries did the bottom 20 per cent receive more than 4 per cent. In Africa, some of the sharpest inequalities have emerged between the income of the top 5 per cent and the bottom 20 per cent: in Gabon it is 45 per cent to 3 per cent; in Senegal it is 36 per cent to 3 per cent, and in Liberia it is a staggering 61 per cent to 5 per cent. The societies today showing the most acute inequalities in Asia are India (25 per cent to 5 per cent), Indonesia (34 per cent to 7 per cent), and the Philippines (29 per cent to 6 per cent).[33]

Who are the rich in these societies? First and foremost, they are the small group of large land-holders, deriving their income from plantations, some associated agro-industries, the renting of land and the lending of money. Some have diversified into commerce, mining, light industries, building, trade, distribution, transport and shipping. Others have gone into banking, insurance and tourism, and more recently have become closely associated with some of the large transnational corporations operating in their countries, and may be found on the boards of directors of the local companies of these corporations. They often include members of the small professional classes of lawyers, doctors, accountants and architects, and the more senior civil servants.

What happens to the landless and near-landless? Those who can, eke out a bare living, if it can be called that, through intermittent labouring jobs in the countryside, sometimes on the large plantations or estates, combined with cultivation of their own meagre plots. Others leave and join the drift of people to the shanties in the cities. It is here that the contrasts between rich and poor are especially stark. In Rio, Santiago, La Paz, Kingston and San Salvador; in Lagos, Ibadan, Monrovia, Abidjan, Lusaka and Nairobi; and in Manila, Kuala Lumpur, Djakarta, Delhi, Dacca and Bangkok.

In many of these now vast cities (by the end of the century Rio, Calcutta and Djakarta will be amongst the largest in the world) the rich (both local and foreign) sometimes live under guard, sometimes even in private compounds, protected by high fences, night lights, guard dogs and security patrols. This is hardly surprising, given the breathtaking luxury of their houses, cars, clothes, foodstuffs and styles of life generally, compared with that of the urban poor and unemployed, who live in shacks, often made out of pilfered bits of cardboard, corrugated iron and wood, and some of whose food may come from rubbish dumps, begging and theft. If one seeks an explanation for some of the explosive urban violence of Latin America, one does not have far to look. The same is true for the crime waves in major African cities, or the banditry and hold-ups in parts of rural Africa and Asia.

At this point it is worth recalling the earlier discussion of famine in chapter 6 (see pp. 111-12). For the factors examined in the present chapter help to explain the outbreak of famine far better than the more commonly held view that it is caused by a sudden food shortage. Most recent famines in Third World societies have *not* been associated with serious declines in food availability. Indeed, it has sometimes been the case that famines have occurred in years of relatively high domestic production. The famine in Bangladesh in 1974 is a case in point.

In that summer, severe flooding occurred in Bangladesh. Although this affected one of the three annual rice crops, it did not affect the total output of rice for the year, nor the *per capita* output. In fact, it was higher that year than in the previous four years. The same was true for other food-grains. So the sharp increase in rice prices which occurred during and after the floods cannot be attributed simply to scarcity. Moreover, the increase in rice prices started *before* the floods. So there were clearly other factors involved, and they included some anticipation of scarcity, and speculative hoarding by large farmers and traders who hoped to make a killing on the market. And there were other factors which had nothing to do with the floods. In the event, prices rocketed throughout the summer, and famine raged.

By the end of the year the official death figure was 26,000, but other sources indicate a number much closer to 100,000. The people who suffered most, it is important to note, were the urban poor, village craftsmen, producers of local services, petty traders, other similar occupational groups and - *especially* - agricultural labourers (particularly *landless* labourers) who all lived on the edge of poverty by selling things, notably their labour.

If food availability did not decline, why the famine? It seems clear that the increase in the price of food, the decline in daily employment opportunities because of the floods (especially for casual rural labour, and hence the collapse in their incomes), and an associated drop in the demand for numerous other services (for instance those of boatmen and transport workers) all contributed cumulatively to the savagery of the famine. For what happened was *not* that the aggregate availability of food declined – the opposite was true – but that people's extremely precarious capacity to buy it was undermined, by a decline in their income relative to the price of food. In short, there was an adverse shift in the terms of trade between the earning (and hence buying) power of their labour and the price of rice. There was yet a further factor. Even as the famine commenced and mounted, urgent food-grains needed by the government of Bangladesh for its general (and then emergency) relief programme for the poor were witheld by the US government in order to compel Bangladesh to cease selling some jute bags to Cuba. By the time food aid was restored by the USA, the worst of the famine was over.

This underlines a central theme of the argument here. Many problems in the Third World (and famine is typical) need to be seen as part of a wider network of the politics of production, distribution and control in a society, and as part of its relations with other societies. Shifts (natural, social, or both) in these relations can precipitate appalling famines even without decline in the availability of food. For it is people's *access* to food, or their earning power to get it, which is affected by such shifts, not only or most importantly the availability of food itself.[34] This is so because millions of poor, landless, intermittently employed or unemployed people in Third World societies now live constantly so close to destitution (without effective social or public insurance systems) that even the slightest fluctuation can tip them over the edge.

IX

Turning now to the social structure and organization of Third World societies, it is important to start by recognizing that there are few societies anywhere in the modern world which are fully homogeneous with respect to their ethnic, cultural, religious or linguistic composition. Centuries of trade, emigration, war, conquest, the rise of new religious movements, and the drawing and redrawing of national boundaries (for instance after the First and Second World Wars) have left many societies with more or less diversity in these respects. The United States and Australia, for example, have been constituted almost entirely from immigrants, mostly free but sometimes forced, as in the case of the descendants of the slave population in the USA. The Soviet Union and Yugoslavia are further cases of societies composed of very distinctive ethnic and cultural groups. So too are Switzerland and Cyprus.

Before the imposition of their modern boundaries during the colonial and immediate post-colonial era, societies in the Third World also contained heterogeneous ethnic and cultural populations. In Africa the great historical empires, such as Mali, Ethiopia and Dahomey, are cases in point. But there are many other more recent examples, such as in Rwanda, where Tutsi rulers dominated

Hutu serfs and the Twa people; and the Ngoni of nineteenth-century South-Central Africa (modern Zambia) whose society was largely made up from groups recruited outside itself in the course of a long migration from the south, which had commenced when they fled from the expanding Zulu empire under Shaka. In Asia there was also a rich diversity of groups within, or associated with, particular societies. In the Indian sub-continent, for instance, there were Hindu and Muslim communities and a very large number of quite distinct local societies throughout. In most parts of South-east Asia, Chinese communities lived amongst numerous indigenous societies. In Latin America, from the time of the Iberian conquests, the descendants of slaves, European settlers and native Indian communities (where they survived) came to form the more or less complex social compositions of most societies there.[35] The European immigrants were not only Spanish or Portuguese, but later Irish, German, Italian and English.

But the boundaries drawn by the imperial powers round their often enormous colonial territories, and the diverse peoples brought together within them (sometimes for the first time), especially in Africa and Asia, added greatly to this pluralism, and gave rise to many problems which have faced some of the new societies of the Third World. Hence, in a country like Nigeria, distinct social groups, divided broadly between the Islamic north (the Hausa and Fulani) and the non-Islamic south (for instance the Ibo and Yoruba people) were incorporated in one state. A large number of peoples with diverse languages and cultures were likewise included in the Sudan and Zaire (the former Belgian Congo). In Zimbabwe, Rhodes and the British South Africa Company claimed a huge territory which included two large and distinct groupings – the Shona and the Ndebele. And in Malaysia the pre-colonial pluralism of Malay and Chinese communities was further compounded with the inclusion in 1963 of Sarawak and Sabah – 500 miles away – on the island of Borneo. This came about as a result of an agreement between the British and Malayan governments, and without effective consultation with the people of Sarawak and Sabah. It added many non-Malay peoples (for instance the Ibans and Land Dayaks) to the Malaysian population.[36] And it is not uncommon, in Sarawak for instance, to encounter sentiments of quite strong dislike for the association with Malaysia, and especially the terms of it.

Moreover, as mentioned in the previous chapter, some of the current pluralism of Third World societies was a direct consequence of colonial labour policies, which moved large numbers of people from one part of the world to others. This explains why Tamils from South India came to be in Sri Lanka, and why many thousands of Indians could be found in places as far apart as Trinidad, Jamaica, Guyana, Kenya, Uganda, Mauritius and Fiji, at the time of their independence.

Thus, it is not surprising that inter-communal tension, violence, civil war and regional secessionist movements have punctuated the modern politics of some of these societies, though it is important to recognize that this is *not* a phenomenon confined to the Third World alone. The Basque separatist movement in northern Spain, as well as that of the French-speaking Quebecois in Canada; the conflict between Walloons and Flemings in Belgium, between the Protestants and the Roman Catholics in Northern Ireland, and the Greek and Turkish communities in Cyprus are all cases in point.

It is even more important to recognize that while such conflicts may often flow along regional, cultural, ethnic or linguistic lines, they do *not* arise out of those differences *alone*. In almost every case they merge with conflicts of one kind or another over resource use, access, availability and distribution. They arise because the different social groupings have either come to be differentially advantaged (or disadvantaged) in relation to some national resource or other, or believe themselves or others to be so, or fear that it will become so, or wish to alter the existing pattern of distribution in their favour, and so on. The resources at stake may be land, mineral wealth, educational facilities, credit and bank loans, votes in relation to seats in the legislature, or control of the often important resource of central government power in the new state itself. Or, such groups may resent discrimination against them, or in favour of others, for jobs, scholarships, contracts, promotion prospects, or government projects in their region or community, by virtue of their language, religion or culture. In each instance careful analysis is required of the historical conditions of incorporation of the different social components, the patterns of distribution between them, and the often unpredictable 'trigger' events which spark off the conflict.

Two bloody and bitter post-colonial civil wars in Africa - in the Congo (Zaire) and Nigeria - were brought about by precisely this mix of factors. In the Congo the secession of Katanga province in 1960 contained all these elements. The dominant Katangese political movement, Conakat (the *Confédération des Associations Tribales du Katanga*), was based largely on the Ba-Lunda and Ba-Yeke people of the area. But Katanga itself was the richest province in the Congo, containing great mineral wealth in copper and cobalt. Furthermore, it was the region which had the greatest concentration of European (primarily Belgian) interests and investments, which they feared they might lose to a left-wing Congolese central government. Thus, there were certainly external factors involved in the secession.[37]

The Nigerian civil war, following the secession of the Eastern Region in 1967 (which called itself Biafra), arose out of a classic combination of social pluralism, regional interests and resource conflict.[38] Under British colonial rule the three regions, composed of mainly Hausa, Yoruba and Ibo, were incorporated in one federal state at Independence in 1960, with varying degrees of reluctance and enthusiasm. Ethnically based parties emerged in each region, and dominated them. From before Independence they came to compete increasingly with each other for control of the central federal government and its resources. Mutual suspicion between the regions, and profound differences in their histories and politics, made for extremely unstable relations in the new federal state and its armed forces. The absence of sufficient appropriately trained personnel in the north also meant that many posts there in government services and educational institutions were filled by people from the south, notably Ibo. In the first five years of Nigerian independence, mistrust and hostility between the regions and their political parties increased – even over such matters as the true census figures, for this would determine the number of seats in the Federal Assembly and hence, potentially, the control of the central government. Public money was corruptly channelled to parties and their leaders.

A military coup in January 1966 sought to brush aside the mess, eliminate corruption and impose unity on the society. But the different histories, objectives and interests of the three major groups made this next to impossible. As one observer commented:[39]

> It's no good ducking ... the single immutable political reality of this country, which is: in any race for the material benefits of life, starting at the same point and on the basis of equal opportunity, the Easterners are going to win by a mile. This is intolerable to the North. The only way to prevent it happening is to impose artificial shackles on the East. This is intolerable to the Easterners.

It was largely for this reason that this first Nigerian coup achieved little. The regime which it instituted did not last more than six months. In the north, fear that the Ibo sought to dominate Nigeria through the first coup unleashed a wave of massacre and violence against Easterners. This was backed up by a second coup, this time led from the north, which sought revenge on the Ibos and probably had northern secessionist objectives at heart. Further massacres of Easterners followed in the subsequent months. Those of them who could do so fled back to the east. And despite various attempts at negotiation to save what was left of the now disintegrating Nigerian Federation, the Easterners could not be persuaded that their lives or property would be 'protected by any government based outside Eastern Nigeria'. At the end of May 1967 they declared their independence, as Biafra. Within weeks the civil war commenced as the Federal government launched attacks on Biafra to crush the secession. It was to take three bitter and bloody years before that was achieved. None of the politics before or during those years was made any less complicated by the fact that Nigerian oil resources were concentrated largely in the east.

Secessionist movements of this kind have usually failed, and the region or province has in the end been dragged back into the state. Sometimes, this has been accompanied by new constitutional arrangements being developed to break up large concentrations of power at the centre and to decentralize it more evenly. Elsewhere, an even more powerful military or military-backed government has emerged. But not always. In the Indian sub-continent before 1947, the forces of hostility between Hindu and Muslim were too strong to resist, especially in the north, and hence the partition of the region into Pakistan and India. But even then, tension between the two separated wings of Pakistan began to mount, based largely on the deep sense of resentment amongst the Bengali population in East Pakistan that they were being exploited by West Pakistan. A war of independence broke out in the late 1960s which gave birth to Bangladesh.

Such civil and seccessionist wars have usually been particularly bloody. But other more or less violent conflicts of a communal kind have often erupted in the post-colonial societies of the Third World - in Trinidad between Indians and the descendants of the slave population; in East Africa between Asians and Africans; in Malaysia between Chinese and Malays; and in Sri Lanka between Tamils and Sinhalese.

In assessing the politics of these incidents, it is important to remember the central point: the problems which give rise to them flow *partly* from the plural character of these societies, and *partly* from the way in which power, advantage, resources or opportunities may be distributed within them between the component social groups. And it is not surprising that those who benefit from the prevailing distributional pattern (or who believe they will do so) will seek to maintain it. Conversely, those who do not will seek to alter it.

X

These aspects of the social composition of some Third World societies overlap with other features of their social structure, which are closely related to the productive and distributive characteristics discussed earlier. Two in particular are worth mentioning.

First, the division between the export-oriented and often urban-related sector on the one hand, and the largely subsistence, rural sector on the other, has come to be associated with two increasingly distinct ways of life, or cultures, though it is important to realise that there are complex relations and much continuity between them. These ways of life are largely rooted in the productive cores and material cultures of the two sectors.

In many cities of the Third World one may find large hotels, new office blocks, shopping complexes, some factories, and around them suburban estates, government-built housing and high-rise apartments. Those lucky enough to have secure jobs - they seldom form more than one-quarter of the urban population - have a lifestyle which has come increasingly to resemble that of city dwellers in the First and Second worlds, but especially in the West because of its generally much more dominant influence on behaviour and consumption. In the business areas of these cities one finds air-conditioning systems, telephone and other communications networks, electric typewriters, computers and all the standard paraphernalia of commerce, though the extent of this varies considerably. An old city - like Colombo in Sri Lanka - is very different from a new one - like Brasilia in Brazil.

None the less, in the homes of those people who work in these cities one may find most items which are familiar to people in 'the North': electric or gas cookers, refrigerators, television sets, hi-fi systems and so forth. It is almost universally the case now that the smaller nuclear family is increasingly the norm in such homes, though more or less recent connections with kin and clan in rural villages are often still sustained, but decreasingly so the longer the family has been an urban one. The patterns of consumption - with regard to food and clothing, for instance - begin to look very much like those found in the North, though there are obvious local variations which one would expect to find in such different climates and ecologies. For example, local fruits, vegetables and fish may be found side by side with sliced bread, cornflakes, a variety of instant foods, imported alcohol and local or foreign canned goods, plus the whole array of cars, mopeds, gadgets, toiletries and cosmetics. Likewise, some *very* expensive and *haute-couture* saris, sarongs, other tradi-tional robes for both men and women, and the now familiar smart executive safari-suits may be found in the same wardrobe as the latest European fashion in shirts, suits, dresses and high-heeled shoes. Living in more individualistic contexts in the towns, leisure is much less something which people *produce* together but is *consumed* individually, like watching television or films. Amongst the usually *very* small élite of urban rich - in government, the armed forces, business, the professions and the expatriate community - one finds a remarkable continuity between Caracas, Kingston, Cairo, Calcutta and Kuching. All of their lifestyles bear a much closer resemblance to what one may encounter amongst the wealthy of New York, Paris, London or Melbourne than to what one may find in the villages of their societies.

The lifestyle and culture of the rural areas is very different.[40] People generally live in small villages which may be widely scattered. Simple houses or huts are the rule and it is rare to find electricity, gas, clean piped water or the domestic appliances of the city. The extended family remains the norm, and many families will have one or more of their members away working in the towns, plantations or oil-fields, or looking for jobs. It is usually the men who are migrant workers, but not exclusively so. Some are able to send cash back to their families. Others cannot or do not. Women carry a major burden of agricultural and other work in the villages. Local staples (where available) constitute the bulk of food intake, though village stores and trading depots carry cans of powdered milk, fish, meat and soft drinks. Television sets can occasion-ally be seen in the rural areas but the transistor radio is much more common. In general, in these villages, people talk more with each other, work from sun-up to sun-down and often share certain productive and domestic tasks with each other - like clearing fields, harvesting crops or pounding corn or rice. Their tools are simple. They produce their leisure out of the fact of the village community, though there are quite sharp divisions between rich and poor in many villages, especially in Asia. Children play together, though you seldom see manufactured and bought toys. Music is made on traditional instruments like pipes, drums and gongs.

It is not an exaggeration to say that, in general, the urban communities often regard rural people as simple, superstitious, backward and slow: in short, as hicks. One may encounter such attitudes even amongst some officials, in administration and various extension and social services, who work amongst them. On the other hand, rural people are often fascinated and attracted by the urban life, and may aspire to it, but they are at the same time cautious of townspeople.

Rural people may often appear slow to innovate, for instance in agricultural methods. This is not because they are in some sense intrinsically 'conservative' or 'traditionalist' in their ways or outlook, but because they have a very clear idea of what the costs of innovation to them may be, especially if the new methods fail. For instance, consider a group of small peasant farmers who have plots of poor land, without irrigation. Many of the new 'high-yielding' varieties of seed which extension services often recommend may require not only better irrigation, but also regular application of fertilizers and systematic weeding. Not only does this cost more, but it will also certainly involve more labour time. The farmers may have little cash available to buy the fertilizer, and hence may have to borrow money. Moreover, they (or other members of their families) who help on the land may have part-time jobs in the neighbourhood and may not have the time to devote to tending the crops in the way required. If, then, for any of these reasons, the crop fails, the family may be worse off than if they had stuck to the older seed. Moreover, they will not then be able to repay their loan for the fertilizer and they will get sucked further into the downward spiral of debt. Rural people understand very clearly in terms of their own experiences the risks of innovation when they have so little insurance against failure.[41]

Just as it is important to remember how few of the urban population really benefit from town life, it is equally important not to glamourize village life. For most people – for instance in the now barren areas of North-east Brazil or the High Andes, in the hinterland of the Caribbean islands, in the arid marginal lands of Africa, or the vast rural areas of Asia – life is very hard, and often short, for all the reasons discussed earlier. Such conditions are not made easier to bear when people know of, and sometimes see, the sharp contrasts with the urban (or even rural) rich, or foreign tourists who may pass through.

The broad differences between these urban and rural cultures are of course in part bound up with the universal differences one may find between town and country. They must also be understood in terms of the inequalities which have developed as a result of the 'urban bias' in the politics of 'development' in the Third World mentioned before. But there is a further factor which needs to be discussed here. This is the second feature of social structure in these societies which is of increasing importance: that of *class*.

XI

The concept of class is a problematic one, and some discussion about it will be found in the next chapter (see pp. 235-6). Its use in relation to the Third World is also contentious.[42] For present purposes here it refers simply to various social groups which are defined by certain common characteristics they share by virtue of their degree of control of, or access to, important resources in the society.

Thus, in the rural areas, the composition of the main classes may be defined by the single most important criterion: whether people own any land or not. Hence one may distinguish broadly between the small class of large landowners, the class of middle and small peasant farmers, and the usually largest class of near-landless or landless labourers.

In the urban areas, the most numerous class is that of the urban poor, who own next to nothing, do not have stable jobs, whose income is both irregular and very low, and who get by as best they can. They are sometimes referred to as the 'lumpenproletariat' or 'marginals'. These are the shanty-town dwellers, who are often made up of the most recent urban migrants, though others have been there for at least a generation or more. Next, one may identify those whose education, good luck or well-placed connections may have enabled them to find more or less secure employment - perhaps in the public service (such as on railways or in the ports), or in local or foreign owned enterprises (such as mines, assembly plants, and light industries - like cigarette, textile, clothing and canning factories). They too own little, but some may have begun to buy or build their own homes, or are fortunate to be able to rent low-cost government housing. It is largely this group that forms the *organized* working class - in trade unions, where allowed.

There are those who would argue that, given the scope and depth of external control and influence in the productive systems of Third World societies - notably through the activities of transnational corporations in plantation agriculture, mining, private and public finance, light industry and assembly plants, marketing and shipping - it is not really possible to talk about a full-fledged local 'ruling class' in referring to those who own, control or direct the major productive activities. There is much to be said for this view. But it does not mean that one cannot speak of the most *dominant* local class in these societies, however inextricably bound up some of its members may be with foreign interests, or subject to them.

It is therefore important to identify that very small group of government ministers, senior civil servants, high-ranking members of the military, officials in state or parastatal corporations, private entrepreneurs, and the local managerial or executive employees of foreign companies and banks as constituting this class. Some have in recent years accumulated substantial land-holdings - Kenya is a case in point, as is the Ivory Coast - or have more or less close relations with large land-holders, as in India and Bangladesh. Elsewhere - especially in Latin America - some members of this class can trace their wealth and power back to the colonial period, when large estates and *latifundios* were carved out and have been handed down from generation to generation. While they are now usually urban dwellers (and hence often absentee landlords) they have been able to use their rurally accumulated capital to diversify into other urban-based productive and financial activities. Finally, there is that section of the dominant class which is sometimes referred to as the 'bureaucratic bourgeoisie'. This term refers to those senior members of government and the state administration whose power (and often whose wealth) derives directly from their control of the apparatus of government, and who may have used their positions (sometimes corruptly, as in bribe-taking for awarding government contracts) to accumulate wealth in land or property in the private sector.[43] Some leading members of the governments of Third World societies have come to own houses, land, other real estate, substantial investments and bulging bank accounts in Europe. President Mobutu of Zaire and some other leaders of some former French colonies in West and Central Africa are especially well known examples of this.

Such class inequalities have not gone unchallenged, as the next section will show. But the kinds of regional and social pluralism discussed earlier have sometimes made the organization of opposition difficult, or have constrained the development of unity amongst different groups of poor. For instance, the majority of tea plantation workers in Sri Lanka are Indian Tamils, and have for long received pitiful wages and lived in appalling conditions in the 'line rooms' of the tea estates. But many of them have been kept off the voting roll in Sri Lanka since independence, and they have seldom had the support of organized groups of Sinhalese rural or urban workers. Similar ethnic tensions have sometimes inhibited the growth and unified action of the small urban working classes in Third World societies, and it has not been uncommon to find trade unions organized along ethnic lines, as in Malaysia. In Africa, ethnic factions within unions have sometimes disrupted the unity of such organizations.[44]

In summary, therefore, it is important to recognize how overlapping conflicts of these kinds - between regional, ethnic, cultural, religious and class forces - have both reflected and shaped politics in many Third World societies.

XII

Conflict is now endemic in most societies in the Third World. It should be clear why. It flows through and around the general characteristics described in the previous sections: scarcity; imbalance in their productive systems; landlessness, food deficits and hunger; rural and urban unemployment; dependency, debt and often far-reaching external influence; inequality and corruption; small, powerful and rich urban élites surrounded by massive urban poverty; regionalism, pluralism and an increasing definition and differentiation of classes. In each instance a different mix of these factors combines to produce and shape the conflicts which thus vary considerably in scope and form.

It may be wondered why, under the kinds of conditions described earlier, there has not been more revolt and resistance. Historically, rural people in particular have found it difficult to organize and act collectively on a wide scale, for the obvious reasons of distance and communications problems. Hence rural revolts and rebellions have usually been fairly local in scope, and the Third World has been no exception in that respect. But not always: some of the major 'liberation' or 'revolutionary' wars of the twentieth century have involved direct and widespread action by peasants - as in Mexico, China, Algeria, Vietnam and Cuba - some of which will be discussed briefly later.[45]

But conflict is not always expressed in such open confrontations. In the rural areas it persists widely as a tightly contained but potentially explosive undercurrent in the daily politics of village life. Asia provides some of the best examples of this, which arise from one of the most widespread features of the region: debt. For whatever reason people may be poor, they cannot live on nothing. They need money for food, for seed and for tools. They also require it for important social and ceremonial purposes, like marriages, funerals and illness, as well as other basic consumption needs. Since they have so little money, they must borrow. But having no security against which to borrow from institutions like banks or cooperatives, they must borrow privately - from landlords, traders or money-lenders. 'The village economy has always been riddled with debt', commented one observer of Sri Lankan history.[46] So borrowing and debt is not entirely new. But as the processes of commercialization have increased, and as dependence upon the cash economy has become crucial to life, debt has become chronic. The interest rates charged on loans can be crippling. One study in Sri Lanka found instances where as much as 300 per cent was charged. But more widely in Asia it may vary from between 25 and 100 per cent.[47]

Indebtedness has become a permanent condition for many rural poor. Unable to shake off their debts, they have to pay a substantial part of the produce of their land (where they have any) to their creditors, and this often becomes the penultimate stage before they too sink into landlessness. Alternatively, they must provide their creditors with long periods of unpaid labour in order to pay off their debt. Others have become 'bonded' labourers or serfs, though this is now officially illegal in many parts of Asia. Such a vice-like grip also renders the poor powerless in negotiations with local employers over wages or conditions of land tenancy.[48]

But such circumstances of rural politics also give rise at times to open violence in the villages. This is especially the case where landless or poor people attempt to negotiate for better wages or conditions with the landlords, who are often backed up in imposing their terms by the local police who may be in their pay - a condition which is commonly reported in Bangladesh. Such incidents have often been especially brutal, for instance in those parts of India where violent conflict over land, wages, debt and other central components of rural politics has broken out between landlords and organized peasants, particularly low caste 'untouchables' (*harijans*).[49]

Wider movements of peasant rebellion and resistance have occurred throughout Asia. In the case of Indochina, support from the rural poor was a major factor in the victory of the communist guerrillas. In the Philippines, the Huks have been involved in rural resistance since the Second World War, and currently the New People's Army has become active with peasant support. In India, perhaps the best-known recent instance of militant rural activism was the Naxalite movement. In Sri Lanka in 1971 there was a short-lived but bloody insurrection, organized by the *Janata Vimukthi Peramuna* (the JVP or People's Liberation Front).[50] While a significant number (about 12 per cent) of the insurgents were young, well-educated left-wing students, over 50 per cent of them were small peasant cultivators, casual rural labourers and rural unemployed.[51]

On the other side of the world, in Latin America, there has also been a long history of peasant revolt and rebellion. Peasant involvement in the Mexican 'revolution' of 1910 was a major factor in its success, for example. But more recent instances of peasant revolt have occurred in modern Mexico and in the more densely settled Indian areas of the Andes. Elsewhere - in Peru for instance - landless peasants have 'invaded' and occupied land in rural areas in attempts to force the pace of agrarian and land reform. In the years since 1960 more organized rural guerrilla movements have emerged throughout the continent - in Guatemala, Venezuela, Peru, Colombia and Bolivia, many of them (unsuccessfully) drawing inspiration from the success of the Cuban revolution in 1959.[52] But, perhaps because of their dramatic activities - like kidnapping, assassination and bombing - the most well-publicized forms of conflict in Latin America (and elsewhere) have been the *urban* guerrilla movements which have burst into action in country after country, especially where urban populations are relatively high. Amongst the better-known groups have been the *Montoneros* in Argentina, the MIR and the FALN in Venezuela, the ALN in Brazil, the *Tupamaros* in Uruguay and the recently successful *Sandinistas* in Nicaragua, who - at their peak - combined urban guerrilla tactics with wider mass action.[53]

Such groups have unleashed ferocious violence, and have in turn provoked massive counter-violence from the police, para-military security services and armed forces of the state. Thousands have died, been tortured, murdered or simply disappeared. In Colombia alone, it has been estimated that 200,000 people have been killed as a result of murder, banditry, civil war and guerrilla action and counter-action since 1948.

One may regard these events either as examples of terrorism or heroic freedom-fighting (or a mixture of both) on the one hand, or naked counter-terrorism by the state or the imposition of law and order (or a mixture of both) on the other. Either way, the really important point to recognize here is the context of inequality, poverty, rural misery and urban squalor from which they spring. And it is this which explains the astonishing levels of hate and brutality which occur in the course of these struggles to alter or maintain the existing patterns of resource use and distribution in Third World societies.

Throughout the Third World, organized labour movements have also played a significant role in politics, and continue to do so on a wide front. Both historically and in the contemporary world, the best-organized and most militant workers have often been those concentrated in particular sectors of productive activity in these societies - the mines, railways and ports. Rural workers - for example agricultural labourers, cane-cutters and tea-pickers on plantations in the Caribbean, East Africa and Asia - have not always been able to organize and act as effectively for some of the reasons discussed earlier.[54] Although many trade union activities - where allowed - have followed the universal patterns of bargaining and negotiation, there have been regular instances of more violent conflict.

There has been a long tradition of this in Latin America, especially in the mining industries. These have sometimes been dominated by foreign companies and control, for instance in the nitrate and copper mines of Chile. Elsewhere, as in the case of Bolivia, a few local families have controlled the tin mines, but often from headquarters outside the country and in conjunction with foreign capital. Some of the most bloody episodes of industrial conflict have occurred in and around such mining activities, for instance at Iquique in Chile in 1907, when between 1000 and 3000 nitrate workers were mown down in the course of protesting at conditions in the mines and against the policies of mass dismissals.[55] More recently, a wave of bitter strikes swept through the mining camps of the Peruvian Andes between 1969 and 1971.[56]

Moreover, in the conditions of dependency, debt, inflation and the fluctuating fortunes of their societies in global politics, the larger federations of organized urban labour have played an active, sometimes violent, but often complicated role in national politics in these societies, for instance in Bolivia and in the Peronist unions in Argentina.

In Africa, movements of organized workers were active in the independence struggles, usually being closely associated with the main nationalist parties.[57] Often, organizations of white-collar employees - like teachers and junior civil servants - were especially prominent in the nationalist movements. But, again, important contributions were made by miners, dockers and railway workers especially, and their struggles go back to the early years of the twentieth century, especially in East and Southern Africa.[58]

In the years since independence in many African and Asian societies, the position of organized labour unions has become much more complicated. Initially associated with the parties which came to power at independence, they were often very closely identified with the new government. But in the last twenty years (or more in the case of the Indian sub-continent) organized groups of workers of all kinds have found their interests to be diverging sharply from those of the state, and direct conflict with it has ensued. This has been the experience, for instance, of railway workers in India, miners in Ghana, and general organizations of urban workers everywhere.[59]

Such conflicts with the state have been especially marked where the government has come to have a major stake in key areas of productive activity (through nationalization or partial nationalization of mines, for instance), and also where it has in effect assumed the role of policing industrial relations between unions and foreign-owned companies, to attract and retain investment. This has ranged from the outright banning of strikes and picketing (as in the Philippines), the arrest and imprisonment of union leaders (widespread in Latin America), and varieties of new 'codes of practice' everywhere for unions which aim to curtail their independence or activities. Many of these crack-downs on organized labour have represented aspects of wider efforts to stamp out opposition more generally, often by military or military-backed regimes, which will be discussed in the next section.

The main incidents of insurrection usually do make the headlines in the Western press and media. But if one scours the daily newspapers closely - especially the short reports, often tucked away in middle pages under such headings as 'Other foreign news' - one regularly discovers brief items about the persistent outbreaks of other, more localized forms of urban and rural conflict. These now erupt and subside, again and again, in the daily politics of scarcity, inequality and imbalance of Third World societies. For this reason, the following excerpt from a daily paper is not an unrepresentative example:[60]

> Police have shot three striking copper miners and a schoolboy in a second day of violence . . . . Zambia has been hit by a series of strikes, first by miners in the copper industry, then by bank employees and teachers . . . . Many Zambians have been disappointed that their economy has not picked up now that the war in Zimbabwe has ended . . . . The shooting occurred at the Mindola Mine, near Kitwe, near the Zaire border. Police said they fired to quell a riot.

XIII

The sharp differences between rich and poor, between town and country, between regions and sectors; the volatility and conflict in their politics; and the sometimes radically contrasting proposals and interests of competing political parties as to how resources should be used and distributed - that is to say, the direction of 'development' policy - have all given rise to a further set of related characteristics in Third World societies. That is the increase in the power of the state and its militarization; the ferocity of some struggles for its control; and the extraordinary brutality often used in eliminating or suppressing opposition.

Global military expenditure now stands at almost $650 billion, and the non-oil producing societies of the Third World have together almost doubled their spending on armaments, from about $22 billion in 1972 to $35 billion in 1981. Some individual examples of this are to be found in Table 1.[61]

Table 1

	1972 (m)	1981 (m)
Bangladesh	49.1 (1973)	140
Philippines	279	688
Ethiopia	115	427
Malawai	3.4	22.2 (1979)
El Salvador	29.1	85.9
Chile	360 (1973)	949
Taiwan	1301	2450
South Korea	1108	3519
Thailand	564	1036

Not surprisingly, the size of the armed forces of the Third World jumped too, between 1960 and 1980, from 8.7 million to 15.1 million persons.[62]

These raw facts only tell part of the story. Another aspect of it is to look at the percentage of government spending which has gone on 'defence', compared with the percentage on education and health, as shown in Table 2 (the figures given are for 1977).[63]

Table 2

	Defence %	Education %	Health %
India	19.9	2.1	1.7
Korea (S.)	34.3	16.0	1.6
Malaysia	17.5	23.6	7.4
Nigeria	17.9	9.6	2.2
Pakistan	33.1	2.7	1.6
Philippines	21.1	13.2	5.1
Somalia	20.1	14.0	6.1
Taiwan	51.8	7.1	1.1

For comparative purposes, British public expenditure on these items in 1981-2 will be roughly 12 per cent on each.

Other societies with high defence expenditures are Sudan, Argentina and Singapore. If data were easily available for expenditure on police and paramilitary services, many of the above figures would be much higher. It is important to note that not all Third World societies have records like this. For instance, Brazil spends roughly the same amount (about 6 per cent) on all three items, while Jamaica, Malawi, Venezuela, Mexico, Kenya, Peru, Sri Lanka and Tanzania all spend more on education than on defence, but most spend more on defence than on health.

It is of course necessary to say that the reason for high military expenditures in some instances is that these societies have been or are involved in military confrontations or conflicts (or fear them) with neighbouring states (such as India and Pakistan; Somalia and Ethiopia; South and North Korea; Indonesia and Malaysia). But the powerful armies which have been built up are extremely handy, and have been widely used for purposes of internal control.

The other side of this particular coin is the very high level of profitable arms sales by countries in the First and Second worlds, notably the USA, the Soviet Union, France and Britain. (Britain maintains a Defence Sales Organization solely for this purpose in the Ministry of Defence.) The US Pentagon predicts that the value of American foreign military sales in 1982 may reach as much as US $30 billion.[64] While a high proportion of sales and direct military aid has gone to societies in the Middle East (and earlier in Indochina), most Third World societies have expanded their arms purchases.

The rise in the overt coercive power of the state, and the increasing levels of militarization, have been associated with the widespread involvement of the military in Third World governments. It used to be the case that military intervention was thought of as a 'Latin American syndrome', but this is no longer so. There are (in mid-1982) more than 56 Third World societies under direct military rule, and even more if one adds those countries where the army plays a major role in the government. There have been more than 76 military coups since 1960, including at least 22 in Latin America, 31 in Africa, 5 in South Asia and 9 in East Asia. In some countries there have been repeated coups and counter-coups.[65] Often, when the armed forces have taken over, or where they have become closely associated with the regime, the expenditure on defence and the size of the military forces has gone up. For instance, in Chile it more than doubled after the coup of 1973; and in the Philippines the full-time armed forces personnel (*excluding* paramilitary and 'reserve' forces) rose from 43,000 in 1972-3 to 113,000 in the eight years after the imposition of martial law.[66] Throughout the Third World, even where the military has not intervened directly, there have been repeated impositions of 'states of emergency' for more or less sustained periods.

Why do the military intervene? The first point to be made is that, like all other institutions, the armed forces are political. They command a monopoly of the directly coercive resources and capacities in a society; their systems of decision-making and social organization are characterized by tightly organized hierarchies with firm and quick lines of command. In many, the cultures and ideologies of internal 'national security' have come to dominate. Thus, from a strictly operational point of view, it is a relatively easy matter for the armed forces to take over. Seizure of key agencies - like the main government offices, the banks, the ports, airport, radio and television studios - is no real problem, especially if all branches of the military are united in their objectives. It is, however, far harder for a military government to make major changes or improvements in the politics of a society, that is in the organization of production and the distribution of resources, for the same reasons that civilian governments find it hard. But what the military can do, and usually do, is to stamp out opposition, at least in the short run.

Secondly, the military usually offer two main types of reason for intervening, which sometimes coincide. One is that they have taken over to eliminate corruption, crush disorder and establish an efficient administrative basis for effective 'development'. The other is that they have intervened to 'save' the country from subversive and disruptive forces which are threatening its 'development'. Of course, once the military is in power it is almost impossible to dislodge it peacefully unless it abandons power voluntarily. Hence counter-coups may occur from within the ranks of the armed forces, sometimes led by junior officers, or by a section of the military (perhaps regional or ethnic) which fears domination of the society by another section, as happened in the Nigerian case mentioned earlier. Whatever the stated reasons for intervention, it is normal practice (with some important recent Latin American exceptions) for the military government to declare that, as soon as possible, it will return to the barracks and restore the country to civilian rule. This may take months – or decades. But, as has happened widely in Africa and Latin America, even when the army does return to the barracks, it often retains a strong presence in the government. And it is not uncommon for the army to intervene again and again.

Finally, it needs to be said that, with a few important exceptions (for example Peru in 1968, Ethiopia in 1974 and Ghana in 1981), the general policies pursued by military governments (and military-backed governments) have *not* been redistributional in character, but much more supportive of the existing patterns of inequality. Regimes of this kind (in Brazil, Nigeria and the Philippines, for instance) have usually enjoyed close relations with the governments (and military establishments) in the West. The ideologies of 'national security' mentioned before have often been fostered by Western powers (especially the USA) in the course of helping with training agreements and 'counter-insurgency' programmes which have been stepped up for both the armed forces and the police. The United States Agency for International Development (AID) has estimated that, between the early 1960s and 1970s, over a million foreign policemen received training through the US 'Office of Public Safety' (OPS) at home and in the USA. This particular programme was cancelled in 1973 and 1974 because of repeated scandals associated with it, but others have taken its place. In addition, more than half a million army personnel from Third World societies have been trained on US bases in the Americas and by other Western military agencies elsewhere. In recent years, too, the Soviet Union and other Eastern European regimes have provided military equipment and training for countries in the Third World that are sympathetic to them.[67]

It is almost inevitable that the conflicts generated in the politics of scarcity, inequality and imbalance produce deep divisions and hence violent tensions. A good illustration of how these relations occur in practice is provided by the example of the coup in Chile in 1973. It is particularly illuminating because that country had such a long history without military intervention. It thus bears looking at here briefly as a short case study in this aspect of Third World politics.

XIV

For most of the present century, at least, the 'Social Question' has been at the heart of Chilean politics.[68] This has been defined by three main features: conditions of poverty and deprivation for the substantial bulk of the population; a growing awareness of this and a determination to do something about it; and an unwillingness on the part of a small and highly privileged minority to initiate or allow significant change. While there has been slow change in the composition and size of this élite, it has remained a minority, getting the best and the most of jobs, housing, education, health care and food, largely through its ownership of major forms of wealth in the society (such as land), or through close association with those who have owned it (like foreign companies in the case of the mines).

These characteristics have been associated with a very narrow resource and productive base in Chile. After its independence from Spain in 1818, Chile was essentially an agricultural society. Landowners had much power and prestige which they have retained to the present, and purchasing land has always been a sign of social 'arrival' for those who have made good in other productive activities, such as mining, the professions or commerce. But after 1880 Chile came to be heavily dependent on its nitrate industry, and between 1890 and 1924 this accounted for almost a quarter of Chilean GNP and about half the government revenue. When the international demand for nitrate declined (largely owing to the development of synthetic substitutes), and after the Great Depression of 1929, Chile's fortunes sagged. Its GNP dropped more than 50 per cent, and its capacity to import fell some 82 per cent in three years.

But Chile has considerable copper resources. New developments in technology and the inflow of foreign capital enabled these to be exploited. And from the 1940s onwards, especially, copper came to play the part which nitrate had done before. Up to 1970 it accounted for 60 per cent of export earnings, while minerals as a whole accounted for 85 per cent. However, the fluctuating price of copper did not make this a particularly secure basis for development, and in any event Chilean control over this major resource was tenuous. Before nationalization of the mines in 1971, two US corporations controlled over 80 per cent of Chilean copper production.

The distributional features of Chilean society have been very similar in most respects to those described for Third World societies in general. In so far as land is concerned, some 81 per cent of it was owned by less than 5 per cent of the landowners before 1950. A census in 1965 showed that less than 3 per cent of the total number of farms contained 73 per cent of all agricultural land. Poverty has been the common experience for most Chileans, and in the early years of the present century, for instance, the average wage of rural workers was about 20 *centavos* a day. Male industrial workers got 3.80 *pesos* a day, while women and children had to accept half of that. The 'affluent' nitrate workers, in the grim conditions of the Atacama desert, might have made 5 or 6 *pesos* a day. By contrast, a better-off family in the capital, Santiago, would enjoy an evening at the fashionable *Teatro Municipal*, where a box could cost anything from 1000 to 20,000 *pesos* for the evening. In the 1970s, the top 5 per cent of households received 31 per cent of total income, compared with less than 5 per cent for the bottom 20 per cent of households.[69]

The decline of agriculture, the rise and collapse of the nitrate industry, and then the emergence of copper, produced government revenues which, although fluctuating, enabled the state to invest quite widely in infrastructural development, but of a largely urban nature. Some industrialization grew up around this, as did the important and ambiguous 'middle' classes of Chilean society. Equally important was the growth of the urban population, from 28 per cent of the total in 1930 to about 70 per cent in 1970. With a long tradition of political parties and an active trade union movement, the demands and interests of the urban poor were expressed through these institutions. Throughout the post-war years their experience of poverty radicalized significant sections of the Chilean working class in the towns. And the failure of successive governments to solve the 'Social Question' (for instance by the Frei government's 'Revolution in Liberty' between 1964 and 1970), pushed many of them leftwards to embrace more directly socialist parties promising solutions which involved wresting control of the copper industry from foreign hands, and enacting serious and far-reaching domestic redistributional programmes.

Class conflict, always present in Chilean politics, was heightened when Salvador Allende was elected president in 1970 (but with just over 36 per cent of the vote). He declared his party's victory had been 'a triumph of the workers', and commenced to implement a programme of radical reform which aimed to re-establish Chilean control of its own politics. This included agrarian reform; nationalization of foreign enterprises (notably the copper mines), banks, financial institutions, major industrial monopolies and distributional services, plus various public service companies. The new government also sought to ensure far greater worker participation in the control of productive activities.

This all involved a major redistributional attack on local and foreign interests, but Allende was determined to do this by constitutional means. However, as his vote in the 1970 presidential election indicates, he did not enjoy the unanimous support of a majority of the electorate. But, by 1973, his support had grown to just short of half of the population, as shown in the legislative elections that year. Be that as it may, Allende was forced to govern with a coalition of parties that went some of the way with him, but not necessarily all the way or the same way. As the programme of the *Popular Unity* government was implemented, it provoked substantial opposition from another coalition of domestic and foreign interests. On the domestic front this included significant sections of the 'middle' classes, the self-employed, the local élite and foreign corporations operating in Chile. Their control of major resources made the programme of reform difficult. Factory owners sabotaged production; merchants hoarded stocks, thus helping to create shortages; landowners impeded agrarian reforms; newspapers spread alarm. The repeated strikes of some 40,000 lorry owners disrupted distribution of goods and food, and acted to stall the reforms and engender conditions of crisis. The opposition parties in congress – allied with some of these forces and groups – made the most of these difficulties, claiming that the constitution was in danger. From abroad, an embargo was placed on Chilean copper after the mines were nationalized, very powerful transnational corporations (like the ITT) contributed to the 'de-stabilization' of life in the country, and the government of the USA was able to persuade the World Bank to suspend loans to Chile.[70]

Under these escalating conditions of crisis, the military under General Pinochet struck on 11 September 1973. The new regime restored the 'free market' in Chile and reversed the reforms. But it also initiated some of the bloodiest repression seen in modern Latin American history, as the military systematically eliminated the organized basis of *Popular Unity* support. Allende died in the coup, and within a fortnight nearly 3000 bodies were recorded in the Santiago city morgue. Many thousands more were killed, tortured or disappeared – perhaps as many as 30,000 – and others fled the country.[71] Since then there have been further widespread violations of human rights, and even after a decade the military has not made it clear as to when it will return to the barracks.

What happened in Chile may have been new for that society, but it was not unique in the Third World. Wherever military or military-backed regimes have come to power under such circumstances, the repression of opposition which has ensued has often been severe. It is not without significance that the code-name for the generals' coup in Chile was 'Operation Djakarta'. This recalls the coup in Indonesia in October 1965, following which *at least* half a million, and perhaps as many as one million, people (mainly members of the Indonesian Communist Party) were killed.[72]

The reports of such organizations as Amnesty International read like a history of modern horror in the repression of dissent and opposition, from Angola and Benin in Africa, to Argentina and Uruguay in Latin America, and from Bangladesh to Vietnam in Asia. They refer to such things as detention without trial, appalling treatment and torture of political prisoners, political killings, thousands of 'disappearances', suppression of trade unions and opposition parties, judicial amputations and floggings, house arrest, administrative banishments, assassinations, military tribunals, deaths in police custody, and 're-education' camps.[73]

It takes little more than common sense to recognize that such generalized brutality and repression often produces counter-brutality, violence and revenge. It has done so elsewhere, for instance in Europe during and after the French and Russian revolutions, and the Nazi occupation. Hence, generally 'right wing' regimes - in Chile, Argentina, Zaire, Indonesia or the Philippines - have not had a monopoly of such behaviour. In the course of guerrilla and other forms of revolutionary war - in Cuba, Nicaragua, Angola, Mozambique and Vietnam for example - counter-terror has been waged by liberation movements. And where 'left wing' regimes have come to power, usually after more or less protracted periods of armed struggle, there has also been repression and elimination of old regimes and old enemies. Perhaps the most gruesome recent example of this was in Kampuchea in the late 1970s, where the political disruption which this caused also precipitated famine on a vast scale.

But the really important analytical point to stress here is that none of this is satisfactorily explained if thought of simply as conflict between 'communists' and 'capitalists', or 'fascists' and 'democrats', as if these were more or less independent ideological options between which people choose, just like that. It is only really understood if viewed within the kind of politics described in this chapter. For such repression and counter-repression is always associated either with attempts by regimes or social groups to *resist* redistributional demands by the disadvantaged (for resources or power or both), or with attempts by other regimes to *enforce* redistributional programmes on the advantaged. Either way, it is the politics of poverty, inequality and imbalance which ultimately holds the explanatory key. Historical and contemporary evidence suggests very strongly indeed that the *maintenance* of gross inequality in a context of scarcity always requires force and repression; equally, *changing* such a structure of relationships may also involve force and counter-force.

XV

Are these problems insoluble? Have any societies in the Third World been able to break out of the cycle of poverty, inequality and imbalance? There are some instances of attempts at this which are worth looking at briefly, and the first example is that of China - the largest society on earth.[74]

Writing in the 1930s, R. H. Tawney compared the lot of the Chinese peasant in some areas to that of a man 'standing permanently up to the neck in water, so that even a ripple is sufficient to drown him'.[75] The predominantly rural population was cruelly taxed, oppressed, exploited and bullied by landlords, officials and generals, and was sunk in debt. A small ruling class - perhaps 2 per cent of the population - extracted something like one-third or more of what the peasants produced. The small peasants, accounting for some 70 per cent of the population, owned barely 10 per cent of the land. Living thus constantly on the 'brink of actual destitution', as Tawney described it, the slightest disruption threw them into starvation - a situation common elsewhere in the Third World, as the earlier discussion of Bangladesh and famine showed. Conditions had been growing steadily worse for more than a century. The penetration of China by the West, as described in the previous chapter, had acted further to disintegrate a supine and corrupt central regime. Local 'warlords' struggled for power and control with each other. A largely urban-based nationalist movement, supported mainly by intellectual groups from the end of the nineteenth century, never found roots or support amongst the vast mass of rural people, and hence was unable to make any significant changes in Chinese politics. From the 1920s, more radical groups emerged, civil war ensued and the Japanese invaded. Chaos followed, and famines struck. In one, at the end of the 1920s, between 3 million and 6 million people died in north China alone.

Under these circumstances, the Chinese Communist Party turned to the countryside and the peasant population to gain support to expel the Japanese and transform the politics of China. A long and bitter war followed which resulted in the victory of the Communist Party in 1949. In the last thirty years the revolution has produced far-reaching changes.

What the Chinese had to do was achieve both a major redistribution of resources and at the same time boost production, especially of food. The broad line of policy which they pursued was called 'walking on two legs'. This meant relying on the old and known practices (for instance in agriculture and health), but also introducing new skills, technologies and practices, and stimulating industrial activity. In thirty years the worst excesses of rural poverty, hunger and inequality have been eliminated. This was achieved largely through an initial and far-reaching programme of land reform which ensured a much more even distribution of access to key rural resources; by concentrating on food production first, as a basis for industrialization; by insisting on collective and cooperative farming so as to ensure a better utilization of the scarce technical and ample human resources, and so that both production and consumption could be shared better; by encouraging local self-sufficiency and a considerable degree of local autonomy; by developing appropriate kinds of mechanization and innovation; and by recognizing, decentralizing and institutionalizing the essentially *political* character of development. The results have been remarkable.

In most years now the Chinese are able to feed themselves. Grain production, for instance, increased from 108 million tons in 1949 to 285 million tons in 1975. The Gross National Product *per capita* in 1979 was estimated to be US $260 (compared with US $90 for Bangladesh and US $190 for India); life expectancy at birth is now 64 years (compared with 49 for Bangladesh and 52 for India); a massive educational drive has brought literacy up to *at least* 75 per cent in 1980 (compared with 36 per cent in India, 26 per cent in Bangladesh, and 24 per cent in Pakistan); an all-out attack on disease and ill-health involved increasing the number of appropriately trained personnel (like the famous 'barefoot doctors' and para-medical staff) so that in 1977 there was one 'doctor' for every 1160 people (compared with 8780 people in Bangladesh and 3620 in

India) and - amazingly - one nurse for every 480 people (compared with nearly 56,000 in Bangladesh and 6430 in India).[76]

None of this has been achieved without costs. The individual rights and freedoms associated with liberalism in the West have been severely restricted. The People's Liberation Army and the Communist Party continue to play major roles at all levels in organizing, controlling and supervising productive and distributive activities, and in making sure that people toe the line. Vast public campaigns - like the Cultural Revolution in the 1960s - attacked and vilified 'rightists', as they were called, at all levels of education and the administration. Many were dismissed from their posts to be 're-educated', and considerable disruption occurred in the politics of China for some years.

But the Chinese have not necessarily seen these as constraints on the revolution, but as conditions of its success, if increased production and equality in distribution and social esteem were to be achieved quickly against the legacy of Chinese history.

But there are still inequalities within and between the major groupings of the people (in the communes) and between the countryside and the towns. However, although the data is patchy, it shows that these inequalities are low by other Asian and Latin American standards, for instance. One estimate suggests that the difference in income between the top 20 per cent and the bottom 20 per cent is in the order of about 3 to 1.[77]

Few people now seriously dispute that there has been a massive transformation for the better in the conditions of most Chinese, in one generation, though life is still austere. China has also been able to avoid the worst aspects of dependency; it has eliminated the massive inequalities and gross poverty of pre-revolutionary days, and has prevented the growth of urban slums and the sharp social divisions and conflicts seen in so many other Third World societies. At the core of this transformative process, indeed the very process itself, has been a revolution in politics, that is a radical change in the control, use and distribution of resources, especially rural resources.

Such revolutionary change in politics - and that does *not* mean simply a change in *government*, as the above should have made clear - cannot, however, be had to order. The combination of conditions which gave rise to the revolution in China was unusual. Nor is the revolutionary seizure of power always possible, necessary or even desirable to achieve at least certain basic changes in some aspects of the politics of a society, for instance to make sure that the country produces sufficient food, or that incomes are sufficient to be able to buy it. In both South Korea and Taiwan - societies whose governments pursue *very* different policies from those of China - a variety of land and agrarian reforms after the end of the Second World War and the liberation from Japan brought important improvements in the distribution of rural resources, and was followed by a substantial increase in food production.

In Taiwan, for example, land reform measures by the government reduced rents and abolished absentee landlords; there was inducement for investment in agriculture; agro-industries were encouraged – in things like canned foods – thus avoiding major imbalances; and the government encouraged the dispersal of industries through the countryside (textiles, food processing and construction materials), which provided local employment prospects as agriculture became more mechanized.[78]

Similar measures in South Korea helped to feed increasingly urban populations which in both societies are now about 50 per cent of the total. Many of these are engaged in the manufacture of electronic goods, clothing and footwear – mainly for export, as mentioned earlier – since both countries are largely deficient in good natural resources. There have been persistently strong rates of growth in their productive systems: savings have been encouraged and utilized: illiteracy has all but been eliminated (the adult literacy rates for both are over 80 per cent); *per capita* income has tripled; and there has been significant redistribution of income in the course of this. In Taiwan (in 1966) the top 10 per cent of households received 26 per cent of all family income, compared with 37 per cent in Sri Lanka and nearly 40 per cent in the Philippines. The current patterns of income distribution in both Taiwan and South Korea are significantly better (especially in Taiwan) than in India, Chile, Brazil or even Tanzania.[79]

That being said, it also needs to be pointed out that in both societies the direction and character of growth has been achieved by a very strict and tough combination of government intervention (for instance in the rice market and in directing industrial locations), private enterprise and substantial foreign transnational investment and activity. What makes societies like these attractive to transnational corporations are of course the low costs, especially in wages, and favourable tax treatment. It is therefore not surprising that growth in both South Korea and Taiwan has been associated with severe control, by the government, of trade unions and political opposition, backed by some of the strongest military, paramilitary and security forces in the Third World.[80]

This shows that a revolutionary seizure of power is not a *necessary* condition of political change. Nor, however, is a revolutionary seizure of power a *sufficient* condition for overcoming the enormous legacy of a colonial past and a neo-colonial present, in the form of dependency, poverty, inequality and external control or influence. Cuba is a good case in point.

XVI

Before the Batista regime was overthrown in 1959 after a guerrilla struggle, the condition of the majority of Cuban people was appalling. Like many other parts of the Third World, Cuba was utterly dependent on one crop – sugar. It has been estimated that about 9 per cent of the population owned 73 per cent of the land. Some eighty-three individuals (half Cuban and half foreign) controlled the sugar mills. Major areas of Cuban politics were under US control. In the sugar business, US companies controlled 40 per cent of the island's crop and 54 per cent of its grinding capacity. US government revenue from Cuban sugar in 1927, for instance, was double the total annual revenue of the Cuban government in that year. US companies or citizens owned 90 per cent of telephone and electricity services on the island, half the railways and a quarter of all bank deposits. In other ways, US intervention in Cuban politics - even in the Presidential elections - was direct and open. A vast, largely landless rural proletariat and a substantial unemployed, underemployed or intermittently employed urban proletariat lived in gross poverty. In 1956-8, for instance, the real average income per head in Cuba (in constant prices) was not different from what it had been fifty years before - about US $200. Illiteracy was the norm. Undernourishment and disease were a direct result of these circumstances. Major social inequalities were pervasive. The Cuban government, supported by a narrow band of local wealth and foreign interests, was corrupt, impotent and brutal. Havana had become the major vice and crime centre of the Caribbean.

The guerrilla movement, as in China, gained wide rural support in these conditions. When the new regime came to power, it moved fast to alter the politics of these circumstances. Given the pattern of ownership and control of resources in Cuba, it is hardly surprising that they encountered major problems and substantial opposition, both within and without the country. Far-reaching land reform took place and productive assets were nationalized and redistributed. Much of the urban squalor of Havana has been cleaned up. The leaders of the crime rings fled or were exiled or imprisoned. The same was true for the supporters of the old regime and for opposition which has emerged since the revolution. Rural poverty has been greatly reduced, literacy is now the norm, and educational and health facilities have been well established. The old inequalities have been largely eliminated, and mass organizations have been set up to facilitate wide and active participation in politics. It is clear that the majority of the population supports the regime and feels part of it. Again, this transformation in Cuban politics has turned centrally on the redistribution and changed use of resources.

But the problems facing Cuba are immense. The legacy of the past is deep. It is still heavily dependent on its sugar crop, though now to the Soviet Union for buying it. There has been some growth, innovation and diversification in its productive system. But given its few natural resources and its long history of illiteracy and deprivation, this has been slow. External pressure - including invasion attempts, trade blockades and the punishment of countries which trade with Cuba - have not made things easier. And a plunging sugar price has forced Cuba to delay repaying a debt of some $1.8 billion to Western banks (apart from the estimated $7.5 billion it owes the Soviet Union.[81]

What this illustrates - amongst other things - is that the seizure of state power after more or less protracted periods of armed conflict does *not* signal the successful completion of what is loosely called a 'revolution'. On the contrary, it is only the beginning of a much more difficult and lengthy process in the politics of revolutionary change, that is in the organization of new ways of using, producing and distributing resources. Similar problems to those in Cuba - although on a much larger geographical and social scale - have faced Angola and Mozambique since their independence from Portugal in the mid-1970s, and Nicaragua more recently.

XVII

In chapter 1 it was argued that the politics of a society can only be properly understood by tracing the 'relations between its past and its present, between internal and external factors, between its history and its structure' (see p. 21). In the previous and present chapters I have shown how this web of relations has acted to shape the politics of Third World societies, and the problems which they experience. The historical legacy is crucial, as is the continuing role of transnational corporations, banks and international financial and trading factors in their affairs. But internal factors in their politics - of ethnicity and class, for instance - help to sustain and deepen their inequalities, imbalances and repression. Moreover, the chapter has sought to underline the general argument of the book that politics is far more than the activities of parties and governments, but consists of all the activities of cooperation and conflict within *and between* human societies in their use and distribution of resources. That, too, is *really* what the subject of 'international relations' is about.

Now it is true that over the last thirty years most of the societies discussed here have experienced growth, if measured in the aggregate terms of such criteria as output per head, or available real income per person.[82] Yet, with few exceptions, the majority of people in these societies have not benefited from this and remain in great poverty, both relatively and absolutely. In most, the distribution of growth has been grossly skewed. Imbalance and inequality remain deeply entrenched structurally. Conflict and repression go hand-in-hand with this.

Can many of these societies escape from such conditions? It is doubtful if any of them can do this on their own. Groups of them would have far better chances, but this would need careful cooperation and planning within and between them. Moreover, aid - in the form of capital, technology and expertise, for example - will never of itself help to overcome their problems. And if aid is not to deepen yet further the inequalities and imbalances, far-reaching changes in the politics of most Third World societies are necessary. But powerful interests with powerful support at home and abroad make this difficult. Though bleak, the future remains open. Yet what happens in the Third World may also depend on the politics of industrial societies in the North. And so, it is appropriate at this point to turn finally to examine their major characteristics, using Britain as a case study. That is the subject of the next chapter.

CHAPTER NINE

Equal rights, unequal opportunities: politics in industrial societies, the case of Britain (part 1)

I

It is now time to turn back from distant and perhaps unfamiliar societies to look at politics in Britain, which will be used as the major example of an industrial society. The broad framework of enquiry which has been developed in earlier chapters will be used here in the same way.

There is a great deal of ground to cover, even in an introductory account of this kind. For this reason, the material is divided between this chapter and the next. They are designed to stand together, but it may be sensible for readers to attack them in two bites, since some of the evidence is quite dense in places. This first part of the account sets out the broad lines of the argument and then concentrates on the main productive and distributive patterns in Britain. The second part, in the next chapter, examines the systems of power, social organization, culture and ideology in the society which are associated with them.

The central thesis of these chapters is that the major features of British politics are best understood when seen as part of the activities of cooperation and conflict which continually occur over the use, production and distribution of resources. The patterns which this has produced reflect considerable inequalities across a wide range of matters. It follows that politics in Britain, as is similarly the case with all major Western industrial societies, is inescapably the politics of conflict which arises both from these inequalities and also from efforts to change or maintain them.

II

It is important to start by pointing out that it may actually be more difficult to study one's own society than other unfamiliar ones. This is because we are so much part of that which we seek to explain. In other words, most of the activities of our society are so familiar to us that we tend to take them for granted and we are not easily able to stand back from them and subject them to careful scrutiny.[1]

For this reason it is quite a useful device (but only a device) to ask initially what features of British society would be most likely to strike outsiders as distinctive, if it were the first industrialized society they had ever visited. Of course, it would depend on who they were, where they came from, what they might be looking for, and where they went. But by referring to some of them here one can highlight a few of the more obvious points of contrast between the politics of industrial society in Britain today and those societies which have been discussed before.

Perhaps the first thing that would strike visitors to Britain would be the sheer size of the population. Moreover, outside the limited circle of family, friends, work-place, clubs and associations, most people do not know each other, nor can they immediately 'place' other people. Visitors would find very few people living on the land and engaged in agriculture. Most are in towns. In and around these urban centres they would see a constant coming and going of ships, planes, trains and trucks, ferrying raw materials, manufactured goods and people. In these areas they would find concentrations of people working in factories, offices and shops. They would notice the sudden rush of people at the start and at the end of the working day (and for others at unusual shift times), entering and leaving these places of work, crowding onto buses and trains which take them to and from the residential areas. They might also actually see some of the unemployed people in the cities, perhaps queueing up at Social Security offices, congregating at Job Centres or - especially the youth - just hanging around and kicking their heels in city centres. They would not be likely to see the less visible, but significant, groups in the society - some old-aged pensioners, the mentally ill, the handicapped and the imprisoned, as well as the very large number of people who work at home, mainly housewives.

Sooner or later, either directly or through the media, visitors would encounter industrial disputes; strikes; go-slow campaigns; announcements of company closures or redundancies; the delivery of petitions to Parliament, Downing Street or County Hall; marches; demonstrations, and perhaps the occasional sit-in, squat or even inner-city riot.

Travelling up and down the country, such observers would note certain broad similarities, for instance in culture and in the structure of families. But they would also see the symptoms of social differentiation and inequality, within regions and between social groups in them. For example, the outward signs of poverty would be especially noticeable in some of the inner-city areas, particularly in respect of grimy environments, run-down housing and poor facilities. Casual observation might lead visitors to conclude that, in general, ethnic minorities in Britain are the most disadvantaged, and official government publications would confirm such a view.[2] More broadly for the society as a whole, they would notice differences in the quality and style of dress, and in the residential patterns, for example as between the leafy suburbs of large detached homes and the rows of more or less identical terraced housing or high-rise flats. This would be apparent not only between regions (for instance the North-east as contrasted with the South-east) but also within them.

If they remained in one particular community for long enough, visitors would soon become aware of the enormous number of voluntary organizations which exist within the society. These include sporting groups, tenants' associations, youth movements (like Guides and Scouts), amateur dramatic groups and charities. They would soon also encounter other associations and institutions, like the political parties, pressure groups and trade unions. If they were in the country at the right time they would hear of, or see, the grand conferences of such organizations, like those of the political parties, the Trades Union Congress and the Confederation of British Industry. Through the press, radio and television they would soon become familiar with the faces and voices of officials in the parties, unions, industry, education, pressure groups, sport, police and other institutions.

As the visitors moved around the country they would observe some of the more unusual costumes and uniforms which are worn, some of which might raise a giggle or two. For example, there are the remarkable outfits of the judicial profession, with their wigs and gowns, or the dark-suited and bowler-hatted gents of the City of London, or the various garbs of different religious institutions and officials (whether the Salvation Army or the Archbishop of Canterbury), or of schoolchildren, waiters, waitresses, policemen, porters, bus-conductors, 'punks' and many other social groups.

Over the course of a year, as seasons changed, they would see some of the peculiar local rituals, ceremonies and institutions of British society. They might watch university graduation ceremonies, harvest festivals, Royal visits to provincial towns, the presentation of various honours (like knighthoods), the rituals of Ascot horse-racing, or miners' galas, or the opening nights of major theatrical performances, or Remembrance Day services in London and elsewhere. As the end of the year approached they would see the frantic build-up to Christmas, with its increased pace of consumerism, the decoration of streets, shops and homes; and with lights, artificial snow and trees being placed inside buildings. In between these seasonal events, they would be able to observe the regular rituals of the christening of babies and the disposal of the dead, as well as various kinds of marriage ceremonies, civil and religious, amongst different classes, with all their associated activities (like stag nights, wedding parties, the reading of telegrams, and the sometimes noisy send-offs of honeymoon couples).

In noting these things it would be surprising if the visitors did not come to recognize a pervasive ideology and practice of competition in the society. This could be identified not only in the productive activities, as expressed so vividly in advertising, but in many other spheres of life as well, for example in consumption, leisure and sport. They would find it in competition between individuals (whether for the best brain, brawn or beauty) and teams (as in football, cricket and rugby) with all their associated crowd behaviours, the symbols of team identification and support amongst followers, such as songs, colours, scarves and the rest. Against this, there would be the noticeable –

though less sharp - ideology and practice of cooperation, in the countless clubs and voluntary associations of people in all walks of life, private and public, recreational and 'party political'.

Finally, it would be difficult for visitors to avoid coming to the conclusion that while the Maasai often talk about cattle and pastures, and the !Kung about game and hunting, the British regularly talk about money, jobs, prices and the cost of living.

Now it is central to the general argument of this book, and the present two chapters in particular, that these and other aspects are not more or less quaint features of the 'British way of life' which, depending on your point of view, are either amusing or irritating or good or bad. Rather, the point is that these things are fundamentally *important*, even if obvious, because they are the symptoms, even if superficial, of the wider politics of the society. And the central purpose of this chapter is to offer an explanation of the broad features of British politics which underlie some of the things referred to above.

But if you turn to the substantial literature on British politics you will find little analytical help.[3] This is because the major focus of such literature is in general not on *politics*, as the term is used here, but on *government*, and all the associated party political, constitutional, electoral, legislative and administrative issues which usually concern the central (and sometimes local) public institutions of the state. Although such an approach may be useful for the study of government, it tells one little about the politics of the society. And it should be clear by now why the study of politics, and hence British politics as well, is regarded here as being far wider, more inclusive, more interesting and more important than the traditional focus on parties, personalities, cabinets and government institutions. The latter are of course *part* of British politics, but only a small if important part. For politics is to be found wherever you look in the society and *far* more widely than at Westminster. It is found in feminist groups, parents' groups, staff associations, protest groups, professional bodies, trade unions, women's institutions, chambers of commerce and countless others. It is also to be found in such institutions as schools, universities, factories, banks, law firms, hospitals, stores, insurance companies, services, nationalized industries, cooperatives and student unions, *and* in the network of relations between them, and *not only* in Whitehall or County Hall. Politics is also to be found in all the campaigns by various *ad hoc* and established groups which aim to secure facilities for the elderly or the disabled, or the poor or the young; to obtain crèches for working mothers or to have the lead level in petrol reduced; to ensure 'No to building nationalization' or 'to save our grammar schools'; to persuade people and government against or for nuclear disarmament, the conservation of the countryside, new airports, trunk roads or coal-mines; to protect or expand commuter transport services; to counteract smoking in public places or the closure of village schools, and many other matters. Politics is also expressed in advertising campaigns by private or public bodies which seek to persuade people to use or consume resources in particular ways.

Moreover, the major problems which face modern Britain are really only explicable when seen as the product of the way in which resources have come to be used and distributed. Such problems in the modern era occur against a background of what is loosely called the 'economic' crisis, and they include regional decline and inequalities, as in Scotland and Wales for instance; unemployment and its distribution between classes, sexes, regions and ages; the disease patterns across the country as between such groups; inner-city decay and urban violence. There are of course many ways of looking at such problems, and of treating them. But the point here is that they are essentially *political* problems in that politics is directly involved both in the creation of such social problems and in attempts to resolve them. Nor are they only insular problems. Their origins and explanation lie also partly in the history of this society, *and* its relations - past and present - with other societies.

It will be argued, therefore, that across the full sweep of the society - from village to capital, from the smallest local government department to the largest state agency or private corporation, and in the relations between them - all the conflicts, campaigns and problems of British politics (in the private and public sectors) flow from and around the central coordinates of resource use and distribution, and power over decisions about such matters.

It goes without saying that to analyse British politics in detail in these terms in two chapters, or even one book, is simply impossible. It cannot all be explored. Thus the chapters will concentrate mainly on the broad structure of national politics and will illustrate the central themes with appropriate evidence for that level. But this provides the context for politics at local levels, within particular regions, institutions and campaigns. Readers may be tempted to use the general framework adopted here to examine aspects of their local politics more closely, with a view to testing the usefulness of that framework and the notions of politics which underpin it.

But first it will be useful to sketch the main outline of the argument which follows.

III

At the heart of the present argument are three propositions about the politics of modern British society.

First, it is unquestionably true that most people in Britain today live in conditions of material welfare and enjoy opportunities which are far better than those which prevailed a century ago. It is none the less the case that the *distribution* of material well-being, opportunities and life-chances in general remains extremely uneven. In that sense it is still a most unequal society. This applies both to regions as well as social groups. This will be illustrated in relation to the distribution of land, wealth and income, as well as health care, employment, educational provisions and other social indicators. These kinds of inequalities compose the structure of relations within which most politics in Britain takes place. For all the major activities of cooperation and especially conflict flow from or give rise to this structure of inequality, both in the private and the public sectors.

Secondly, Britain is often regarded as one of the foremost among the *liberal-democratic* societies of the world. With the possible exception of the increasingly vexed question of 'race' and community relations in Britain, it is certainly the case that it is a remarkably *liberal* society. Dissent, eccentricity, unusual behaviours and odd opinions are tolerated to a very considerable degree, though this is probably more true for the large cosmopolitan cities than the smaller towns and villages. That being said, closer examination does not suggest that the politics of British society is in any way as *democratic* as it is often claimed to be. Of course, such a claim depends on what is meant by the term 'democracy'. Democratic politics involves far more than the undoubtedly important institutions of free elections, free speech and the existence of certain kinds of rights and liberties. What is central to democratic politics is both the right *and* opportunity for effective participation in decision-making about the use, production and distribution of resources. This means thinking about democracy in terms that are wider than the election, control and accountability of *government*. And it means asking this: are the productive affairs of the society, in the private and public spheres, as they affect resource use and distribution, under the effective and popular control of the community?

The fact of the matter is that both in the public and private sectors of British society, decision-making power is confined to a remarkably small number of people within all the main institutions, whether these be local and national government departments; private companies, banks and corporations; factories, insurance firms, nationalized industries, political parties, pension funds and so forth. Whether this is good, bad or inevitable in such a large and complex society is a separate issue: all that needs to be stressed here is that it seems clearly to be the case. It is in this respect that while Britain may be regarded as a very *liberal* society, it is necessary to question sharply the widespread assumption that politics in Britain are democratic.[4]

It is a further part of the argument here that these two central features of British politics - the uneven distribution and control of *both* resources *and* power - are related to each other through a third major factor. This is that the ownership and control of the bulk of productive and other resources in the society are in private hands. Those who control the use and distribution of these resources have no real obligation or accountability to the wider society, nor are they required to, although they may be constrained by various laws which specify in some areas (like health and safety regulations) what they may or may not do in the public interest. The central fact of private resource use and distribution in Britain is that those who own or control resources may and do use them more or less as they wish in pursuit of their private interests, and *not* those of the society. For this reason, private ownership is a major source of power and authority in the society. Moreover, the tight state direction of public funds (through government control of public expenditure) means that in the public sector as well there is very little effective participation by the community in decisions which have far-reaching effects on the society as a whole. Thus the private ownership and control of the major productive resources, plus state control over raising and spending public funds, are together the paramount factors influencing the broad contours along which politics in Britain flows. This serves to explain much of the inequality in the society which was referred to above, as well as the absence of the democratic processes. The essential point here is that both private ownership *and* state control *necessarily* exclude the democratic management of resource use and distribution by communities, for neither allows or encourages active public participation.

More generally – since this is more or less the case in all Western industrial societies – this raises the question as to whether the productive and social system we refer to as 'capitalism' is at all compatible with the central principles and ideals of 'democracy'. The same general issue can be raised with respect to the so-called 'communist' societies (or 'state capitalist' societies as some would call them) of the Eastern bloc. There, very tight state control in all sectors of the society seems to be in stark contrast with the democratic and participatory principles of the socialist ideal.

The rest of this chapter and the next one will amplify and illustrate these central strands of the argument.

IX

As was shown in the previous chapters, the starting-point for the analysis of the politics of any society must be an understanding of the central features of its system of production. For Britain this means industrialism.

Regarded strictly as a productive system, industrialism is characterized by the systematic application of machines to raw materials in order to make things (sometimes other machines), supervised by human labour, though increasingly by programmed computers. It involves, also, a constant modernization of technology. Such productive activities consume huge amounts of energy, the vast bulk of which is provided by the conversion of inanimate energy sources into productive power. Human and animal energy is, by contrast, quite insignificant.

The transformation of Britain from an agricultural society into a primarily industrial one, which was discussed briefly in chapter 7, can be illustrated with appropriate figures. Towards the end of the eighteenth century, in 1770, agriculture still accounted for nearly half (45 per cent) of national income. Manufacturing, mining, building and commerce together only accounted for about 37 per cent.[5] Throughout the nineteenth and twentieth centuries the process of industrialization continued to shift the focus of productive activities (and hence population) from the countryside to the towns, from agriculture to industry, and created an urban society from what had been a rural one.

Thus, by 1978, some two hundred years later, agriculture contributed only some 2.5 per cent to the Gross Domestic Product, while industry and related activities (for instance mining, manufacturing, construction, energy supplies, transport and communications) together accounted for nearly 48 per cent.[6] Not surprisingly, the single largest sector of employment today is in manufacturing and construction (35 per cent), followed by financial and professional activities (20 per cent), distribution (12 per cent), and the public services (7 per cent).[7]

Now a society built around industrialism is necessarily an urban one, though not all urban societies are, or have been, industrial. In modern Britain today more than 90 per cent of the 56 million people live in towns. This figure contrasts sharply with the agricultural (and hence primarily rural) societies like Bhutan, Nepal and Burundi, where less than 5 per cent of the people live in towns, even small ones.[8] In this obvious and most striking way it can be seen how important aspects of social organization (in this instance residential patterns) are decisively influenced by the character of the productive system.

But what does an industrial society like Britain actually *produce?* How, in general, does it make a living? To answer these questions it is necessary to look at some apparently rather dull facts, but they are of the greatest importance if we are to understand the productive and social activities which form both the context and core of British politics.

Until the early nineteenth century Britain was still self-sufficient in food. But with the growth of industry, urbanism and population, this self-sufficiency declined. Already by the 1870s some 50 per cent of wheat and flour consumed in the country was imported, and the volume was increasing. With the development of refrigeration techniques, the first imported meat was beginning to arrive and the *per capita* consumption of items like tea and sugar had increased fourfold since 1815.[9] Today, there is still an active and highly productive farming sector in Britain, although its contribution to the Gross Domestic Product is very small. But Britain is no longer self-sufficient in food. The notion of self-sufficiency is a complicated one and can be measured in various ways. Depending on how this is done, the degree of self-sufficiency, expressed in percentage terms, ranges from about 52 per cent to 70 per cent.[10]

To give some concrete examples of this, Britain (in 1976/7) was largely self-sufficient in barley, oats, milk, eggs, veal and poultry. But it was not at all self-sufficient in wheat, fresh vegetables, sugar, fresh fruit, butter, sheepmeat, oils and fats.[11] When you look at other figures it soon becomes clear that Britain *imports* far more food than it exports. Indeed, over 16 per cent of British imports in 1975 (out of a total of £24 billion) were taken up with live animals and food, including such items as meats, dairy produce, fish and seafood, rice, grains, fruit and vegetables, coffee, tea and cocoa, as against less than 5 per cent of exports (of a total of £20 billion). In short, when you think of the typical diets in Britain and the staple items in them, it soon becomes clear why food is such an important component of imports. Hence, the politics of food production and purchasing is very important. This is true not only with respect to Britain's trading relations with the European Community but also with many Third World societies, from where some items (fruit, sugar, non-alcoholic beverages such as tea and coffee) originate.[12]

But it is when one turns to the other productive sectors of the society that one begins to get a broader sense of what industrialism is about. The import-export figures are again useful indicators of this. In addition to live animals and food, Britain imports vast quantities of raw materials and fuels, which in the 1970s together accounted for nearly one-third of all imports.[13] Some of the things which are included in these categories appear very traditional, in terms of the issues which were discussed in chapter 7. They include skins, groundnuts, rubber, timber, wood pulp, wool, cotton, stone and so forth. But they also include very modern items such as synthetic fibres, minerals like asbestos, lead, zinc, aluminium and copper - and of course iron - and a remarkable range of 'raw' chemicals.[14]

With these and other primary materials, firms and factories produce the bulk of industrial exports which enable the society to make a living within the global system of politics. Well over 70 per cent of British exports are accounted for by manufactured goods, machinery and transport equipment. What are some of the items which fall into these categories? The list is enormous, but a few examples will help to give the flavour. They include yarns, textiles, carpets, glass, metal components, sheet metal, tubes, pipes, containers, boxes and tools. Then there are machines like boilers, engines, tractors, buses, cars, office machinery and machine tools. There are various parts like taps, valves, electrical components, cables, railway gear, telecommunications equipment, and large items like aircraft, ships and boats. There are also precision items like instruments, medical equipment and pharmaceuticals, but also mundane things like furniture, books, corset busks, paint rollers, central heating systems and toilet equipment. Data on arms exports are hard to come by, but between 1973 and 1977 Britain supplied about 5 per cent of world armaments, being fourth in line after the USA (38 per cent), the Soviet Union (33 per cent), and France (6 per cent). Investment in military production accounted for nearly 17 per cent of investment.[15]

The production of goods of this kind requires both secure sources of raw materials (including especially energy sources) and foodstuffs, as well as markets in which to sell such products. While Britain ruled an empire the procurement of raw materials was seldom a major problem and costs could be kept low. And so long as Britain was the leading manufacturer of industrial goods, she was able to dominate the markets for them. But as other societies (the United States, Germany, France and latterly Japan) industrialized during and after the nineteenth century, and as the empire came to an end in the twentieth century, Britain has had to compete more sharply to sell its goods, and it can no longer obtain raw materials and foodstuffs as easily or cheaply as before. Today, most other industrial societies (including the 'Newly Industrializing Countries' - the NICs - like Brazil, Singapore and Taiwan) are also making very similar products which they sell in each other's markets. Indeed, so far as Britain is concerned, more than 60 per cent of its selling is done in the industrial societies of Europe and North America.

All this underlines the point that Britain, while still in a very advantageous position by comparison with most other societies, is also embedded in a global system of relations which has many repercussions for domestic politics on a wide front. International competition directly affects what governments, managements and trade unions do and argue about in relation to resource use and distribution in the productive and social core of the society. British politics in this respect is reflected in all the conflicts between various groups over the rewards, costs and benefits of current patterns of production and distribution, and also in conflicts about proposals to change them in response to international factors. For instance, the fate of formerly dominant industries (textiles or cars) in the face of low-cost competition from abroad has stimulated calls for 'protection'. Likewise, technological innovations - prompted often by foreign competition - have had implications for labour arrangements. The attraction of highly profitable investment opportunities abroad has also had implications for employment levels at home, which in turn have provoked demands for controls on capital movements. In all these and many other respects, the politics of industrial societies like Britain are not autonomous, nor are they insulated from external factors and historical legacies.

V

Before turning to look at some of the facts of resource distribution in Britain, there are some general points to be made about the distributional principles which lie at the heart of its productive system of industrialism, which is a capitalist one. That is to say, a capitalist industrial system is one in which the means of production are predominantly *privately owned*, and the central purpose of production is *profit*.

Unlike pre-industrial Britain and most other non-industrial societies discussed in earlier chapters, all the main productive activities in modern Britain have become separated from the domestic domain and its immediate locality. Thus, at the heart of industrial capitalism in Britain is the factory system where financial capital is combined with machinery, tools, human intelligence and labour to produce the goods. More important for understanding the character of politics associated with this system of production, is that it is almost universally the case that the capital, tools and equipment which are used in the productive processes are *not* owned by the labour force but by those who own or finance the factory, whether private interests or the state. The same is true for the raw materials which are brought to the factory to be fashioned into goods, as well as the finished products. Even the very idea, design and detailed specifications of some products and tools are the private property of the owners of the factory, and are defended as such by the law, through the operation of the patent system. And such ownership is confined to a very narrow band of people.

It is worth pausing to note the contrast with some of the major features of the productive and distributive systems of other societies which have been discussed before. Amongst foraging, pastoral and subsistence agriculture societies, there is of course private ownership of many items, such as cattle, some food that is collected or grown, weapons, tools, houses and so forth. But the main productive resources on which people depend crucially for their subsistence and survival - such as the land, the rivers, the grass, the game, the flora and the waterholes - are generally regarded as belonging to the community, not to individuals or families. All members of the community usually have equal rights in them. In some societies, land which has been cleared and claimed by a family is theirs to *use*, but not to own. When and if they no longer use it, such land reverts to the community and others may claim and use it, or it may be re-allocated. Often, neighbouring communities (camps, bands, village or 'tribal' sections for instance) may be excluded from automatic rights in the resources (except in an emergency) but have their own resources of a similar kind, to which similar rules about use apply.

Thus, in general, it is true to say that in pre-capitalist and non-capitalist societies, people have not been separated from their means of subsistence by the development and intervention of highly defined property rights which exclude some of them from access to necessary resources. In many 'tribal' societies in Africa, for example, the land was held in trust for the community by the chief or headman. His responsibility was to allocate it to members of the tribe (or section of it) so that no one would be deprived of access to this central productive resource. The development of private ownership (and hence the buying and selling) of land - which proceeds apace in Africa and Asia - is often associated with the emergence of new forms of hierarchy and inequality in power, status, wealth and social organization. Moreover, this has been one of the major factors which has contributed to the problem of rural landlessness and unemployment which did not exist until the intensive commercialization of agricultural production occurred. In many parts of Africa, Asia and Latin America this was either initiated or rapidly intensified by European colonial penetration in the variety of forms discussed in chapter 7. These processes continue today.

By contrast, in Britain as in other capitalist industrial societies, very sharp property rights have existed for a long time. They went hand-in-hand with the much earlier processes of commercialization of agriculture and of capitalist industrialization. The private ownership and control of the major productive resources - of land, capital, factories, equipment, buildings and so on - by a small minority has meant in practice that the connection of most people with these crucial resources of subsistence has become indirect and usually insecure. Most people today derive their subsistence from wage or salaried employment: there is only a small fraction of self-employed people. That is to say we *depend* on being able to sell our labour, our skills and our experience in order to earn money, so that we may buy what we require to enable us and our families to subsist - food, clothing, housing and other needs. Few people have independent means of survival outside employment, except for the safety net of social security arrangements provided by the state, which are widespread but not universal in the industrial capitalist societies. But we have no *rights* to employment as the mainstay of our subsistence, by contrast with the rights of access to pasture for the Maasai, or the rights of access to agricultural land amongst Iban shifting cultivators, or the rights to game and wild plants amongst !Kung foragers.

The relevance and implications of this for politics in Britain should be clear. These distributional principles and organizational characteristics of the productive system of industrial capitalism lie at the root of British politics. They give rise to a whole series of disputes and conflicts, claims and counter-claims, demands and rejections, organizations and counter-organizations, micro-cultures (often associated with classes) and contrasting ideologies, theories and policies. The political activities associated with these disputes are found both in the public sector and in the enormous range of institutions, companies and firms in the private sector, as well as those institutions which overlap both the private and public. One needs only to look, for instance, at the interests, claims and policy proposals of broadly opposed organizations such as the Confederation of British Industry (CBI) - see their publication *The Will to Win* - or the Trades Union Congress (TUC) - see their publication *The Reconstruction of Britain* - to recognize that the origins and continuing condition of their differences lie in the organizational and distributive arrangements of industrial capitalism in Britain.[16] The central point here is that it is simply not possible to understand the politics of such disputes and differences unless one relates them directly to these inequalities of ownership, control, resources and power.

In the light of these wider considerations it is now appropriate to look at some of the facts of resource distribution in Britain. These are dealt with in terms of land, wealth, shares, productive enterprises and incomes.

VI

Land

In an industrial society the major components of wealth are *physical assets* like houses, factories and consumer durables, and *financial assets* like stocks and shares.[17] By comparison, ownership of land (which is a physical asset) is much less important since it is not (or no longer) a major *productive* resource, whereas in an agricultural society its role is paramount. None the less, the ownership of land in an industrial society like Britain is not without significance. In a very basic sense, those who own the land may be regarded as owning the very ground upon which the society is built and on which people live out their lives, and they can thus directly and indirectly influence many features of the productive and social life of a society. For instance, extensive private ownership can affect the availability and cost of land, and hence the location and design of factories, schools and houses, especially in and on the edge of urban areas where land is often particularly expensive. Ownership of agricultural land can influence agricultural policy and practice, with implications for the cost of living, food availability and diet. Likewise, ownership of land confers the power to grant or deny access to places of interest or leisure, and can also affect employment and welfare in rural communities. In all these respects, therefore, the control of land has important implications for the politics of a society, though these influences are seldom obvious and even more rarely discussed. This issue is one of the many which we tend to take for granted. So, who owns the land in Britain and how is it distributed?

There is an important point to make here about information on land ownership, or rather the lack of it. All attempts to obtain a detailed and accurate picture of land ownership and usage in Britain have met with powerful resistance from landowning groups who do not seem to believe that the facts of ownership should be open and public information.[18] An official government commission on agricultural land (the Northfield Commission) declared with great frustration in 1977 that throughout its work it 'was hampered by the lack of detailed information on many topics' it studied. The Royal Commission on the Distribution of Income and Wealth (the Diamond Commission) likewise complained that 'The paucity of comprehensive up-to-date information on land ownership is remarkable.'[19] Such lack of information, and the associated secrecy about the ownership and distribution of a key national resource, raises questions about how democratic such a society is and how democratic it can be. For without information it becomes very difficult for decisions to be taken by government or the wider community, as the Northfield Commission found.

None the less, despite these problems, the broad picture in Britain is known. The ownership of land remains most unevenly distributed and the bulk of the land is concentrated in a small number of hands. A complete national survey, the New Domesday Survey of 1873, set out to show how land was becoming widely distributed among the population. In fact it revealed the opposite.[20] More recent data confirms the general picture.

The total land area of Britain is some 57 million acres, of which 44 million are devoted to agriculture.[21] Another way of expressing this is to say that, of the total land area (in 1971), some 8 per cent was taken up with urban development and the rest was non-urban (including about 77 per cent for agriculture, 8 per cent for woodland and 7 per cent for the rest).[22] But although most of the land is thus non-urban, it only accounts for about 10 per cent of the *value* of all land in Britain, while the 8 per cent of land taken up with urban development accounts for some 90 per cent of the value. This underlines how important the *use* of land is in determining *value*, and the importance of the urban-industrial areas in this society.

In 1978, some 19 per cent of the total acreage of Britain was owned by the state (including central government, local government and various other government agencies, such as the conservation authorities). The Crown Estates, the Monarchy, the Church, the universities of Oxford and Cambridge and various charities together own a little more than 4 per cent. The vast bulk of land in Britain - well over 50 per cent - is owned privately, by individuals and companies. Of this last amount, the great private estates accounted for at least 31 per cent of the total, and perhaps as much as 40 per cent. That is to say, the landed aristocracy owns at least one-third of the total land surface of Britain.[23] This could amount to as much as 18 million acres, including estates of 5000 acres or more which are owned by some 200 titled families. Much of this is rural and some of the largest acreages are in Scotland, as will emerge shortly.[24]

For all intents and purposes, most people in Britain own no land, or next to no land, other than that on which their houses stand. Just over half the stock of dwellings (54 per cent of houses and flats in 1978) are owner-occupied, and the rest is rented from local authorities or private owners.[25] This accounts for very little of the land in the country, though some of it is extremely valuable. The vast bulk of the land (mainly agricultural and horticultural) in private hands is owned by a very small section of the population, the wealthy. The wealthiest 1 per cent owns some 73 per cent; and the wealthiest 20 per cent owns over 92 per cent of it.[26]

Though land is not the most important or main form of wealth for the rich (stocks, shares and other financial assets are), it is the form of wealth which is most 'differentially concentrated in the top echelon of wealth'.[27] Some 95 per cent of total personal wealth in land is held by individuals with estates of more than £10,000 (in 1973 terms). Of this, some 40 per cent is concentrated in the ownership of individuals with estates worth over £200,000. In short, it seems that this group owns some 38 per cent of the total personal wealth in land in Great Britain.[28]

The regional figures for Scotland are even more dramatic. There are some 19 million acres there. According to 1970 figures, about 2.5 million acres are state-owned, and some 12 million acres of the remainder are owned by a small group of 1739 landlords, out of a total population of 5.25 million. The top 10 landlords own about 1.5 million acres; the top 25 own 2.5 million and the top 50 own 4 million. Two members of one family alone own one-quarter of a million acres. In short, 546 estates cover 9 million acres, or 48 per cent of the surface area.[29]

While the figures for Scotland (and probably for the whole of the United Kingdom) are not as uneven as they were a century ago, it is still quite clear how uneven the distribution of land ownership remains. There has also been a contraction in the number of agricultural holdings during this century. In 1908 there were some 509,000 holdings but this had been reduced to 406,000 in 1960 and more than halved to 224,000 in 1977.[30] This pattern of increased *concentration of ownership* is reflected, too, in the decline of the tenant farmer.

In 1873 some 90 per cent of farmland was tenant-farmed; in the last decade this has been reduced to less than 50 per cent.[31]

This uneven pattern of resource distribution is reflected in other forms of wealth in this society.

Wealth

As was pointed out earlier, wealth is composed of two main types. These are *physical assets* (stocks of goods, vehicles, plant, machinery, dwellings, developed land, agricultural land and consumer durables), and *financial assets* (including deposits, shares, securities, savings, loans, stocks, notes and coins, and so forth). According to the Central Statistical Office, the total net value of *personal* wealth in Britain in 1976 amounted to some £288,314 million (which would perhaps be four times that amount in today's values), of which some 63 per cent was accounted for by physical assets and 37 per cent by financial assets.[32] Using a slightly different means of estimating wealth, the Royal Commission on the Distribution of Income and Wealth found that the distribution of wealth for the total adult population was still remarkably uneven, and had become still more concentrated at the top in the mid-1970s. They found that the vast majority of people in Britain in fact own very little wealth indeed. More than 50 per cent of the population have wealth to the value of only £1000 (perhaps £5000 in 1982 values) or less; more than 70 per cent of the population have wealth to the value of £3000 (perhaps £15,000 in 1982) or less; while some 1 per cent of the population have wealth to the value of £50,000 (perhaps £250,000 in 1982) and more. Put another way, this means that the wealthiest 1 per cent in 1976 had some 25 per cent of the total personal wealth, while the bottom 50 per cent had less than 6 per cent of the wealth.[33]

In this wider context, land constitutes only about 5 per cent of the total personal wealth in Britain. But its contribution to the wealth of the rich is far greater than its contribution to the wealth of others. Land constitutes 15 per cent of the net wealth of the top 1 per cent of land-holders, but only 1 per cent of the bottom 80 per cent.[34]

Despite these figures, there is no doubt that there has been 'an appreciable reduction in inequality' in the last fifty years. For instance, it has been estimated that in 1923 the top 1 per cent of the wealthy then had over 60 per cent of total personal wealth, while in 1954 this figure had declined to about 43 per cent. However, the main redistribution of wealth which has occurred seems to have taken place mainly *within* the top groups, that is the top 10 or 15 per cent, and not much more widely or significantly than that.[35]

Shares

There is a further important respect in which the inequalities in the distribution of resources show up dramatically, and that is in the ownership of company shares. It is true of course that today more than 50 per cent of shares are owned by institutions such as banks, insurance companies and pension funds.[36] This gives them important power over the major productive resources of the society and enables them to influence the life-chances of more people more directly than most actions of government. Most individual and small contributors to these institutions play no significant role in decisions that are taken about the funds at their disposal. Hence, two main groups in the society, the large private shareholders and the managers of institutions which hold shares, have a decisive influence on the single most important social activity of people in Britain today, their jobs. When one considers, furthermore, the degree to which there is an élite of overlapping directorships on company boards and also close connections between financial institutions and industrial enterprises, this underlines the extent to which both resource control and power in the productive system of the society is narrowly concentrated.[37] For all intents and purposes, the vast majority of people in Britain simply do not participate in decision-making about these matters, since they hold no shares at all.

What is true for the institutional shareholders is also true for the personal shareholders. Here, the distribution of wealth is starkly uneven. Some 93 per cent of the adult population in the 1970s in Britain held *no shares* at all. The majority of those who do have shares hold only a few. But about 1 per cent of the adult population holds some 80 per cent of these personally held shares, and some 5 per cent of the adult population holds about 96 per cent.[38] As will be stressed later, this structure of ownership and control has a strong influence on the politics of British society.

Industrial concentration

The previous point is underlined when one considers a further important factor. Not only is the ownership and control of the major productive resources confined to a relatively small group in the society, but the *number* of productive enterprises accounting for most of the output, employment and investment is also small, and *getting smaller*. In short, throughout the present century there has been a concentration of industrial wealth and power. The process continues today in Britain where the private sector still accounts for nearly 75 per cent of the gross domestic product and over 70 per cent of all employment.[39] Production is dominated by a small number of large corporations, and this can be illustrated in a variety of ways.

First, there has been a steady decline in the number of small firms and the emergence of the 'giants'. Firms having fewer than 10 employees *declined* in number from 93,000 establishments in 1930 to 35,000 in 1968. And in 1978 about 71 per cent (some 76,000 in all) of the total number of manufacturing establishments accounted for only 7.3 per cent of total employment: these were firms employing fewer than 20 people. At the other end of the scale, over 33 per cent of total employment was accounted for by 0.5 per cent (or 594 in number) of manufacturing establishments, which were firms employing 1500 or more people.[40]

Secondly, the share of output of the 100 largest manufacturing firms in the society has *risen* from about 16 per cent in 1909 to 32 per cent in 1958 to almost 41 per cent in 1970. Similar trends are evident in retail distribution, where today the multiple stores (like supermarkets and large self-service shops) take some 54 per cent of retail turnover. The same is true in finance and many other services. For example, the number of building societies in the United Kingdom decreased from 460 to 257 between 1972 and 1981.[41]

Put in a slightly different way, before the First World War about 2000 of the biggest firms accounted for half the manufacturing output. Today, that half is accounted for by only about 150 firms. Those firms are household names: they include BP, Shell, British American Tobacco Industries, ICI, Unilever, Ford, British Leyland, General Electric, Allied Breweries, Guest, Keen & Nettlefold, Rank, Hovis, McDougall, and Cadbury-Schweppes.[42]

In the early 1970s the 100 largest privately owned companies accounted for not only 41 per cent of manufacturing output but also for one-third of employment and just over 40 per cent of capital investment. They also carried out 70 per cent of industrial expenditure on research and development.[43]

Incomes

What is true for the distribution of wealth is also in general true for the distribution of income. On the one hand, while the real incomes of most people have risen considerably over the century, and the distribution of income has become less uneven than it was towards the end of the nineteenth century, it still remains clearly uneven. Moreover, the *re*distribution that has taken place has mainly been from the top 1 and 10 per cent to the top 50 per cent.[44] One calculation even shows that the percentage of income received by the bottom 30 per cent of earners actually *fell* between 1949 and 1967 from 12.7 per cent to 10.4 per cent (before tax) and from 14.6 per cent to 12.0 per cent (after tax).[45] The figures of the Royal Commission on the Distribution of Income and Wealth are shown in Table 3:[46]

Table 3

Changes in shares (per cent) of total personal income: 1949, 1959 and 1976/7

Before tax	1949	1959	1976/7
Top 1 per cent	11.2	8.4	5.4
Top 2–10 per cent	22.0	21.0	20.4
Top 11–50 per cent	43.1	47.5	49.7
Bottom 50 per cent	23.7	23.1	24.5
After tax			
Top 1 per cent	6.4	5.3	3.5
Top 2–10 per cent	20.7	19.9	18.9
Top 11–50 per cent	46.4	49.7	50.0
Bottom 50 per cent	26.5	25.0	27.6

For most people the major source of income is their earnings in employment. In the 1970s about 70 per cent of total personal incomes came from working for an employer, and only about 10 per cent from self-employment, the rest being from such things as rents and income from investment (like shares) which most people do not have. So it is important to look at the pattern of pay which accounts for the bulk of incomes. The figures are illuminating, especially when you compare the relative differences in pay of different groups in the society over the last century.

The important thing to stress here is that the following discussion is about the *relative* pay of different groups and occupations, not the absolute pay. That is to say, while the pay of most groups and occupations has clearly risen in real terms since the 1880s, the relative differences between groups have not changed dramatically, and in some instances not at all. For example, a male manual labourer about a quarter of the way up from the bottom in the manual labour earnings scale earned about 82.8 per cent of what the man in the middle of the scale earned in *both* 1886 *and* 1975. A man who was one-quarter of the way from the top earned 121.7 per cent of what the man in the middle earned in 1886 and almost the same percentage in 1975. In short, 'Eighty-nine years and immense changes stand between, yet the relative shares are almost identical.'[47] When the comparison is broadened out to cover males in various other occupations and categories, the general picture is confirmed, though one interesting aspect is that the relative earnings of professional and clerical occupations declined between 1913 and 1960. But this decline has been against the general trend, which shows remarkable stability in the structure of inequality in earnings. For instance, male manual workers received only 79 per cent of the average earnings in both 1913/14 and 1960. Furthermore, managers and administrators increased their relative earnings from some 250 per cent of average earnings in 1913/14 to 271 per cent in 1960.[48]

Though there are many problems involved in collecting, organizing and interpreting data on earnings, there is general agreement on two main points. First, it is clear that the *real* income of most people, whatever their occupations, is greater than that of people a century ago. However, secondly, the inequalities in pay structure remain very considerable indeed. For example, the *average* earnings for all adult males in full-time work in 1979 was £5200 per annum. Bus-conductors received an average of £4200, secondary school teachers an average of £5564 and coal-face workers received an average of £6600. But the chairmen of nationalized industries received around £30,000 and the chief executives of some large private corporations received salaries in the order of £100,000 or more.

The inequalities are even more apparent when the pay of women is considered in overall terms.[49] For instance, in 1980, the average hourly earnings of women in full-time *manual* employment (excluding overtime) was about 71 per cent of men's earnings; in *non-manual* occupations it was only 61 per cent. And although women represent about 30 per cent of the full-time adult workforce, they accounted for about 60 per cent of the low paid.[50]

Such differences in earnings raise a central issue. Why do some occupations get paid so much more than others? Why are so many women to be found in low paid jobs? Such differences cannot be usefully explained with reference to allegedly 'natural' factors, or to the supposedly impersonal forces of the market, or Acts of God. They are the results of *decisions* about the use and distribution of resources which are taken in the course, perhaps, of more or less complicated bargaining. But with or without such bargaining, these decisions are everywhere and always influenced by the structure, distribution and balance of power, and by the social organization, culture and ideology of the society or institution concerned. For instance, in Britain it is now normal to find women doing secretarial and related jobs; in many parts of Asia it is not in the least uncommon to find men doing such jobs, as it was in Britain in the nineteenth century and before.

In short, decisions about which groups do what jobs and how much they are paid are *political* decisions, and integral to the daily politics of any society. That is why this question has been raised here in the present discussion of resource distribution in Britain.

VII

To sum up this first part of the analysis of politics in Britain, it is sufficient to say that the productive system of industrial capitalism in this country is characterized by sharp inequalities in the distribution of the ownership and control of the major productive resources. This is largely true for most Western industrial societies.[51] Private property - in land or other forms of financial or physical assets, such as stocks, shares, plant and buildings - is unevenly distributed amongst the population. The same is true for the distribution of occupations between sexes, and the flow of income between both occupations and the sexes. A decreasing number of increasingly large firms accounts for the bulk of production, employment and investment, both at home and abroad. These firms play a very dominant role in the productive activities of the society, and hence its politics. They have great power to influence resource use and distribution, and hence the quality of life and the life-chances of the population.

In the next chapter these considerations are explored further, with reference to the structure of power, social organization, culture and ideology, and their influence on politics in Britain.

CHAPTER TEN

Equal rights, unequal opportunities: politics in industrial societies, the case of Britain (part 2)

I

What are the central characteristics of power and the main operational principles of decision-making in the major institutions of British society? How do these influence its politics?

It is important to stress from the start that an understanding of these matters and their influence on British politics cannot be separated from an appreciation of the patterns of ownership and control of the major productive resources, especially in the dominant private sector, which were outlined in the previous chapter.[52] For just as ownership and control of resources in that sector is unevenly distributed, so too is the associated power. Thus, any discussion of power in British society (or any other Western industrial capitalist society) which focused *only* on the institutions of government would entirely miss this vast field of non-governmental (or 'private') political activities which have far-reaching effects on the community.[53]

Control over resources is the essence of power in any society, and hence decisively shapes the way it is distributed. In an industrial capitalist society, this is true for the two main domains of power, the private and the public sectors. In the private sector it is clear that power is in no sense of the term democratically derived. Indeed, it is the opposite. Illustrations of how resource-control in the private sector confers power, and how this in turn conveys the right to make decisions, can be drawn from daily incidents up and down the country. For example, decisions about employment policy - hiring and firing - is a major form of this power. So too is the power to open, close, contract or expand factories, or particular lines of production. There are also decisions about what, where and when to invest - at home or abroad, in new plant or more staff. There are gifts to charities, research organizations, political parties, or the establishment of foundations, pressure groups and scholarship schemes. There is the power to decide where and how to expand investment in research, and the kind of research - for instance in the North Sea. In the sphere of the mass media, great wealth can enable those who hold it to shut down, buy up or amalgamate newspapers. And, through editorial appointments, it can enable newspaper proprietors - the so-called Press Barons - to influence the political line of the paper, as the recent history of *The Times* has shown. The power which comes from the control of resources and wealth can also be used to influence what shall be advertised. The importance of advertisement revenue to a paper has been known to influence whether or not it runs a particular story which may be embarrassing to one of its large advertisers. Control of retail outlets (for example bookshops and news-stands) can influence what books or journals will be sold. In short, across the whole range of productive and social life, decisions of this kind, which flow directly from the private ownership and control of resources, have a profound impact on the life of British society. This kind of power is the dominant or *primary* form of power in the society. It constitutes the main structure of power, or framework, through which the politics of most other disputes get worked out.

Of course, different institutions and groups in the society have other, or *secondary*, forms of power. These derive principally from their control of other resources, such as labour (workers, for instance), expertise (engineers or doctors, for example), and even prestige (perhaps clergymen). And when conflict occurs within or between institutions in the private sector of the society (perhaps an industrial dispute, or a boardroom battle for control of a company, or two firms fighting to dominate a market), the different groups in the conflict use whatever resources they have most of (primary or secondary) to try to turn the outcome their own way. All these activities of cooperation and conflict over the use and distribution of resources in the private sector are of course highly political. And although those who have control of secondary forms of power may influence the outcome of disputes, in the final analysis those who control the productive resources, that is those who have *primary power*, have the right to decide.

II

If this is true for the private sector, what of decisions in the public sector? For instance, what of disputes between local communities wanting, say, pedestrian crossings, or playgrounds or crèches from local authorities? Or conflicts between regions or national interest groups and the central government? This raises the large question of power and decision-making in the 'public' or governmental sector, and its relationship with the private sector. Are the patterns in this sector starkly different from those in the private sector? Does it need separate treatment? Or is there an underlying continuity between them? It will be argued that while there are certain important institutional differences between politics in the public and private sectors, there is no reason to treat them separately for present purposes. The essence of the argument here is, first, that government power too flows directly from its control of resources, public resources, and secondly, that its use of these resources is far less subject to wide, regular or effective popular or democratic *control* than is sometimes claimed in the official ideology of parliamentary democracy. This requires some explanation.

The government is the major agency in the public sector which is primarily responsible for raising public resources in the form of revenue and spending it on, and for, the public. The main sources of revenue are taxes on income (personal and corporation), taxes on capital (like Capital Gains and Capital Transfer Taxes), and the various taxes on spending (like Value Added Tax, customs and excise duties on items like tobacco and liquor, and various licence fees, for instance on motor vehicles). This authority to raise (and spend) revenue gives the government control of very substantial public resources. And this, as is the case in the private sector, is the core of its power. The question here is whether that power can be said to be exercised in such a way as to reflect the wishes, needs and interests of the community, that is democratically.

It could be argued that there are broadly two major aspects of domestic public politics in Britain. The first is to do with how this revenue is raised and how it is spent. The debates and conflicts about these matters reach their conclusions in the strange annual rituals of Budget Day, on the one hand, and in the announcements of government expenditure plans from time to time, on the other. The second major area of conflict is concerned with the rules and regulations (legislation) which governments specify, amend, support and enforce. These cover a large area of industrial and social behaviour, including civil and criminal law, as well as such matters as pollution control and traffic flow regulations, codes for fair retailing practices, the treatment of minors and attempts to regulate industrial relations. All the regulations and codes constitute the broad legal framework in terms of which resources are used, produced and distributed in the society. That, in essence, is what 'the law' is in this, or any other, society.

Now it could be said that, in respect of *both* these broad areas, the government of the day is severely constrained by the 'opinion' of the electorate, by parliament and by the jungle of pressure groups, inside and outside parliament and the parties, and that this makes politics in the public sector different from in the private sector, and hence 'democratic'. There is of course some truth in this. But the central point which cannot be avoided is that what enables the government to enact these things through legislation (and the administrative power which is embodied in legislation) is the majority which it commands in parliament. In much official ideology, and to some extent in popular thought, it is often held that parliament is supreme in matters of taxation, public expenditure and law-making. It is not. It is of course true that parliament (and especially the House of Commons) is *involved* in the processes, as are pressure groups and whatever organized or expressed 'public opinion' gets through. But to suggest that financial or legislative *power* is in their hands, or that it is even *shared* in any useful sense of the term, would be grossly false in most cases. The fact of the matter is that the real core of public decision-making power about these things resides in the Cabinet (*and* the departments of government), and it is derived from the majority which the party in office has in the Commons. While governments of both major parties have increasingly this century had to keep their MPs informed, and have had to engage in some degree of consultation and argument before, during and after their party conferences, they know (and the public knows) that, in all but the most unusual circumstances, they can rely on their backbench MPs who have all been elected on the same broad programme anyway. Moreover, the *vast* bulk of proposals for legislation arises from *within* the government departments, as do suggestions for raising and spending public resources. Thus, as one author on comparative government has written, 'There is a fiction that the House "controls" taxation and expenditure. In fact it does neither', and again, 'The Commons is not a true legislature but an extension of the executive.'[54]

Elections once every five years, or less, decide little more than which party (or coalition of parties) will have a majority and hence which government will be in office to exercise power in implementing its policies and programmes. But the electorate can not be said to *participate* in formulating these policies. They are decided by the parties and usually by relatively small élites within them.[55] So while governments are restrained, scrutinized and generally compelled to do things constitutionally (which also means according to custom and convention, and not only according to law) they none the less enjoy enormous power within the constitutional arrangements to make decisions about the use and distribution of public resources. This is a power which government (including the civil service), as with management in the private sector, guards and defends with great vigour against wider participation or greater decentralization.

There are some aspects of course in which politics in the public sector could be said to be different from politics in the private sector. 'The government' is composed of elected representatives in a way that the owners and managers of industry and commerce in the private sector clearly are not. But to regard government as being confined to the elected personnel who are in 'the government' is to have a *very* limited view of the actual range of governmental activities. There is a substantial and powerful bureaucracy of civil servants and administrators at national, regional and local level, and there are many appointed officials and executives of quasi-public institutions in the society. These are all authorized and empowered to make daily decisions about the use and distribution of public resources (such as regional development grants, house improvement grants, discretionary grants for higher education, social security payments, the opening or closing of mines, steelworks, or railway lines) which have far-reaching consequences for the individuals or communities who may be affected. Of course, such officials do not act arbitrarily. There are detailed rules and guidelines for them to follow. But large areas of discretion do and must remain. This is power.

But could it not be said that such officials are ultimately accountable to elected bodies, or persons (like local government, parliament or the Cabinet), in a way that managers of industry are not - except to their boards of directors, and they in turn to their shareholders? Only to an extent. For in government, as in industry, the lines of accountability are very long indeed. Moreover, of the

4.5 million people who work as public servants, some three-quarters of a million are in the central government civil service, though only about 4000 of these are policy-makers. The Cabinet (usually about twenty ministers) has a Cabinet Office staff of 500 civil servants. There is simply no way in which all the countless daily decisions of such officials can be supervised or monitored by elected authorities, and they are not. Moreover, as we shall shortly see, there are many areas of government (especially at the centre) which are shrouded in secrecy, and this makes investigation and therefore accountability very difficult indeed, especially for any person or body outside government.

What, finally, of the argument that the major political parties have the capacity, when in government, to rearrange the current distribution of resources and also to dismantle the concentrations of power associated with this in both the private and public sectors? In theory, this is so. In practice, it has never happened on any significant scale. It is a truism that the main political parties in Britain, especially in the twentieth century, have broadly speaking represented (and appealed to) different groups in the society. These groups have been characterized by whether in general terms they have, or have not, controlled or owned major portions of the productive resources in the society. Hence the traditional association of the Conservative Party with the landed aristocracy, small business and the industrial, managerial and professional classes on the one hand, and the obvious association of the Labour Party with the trade union and cooperative movements on the other.[56] In broad terms, that is, electoral and parliamentary politics has also been firmly anchored historically in the wider social patterns of resource distribution and control. The main parties have sought government office in order to influence the way resources are used in the society and so to sustain or alter current distributions. And each has employed or evolved differing theories in support of its policies. Over the century, it is true, there have been changes in distributional patterns, notably an overall decrease in the extremes of inequalities, as has been pointed out earlier. But it would be naive to believe that this has been entirely due to governmental action; politics in the private sector has been equally, if not more, important. Despite these changes, there has been clear continuity in the uneven patterns of distribution and an increase in the power and functions of the executive, that is the government, through the coming and going of different parties in office.

This suggests that in practice none of them has been either willing or able (or both) to alter in any significant way the principles and rules according to which this society goes about its politics. Over the last two centuries there have been, and there remain, pronounced differences in wealth, income and power in the society; there have been and there are different parties representing major social groups; there have been and will be times of bitter class antagonism. Through all this, major democratic rights have been gained by the people at large: the *right* to vote, to organize collectively, to demonstrate, to strike, to publish; to a free education, to free medical attention, and so on. But despite all this, in Britain, as in most other societies, radical political change (that is, change in the way resources are used, produced and distributed) is very rare and very slow. There are many reasons why this is so, not least of which is the continued combination and concentration of wealth and power at the top of all major institutions, and it is this which can choke off change from below. The decision-making arrangements and practices have shown remarkable endurance in retaining power at the top, beyond the grasp of advances made by the electorate and its representatives in the parliamentary system. And most people, it would seem, appear to regard this as a legitimate state of affairs, or at least one which is very difficult to challenge.

For all these reasons, it makes sense to treat power and decision-making in both the public and private sectors of British politics as a whole, not as separate. Government is clearly an important one - but *only* one - amongst many interlocking institutions which are all involved in the politics of Britain. In many respects they overlap and reinforce each other in the organization of the national use, production and distribution of resources. For instance, between 1979 and 1982 the evidence suggests that unemployed people, manual workers, semi-skilled and skilled workers, and pensioners had on average become *worse off* in terms of real income, while non-manual, managerial and professional groups had become better off.[57] This was due to politics in the private sector (for instance the relative bargaining strengths and capacities of the various groups during a recession) and also politics in the public sector (in the form of government taxation and social benefit policies). Another example of the intimacy and interdependence of the two sectors is the way in which national and local governments raise loans in the private money markets, the way private institutions invest in government stocks, and the competition between private firms to win government contracts. The evidence does not suggest a condition of fundamental antagonism between the private and the public sectors but a great deal of continuity and mutual reliance.

Moreover, decision-making procedures in both private and public institutions are not dramatically different. They are rooted in common structural characteristics and they reflect similar principles and practices. What are these? One may identify three main ones: those of hierarchy, the restraints on wide and popular participation in decision-making in the institutions, and secrecy.

III

Hierarchy

Given the concentration of power at the top, it is hardly surprising that in most industrial capitalist societies like Britain, more or less steep decision-making hierarchies shape the pyramids of institutional power. This is true of government and the political parties, and also of business firms, large corporations, professional associations, trade unions and educational institutions. The important exceptions are generally to be found in voluntary and small organizations, where the levels of participation and equality can often be high. Within the organizational culture and ideology of Britain this hierarchical pattern is generally held to be proper, a good thing, and - some would say - inevitable. Such phrases (and the ideology underlying them) as that it is the job of 'managers to manage', or 'leaders to lead' or 'governments to govern' reflect and maintain the prevailing practices. Of course, this is not to say that the higher personnel of all institutions are ruthlessly dictatorial. It is common for there to be more or less elaborate forms of 'consultation', 'opinion sounding', 'discussions' and the 'airing of views', often through a hierarchy of committees or consultative procedures. In some organizations (for instance certain trade unions), major decisions require a ballot of all members. But this is very rare. In general, when it comes to the real core of decision-making, the fact of the matter is that in most institutions, and hence across the society as a whole, decision-making power is lodged firmly at the top of the hierarchies.

Moreover, this power is guarded. Most people recognize this instinctively. Wherever we work, nothing is more likely to promote conflict with 'the management' or those in 'higher authority' - supervisors, foremen, inspectors, managers, directors, senior partners, chief executives, headmistresses, professors, bishops, Ministers, Permanent Secretaries and the rest - than attempts by members of the institution, lower down the hierarchy, to seek both the right and opportunity for direct participation in decision-making about resource use or the general running of the institution or department concerned. Make suggestions, offer opinions, prepare papers, voice ideas - yes, so long as they are advisory. More widely, in the society, write letters to *The Times*, contribute to phone-in programmes or chat-shows with Ministers or the chairmen of major industries, and the impression of wide public debate and even some measure of participation may be given. But try to redistribute real decision-making power more widely in an organization or institution and there will be trouble, even where it is in principle and constitutionally possible to do so, which usually it is not. Attempts to open up, broaden out and democratize decision-making in this way, in private and public institutions, are generally regarded as subversive, insubordinate or disruptive by those who hold power, and are firmly resisted.

The hierarchies are, furthermore, ladders up which people are encouraged to scramble. And while all individuals have equal *rights* to compete in this scramble in the Western industrial societies (best typified by the 'rags to riches' or 'log-cabin to White House' idioms of the USA), they do not in practice have equal *opportunities* to do so. This deep tension between rights and opportunities which lies at the heart of much British politics is a theme to be taken up later in some other contexts. For some people are clearly better placed in terms of background, status, education, connections or wealth, and this puts them at a substantial though not consistently winning advantage. Amongst the Maasai, for instance, successive generation *groups* (the age-sets) used traditionally to proceed through a series of age-grades with differing kinds of duties and responsibilities at each stage. By contrast, *individuals* in industrial capitalist (and 'state capitalist') societies compete for control of top decision-making positions in the hierarchies, and also for the personal perks that go with them. This competition in both the private and public sectors is often far from being democratic or open.

One may also often find sharp distinctions between groups in the hierarchies (most noticeable between the top and bottom) in terms of status (ranks, grades, levels) and incomes, and also in terms of associated rights and privileges. These may be functional from an insider's point of view, acting to mark out the rungs in the ladder. But to an outsider, they are also often very revealing about power and privilege, and sometimes amusing. These levels may be reflected in what people wear (not only in the sense of uniforms); different eating facilities; forms of address; titles; size of offices, desks, carpets and hatstands. That is to say, the *internal* social organization and cultures of most large institutions both express and maintain the power hierarchies. You can see this in the civil service, in the armed services, in the professions (like law and medicine), in large businesses, finance houses and the universities.

Moreover, Britain is not unique amongst the Western industrial capitalist societies in having remarkably close informal links amongst the upper echelons of the various private and public institutional hierarchies. In the private sector the institutions are ones which have been mentioned before: they include banks, industries, finance houses, retail firms, the professions, large multi-activity and often transnational corporations, newspapers, and so forth, as well as organizations like the CBI, the National Trust and the Design Council. In the public sector there is an enormous range of institutions, including of course the civil service and the government departments, the judiciary, the armed forces, the police and the Church. Then there are the better-known 'official' but independent' institutions like the BBC and the IBA, (Independent Broadcasting Authority).

Beyond these still, and beyond the nationalized industries, there is a multitude of further institutions, sometimes referred to loosely as quangos ('quasi autonomous national government organizations'). This is a large and diverse category of hundreds of government bodies and agencies. They include art galleries, museums, the Atomic Energy Authority, the Charity Commissioners, the Forestry Commission, the Gaming Board, the Ancient Monuments Board, the Patent Office and Her Majesty's Stationery Office, to mention but a few. There is also a number of advisory bodies on a great range of matters, including various kinds of training boards; and there are tribunals and such institutions as the Celtic Sea Advisory Committee and the Scottish Home Ownership Forum (a few of which have recently been abolished). A senior civil servant estimated that if one considered only the executive, regulatory and administrative bodies, there were some 200 quangos in 1977-8, spending some £3500 million annually. Another estimate suggested that there were some 9600 paid and about 31,000 unpaid posts to be filled in the quangos, of which a majority are part-time. Almost none of the senior executive posts in such institutions or their advisory committees (the trustees of galleries, for instance) are ever elected, and very few are advertised in such a way as to promote open competition. Most (especially at the top of the larger and more powerful quangos) are appointed by processes which originate and take place deep within government departments according to selection procedures which are still shrouded in administrative silence. However, it is known that a Central List (the 'List of the Great and the Good') is maintained from which people may be drawn. It is also generally said to be the case that 'among the sections of the population under-represented on the Central List are women, people under forty, and those from outside London and the South East region'.[58] The democratic and representative process does not penetrate far in these matters, with non-elected people (civil servants) playing a major role in selecting candidates for other non-elective posts of power and decision-making.

Together, these private and public institutions, *and* the persons who occupy top positions in their hierarchies, constitute what is loosely referred to as 'the Establishment', in Britain. In theory, anyone can enter it. In practice, that is not the case. All the main studies which have investigated the social origins of senior people in these hierarchies have shown quite clearly similar social and educational backgrounds.[59] And class, as will be clear shortly, remains of profound significance in these matters.

Moreover, once people have entered 'the Establishment', it is remarkable how often and smoothly they move between various positions within it, confirming that the divide between public and private is not nearly so sharp as sometimes suggested. Most of these activities (and especially the plum jobs) are concentrated in London and the South-east, though not exclusively. This network of institutions forms a well-established structure of posts and opportunities through which top people swing with ease. There is movement, for instance, from senior positions in government and the civil service to directorships of private banks and corporations, to the chairmanships of nationalized industries, to Vice-chancellorships of universities or Masterships of Oxbridge colleges. There is a regular flow from the judiciary, private industry and universities to advisory positions in government, to Royal Commissions, nationalized industries and official bodies (like the old Prices and Incomes Board; the Top Salaries Review Body; the recently disbanded Supplementary Benefits Commission; and the Advisory, Conciliation and Arbitration Service, ACAS); and also to Official Enquiries (into riots or telephone tapping or disasters or industrial disputes in the nationalized industries). Incumbent members of the Houses of Commons and Lords and retired senior members of the armed forces may also regularly be found sitting on the boards of companies, or as advisors to private institutions of many kinds. There is a steady interchange between various positions in the media, for instance from the editorship of a large national daily paper to an executive post in the BBC. More recently, since Britain joined the Common Market, a number of important new positions have opened up there for which members of 'the Establishment' have become eligible. A quick glance at the 'government' of the EEC, its Commission, shows mobility in that direction from Britain (and back) to be occurring.

It is important to add that it is not a necessary part of the argument here to suggest that such people constitute a tightly organized ruling class, though some observers would argue that they do.[60] Yet this informal web of institutions, and especially the people in them, do have or develop a kind of unofficial corporate identity of status which helps to shape and define a top-level national consensus of outlook and loyalties. In part, this is established by the remarkable mobility of people between these positions. But it is also sustained and almost institutionalized by the extraordinary system of honours in Britain, which is also hierarchical.[61]

At the top of the honours tree are the hereditary Peerages, no longer created, the most important of which descend from pre-industrial times. There are some 900 of these, including Dukes, Earls, Viscounts and Barons. Next, there are the Life Peers (about 300), and then the various Knighthoods (there are over 4000 living Knights and Dames), followed by a descending range of lesser honours such as the CBE, the OBE and the MBE.[62] All these are formally bestowed by the Monarch. In fact, the decisions are made by the Prime Minister on advice and recommendations from various official quarters. While the lesser honours are given to a wide variety of people - for their achievements in sport, in the media, in the arts and sciences, for example - the most prestigious honours (the Life Peerages and the Knighthoods) are given to the top people in the major institutions, private and public. These include members of the government and civil service; industrialists and financiers; generals and admirals; senior members of the professions; Commissioners of the Metropolitan Police; diplomats and occasional academics. Look at the top of all major British institutions - British Rail, General Electric, British Leyland, ICI, the National Coal Board, Parliament, the Treasury, the Foreign Office, the BBC, the Oxbridge or London university colleges, the TUC and the Army - and you will find that most of those who are (or were) in executive charge generally have, or are awarded, Life Peerages or Knighthoods.

This whole process at the apex of 'the Establishment' may seem distinctly 'tribal'. Indeed, so far as there may be said to be 'elders' in Britain these are they, situated in different but often overlapping sections. Sometimes they are brought together institutionally, for instance in the Privy Council (whose technical constitutional role is to advise the Monarch) which is made up of about 370 Privy Councillors who are present and former members of Cabinets, as well as 'eminent people' from the Commonwealth, all appointed. Then there are the Peers, who together have the right to sit in the House of Lords, all either hereditary or appointed. The honours system - which is thus also a means of both confirming *and* conferring power - has a remarkable set of rituals associated with it. These include investitures at the Palace, medals, titles, special forms of address, gowns with bits of fur on them, long dark cloaks with elaborate badges, and floppy hats with feathers. It may all seem strangely out of place in a supposedly secular, industrial society at the end of the twentieth century. But these are only the outer symbolic aspects of a system whose primary function is to integrate the diverse and sometimes competing institutional hierarchies into a wider national cone of power, prestige and consensus, which is generally above the level of party dispute and largely beyond the reach of the democratic process.

I V

Lack of participation

An important corollary of this hierarchy of offices and power is that *active participation* in decision-making is in general neither welcomed nor encouraged in the society, nor is it in practice energetically sought. The point has been implicit in much of what has gone before but needs to be elaborated here. In the private sector, companies and organizations engaged in production and distribution are generally not at all sympathetic to ideas or movements for greater participation by the workforce on boards or committees of management. Governments and members of legislatures and parties, in the public sector of politics, are generally hostile to wide public debates followed by binding referenda or plebiscites on major policy issues, whether these be such matters as capital punishment, nuclear weapons, the monarchy, the future of the House of Lords or intra-party policy issues. The same is true of balloting in some trade unions. It is also the case that planning departments, of central or local authorities, rarely go out of their way (nor are they always required by law to do so) to seek actively the views, preferences or participation of communities for whom they are planning facilities, whether these be new hospitals, housing developments or recreational centres.[63]

V

Secrecy

Closely associated with this is a considerable degree of *secrecy* in decision-making about resource use and distribution. In the private sector, given the highly competitive nature of the politics of commercial enterprise, this may not seem surprising. The stakes are often high, and the managements of companies are often extremely cautious about the facts they allow to be made public, about current production techniques and research, or financial circumstances, or future developments and plans. As with the secrecy which surrounds information about land ownership, it is sometimes very difficult, if not impossible, to find out the details of operations of large companies (especially transnationals) given their size and structure, especially in 'sensitive' areas both at home and abroad. This was well illustrated in the course of the Bingham enquiry into the alleged sanctions-busting operations of Shell, BP and other international oil companies in Rhodesia in the 1960s. While the Bingham Commission was able to piece together some of the story, it was not able to find out all the facts. Some oil companies refused – and were entitled to refuse – to cooperate with the enquiry. Moreover, it emerged after the course of the enquiry that a secret decision had been taken (involving only *some* government ministers, senior civil servants and British oil companies) to allow the companies to get oil to Rhodesia by what came to be called 'swap' arrangements between British and French companies. It appears that the full Cabinet was not even told of this deal. A similar difficulty with respect to information occurred in 1976 when a survey of 141 British companies with subsidiaries in South Africa revealed that they were not willing to provide information about the conditions of employment and wages of employees there.[64] Attempts even by small shareholders to influence the policy or obtain more information about the running of British building societies or banks have regularly met with failure in the face of the control exercised by the large shareholders.[65] The inevitable secrecy associated with competitive private enterprise has meant, for instance, that travel companies have continued to trade when their managements must have known that they were on the verge of collapse. The same has been true of smaller banks, financial institutions and other businesses, whose downfall has sometimes left ordinary citizens and other creditors in considerable distress, financially and otherwise.

Such secrecy is not confined to the private sector. When it comes to major areas of official information, especially about decision-making principles and procedures over the use and distribution of *public* resources, and about the facts of government themselves, Britain has 'the most secretive system in the Western world' according to Lord Croham, who, as Sir Douglas Allen, was head of the Home Civil Service.[66] While the USA, with its Freedom of Information Act, is more open with 'official' or government information than Britain, and while the Soviet Union is far more closed, 'the British system starts from the premise that the public have *no right* of access to any information except when it is made available for a particular reason' (my italics).[67]

It may well be, according to some people who have had access to much Cabinet material when working at No. 10 Downing Street, that a great deal of 'official' information is incredibly boring and routine.[68] But that is not really the point. What is important is that the public does not have the *right* to know, that there are today some eighty-nine statutes which include provisions which prevent the disclosure of official information, and that the range of matters closed to public scrutiny is very large indeed.[69] The main Act (in fact a number of Acts) which serves to convert official information into 'Official Secrets' is the Official Secrets Act of 1911, and subsequent Acts in 1920 and 1939. Its peculiar bite derives from Section 2 which makes it a crime for any civil servant or temporary employee of government to reveal *any* information learned in the course of his or her job, and also makes it a crime to *receive* such information, unless the government decides to make it available.

Some examples will help to illustrate how far-reaching is government control of information as a consequence of this and other Acts. There is, of course, the whole field of 'national security' and defence. But there are other areas in which the public have no right to information. For instance, official reports on sanitary conditions in some British food companies (found to be available in the USA) are not available to the public in Britain. The same is true of reports prepared by the Ministry of Agriculture in Britain on food colourings used in commercial food preparation. Many reports on accidents prepared by the Inspectors of Mines and Quarries are 'confidential'. Details of the work of the Alkali Inspectorate (which looks into pollution, especially through the emission of noxious gases) are not made available to the public. This is in large measure due to the fact that such information can, it is said, be commercially harmful to the company. Some critics of the Alkali Inspectorate argue that it fails to recognize the real conflict of interests there is between the firm (which is doing the polluting) and the public (which the Inspectorate is supposedly there to protect).[70] Most people do not know that, as patients in the National Health Service, they have *no right* to see their *own* medical records, except under certain limited circumstances which can usually only be brought about by legal intervention.[71] A further small but typical example of official secrecy occurred in 1981 when the University Grants Committee refused (and had every legal right to do so) to explain openly what criteria it used in the way it allocated public finances to British universities in the course of a severe cut-back of resources. Official Archives - housed in the Public Records Office - are only available to the public after thirty years (it used to be fifty years), and even then they are carefully vetted under the authority of the Lord Chancellor's office, though in practice this means it is done by civil servants in the relevant government departments.

The work of the Cabinet, too, is cloaked in secrecy, or 'confidentiality' as it is politely called. One government publication states that 'Membership and terms of reference of all Cabinet committees are confidential.'[72] This is certainly true of all Cabinet papers and discussions - which contrasts quite sharply with the open discussions of Maasai elders, or the public discussions in Iban longhouses, where everyone is entitled to *hear* the arguments, at the very least. In the industrial societies, governments have regularly launched extensive enquiries into 'leaks'. And when a national newspaper in Britain sought to publish serialized extracts of Richard Crossman's *Diaries*, based on his experiences in the Cabinet, intense pressure was exerted on the paper to prevent publication and then to edit severely what the paper proposed to publish anyway. The source of this pressure was, in the first instance, the Secretary to the Cabinet (a civil servant), Sir John Hunt, who was strongly backed, it would seem, by other senior members of the civil service. And when a London publishing house declared its intention to publish the *Diaries* in full in book form, the state (in the form of the Attorney General) took legal action in the High Court to prevent publication. After a celebrated hearing, the action was not successful, but the nature of the decision of the court and the subsequent discussions in official circles make it seem very unlikely that this could happen again.[73]

But what of Parliamentary Questions? Can MPs not gain information about any matter on behalf of their constituents, the public, by asking questions in the House? Some, yes. But there is a list of ninety-five 'Matters about which successive administrations have refused to answer questions'.[74] Some topics on the list are said to be matters of 'defence' and 'national security', including telephone tapping, the location of Regional Seats of Government (the local centres of government which will become operative in times of national crisis) and the amount of strategic food reserves. But there were other surprising topics on the list, including agricultural workers' wages, arms sales, the accident rate of aircraft, instructions to research councils, the attendance records at the Council of Europe, the details of near air-miss enquiries, reasons for refusing to refer mergers to the Monopolies Commission, and working details of the White Fish Authority.[75] At one stage, even details of the escalating costs of building Concorde were kept from Parliament by the Public Accounts Committee on the grounds of 'commercial confidentiality'.[76]

The main source of information and news for the public is of course the mass media of press, radio and television. There are those who argue that the very way in which controversial national items are reported by the BBC and ITV - events in Northern Ireland, 'the economy', major industrial disputes and so forth - is consistently biased in favour of the government view and against alternative interpretations.[77] They would explain this partly in terms of the similar background and outlook of senior media executives, civil servants, industrial chiefs and members of the government. But they would also point to the close links which exist between the media and officials. 'Regular pilgrimages from Broadcasting House to the Home Office in Queen Anne's Gate have taken their toll of the BBC's independence', writes one critic.[78] Programmes on aspects of the situation in Ulster have been blocked. Programmes on the poor safety record of some British Leyland cars have also been stifled by commercial and official pressure.[79]

In addition to this, the 'Defence, Press and Broadcasting Committee' (the 'D' Notice Committee) in the Ministry of Defence is made up of senior Services personnel, Foreign Office officials and some members of the Press. From time to time, the Committee issues 'D' Notices to editors. These are 'formal letters of warning or request' which specify subjects about which it would not be wise for the editors to run stories since they might endanger 'national security'. The 'D' Notices have no legal binding effect, but people can be prosecuted under the Official Secrets Act for giving or receiving official information. Now and again the system is breached and enquiries are undertaken.[80] These can often reveal quite clearly the extent to which pressure can be put on journalists, editors and proprietors of newspapers to 'kill' a story, as occurred in 1967 with the 'Cable Vetting' story in the *Daily Express*. In this instance, officials in the Security Services, the Foreign Office, the Ministry of Defence, as well as the

Foreign Secretary and others, were involved in a flurry of activity which took place over telephones between London restaurants, clubs, dinner parties in private homes, editorial and civil service offices. In the event, the heavy pressure did not prevent the story being published, and no one was charged with an offence. But it did suggest to some critics of the system that definitions of 'national security' seemed to be very wide indeed to permit such blanket 'vetting' of *all* cables. Similar worries about the implications of this for individual privacy and liberty have been raised by more recent allegations about telephone tapping.[81]

But governments do often want information, or selected information, to be made available. This can of course be done through official Departmental Reports, statements to Parliament, through Reports of Commissions or Enquiries, as well as White Papers and other documents published by the Central Statistical Office or Her Majesty's Stationery Office, and so on. There is a great deal of this, easily available and regularly published, and much of it is of a very high standard indeed. A chapter like the present one could not be written without it. But there is also a less formal and less open system whereby governments (and opposition leaders) can informally but legitimately 'leak' information to a rather select group of journalists called Lobby Correspondents in the House of Commons, and they do so on a regular basis. The Lobby has its own rules and conventions which act to preserve the secrecy of sources. It is this system which is primarily responsible for reports which are attributed, for example, to the anonymous 'sources close to the Prime Minister'.[82] In the middle of a major political row this can be a useful way of providing the media with ammunition which one side or another would like to see used in public.

Visitors, observing British politics, might be told that the main justification for so much official secrecy - about discussions, about decision-making procedures, about appointments, about facts obtained in the course of investigations into an enormous number of matters - is that it makes for 'good' or 'efficient' government. Civil servants can give 'frank' advice, and they and members of the government can take 'cool' decisions about difficult issues on the basis of the 'facts', beyond the glare of publicity and debate. Many of the facts, the argument might continue, are too technical or complicated for the public to understand or might confuse them. As two experienced observers have commented:

> The unspoken heart of the argument for closed government is that private debate among civil servants and ministers produces more *rational* policies, freed from public pressure which is assumed to be irrational. Wise men, cogitating quietly on the nation's problems, will produce 'right' answers if they are shielded from the hubbub of the political marketplace.[83]

Moreover, leaving aside the justification of 'national security' (which some people would contest on the grounds that its definition is far too wide), there is much information which could be damaging to commercial interests, which government must protect, and which would also not be in the public's 'best interest' to know about.

There may be some truth in some of this argument. But why, it might be said in reply, should facts about pollution be kept secret, or information about unsafe cars, or unsanitary methods of food preparation, or citizens' own health records, or full details of lead pollution? What, in short, is the justification for the central operational principle that official information in Britain is officially secret, and that the public have no right to know, except what and when the government decides to tell them? A fundamental requirement for any democratic society is that there be full and open access to information so that people may form views and express opinions about the way their society is run and organized. Without that, effective participation in decision-making is extremely difficult, both in the private and public sectors.

Thus, it is interesting to raise the question: is the degree of secrecy which applies in large areas of British politics consistent with the official claims and ideology that Britain is a democratic society? Is there in this respect (as in the tension between rights and opportunities) a fundamental inconsistency between theory and practice? And is the function of ideology about democracy in this respect rather like the function of all myth, to obscure reality or explain away uncomfortable paradoxes? Is it possible that the productive, distributive and associated power arrangements of an industrial capitalist society are structurally incompatible with the principles and requirements of wide, effective and participatory democratic politics?

Whatever conclusions one may reach on these broader issues, it is clear that the structures of power and the patterns of decision-making in the private and public institutions of British politics are steeply hierarchical, intrinsically hostile to wide participation, and pervaded by secrecy. The *private* ownership of major productive resources is necessarily incompatible with popular democratic control of them. Could it be otherwise? And government control over the raising and spending of public resources (plus the presumption that the official establishment knows best and hence must decide for the public) is one major factor which prevents the development of more open, decentralized and participatory patterns of public politics. The latter would necessarily diminish the power of central government especially.

For these reasons, it would simply not be possible for serious change in the distribution of power and decision-making to occur in Britain (other than the superficial shuffling of personalities and their supporters in various parties) without serious change in the productive and distributive arrangements.

VI

The productive and distributive characteristics, plus the relations of power which have been described above, express themselves in a variety of aspects of *social organization* in Britain. As was shown before, the patterns of urban concentration of both work and residence, for example, are a consequence of the industrial system of production, but there are great differences in the kind and quality of residential areas. Moreover, while the nuclear family is the dominant form of the family in Britain, there is also great variety in the sources and amount of family income, the kind of education children receive, and the patterns of family expenditure. Another feature of social organization in Britain is the number of voluntary associations there are, ranging from the Red Cross and the Round Table to pigeon-racing clubs, élite London clubs and working men's clubs. However, in general, people from different social groups join different institutions. Why?

Underlying most of the major differences in residence, domestic economy, family, leisure and membership of associations is the single most important principle of social organization in Britain from which they flow, that of *class*. In turning now to look at this question it will be argued that the politics of inequality in wealth, income and power discussed earlier is reflected also in profound inequalities in the main social and cultural features of the society. These inequalities together form the basis of class. The relations between classes are at the heart of politics in Britain. Since the concept and reality of 'class' is a complicated matter, some brief introductory comments are necessary.[84]

Some people, following the summary accounts of Marx and Engels on the subject, hold that there are really only two main classes in industrial capitalist societies: those who own and control the means of production and control the state (the bourgeoisie or ruling class), and those who do not (the proletariat or working class). While such a view does provide some preliminary guidance in looking at social structure and social organization, it is in practice far too blunt as an analytical instrument. It obscures much of the actual range and complexity of class structure and class relations. Thus the term 'class' in this argument means, in the first instance, a category of people who share a number of common characteristics which are different from those of other classes. These include such things as wealth, income, occupation, education and - rather more broadly - lifestyles or cultures. These characteristics represent the 'objective' facts of class and can be measured and compared. These sets of facts about different groups of people are what defines and differentiates the classes in this 'objective' sense.

But it is most important to stress, first, that these are not hard and fast categories, and that there are grey areas at the margins between classes. Classification is not a simple matter. Moreover, it does not follow at all that, secondly, the people who may be classified in these 'objective' terms as belonging to a particular class necessarily regard themselves as members of it. That is to say, self-definition (the 'subjective' sense of class) may not square up with the 'objective' classification. It also does not follow, thirdly, that all the members of an 'objectively' or 'subjectively' defined class necessarily regard themselves as a coherent social group, conscious of themselves as a group and united in their opposition to other classes, though as one author writes, they may have a 'disposition to behave as a class, to define themselves in their actions and in their consciousness in relation to other groups of people in class ways'.[85]

Two examples will help to illustrate the difficulties. Consider, on the one hand, a coal-miner who works at the pitface (and hence is a manual worker), who earns a wage which is above the national average for full-time adult male workers, who has no formal educational qualifications other than his school-leaving certificate obtained at the age of 15, and who lives in a council house. While an 'objective' definition of 'class' may place him in, say, the working class, he may *regard himself* and his family as middle class. On the other hand, consider a female secondary school teacher, whose parents were both 'working class', but who was encouraged in her education and took a university degree before becoming a teacher, and who owns her own house. An 'objective' definition of her class position, in terms of occupation, income, living accommodation and status may place her in the 'middle class', but she may *regard herself* as working class.

These problems are raised in order to emphasize the dangers of confusing the 'objective' and 'subjective' definitions of class. The discussion which follows is concerned primarily with 'objective' class. There are a number of ways in which this can be defined, but since the only full data on the population of Britain are found in the ten-yearly national census figures, I follow the basic classification of class adopted for the census by the office of the Registrar-General, which hinges on *occupation*. As will become clear, a considerable number of other social, educational and cultural characteristics are closely associated with occupation, and hence it is a very useful starting-point for exploring the class basis of social organization, and its influence on politics in Britain.

The Registrar-General's classification of social classes and a few of the typical occupations in each are set out in Table 4.[86]

Table 4

Social class	Examples of typical occupations in the class
I Professional, etc.	Accountant, architect, company secretary, doctor, engineer, judge, surveyor, university teacher, lawyer
II Intermediate	Pilot, farmer, manager, proprietor, MP, nurse, schoolteacher, laboratory technician
III (N) Skilled non-manual	Auctioneer, clerical worker, draughtsman, secretary, typist, telephone supervisor
III (M) Skilled manual	Bus driver, bricklayer, electrician, miner, hairdresser, policeman, railway engine driver
IV Partly Skilled	Agricultural worker, barman, fisherman, postman, packer, roundsman, telephone operator
V Unskilled	Charwoman, kitchen hand, lorry driver's mate, office cleaner, railway porter, window cleaner

Before proceeding to look at this in greater detail, there are a few points to note. First, it will be seen that Social Class III provides the main point of division between non-manual and manual occupations. Secondly, unless explicitly mentioned in the text or the notes, I shall be referring mainly to these social classes in the argument that follows and not to the somewhat looser terms (like working, middle and upper classes). Thirdly, though it is far from satisfactory, it is general practice to assume and infer the social class of wives and dependent children as being that of their husbands or fathers, and this generally applies to figures for households too, although it is quite possible and common for married working women to be classified in a different occupationally-based class from that of their husbands. Finally, notions of hierarchy are so deeply embedded in the culture and ideology of British society that, for instance, Social Class I is commonly regarded as 'higher' or 'better' than Social Class V. Whatever 'higher' and 'better' may mean in this context, no connotation of that kind is implied here. What is of interest and importance here are only the facts of difference between the classes and, more especially, the way these both reflect and sustain the inequalities in the productive, distributive and power relations in British politics.

The population of the United Kingdom stands in 1982 at almost 56 million, of whom 5.1 million are in Scotland, 46.4 million are in England, 2.7 million in Wales and 1.5 million in Northern Ireland. The vast majority of the population lives in the main urban concentrations. In England, furthermore, some 30 per cent of the population is in the South-east; 9 per cent in the West Midlands; 8.6 per cent in Yorkshire and Humberside; 6.4 per cent in the North-west and 5.5 per cent in the North.

Of the working population in the 1970s, Table 5 shows the Social Class distribution in percentage terms.[87]

Table 5

	I	II	III(N)	III(M)	IV	V	All
			Social class				
Male	5	18	12	38	18	9	100
Female	1	17	38	10	26	8	100
Both	4	18	21	28	21	8	100

From these figures it is clear that a majority of those in employment are in manual occupations (65 per cent of all employed men and 44 per cent of employed women), that the single largest category is that of Social Class III(M) (skilled manual workers), and the smallest category is that of Social Class I (the professionals).

The distribution of these occupation-based classes between and within the regions is also interesting. Some of the regional characteristics of class will be mentioned later, but the point to note for the moment about region and class is that 'income and employment combine into a powerful force to endow much of the south-east with a better social and economic environment on the whole than other parts of Britain'.[88] The South-east (with London at its core) has 43 per cent of its economically active males in non-manual employment (that is Social Classes I, II and III(N)), compared with 29 per cent for both the North and the Yorkshire-Humberside regions. The North, Yorkshire-Humberside and the West Midlands all have some 70 per cent of their employed males in manual jobs. Mapping out the postal addresses given in *Who's Who* confirms that 'top' people are relatively dense on the ground in the South-east and London.[89] Looked at from a different angle, the data is clear on another point. The distribution of these social classes within the regions shows that although Social Class I only represents 5 per cent of the total male working population, some 42 per cent of the males in this class live in the South-east (compared with 4.6 per cent in the North), though only 32.2 per cent of all economically active males live there. In other words there is a clear bunching of Social Class I (and also II and III(N)) males in the South-east.[90]

The census figures do not provide information on wealth and income, so there is no full nation-wide data on the distribution of such resources between classes. However, it is an overwhelming presumption, supported by a lesser range of evidence, that the uneven distribution of income and wealth referred to earlier is closely associated with class. For instance, the *New Earnings Survey* of 1981 showed that in April 1981 the *average* gross weekly earnings of adult males in *non-manual* occupations was £161.2 compared with £118.4 for *manual* workers. The comparative figures for females were £95.6 (non-manual) and £72.1 (manual).[91] Using a slightly different and more extended system of classification, the Royal Commission on the Distribution of Income and Wealth found clear evidence to support the view that earnings by social class declined more or less consistently from Class I to Class V. For example, in 1978 the average yearly earnings of 'Higher professionals' (in Class I) was £8286. The comparable earnings of skilled manual workers (in Class III(M)) was £4354, and those of unskilled manual workers (Class V) was £3390. The comparable figures for females in these classes were £6712, £2246 and £2275.[92]

If one considers personal wealth, the presumption must also hold that the uneven distribution concentrates the bulk of it in Social Classes I and II, whether one is looking at physical or financial assets. One important indicator, the ownership of houses (and type of housing), confirms the point. *The General Household Survey* of 1977 showed that whereas some 43 per cent of Social Class I and 37 per cent of professional and managerial classes lived in detached houses, only 8 per cent of semi-skilled and 5 per cent of unskilled manual classes did so, when classified according to head of household.[93] Moreover, well over 70 per cent of professional, managerial and intermediate non-manual household heads (Classes I and II) were owner occupiers (that is they either owned their houses outright or had mortgages on them), compared with only 47 per cent of skilled manual household heads, 33 per cent of semi-skilled manual household heads (in Class III), and 19 per cent of unskilled manual household heads (in Classes IV and V).[94] Furthermore, although many domestic appliances and conveniences have spread throughout the population in the last two decades, it is still the case that they are unevenly distributed between the social classes. For instance, regular access to cars, and ownership of such amenities as washing machines, central heating and telephones are much more common amongst Social Classes I and II than Social Classes IV and V. The same is true of bank and building society accounts and credit cards. The regional distribution of types and tenure of houses, and of amenities, in general also favours the South-east by comparison with the North, Yorkshire-Humberside, the North-west and the West Midlands, as does average weekly household income.[95]

VII

The way in which a society educates its young is part of the whole process of 'socialization', that is the way in which the values, norms, ideas, customs, knowledge and expectations of a culture are handed on from one generation to the next. However, in an industrial society like Britain there is more at stake than this. Education also decisively affects life-chances, and hence opportunities in terms of occupation, income, status and power. Thus, while education may be considered as part of culture, it is also of the greatest importance when considering social organization since it both affects and is affected by class. Hence it must be dealt with here briefly.

Until quite recently, the secondary educational system in Britain could be said to have consisted of three main components: the private (or Public) schools, and the two parts of the state system, the grammar schools and the secondary modern schools. The main qualification for entrance to the private schools was, and still is, money. This will be dealt with later. In the state system, a fateful examination was written by children at the age of 11 (the 'eleven-plus' examination) which largely determined whether they would attend the (more academic) grammar school or the (less academic) secondary modern school. It is perfectly clear, too, that the decision taken at that age in turn affected children's later chances of going on to university or other forms of higher education after leaving school, and therefore affected their long-term life-chances in a number of other ways. The rise of the comprehensive school movement, from the 1960s onwards, sought to eliminate this distinction and abolish the eleven-plus examination. But some local authorities (as in York in 1982) still have it.

Over the years since the 1950s, the evidence which has been assembled from various studies is quite consistent about the consequences of this educational system and its relationship with class and mobility. In the 1960s, for instance, it was shown that while children from *all* social classes were in the grammar schools, the proportion of children from Social Classes I, II and III was consistently higher than children from other social classes. Despite changes in the educational system, this pattern prevailed throughout the 1970s. Partly in consequence of this, the figures show that the distribution of public expenditure on education (the second highest single item in government spending after social security) has favoured Social Classes I, II and III. This is because secondary (and especially post-16) education is the most expensive sector of the educational system (including universities), and also because more children from these classes are in that sector, especially the grammar schools, and for longer.[96]

While educational reform since the Second World War, especially following from the 1944 Education Act, did expand the opportunities for all children from all social classes in the state system, the private schools have not been affected much. Of the 11 million children at school in Britain today, only about 6 per cent attend the private schools (which are also concentrated more densely in the South-east of the country than anywhere else). A fierce debate surrounds these schools, and it is a political debate. Whether such schools provide a 'better' education than others depends on what various participants in the debate believe a 'good' education to be. But what is quite clear is that, first, it is generally the case that the facilities at these schools are often better than in the state system, that the teacher-pupil ratio is often lower, and that the choice of subjects or activities is often much greater. Moreover, as one headmaster of such a school pointed out, he had almost twice as much to spend on each pupil (day pupil) than was available at a comprehensive school he knew well. Secondly, the importance of these schools in the politics of Britain is that they have educated (and still do) a substantial bulk (in some cases an overwhelming majority) of those people who have gone on to occupy the 'top' positions in the various hierarchies referred to earlier – in the civil service, the Church, the media, the judiciary, the universities, commerce and industry, Conservative MPs and Cabinets (but not Labour MPs and Cabinets) and the armed forces.[97]

The fees at these schools are very high indeed, which in practice makes them largely exclusive for the wealthy. For instance, Eton, Rugby and Winchester had annual fees in 1981 of £3780, £4050 and £4200 respectively. The better-known girls' private schools have similar fees.[98] It will readily be apparent that such fees, when compared with the typical annual income of people in Social Class III(M), IV and V, are way out of the reach of most people. It is therefore hardly surprising that these schools are attended primarily by the children of Social Classes I and II. A study of the social class of the fathers of children attending private schools in 1968 showed that over 80 per cent of the pupils came from such homes, although men in these social classes accounted for only about 18 per cent of the adult male population in the country.[99]

The advantages which accrue to children of Social Classes I and II in so far as secondary education is concerned – in both the state and private sector – apply also to their chances of higher education, especially in the universities. Of course children from all social classes, and from all kinds of schools, go on to university. But the figures make it clear that those from grammar and private schools, and from Social Classes I and II, are the main beneficiaries of the opportunities. In 1979, children from Social Classes I and II together accounted for 64 per cent of the candidates for admission to British universities, compared with 13 per cent of Social Class III(N), and 16 per cent, 5 per cent and 1 per cent from Social Classes III(M), IV and V. Moreover, those who complete their university education almost always end up in Social Classes I and II, and to a lesser extent Social Class III(N). A 1972 survey found that nine out of ten university men found their way into the professional and managerial classes.[100] Finally, although only 8 per cent of the economically active male population in Britain of 1978 had degrees (and 3 per cent of females), these university graduates were concentrated in Social Class I (60 per cent of males and 67 per cent of females) compared with about 10 per cent for both Social Classes II and III, and less than 1 per cent for other social classes.[101]

There are many other indices of difference between classes. For instance, in the 1930s only the two most prosperous income groups could afford 'an entirely adequate diet', and in the 1970s, the *National Food Survey* showed that richer people had a better diet, eating more fresh fruit and vegetables, meat, milk and cheese, while the poorer ate more bread, potatoes and sugar.[102] Even the average height of children of professional and managerial fathers (Social Classes I and II) is greater than that of Class V children, being some 2 cm greater at the age of three, rising to 5 cm at adolescence.[103] Some of the other cultural differences will be mentioned later.

The evidence outlined above suggests a fairly clear pattern which relates the characteristics of social classes to the productive and especially distributive features of the society. Those with wealth and high incomes appear also to be those who have received higher education, who exercise power in the major institutions of the society and who enjoy high status, largely through their occupations. These advantages are passed on to their children, in part through inheritance but also through access to certain kinds of educational facilities which in turn enhance their opportunities for entry to high-income, high-power and high-status occupations. Moreover, there is a strong tendency for marriages to take place *within* social classes, and also between men and women of similar educational background. This pattern of endogamy (marrying within a given group) is obviously most marked within the broad non-manual and manual categories.[104]

VIII

But is this a closed circle? Is there no mobility between classes? Is the official ideology of equal opportunity entirely empty? The short answer to this is that there *is* mobility but not nearly enough to allow the conclusion that British society is in any sense a fully 'open' one, in which chances of upward (and downward) mobility of people in different social classes are equal. Factors which have contributed to mobility over the years (either within generations or between them) are many. For instance, the occupational structure of the society has changed: between 1911 and 1966 the proportion of manual workers fell from 75 per cent of the economically active male population to 58 per cent.[105] Even between 1961 and 1971 the percentage of men in Class I and II occupations *increased* from 17.8 per cent to 24.1 per cent, while the percentage of men in semi-skilled and unskilled manual occupations *decreased* from 33.8 per cent to 30.7 per cent, and these trends have continued up to the present.[106]

This kind of change has produced more 'room at the top', so to speak, and less at the bottom. This has come about through changes in the productive core of the society, for instance in technological innovation, the associated decrease in blue-collar jobs and the increase in service industries and office work. This helps to explain the *absolute* increase in mobility between classes, that is the sheer number of people who have changed social class (based on occupation) within a generation or between generations. Educational expansion has helped the process. For it has provided the training to enable more people who otherwise would have probably sought and obtained jobs in semi-skilled and unskilled manual occupations (of which there are now fewer) to find them in skilled manual (Social Class III(M)) or even non-manual (Social Class III(N)) occupations.

Despite the general increase in *absolute* mobility of this kind, there does not appear to have been much increase in *relative* social mobility, according to the main studies which have been undertaken since the 1940s.[107] What does this mean? To summarize and simplify much dense and complicated evidence, the main point is this. It is clear that people *have* been upwardly mobile, both *within* generations (intra-generationally) and *between* generations (inter-generationally). There has been upward movement from all classes (except Social Class I, obviously), and downward movement, too (except Social Class V). However, the *chances* of 'upward' mobility across the major divide *between* the manual and non-manual classes are much less than the chances of mobility *within* either the manual or non-manual classes. That is to say, there is more chance that unskilled or semi-skilled manual workers (and their children) will become skilled manual workers, than that they will become skilled *non-manual* workers or enter the managerial or professional classes. Likewise, there is a much greater chance that members of the non-manual classes (I, II and III(N)) - *and* their children - will stay in those classes, or be upwardly mobile between them. In short, and crudely, the chances are considerably better the further 'up' the ladder of classes you start, or your father starts.

IX

The reality of class in Britain is not only reflected in data of this kind about wealth, income, education, power and opportunity - though these are the key indicators. These differences are further and decisively expressed in what might be termed the 'micro-cultures' or lifestyles of classes. For instance, there are clear differences in the newspapers which are in general read by different social classes, with papers like *The Sun* and *The Daily Mirror* being read mainly by people in the manual classes, and papers like *The Telegraph*, *The Guardian* and *The Times* being read mainly by people in the professional and managerial classes. A higher percentage of people in these latter classes buy and read more books; they are more likely to visit hotels and restaurants; in general they are more likely to drink more spirits and wine and, as was shown earlier, in general enjoy more nutritious diets. A higher percentage of them are likely to go to the ballet, theatre or opera, and they are more likely to join clubs, so that, for example, the children of these social classes are much more likely to be members of such youth organizations as Cubs and Brownies. People from Social Classes I and II are more likely to do more swimming, sailing, skiing and jogging, and to play more tennis, squash, golf, chess and badminton. And they are more likely to take holidays abroad.

While the size of families in Britain is today roughly similar across all social classes, there are some important differences between them. For example, the age at which people marry tends to be younger amongst Social Classes IV and V than amongst Social Classes I and II. Likewise, the proportion of first-time mothers under the age of 20 increases from Class I to V. And a higher percentage of Social Class I, II and III mothers breast-feed their babies, and do so for longer.[108]

Looking back at this evidence, one thing is quite plain. Social class flows directly from the system of industrial capitalism in Britain, its division of labour and its patterns of unequal distribution and rewards. Contrary to official claims and some aspects of public ideology, it is quite clear that while there may be equal *rights*, there are not equal *opportunities* for people from different classes for upward mobility, or for gaining entry for themselves or their children to high-paid, powerful or prestigious positions in the society, nor for the equal enjoyment of its cultural, social and scientific fruits. In these respects, class reflects British politics and has a profound effect upon it. Furthermore, as this last section has shown, the 'micro-cultures' of different classes are directly associated with these inequalities and act to sustain them from generation to generation, despite such social mobility as there has been.

X

The previous section has touched on some of the features of culture in Britain. These included monogamous marriage (though cohabitation is more common now than a generation ago), patterns of residence, education, leisure and entertainment. As shown in that section, it is probably more realistic to explore the detailed aspects of culture in relation to particular socio-economic groups, classes or even communities, because these reveal quite distinctive differences, and there is a useful literature on this, though some of it is now a bit dated.[109] The growth of different ethnic minorities in Britain in the last three decades has added to the variety of local and micro-cultures in Britain.

Despite these differences, it is none the less quite possible to talk in more general terms about some of the *central principles* underlying behaviour and belief, culture and ideology, in the society as a whole. To do this it is necessary to bear in mind the main features of the productive and distributive systems described earlier, for these principles flow directly from them. Moreover, in looking at these principles, it is important to remember that the argument here moves at a level of generality above the particularities of class and region.

The first and most important set of related principles which lie at the heart of many behaviours and beliefs in Britain are ones which now permeate the politics of all industrial capitalist societies, and - arguably - are now becoming prevalent on a global scale. These principles are the competitive pursuit of private profit and the accumulation of private wealth and possessions. They flow directly from the system of industrial production by means of private ownership. Observing nineteenth-century capitalism in Europe, but especially England, Marx wrote: 'Accumulate, Accumulate! That is Moses and the Prophets.' He believed that this driving force had been a major and necessary factor in the industrial transformation of Europe. But he also regarded production for profit, as opposed to production for use, as a central cause of the inequality and poverty which he and Engels saw around them, especially in England, which was so vividly portrayed in the fictional writing of Dickens, for instance, and in the classic study by Engels of *The Condition of the Working Class in England*.[110] This, however, was not a view which was widely held in the nineteenth century. Nor is it one which is shared by many today, certainly not in official quarters, by the main political parties, or amongst industrial, social or educational hierarchies. Successive governments, and organizations like the Confederation of British Industry, repeatedly stress the need for individual firms to be both competitive and profitable, in order that Britain as a whole may be so in relation to the world in which it buys, sells and invests. In the daily politics of national and international production, firms seek to expand their profit and compete for 'market shares' or customers or contracts or opportunities. As the Director of the CBI wrote, 'It's all about winning.'[111]

It is central to the argument here that this competitive drive - rewarded by some form of success, like profits or winning - has profoundly influenced the daily lives, social customs, behaviours, goals and beliefs of people in Britain. It is now deeply embedded in diverse aspects of the culture and extends *far* beyond merely the productive system. There are two main elements of all this. The first encourages individuals or groups to stand out, to try to be better than the rest, whatever the activity. From a very young age members of the society are trained and urged to do so, and a complex system of rewards enhances the process. The honours system at the apex of the society has already been referred to, but there are many other prizes which confer social rewards on individuals, groups or companies and which thus help to sustain and encourage the competitive character of politics, in the private and public sectors. There are awards for the Young Businessman of the Year, as there are the Queen's

Awards to Industry. There are competitions and awards for films, books, journalism and television; for hairdressing, fashion, design and slimming. In schools and colleges up and down the country, as well as in sporting clubs and recreational associations, there are prizes for achievement, and especially winning, in thousands of different activities.

The second element, which is clearly related to the first, is the belief that competition - in industry as in all things - is the *only* realistic spur to improvement, innovation and ultimately 'progress'. Without the incentives which go along with competition - profits, prizes or rewards - there would be no dynamism, no change, no advancement worth talking of. Indeed, such beliefs and behaviours are so much part of the culture and ideology of the society that it is often said that these virtues - to compete, to stand out, to accumulate and to win - are part of what is sometimes referred to as 'human nature'. Even when people think of games in British society, most think of competitive individual or team games, which have winners and losers. Thus, it is fair to say that in few societies outside or before the industrial capitalist era has conflict and competition been so endemic - and *encouraged* to be so - in play, in work and reward.

Whether these characteristics are part of 'human nature' or not, it is here worth recalling momentarily the contrast with the !Kung. Above all they avoid conflict, they encourage sharing, they do not like to stand out and seldom promote competition. As was argued in chapter 2, so much of the productive life of the !Kung requires cooperation (as has been the case generally amongst foragers, herders and agriculturalists) that competition and conflict would endanger their very existence. Few of their games, for instance, allow or express conflict, although they involve much physical activity (climbing, swinging, jumping, dancing, hopping) and skill (stick-throwing), 'in which they show their prowess, but no one wins'.[112] As one would expect in two societies so markedly different in their productive and distributive systems as modern Britain and the disappearing !Kung, their cultures and ideologies are poles apart.

Another major feature of the behaviour and beliefs of people in Britain, as in all industrial capitalist societies, is what is generally called 'consumerism'. The structural sources of this are obvious. The division of labour is so complex and detailed in such societies that the vast majority of us, with the exception perhaps of a few craftsmen, never really produce *any* whole thing. Each of us in our own way contributes a bit or a part or a function. Moreover, as workers, we do not directly produce what we individually need. Rather, we are employed to produce a part of something and we are paid a wage or a salary for what we do. We then use our earnings, in the form of money, to provide for our needs and satisfy our wants, in so far as we can afford to do so. Not only must we work in order to live (that is true for all societies) but, with very few exceptions, we must *buy* in order to survive. This is the real source of consumerism.

But surrounding this structural core is an elaborate web of institutions, behaviours and practices which have become part of the culture of the society, which engulfs us from an early age. This includes inducements (advertising), facilities (credit or hire purchase schemes) and steadily changing models (fashion) which all serve to encourage, sustain and direct our patterns of consumption, and which provide talking points amongst different groups of consumers. Our consuming is done as individuals (as children, teenagers, adults, etc.) and as couples, as families and in larger groups or organizations (like clubs, companies and agencies of government). We buy houses, cars, bicycles, tables, chairs, washing machines, crockery, hose-pipes, clothes, food, drink, machinery and a thousand other commodities, services and raw materials. We work, we earn, we buy, we consume. In general this is a private activity, but its scope and pace can be influenced by government action through stimulating or depressing 'demand' - for instance in adjustments in the income tax rates and forms of tax relief, in VAT levels, and in public expenditure. This once again underlines the continuity in politics there is between the private and public sectors. For just as governments must promote competition, so too must they promote consumption. In industrial societies we could not now survive for long without specialist production, commerce and trade. But equally, industry and commerce could not survive without the consumerism that sustains it. The role of advertising in all this is not only to ensure that we know what is available to meet our *needs* (that is generally a simple matter), but actually to create *wants* which strengthen and extend the pace and scope of consumerism.

For all these reasons, shopping is now not only a necessary activity but has become very much part of our daily life, our culture. The things which people buy vary from group to group, and are influenced by many factors - advertising, wants, fashions and preferences of the group, image, need and available cash. But what are the politics of shopping within families, for instance? Given competing demands on the family - for dinner money, pocket money, transport, food, decoration, payment of bills and rents or mortgages - how are resources distributed? Take food, for instance. We know that most shopping for food is done by female members of households in Britain, as is cooking. It was shown earlier that different social classes tend to buy different kinds of food. But what about differences *within* the family, between ages and sexes? What factors influence the choices of female shoppers as far as food for their families is concerned? Studies now being undertaken are beginning to suggest that *male* preferences in food and type of dishes in general may strongly influence consumption patterns in this respect, and that where food resources are scarce, adult or adolescent males may get more than females.[113] How far could this be true in other aspects of domestic politics? Moreover, is there a connection between competitive accumulation and domestic consumerism? The behaviour which is referred to as 'Keeping up with the Jones's' is both competitive and consumerist, and deeply influenced by commercial advertising. This element of our culture is best understood as part of the politics of industrial capitalism, and *not* as an expression of 'human nature'.[114]

These are not points which can be developed further here. The purpose, however, in merely touching on these questions was to illustrate how far-reaching are the influences of the productive system on culture, and vice versa, ranging from the principles and purposes of games, through to the patterns of intra-family consumption and competitive inter-family consumption, which is widespread in all social classes, and between them.

X I

Competitiveness and consumerism are amongst the dominant principles which shape many of the central institutions and beliefs of the society. But they are not the only ones. Running counter to these – at least in some respects – are principles and activities which promote cooperation and sharing, but these are only minor elements within culture and ideology. Broadly speaking, Britain is a Christian society. Although the Anglican Church (Church of England and Scotland) is the established and largest church, of which the Monarch is the 'supreme governor', there is a variety of other Christian churches, but technically no 'official religion'. Despite this, and despite religious education in the schools, Britain is now very largely a secular society.[115] As an institution, the church has only a limited cultural and ideological influence on politics, though the two Anglican archbishops and some twenty other bishops are appointed by the Monarch (advised by the Prime Minister) and are fully integrated into 'the Establishment' through their position as members of the House of Lords. Yet only some 18 per cent of the population in 1979 were members of any church, and barely 11 per cent were regular attenders, though about half the marriages still took place in church, compared with 68 per cent in 1966.[116]

The steady decline in the influence of Christianity over the century is not really surprising. Its central social teachings – to love and care for others and avoid material greed – are not easy to reconcile with the powerful influence of the competitive and acquisitive features of British society discussed earlier. Indeed, the Christian injunction to love and care for one's fellow beings is interpreted almost entirely – in private and public circles – in largely individual and personal terms. For instance, considerations of this kind rarely enter the calculations of private or public agencies when deciding on investment programmes – perhaps in run-down inner-city areas. Considerations of profit and success are what matter here. In general, the churches say little or nothing about such matters. Yet arguably, the causes of much human suffering – such as poverty, unemployment and ill-health – are due precisely to the maldistribution of resources, as will become more clear in the next section. The 'official' morality of Christianity has little influence on the politics of the society in that respect. Finally, the efficacy of prayer seems to many people rather flimsy compared with that of science in the treatment of some personal problems, such as ill-health.

But in addition to the churches, British society is one which is remarkably rich in charities of all kinds, operating at home and abroad. Giving to charity is regarded within the society as a virtuous and generous activity and it is especially expected of rich people or large organizations. Those who do not do so are thought of as mean or stingy, just as 'big men' in many non-state societies are expected to redistribute their wealth through feasts.[117] Even large companies like to be associated with giving, for instance through sponsorships, trophies and grants. The charities are numerous and enormously varied. They are concerned with the interests of children, the elderly, the sick, the injured, the homeless and the handicapped – as well as dogs, cats and donkeys. They raise funds to look after them, above and beyond what the state may do on their behalf. Amongst the better-known of these organizations are Shelter, the Red Cross, the Round Table, the National Society for the Prevention of Cruelty to Children, Age Concern, St John's Ambulance, the Salvation Army and Oxfam.

There is also a cooperative movement in Britain, no longer nearly so widespread as it once was. It seeks to demonstrate the moral and material advantages of cooperation (in production, saving and consumption) over that of competition. In most towns and cities of Britain you will find a few, small cooperative ventures – perhaps baking and selling bread, fixing bicycles, or sometimes producing furniture or light machinery. By comparison, however, with the vast resources and powerful interests which promote competition, capital accumulation and consumption – and with the dominant form of the large capitalist firm – this tradition, with its roots in both Christian and nineteenth-century socialist teaching – is neither widespread nor strong.

The important point to recognize is that the dominant elements of culture and ideology in Britain are not detached, autonomous or self-generating sets of activity and belief. They reflect and are associated with the productive and distributive characteristics of the society and its past, and they influence its current politics accordingly.

Before drawing the threads of the argument together in the concluding section, it is important to show here how some of the major problems of the society are best understood as products of its politics, and in turn fuel its conflicts. The examples that will be used to illustrate the point are poverty, unemployment and ill-health.

XII

Poverty

Britain is by no means a poor society. By international comparisons it is amongst the wealthiest, if you take a basic indicator such as the gross national product *per capita*.[118] The internal inequalities in Britain which such an indicator disguises are to a limited extent compensated by redistributive measures undertaken by the state, through a complex of transfers including tax, cash benefits and benefits in kind. Almost every society has some form of social insurance system to protect and cater for disadvantaged groups, whether they be the old, the young, the disabled, the poor, the ill or the unlucky. Sometimes this operates informally through networks of kin, or age-sets, or clans, or bands – as was shown for the !Kung and the Maasai. In Britain, while families and relatives of course look after their own to some extent, there are also in the private sector various pension plans, health-care programmes and insurance schemes. But the main form of social insurance is operated by the state through the social security system which is the largest single item of public expenditure, accounting for more than 20 per cent of the total.[119] It includes retirement benefits, child benefits, sickness benefits, unemployment benefits and supplementary benefits.

But despite these redistributive measures, there is poverty in Britain. How wide this is depends on how you define it. A recent massive study of poverty in the United Kingdom, by Peter Townsend, showed that, if you took the official (or state) definition of poverty (the supplementary benefit level which is a minimally defined, or subsistence level), some 9 per cent of the population, or nearly 5 million people, were living in poverty. And if you add to this the number of people living *on the edge* of poverty, the figure jumps dramatically: 'By the state's own definition . . . there were between 15 and 17½ million in a population of some 55½ million who were in or near poverty.'[120]

Moreover, poverty is not like a virus which may strike indiscriminately. As one might expect from the earlier analysis, the concentration of people in or near poverty is much greater amongst semi-skilled and unskilled manual occupational groups than amongst professional or managerial ones, and especially amongst the old-aged and children in those classes. There is also a higher incidence of poverty in Northern Ireland, Scotland, the North-west, the North, Wales and the South-west, while Greater London and the South-east has the smallest proportion of poor people.[121]

It may well be that everyone in Britain, even the very poorest, is much better off than the poor, or even the majority of people, in Bangladesh or Haiti. But that is not the point. What poverty means in this context is that there is a significant minority in Britain whose income exludes them from the 'living standards, the lifestyles and the fellowship' of their fellow citizens, from the conditions of living which are regarded as the right of all in *this* society. That is, poverty must be understood *relatively*, within societies, not between them. As one author puts it, this means that poor people in Britain may not be able to ensure that they and their children are reasonably fed and dressed, or to keep their homes warm, or to be able to visit friends and relatives, to give presents on birthdays or at Christmas, to buy and read newspapers, to pay their television licences or maintain their membership of associations, like churches or clubs or trade unions.[122]

This is not a subject which is generally discussed in books on British politics. But Professor Townsend's conclusion is of the greatest importance. He writes that:[123]

poverty is more extensive than is generally or officially believed and has to be understood not only as an inevitable feature of severe social inequality but also as a particular consequence of the actions by the rich to preserve or enhance their wealth and so deny it to others. Control of wealth and the institutions created by that wealth, and therefore the terms under which it may be generated and passed on selectively or for the general good, is therefore central to any policies designed to abolish or alleviate the condition.

Translated into the terms of the argument used here, this means that both the causes and incidence of poverty are *not* simply technical or administrative matters, nor can it be explained with reference to impersonal market forces. In our politics we *create* poverty. Its occurrence, persistence and distribution flow directly from the way resources are controlled, used and distributed. And the conflicts which poverty in turn generates are equally and decisively about efforts to change this. In short, politics is central to the causes, conditions and cures of poverty.

For example, there are those who have long argued that effective minimum wage legislation, at one end of the scale, would help to reduce the incidence of poverty. Others argue for a wealth tax (or a tax on income from wealth) at the other end of the scale, which could promote greater equality. Neither measure would be easy or without problems.[124] Articulate pressure groups, working across the private and public sectors of politics, are ranged against each other. They represent far more than detached philosophical views or different strategies for the promotion of social welfare: they represent interests, anchored in the inequalities which have been described, and most dramatically symbolized by the poverty data. Trade unions, representing the low paid, campaign publicly and take industrial action for better wages and conditions.[125] Other organizations, like the Claimants' Union, associations of pensioners and pressure groups like the Child Poverty Action Group and Age Concern, press for better treatment and improved benefits for the poor, the young and the old. Apart from any strictly moral arguments they may advance, such groups would claim that it is a costly and wasteful use of *human* resources to have large numbers of people in the society who may be poorly fed, badly housed, inadequately educated, untrained and alienated, and who thus find it difficult to escape the 'poverty trap', and become dependent on the state. In reply, others argue that a wealth tax would dampen enterprise and initiative, that minimum wage legislation might increase unemployment, and that higher social security benefits for the poor or the unemployed would only be a disincentive for people to work. They believe - in line with the kind of ideology discussed above - that it is important to reward success, not failure. They say that each generation must be spurred on to attain, to achieve, to improve, for that is the only way forward. In the real, tough world, they argue, there must be winners and there must be losers. Why should the winners subsidize the losers?

Wherever one may stand in relation to these conflicts, the important point to grasp is that the problem itself, and the debates about it, arise *directly* from the uneven distribution of resources and power in the society and hence the unequal opportunities which this confers to alter the balance, especially in the private sector. In general, it is those who *do not* own or manage resources who seek public (that is state) intervention to compensate for their powerlessness or poverty, while those who *do* own or manage resources in the private sector seek to prevent the state from intervening.

Unemployment

The same is true for another central and very costly problem of all major industrial capitalist societies in the modern world, and increasingly for all other contemporary societies as well: the problem of unemployment. It is not a new problem, and at various times in the history of the industrial societies the immediate causes of increases in the level of unemployment have been various but often related. In recent years, however, these have become more complex and often more sudden in an increasingly competitive, interdependent and unequal world. They include the decline of traditional industries in the face of foreign competition; technological innovation which may lead to a decrease in labour requirements (consider the effect of the micro-chip and computer); an increase in wage levels which may in turn lead to a fall in the levels of profit and so induce investors to look abroad for more profitable opportunities, thus depriving their own societies of job-sustaining industries and regions; a sudden increase in the price of a vital commodity like oil - and many more.

But what must be kept absolutely in the forefront of a discussion of this kind is the central point that unemployment, like poverty, is *not* an accidental feature of industrial capitalist societies or the relations between them, but is intrinsic to them. It flows directly from the way they use, produce and distribute resources; that is from the predominantly private ownership of the major productive enterprises, the competitive relations between them and the necessary pursuit of profit and capital accumulation associated with this. Indeed, any form of private ownership of the major productive resources, which requires wage labour but *does not guarantee it*, must contain within it the possibility of unemployment. This of course can be stimulated by any of the factors mentioned above, but is *always* present to some degree. For wherever and whenever in human history people (in families, villages or wider communities) have become separated from the ownership or control of the means of their own subsistence - land, tools, capital, machines, jobs - unemployment appears. It must. In the industrial capitalist societies this process has been taken to the furthest known extreme.

In short, in the politics of these societies we *create* unemployment. The vast majority of young people, emerging today from school or college, seek jobs whose availability and kind is largely controlled by the decisions and actions of others. This is one of the sharpest features which distinguish industrial capitalist societies from some of those which have been discussed before, in which access to the life-sustaining productive resources is equally open to all, because private ownership of these resources (and hence *socially created* scarcity) has not developed. Societies such as those of the !Kung or Maasai - or even feudal Britain - certainly experienced other problems, as a result of the vicissitudes of nature, or their relatively simple technologies, or diseases which they could not control: but they did not have unemployment.

In late 1982 there were more than 3 million people unemployed in Britain, or 13.4 per cent of the working population.[126] Reliable evidence about the distribution of unemployment between social classes is hard to come by. The available evidence for the 1970s suggests, as one might expect, that although unemployment is found in *all* social classes, it is most densely concentrated amongst semi-skilled and unskilled manual workers.[127] Moreover, the regional incidence of unemployment is also uneven. The areas of highest unemployment in Britain are in the North, in Yorkshire and Humberside, the North-west and the West Midlands. In some of these regions there are towns where the unemployment levels go well over 20 per cent. Amongst the worst hit areas are Liverpool, Glasgow and Tyneside.[128] And within the composition of the unemployed there is a very substantial number of young people. In Liverpool, for instance, perhaps one-third or more of school-leavers have been unemployed in recent years.[129]

Just as the politics of industrial capitalism creates unemployment, so unemployment stirs further conflicts, problems and disputes in these politics. This gives rise to new arguments, theories, policies, organizations, campaigns, hostilities, violence and even ill-health. In all these and many other respects the causes and consequences of unemployment flow from, and work back on, the fundamental core of all politics, the ownership, use and distribution of resources. For instance, each month when the official figures are released there is more or less uproar in Parliament, echoed by comments from major private institutions, like the TUC and the CBI. Governments come under pressure from some quarters to increase public expenditure so as to 'stimulate' productive activity which might in turn generate more jobs. Others urge cuts in what they consider to be the high levels of taxation so that investors may be encouraged to invest by the attraction of higher profits. Trade union leaders point to the enormous rise in overseas investment by private institutions in the UK since the lifting of exchange controls in 1979. It rose from £4634 million in 1978 to £10,637 million in 1981.[130] And they urge the re-imposition of controls so that these resources may be directed back into domestic investment and hence job creation. Those, on the other hand, who control such resources and who have worked for and now welcome the freedom to invest abroad, respond by saying that if unions did not press for high wages they would invest locally, but not under these high-wage circumstances. Individuals, organizations and political parties line up around these conflicts.

But outside and beyond these debates within and between the major institutions of 'the Establishment', there are other responses and initiatives from the unemployed directly, and those who speak for them. Unemployed people have organized demonstrations, 'right to work' marches and campaigns. Others have occupied factories which are scheduled to close or where large numbers are threatened with redundancy. Their unions try to negotiate various redundancy pay deals. Where public expenditure cuts have caused unemployment in the public sector, resistance has been mounted by a wide variety of groups - trades councils, students, civil servants and employees in the health services. Vicars, Chief Constables and social workers also enter the debate. They point to the wider politics of unemployment, and the response of some unemployed to their impotence, frustration and sense of deprivation - the increase in levels of crime, especially among the young, as well as the ugly outbreaks of rioting and urban violence that have occurred in the late 1970s and early 1980s. People working in the medical field underline the expensive health implications of unemployment and the consequences of this in terms of family politics - and wider social costs. For the medical evidence suggests an increase in depression, insomnia and hypertension amongst unemployed people, as well as increased smoking and drinking, grave strains on family relationships, and sometimes higher risks of suicide and heart attacks.[131]

Ill-health

This leads on to the third example of a major social problem which flows from the patterns of British politics - the distribution of ill-health in the society (and hence the costs to the society in a variety of ways), as well as the distribution of health care.

Now it is of course true that people in *all* social classes get similar diseases, but the *incidence* of the major diseases is almost always higher amongst Social Classes III, IV and V. Moreover, chronic ill-health is more common amongst the poor and in certain regions, for instance Merseyside and Scotland. The death rate, for example, from tuberculosis, bronchitis, lung cancer, stomach cancer and duodenal ulcers is much higher in Social Classes III, IV and V than it is in Social Classes I and II. The same is true for neo-natal death rates (deaths within the first month of life) and post-neo-natal death rates (from one month to a year). Also, a higher percentage of people from Social Classes IV and V report illness than do people from Social Classes I and II. It is also the case that fatal accidents (especially industrial accidents, but excluding road accidents) are far more common in the poorer social classes. In short, almost whatever data are chosen, 'they show inequalities in health to be a salient feature of British society'.[132]

Ill-health in a society is costly, not only to the society as a whole but to individuals and their families. The main finding of the Black Report (*Inequalities in Health*) was that the most plausible explanation of these patterns of ill-health amongst different social groups lies in the social and economic circumstances in which different groups of people work and live. For 'Human health is a part of the organization of material existence. It is both produced and endangered by the work which men and women do in order to earn their livelihood.' Moreover, the uneven patterns of ill-health and death in old age amongst different social classes is a reflection 'in a dynamic sense of inequalities in the social division of labour. In the collective effort of social production, some workers literally give more of themselves than others and hence their bodies wear out first.'[133] In short, the cumulative effects of the kinds of inequalities discussed earlier - income, wealth, housing, domestic amenities, and the causal relationship of these factors to different kinds of work, education and opportunities - express themselves in the patterns of ill-health experienced in the society. An understanding of them must be directly related back to the character of the systems of production and distribution. Thus, just as the politics of British society causes the problems of poverty and unemployment, so too is it a major factor in the cause and condition of ill-health.

But there is a further dimension to this. The National Health Service in Britain is still one of the most remarkable of its kind in the industrial capitalist world, even if a bit creaky and starved of funds in the 1980s. All people in Britain have the *right* to what is, in effect, free medical care. Yet the research which has been done shows that the actual *use* of the health service, in relation to need, is far greater amongst the 'higher' social classes than others. This is true for instance in relation to radiography, cervical screening, pregnancy, infant care, dental treatment, breast operations and hospital referrals, as well as vaccinations against smallpox, diptheria and polio.[134]

Why should this be the case? Why should some people, with equal rights to a free public service, use it less than others, and why should this be the case amongst the poorer social classes in particular? Some part of the explanation may lie in ignorance of available services, but the explanatory burden is better carried by the same kinds of factors which explain the incidence and distribution of ill-health: the broadly 'socio-economic' factors associated with class. That is to say, while people have equal rights to use the services, they do not in practice have equal opportunities. In simple terms, there may be fewer doctors or dentists or hospital beds available in certain areas than in others.

But there is a further related reason which may be more important. Many people in Social Classes III(M), IV and V do not have fixed yearly or even monthly salaries. Many are paid by the hour. It is uncommon for such employees to be given *paid* time off to go to the doctor or the clinic, or to take their children. Moreover, their access to cars, as shown earlier, is far less than in Social Classes I and II, which means they must rely on public transport or private taxis which are both expensive. It is also easier to make appointments with the medical services if you have a telephone, and there are far fewer phones amongst these social classes than others. In a nutshell, the evidence suggests that it is both more difficult and more expensive for people from these groups to attend regularly at medical centres or to follow up with necessary subsequent visits. They may, too, receive fewer visits from health workers than other social groups. There may also be real problems in communication and mutual understanding between patients and doctors coming from very different social and educational backgrounds.[135] But the central point seems to be that the uneven distribution of resources, education and opportunity, as well as the distinctive character of different types of work, together account best for *both* the greater incidence of diseases (which prosper in poor environments) *and* for the less frequent use of the free medical services.

It is important to recognize that such problems as these in British society, as with others (for instance inner-city decay, or the decline of certain regions, or even inflation) cannot simply or only be attributed to 'technical' or 'administrative' errors or failures. They are intimately bound up with the way in which the society goes about using, producing and distributing resources - its politics. Likewise, the elimination of the causes of such problems would require far more than technical adjustments or innovations, whether they be fidgeting with the money supply, reorganizing the National Health Service or shortening the working day. They would require fundamental changes in resource use, control and distribution, and this in turn would bring about and require changes in access to opportunities, in social organization, culture and ideology. Such changes would in many ways strike at current inequalities, and hence at the interests and outlooks of some of those who presently enjoy the fruits of advantage in both the private and public sectors. And that is precisely what makes the resolution of these problems not only so difficult, but so deeply political.

XIII

When one stands back from the detail, what patterns emerge?

There can be little doubt that the last two centuries have brought remarkable advances in the absolute levels of welfare for all people in Britain, and have lessened the distributional inequalities, especially in the twentieth century. This is largely true for most of the Western industrial societies as well. The availability and standards of housing, education, food, clothing and social services are far in advance of what they were in the early nineteenth century. Technology has liberated people from exhausting and dangerous tasks, though it has also created new threats and dangers. Improvements in the material conditions of living, plus important advances in science, have helped to prevent or cure diseases, and to shelter people from the sharpest edges of nature. But the productive systems and associated lifestyles of industrialism have in turn promoted other diseases and health hazards. Finally, by comparison with much of continental Europe and the United States, domestic politics in Britain since the end of the Napoleonic wars has, in general, been relatively non-violent, though this has not been the case for imperial politics abroad.

That being said, British politics has clearly failed to resolve what has always been the central problem for all societies: the problem of the distribution of both resources and power. There are still sharp inequalities in the ownership, control, use and distribution of resources in the society. These are sustained through its structures of private and public power, and its systems of social organization, culture and ideology. In particular, they are sustained by two major characteristics: the predominantly private ownership and management of the major productive resources, and by the very partial and largely ineffective nature of democratic participation in decisions about the use, production and distribution of these *and* public resources in all areas of politics.

None the less, Britain is by any modern comparison a remarkably 'free' and 'liberal' society. There are few constraints on what individuals can do or say, or where they can go, by contrast with the Soviet Union or South Africa. These are important and hard-won rights. But, together with the clear inequalities described earlier, they produce the fundamental tension at the root of the conflicts in British politics, that is between formally *equal rights* and *unequal opportunities* in practice. Most people, in their bones, know this, though it is not always easy to recognize it outside one's own sphere of activities, and it applies with more or less consistency to the other Western industrial societies as well.

This fundamental tension, in the context of inequality of resource and power distribution, expresses itself in all the disputes which occur within the society at every level – from village to Westminster, from local pressure group and trade union to large corporation. It is this which is the real source of the most obvious and persistent manifestation of political conflict in Britain, in so-called 'industrial relations', and not simply bloody-minded trade unions or mean managers.

It is equally at the root of countless other instances of political conflict in the society, from disputes over access to the countryside to various kinds of community action against private companies or public bodies. For instance, in 1932, in a celebrated encounter, some 400 ramblers confronted gamekeepers and police on moorland in the Peak District of the Midlands. They wished to make their 'right to roam', as they called it, a reality on thousands of acres of fine walking country which were privately owned and which had been closed to the public by the landlord. Such incidents still occur today.[136] More recently, the rise of various kinds of consumer associations has been a significant feature of community politics. Such organizations campaign for fair deals in terms of the price, quality or safety of a great variety of goods and services, both public and private. They represent another aspect of the politics of commercial conflict which necessarily arises in a society where the central purpose of production and sale is profit, and where the consumer has little real say in what shall be produced or how. Other actions by organized groups are sometimes primarily defensive, such as rent strikes by council-house tenants. These are political responses by people who have little influence over decisions which directly affect their lives and in general circumstances which are entirely beyond their control, that is where the increase (if any) in their incomes does not match the increase in rents.

At a national level, debates between parties and pressure groups about the kind and level of public expenditure represent *much more* than merely ideological or theoretical differences. For instance, disputes about whether private education or private health insurance schemes should be encouraged or not, are more than only arguments about individual rights and freedoms, for example to use one's money as one wishes. They are also arguments about *opportunities*, and they frequently merge with wider debates about the priorities of public expenditure. For example, those who may be able to afford private medical insurance or education may be less concerned with expenditure on social security, the National Health Service or the education system, and may prefer more expenditure on defence, or law and order. Those without such opportunities may have very different priorities as to what should be done with their taxes.

All the disputes, differences and conflicts in British politics of this and many other kinds are rooted deeply in different interests. But these are seldom merely abstract, philosophical or idealistic interests which are plucked reflectively from a range of possible theoretical options. They regularly and widely arise from the pattern of inequalities discussed above, from attempts to preserve or change them, or from the wish to make use of the unequal opportunities which they generate. This is what British politics is really about.

XIV

Are such conflicts intrinsic to the politics of industrial capitalist societies? It would seem so. Are there any alternatives?

While the Communist (or 'state capitalist') societies of Eastern Europe seem more concerned with the promotion of equality in the distribution of resources and opportunities, they currently experience (or soon will) deep conflicts. These arise from the lack of democratic participation in the main decision-making processes in the institutions of their societies, where power is also concentrated at the top. In some respects, their problems are thus not entirely different.

But is it possible that the industrial societies (of both West and East) are simply too large for more effective systems of participation? Or will they have to face this issue, along with the directly associated issues of ownership and control, in the near future? Is it possible to *organize* more effective participation? Is it possible to continue in the way they are going without far more public involvement in planning? Can planning be undertaken in a democratic, decentralized and participatory fashion? Can planning work *without* it? Who will control the transnational corporations, and how? Are bureaucracies essential? Do people prefer inequality to participation? Would greater equality in the distribution of resources and power in these societies mean a much slower pace of innovation, and a narrower choice of goods and services? And would people mind that? Can problems of this kind be resolved within the framework of any one society alone? How could change come about, if at all? It certainly seems that, until there are changes in the direction of greater equality and participation, there is little significant that the industrial societies will be able to do to help the societies of the Third World.

These questions and issues signal the start of a different book with a different purpose. But they are worth thinking about. For the present, the main point of this book and the present chapters must be re-stated. When we think of *politics* in Britain, or any other society, we must cease to think only in terms of the activities of its politicians, parties, governments, ministers and civil servants. These tell us little. We must look at and analyse the resources of the society, and its systems of production, distribution, power, decision-making, social organization, culture and ideology - and the relations between them. Therein lies the clue to understanding its politics. The rest is merely detail.

PART THREE

CHAPTER ELEVEN

Conclusions: the poverty of Politics; the possibilities of Politics

I

These conclusions will first underline the main themes of the book and, in the light of these, suggest some of the reasons for the title of the present chapter. I will then indicate some of the considerable possibilities for expanding the discipline of Politics with respect primarily to content, but also teaching methods. Finally, I will explain a little more fully the 'democratic bias' which has been implicit in much of the argument.

II

Throughout the book I have been concerned to argue that politics is a universal feature of *all* societies and *all* institutions and groups within them, not just some of them. It is an inescapable part of the activities of cooperation and conflict which occur in the use and distribution of resources and which are everywhere involved in the production and reproduction of our social and biological lives. Indeed, politics is one of the defining characteristics of human beings as a species, though its forms and particulars differ widely from place to place and time to time.[1]

Moreover, it has been central to the argument here that the problems which arise in societies are seldom random and inexplicable eruptions in human affairs; nor can they often be said to arise exclusively from within such artificial abstractions as 'the political system' or 'the economy' or 'the social system' or 'nature'. They more commonly arise from the wider complex or relations within the social world, and between it and the natural world. In each and every instance it is our *politics* which has organized these relations. Hence it is to politics - and not merely technological or scientific advances - that we must look for the resolution of current problems, global and national.

For all these reasons it is important to assert the *primacy of politics* in the affairs of human societies, and hence the importance of studying and understanding it, at least as defined here. It is therefore crucial that the very conception and definition of politics be detached from its usual identification with 'government' and that it be expanded to include the kinds of matters discussed in previous chapters. It will be clear, too, for the same reasons, why an interdisciplinary approach is needed to do that.

The examples which have been used to support the argument were chosen because they were either interesting to me or unusual, or both, and because they helped to clarify and illustrate this wider notion of politics. But there are clearly countless other examples of societies, institutions or problems which might have been used for this purpose. For instance, one reader of the manuscript of this book thought that the question of inequality between the sexes was not adequately explored. Another pointed out that there might have been a fuller comparative treatment of the politics of the authoritarian societies in the Soviet bloc. And it is also the case that I have given little attention to international relations in the conventional sense, or to slavery or slave societies, or to the politics of the enormous variety of institutions in contemporary societies, like churches, factories or voluntary organizations.

Now it is obvious that one cannot cover everything, and any one author has only limited competence. None the less, my overall objective in the book - expressed in the title - has been to redefine the conception of politics and, equally important, to offer an introductory framework which might be used to analyse it. It is to be hoped that readers who have particular interests in topics not covered here will be tempted to pick up the framework of questions outlined at the end of chapter 1, and to apply them to the problems, societies and institutions which concern them. In so doing, they may find it possible to develop and refine the approach suggested here. For it is the definition of politics and the framework for its analysis which is the important part of the book, and not really the particular examples which have been used, however interesting they may be to some. Thus, if one is concerned to explain the patterns of inequality between sexes in any given instance, it is worth starting by asking about the control and distribution of resources; about how these both reflect and sustain the systems of power, social organization, culture and ideology; and how these are all expressed in sexual inequalities. Likewise, in seeking explanations for the politics of societies in the Eastern bloc, it is not sufficient to look only at the institutions of government there. It is also necessary to focus historically on the relations between resource use and control and the other 'systems' referred to above, which of course include the relations with other societies.

III

Now most graduates in Politics emerge from their degree courses with some understanding of the major features of *government* in their own and perhaps other societies as well. But how many have a firm grasp of the main patterns of resource ownership, control and distribution in these societies? How many Departments of Politics concern themselves analytically with the politics of the critical modern problems in their societies - such as unemployment, poverty, inequality or health? How many courses are concerned with the comparative analysis of the politics of non-contemporary societies? Or the politics of families, in the West or elsewhere, or of villages, or rural or regional development, or global food issues, for instance?

Such problems and issues are generally not found in courses in Politics in most educational institutions; nor are they generally defined as political by the media. Ecologists, medical scientists, economists, social administrators, anthropologists, industrial relations experts, agronomists and other specialists have important things to say about certain aspects of these matters. But such experts in these fields, understandably, almost always leave off just when they edge close to the 'political' issues involved; that is, when questions about the social causes and conditions of such problems arise, when it becomes necessary to explain the *relations* of resource use and distribution, power, social organization, culture and ideology which are involved in their occurrence. It is here that one would expect to find the discipline of Politics in the forefront, trying to fill these interdisciplinary gaps. With a few notable exceptions, it currently is not.[2] And it is this, I suggest, which highlights the poverty of Politics.

Can it really be said that these kinds of issues are unimportant or that they are *not* political? Some of them are at the centre of public debate in Britain and elsewhere. But generally not in Departments of Politics. Why?

I believe that this can largely be explained by the traditional, but still dominant bi-focal preoccupation of the discipline with the institutions and sociology of government, pressure-groups, parties, elections and so forth, on the one hand, and with the more or less detached and generally *non-applied* study of the reflections of political philosophers and theorists, on the other. These are all important and interesting matters. It is right and proper that they should be studied. But can such a narrow and largely institutional definition of what constitutes politics really continue to be justified, and to dominate the discipline of Politics? Does such an approach provide students and a wider public with the intellectual skills and frameworks of understanding which they can *use* in their own ways and lives to interpret the daily politics and problems they encounter around them, locally, nationally and internationally?

IV

Writing many years ago, the late Peter Nettl observed that 'the scope of politics as an academic subject is rarely formally discussed in course planning', and that remains largely true today.[3] That is why this book has sought to redefine and widen the conception of politics, so that the fascinating range of all the activities of cooperation and conflict over resource use and distribution (and debates about it) can become the legitimate scope of the discipline of Politics. In undertaking the analysis of such activities in human groups, institutions and societies – historical or modern – a much richer haul of comparative understanding could well emerge, and it may become possible to identify the patterns and regularities in these processes of politics. And if there is ever to be a science of

Politics, the principles which will underlie it will be rooted in these wider comparative understandings.

It should therefore be clear that it is not part of the argument here to suggest that all the societies, problems or issues which have been considered in this book should be part of every syllabus. Not at all. They are mainly illustrative of the wider general purpose. Almost any examples can be used for the purposes of teaching and learning, so long as they serve to explore and illuminate the processes of politics in human societies and to develop the necessary interpretative skills. The claim here is that the kind of redefinition and analytical framework offered in this book can at least provide a starting-point for such an enterprise, and I have tried to show how by using a wide range of different examples.

There are many other *local* issues and problems which might be explored in Politics courses and which would serve to cultivate the appropriate analytical skills and help to uncover principles and processes. They could include the *politics* of local chambers of commerce, factories, cooperatives, trade unions, students' unions, universities, women's groups, voluntary organizations – and the relations between some of them. They could include the study of the countless issues which occur up and down the country – for instance, the politics of disputes about whether companies (private or public) should open or close factories; the kinds of technologies and labour arrangements used in them, and the employment consequences of such decisions for local communities.

There are also many contemporary problems which raise fundamental issues of political philosophy which have to do with issues such as 'justice', 'fairness', 'equality' and 'freedom'. For example, one such question has to do with comparative wage and salary levels which is at the centre of much of the politics in many societies today. Another is the question of the powers of the police or other agencies of the state with regard to the rights of citizens. For instance, is it legitimate to deprive individuals of their civil liberties (say, by detention without trial) if it is thought that they may have information about threats to law and order, property or life? And can government secrecy be justified in terms of democratic theory?

Then there are issues to do with whether and where new trunk roads or reservoirs should be built in the countryside, or where to place new coalmines, or power stations, and the implications of such decisions locally and nationally. Such questions raise profound issues for political theory in general, and democratic theory in particular. For instance, disputes of this kind over the use of public and private resources may involve conflicts between national or social needs and interests on the one hand, and individual rights and freedoms on the other. How, in practice, *do* such matters get resolved? How *should* they get resolved? What does a comparative analysis of such conflicts in different societies reveal? Are the procedures and outcomes different in societies where, for instance, resources are largely owned and controlled communally, or by the state or privately? Or where there is more or less equality in terms of income, wealth and opportunities, or in terms of access to, and participation in, decision-making procedures?

Now, despite the important contributions which some writers - like Rawls and Nozick - have made in recent years to the philosophical clarification of some issues of this kind, it remains in general true to say that it is not common - though not unknown - in undergraduate courses in Politics for contemporary *practical* problems and conflicts of this kind to be considered in detail as illustrative examples of such fundamental questions in political philosophy and theory.[4] Why? Are such issues not central to many aspects of the problems of modern societies? And, from a strictly educational point of view, does it not make more sense to start by focusing on concrete problems as a means of introducing students to the broader issues of political philosophy and theory? How often is this done? Is it not more commonly the case for students to be required to study the content of particular political philosophies and theories - in abstract - without applying them to the politics of their own societies?

Abroad, in the Third World, it is not only the rise and fall of governments and *juntas* that should form the focus of attention for students of politics, but also the crucial issues to do with land, debt and the control and distribution of rural and other resources amongst both social and regional groups. I have tried to suggest in earlier chapters why the analysis of these matters is essential for an understanding of much of the conflict and repression found in the Third World (but not only there, of course). The whole question of the 'development' of those societies turns on an appreciation of their politics in the sense defined here, and underlines the need for interdisciplinary work. For 'development' is not simply a *technical* or 'economic' matter, which may be hastened by financial aid or technological assistance. It is a profoundly *political* matter. And it is the politics of these societies, in their relations with other societies and international agencies, which determines how such resources, as well as local ones, get to be used and distributed. And these politics occur far beyond the domain of national governments in the capital cities.

But the central point in all this has been to emphasize that for students of Politics the range of problems, issues and dilemmas in various societies round the world is simply endless, though it is not necessary or essential that these be drawn from contemporary societies or institutions. The possibilities of expanding the scope of the discipline of Politics to include such matters are both enormous and exciting. It is a matter of urgency that we do so. And since it is not likely that many older and more established teachers and scholars in the discipline will be willing to do this, the book is addressed primarily to newcomers to the social sciences in the hope that they will undertake this task in due course.

V

It is not possible here to discuss in any detail the full pedagogic or syllabus implications of the view of politics adopted in the book.[5] But there is one central point that is worth mentioning.

Part of the wider objective of the book is to argue that students in Departments of Politics should emerge from their studies with analytical and diagnostic skills, which have as their purpose and central point of reference the explanation of the *politics* of historical or modern societies, institutions and problems. The study of politics, I would argue, is an intensely *practical* matter, as is the study of medicine, and it is no less or more academic or theoretical. It is, in my view, much *less* important for students of politics – as defined here – to be able to give an account of what Plato, Rousseau, Mill, Marx or Weber *said*, for example, than to be able to *use* such theories, if appropriate, to help *explain* the politics or resolve problems in their own and other societies. For the study of politics is not in the same category as the study of political philosophy or the history of ideas, just as it is not synonymous with the study of government, however productive some of the points of overlap and connection may be. When I say that the discipline should be concerned with 'practical' matters, I mean events, processes and problems occurring in the politics of human societies, some examples of which have been given in the previous chapters. From a pedagogic point of view it is these which should form the starting point for students of politics, and not wider general theories which are usually taught and studied in abstract, and which many students experience as having little relevance for, or connection with, the politics of societies past or present.

VI

There is a final point to make which merges with the argument of the previous sections, and which underlines the urgency of developing understandings of politics discussed in this book.

It is necessary to admit a strong 'democratic bias' in the thinking behind the book. By that I mean the *necessity* and *importance* (not just the desirability) of *participation* by people in the decisions which affect their lives and life chances, whether these concern domestic arrangements, work, community or national affairs. There is good evidence to suggest that the more openly, actively and equally people participate in such decision-making processes, the less suspicion, the less conflict and the more balance there is in the development of their institutions and societies.

But there is more to the question of participation than this; for there are many obstacles which stand in its way. Some societies are so large that regular participation is not easily organized. Perhaps more important in practice is the complex question of the *current* control and distribution of resources and power, both private and public, which may act to hinder wider participation. For it seems clear that the greater the *equality* of resource and power distribution, or of access to them, the better are the opportunities for fuller participation, and the more of it there is in practice.

Another obstacle is the role of experts. The evidence of the present century, especially, suggests that the design and direction of 'development' in the industrialized and Third worlds alike is not safely left to them alone. It is not good for us and it is not good for them. This applies across the whole range of specialist matters - such as preventive medicine, technological innovation, urban and other forms of planning, social services, educational policy and practice and rural development. Now, it would clearly be absurd to suggest that we can do without their expertise. But it is equally important to stress two things. First, there is the necessity for more effective democratic control over experts, and the need for far greater accountability by them to the societies and communities they serve. Secondly, in order for this to happen, much wider participation is needed by communities in the decision-making processes which affect their lives.

But this raises the third obstacle to participation, and one of the most important: that of ignorance and one of its consequences, various aspects of deference. Indeed one form of 'expertise' or specialization which dominates modern societies is 'political expertise' which comes largely from the professionalization of politics and its tendency to be regarded as a specialist concern, confined to the formal political institutions. The point to stress here is that the more we understand about our social and natural environments, and the relations between them, our technologies, institutions and problems - that is our politics generally - the more we become able and willing to participate in their management, and not simply leave any or all of this to the 'experts' alone; and the more democratic our societies become.

What, then, constitutes the real core of 'democratic politics'? It is not, in my view, the usual identification of 'democracy' with only the *principles* of 'liberty', 'equality' and 'justice', or with only the *processes* of free elections and the like. Such important principles and processes are emptied of content and are hardly meaningful in practice when detached from the central democratic question of the ownership, control and distribution of resources. Thus in any society, whether that of the !Kung San or modern Britain, whatever its productive characteristics or particular institutional arrangements, the core of democratic politics must consist of *participation in decision-making about the use, production and distribution of resources*. The point may be emphasized by referring to the vast number of decisions in the institutions and societies of the West, East and Third World alike, in the private and public sectors, which are taken by tiny minorities who rarely or barely even consult with those who will be affected by them.

For these related reasons, understanding is *one* of the necessary conditions for participation and hence for democratic politics, as is the promotion of equality in both resource and power distribution. And if this book has contributed in some way to such understanding of our societies and their politics, it will have helped to achieve its implicit democratic purpose.

Notes

INTRODUCTION AND BACKGROUND

1 Charles Dickens, *A Tale of Two Cities* (1859), London, Oxford University Press, 1967, 1.
2 A useful introduction to some of the problems of the Third World may be found in Paul Harison, *Inside the Third World*, Harmondsworth, Penguin, 1979. See also J. E. Goldthorpe, *The Sociology of the Third World*, Cambridge University Press, 1975. The notion of 'absolute poverty' is defined by Robert McNamara as 'a condition of life so characterized by malnutrition, illiteracy, disease, high infant mortality and low life expectancy as to be beneath any reasonable definition of human decency'. See R. S. McNamara, *Address to the Board of Governors of the World Bank*, 1978, Washington, DC, The World Bank, 1978, 2. See also The World Bank, *World Development Report, 1978*, Washington, DC, The World Bank, 1978, chapter 1.

CHAPTER 1
REDEFINING POLITICS: THE ARGUMENT

1 The view that politics is found only in certain societies is held both by some very 'mainstream' political scientists and also some who work within a broadly 'Marxist' tradition. See, for instance, Bernard Crick, *In Defence of Politics*, Harmondsworth, Penguin, 2nd edn, 1982; and Barry Hindess and Paul Q. Hirst, *Pre-Capitalist Modes of Production*, London, Routledge & Kegan Paul, 1975. For rather different approaches, drawing on a much wider range of comparative materials, the following books are useful: Meyer Fortes and E. E. Evans-Pritchard (eds), *African Political Systems*, Oxford University Press, 1940; Isaac Schapera, *Government and Politics in Tribal Societies*, London, Watts, 1956; Lucy Mair, *Primitive Government*, Harmondsworth, Penguin, 1962; and George Balandier, *Political Anthropology*, London, Allen Lane, 1970. Though the comparative range of these latter studies is much wider than the usual focus, they are still trying to identify and define a set of *particular* activities within societies which are their 'politics'. A helpful survey of different definitions of 'politics' is that of Peter Nicholson, 'What is Politics: determining the scope of political science', *II Politico*, XLII (2), 1977.
2 One can do no better than look at the following books for good introductory accounts: Andrew Sherratt (ed.), *The Cambridge Encyclopedia of Archaeology*, Cambridge University Press, 1980; Richard E. Leakey, *The Making of Mankind*, London, Michael Joseph, 1981.

3   For good accounts of the Ibo see M. M. Green, *Ibo Village Affairs*, London, Sidgwick & Jackson, 1947; and Phoebe Ottenberg, 'The Afikpo Ibo of Eastern Nigeria', in James L. Gibb Jr (ed.), *Peoples of Africa*, New York, Holt, Rinehart & Winston, 1965.

4   Interesting descriptions of these West African Empires may be found in R. Oliver and J. D. Fage, *A Short History of Africa*, Harmondsworth, Penguin, 1962, especially chapter 4; Jacques Maquet, *Civilizations of Black Africa*, New York, Oxford University Press, 1972; and Walter Rodney, *How Europe Under-developed Africa*, Dar Es Salaam, Tanzania Publishing House, 1972, especially chapter 2.

5   The best single account of Dutch society and history in this period is that of C. R. Boxer, *The Dutch Seaborne Empire, 1600-1800*, Harmondsworth, Penguin, 1973.

6   One measure of inequality in a society is shown by contrasting the percentage of private income (sometimes in both cash and kind) received by the richest 5 or 10 per cent of the population with that of the poorest 10 or 20 per cent. Data on this question for British and some Third World societies will be found in chapters 8, 9 and 10.

7   See William W. Murdoch, *The Poverty of Nations*, Baltimore, Md, and London, Johns Hopkins University Press, 1980, especially section I.

8   A good introduction to 'ideology' is Nigel Harris, *Beliefs in Society. The Problem of Ideology*, London, Watts, 1968.

9   A fine account of the evolution and variety of human societies, which is rich in examples, is that of Marvin Harris, *Culture, Men and Nature: an Introduction to General Anthropology*, New York, Crowell, 1971.

10 Crick, op. cit., 32.

11 The relationship between kinship, politics and economics in 'tribal' societies is explored interestingly in Marshall D. Sahlins, *Tribesmen*, Englewood Cliffs, NJ, Prentice-Hall, 1968. The politics of all families everywhere are influenced by a complex of power relations, norms, roles, social pressures and ideologies operating within it, and on it from outside.

12 For some indication of this in Britain, see the report of the Equal Opportunities Commission on *Women and Public Bodies*, London, Equal Opportunities Commission, 1982.

13 See Andy Chetley, *The Baby Killer Scandal*, London, War on Want, 1979; Alan Berg, *The Nutrition Factor*, Washington, DC, Brookings Institute, 1973; Alan Berg, 'The economics of breast-feeding', *Saturday Review of Science*, 1 May 1973; Ted Greiner, *The Promotion of Bottle-feeding by Multinational Corporations*, Ithaca, NY, Cornell University Nutrition Monograph Series, no. 2, 1975.

14 Vittorio Lanternari, *The Religions of the Oppressed*, New York, Mentor Books, 1963; Bryan Wilson, *Magic and the Millennium*, London, Heinemann, 1973; and Peter Worsley, *The Trumpet Shall Sound*, London, McGibbon & Kee, rev. edn, 1968.

15 E. J. Hobsbawm and George Rudé, *Captain Swing*, London, Penguin University Books, 1973; see also *The Observer*, London, 16 November 1980, for an interesting report on the outbreak of rural rebellion and its suppression in Spain in recent years.

CHAPTER 2
SHARING AND EQUALITY IN THE KALAHARI:
THE POLITICS OF THE !KUNG SAN

1 R. B. Lee and I. de Vore (eds), *Man the Hunter*, Chicago, Aldine, 1968, 3. See also C. S. Coon, *The Hunting Peoples*, Harmondsworth, Penguin, 1976, and Elman Service, *The Hunters*, Englewood Cliffs, NJ, Prentice-Hall, 1976.

2 Lee and de Vore, op. cit., 3.

3 The best accounts here are those of R. B. Lee, *The !Kung San*, Cambridge University Press, 1979, together with the articles he has published previously on the people of the Dobe area, and Lorna Marshall, *The !Kung of Nyae Nyae*, Cambridge, Mass., Harvard University Press, 1976, and her earlier articles. The orthographical symbol ! preceding a word (as in !Kung) denotes the alveopalatal click sound typical of San languages. See Lee, op. cit., xxv. Other extremely useful works are Nancy Howell, *The Demography of the Dobe !Kung*, New York and London, Academic Press, 1979; and R. B. Lee and I. de Vore (eds), *Kalahari Hunter-Gatherers*, Cambridge, Mass., Harvard University Press, 1976.

4 George B. Silberbauer, *Hunter and Habitat in the Central Kalahari Desert*, Cambridge University Press, 1981, 78 and 291. An early and important contribution to the literature on the San may be found in Silberbauer's early work, *Bushman Survey*, Gaberones, Bechuanaland Government, 1965.

5 Lee, *The !Kung San*, 236.

6 Silberbauer, *Hunter and Habitat*, 193-4. See too H. J. Heinz, 'Territoriality among the Bushmen is general and to !Ko in particular', *Anthropos*, 67, 1972, 405-15, and his 'The social organization of the !Ko Bushmen', MA thesis, University of South Africa, 1966; and Aram Yengoyan, 'Australian section systems - demographic components and interactional similarities with the !Kung Bushmen', *Proceedings of the Eighth Congress of Anthropological and Ethnological Sciences* (1968), Tokyo and Kyoto, 1969.

7 Pierre Clastres, 'The Guayaki', in M. G. Bicchieri (ed.), *Hunters and Gatherers Today*, New York, Holt, Rinehart & Winston, 1972, 168-70.

8 Marshall, op. cit., 303.

9 ibid., 311.

10 G. B. Silberbauer, 'The G/wi Bushmen', in Bicchieri (ed.), op. cit., 309.

11 Lee, *The !Kung San*, 31.

12 Marshall, op. cit., 53.

13 Lee, *The !Kung San*, chapter 13; and Marshall, op. cit., especially chapter 9.

14 Colin Turnbull, *The Mountain People*, London, Picador, 1974.

15 J. E. Parkington, 'Seasonal mobility in the Late Stone Age', *African Studies*, 31 (4), 1972.

16 A long-held view in political theory, which can be traced back to Thomas Hobbes and no doubt earlier, is that where there is no 'common Power', like a ruler or a state, to hold people 'in awe', there is a state of 'Warre' as Hobbes called it. In such a state, he argued, the lives of people were 'solitary, poore, nasty, brutish and short'. See Thomas Hobbes, *Leviathan* (1651), London, Dent, Everyman edn, 1957, 65. This view of the 'uncivilized' and 'native' people of the world has a long history in the thinking of Europeans. It is extraordinary that such a view is still taken seriously. Moreover, relative to their *needs*, foraging societies have

enjoyed abundance and, as mentioned, worked only three or four days a week. For these and other reasons Marshall Sahlins refers to this type of society as being 'The original affluent society'. See the chapter of this title in his *Stone-Age Economics*, London, Tavistock, 1974.

17 Elizabeth Marshall Thomas, *The Harmless People*, Harmondsworth, Penguin, 1969. Two other delightful studies of a foraging society may be found in Colin Turnbull, *The Forest People*, London, Picador, 1976 (first published 1961), and his *The Wayward Servants: the Two Worlds of the African Pygmies*, London, Eyre & Spottiswood, 1966. Both illustrate the friendly and cooperative character of these people.

18 See Howell, op. cit., especially chapter 3.

CHAPTER 3
PREDATORY POLITICS: THE AZTECS

1 Bernal Díaz, *The Conquest of New Spain*, trans. J. M. Cohen, Harmondsworth, Penguin, 1963, 214. For further background see J. H. Parry, *The Spanish Seaborne Empire*, Harmondsworth, Penguin, 1973; and Charles C. Cumberland, *Mexico: the Struggle for Modernity*, Oxford University Press, 1968, especially chapters 1-3.

2 Marvin Harris, *Culture, Man and Nature*, New York, Crowell, 1971, 189.

3 Díaz, op. cit., 235.

4 Jacques Soustelle, *Daily Life of the Aztecs on the Eve of the Spanish Conquest*, trans. P. O'Brien, Harmondsworth, Penguin, 1964, 20-1; and V. W. von Hagen, *The Ancient Sun Kingdoms of the Americas*, Frogmore, St Albans, Paladin, 1973, 52.

5 Thomas C. Patterson, *America's Past: a New World Archaeology*, Glenview, Ill., Scott Foresman, 1973, 24-6.

6 Marvin Harris, *Cannibals and Kings: the Origins of Cultures*, London, Fontana, 1978, 31; Eric Wolf, *Sons of the Shaking Earth*, University of Chicago Press, 1970, 48-9; and Michael Coe, *Mexico*, London, Thames & Hudson, 1962, 33.

7 Carlo Cipolla, *The Economic History of World Population*, Harmondsworth, Penguin, 1978; and Harris, *Culture*, 174-99.

8 For an extended and brilliant account of the theory, backed up by fascinating evidence, see Harris, *Cannibals*, and also his *Cows, Pigs, Wars and Witches: the Riddles of Culture*, London, Fontana, 1977. Another interesting version of this approach may be found in Richard G. Wilkinson, *Poverty and Progress: an Ecological Model of Economic Development*, London, Methuen, 1973. See also John O'Shea, 'Mesoamerica: from village to empire', in Andrew Sherratt (ed.), *The Cambridge Encyclopaedia of Archaeology*, Cambridge University Press, 1980, chapter 58, which deals with the emergence of empires in Middle America; and also Sherratt, 'Interpretation and synthesis, a personal view', chapter 61 in the same book.

9 Patterson, op. cit., 52-7; and also R. S. MacNeish, 'The evolution of community patterns in the Tehuacan Valley of Mexico and speculations about the cultural processes', in P. J. Ucko *et al.* (eds), *Man, Settlement and Urbanism*, London, Duckworth, 1972 (Proceedings of the Research Seminar in Archaeology and Related Subjects). See too R. S. MacNeish, 'Speculation about how and why food

production and village life developed in the Tehuacan Valley, Mexico', *Archaeology*, 24 (4), 1971; and Kent V. Flannery, 'The origins of the village as a settlement type in Mesoamerica and the Near East: a comparative study', in Ucko *et al*. (eds), op. cit.

10 Wolf, op. cit., 20.

11 Patterson, op. cit., 111; Harris, *Culture*, 195-7.

12 Wolf, op. cit., 144.

13 O'Shea, op. cit., 389.

14 Nigel Davies, *The Aztecs: a History*, London, Macmillan, 1973; 8-9; Harris, *Cannibals*, chapters 7 and 8; and Michael Harner, 'Population pressures and the social evolution of agriculturalists', *Southwestern Journal of Anthropology*, 26, 1970, 67-86.

15 Davies, op. cit., 112.

16 Soustelle, op. cit., 90-4; Davies, op. cit., 92-3, 78-9, and 112; G. C. Vaillant, *The Aztecs of Mexico: Origin, Rise and Fall of the Aztec Nation*, Harmondsworth, Penguin, 1951, 123-4.

17 Soustelle, op. cit., 59-108; Wolf, op. cit., 135-44; Davies, op. cit., 78-80; and von Hagen, op. cit., 66-7.

18 Davies, op. cit., 78-9; and Soustelle, op. cit., 96-7.

19 S. F. Cook, 'Human sacrifice and warfare as factors in the demography of pre-colonial Mexico', *Human Biology*, 18, 1946, 81-102; and Michael Harner, 'The ecological basis for Aztec sacrifice', *American Ethnologist*, 4, 1977.

20 Harner, 'Ecological basis', 120.

21 Harris, *Cannibals*, 124.

22 Harner, 'Ecological basis', 129.

23 The need for interdisciplinary work is regularly stressed, but it is all too uncommon. In our teaching, the walls between the disciplines are firm, preventing the focus of attention on the problems of our time. Others who would make similar points from diverse perspectives include Gunnar Myrdal, *Economic Theory and Underdeveloped Regions*, London, Methuen, 1969, 10; and Immanuel Wallerstein, *The Modern World-System*, New York and London, Academic Press, 1974, 3-11. For a brisk but apt description of the consequences of non-integrated specialisms, see Harris, *Cows, Pigs Wars and Witches*, 7-9.

24 For some of the evidence about diet and nutrition in the modern world, see Lesley Doyal with Imogen Pennell, *The Political Economy of Health*, London, Pluto Press, 1979; and Diana Manning, *Society and Food: the Third World*, London, Butterworth, 1977.

CHAPTER 4
CATTLE, KRAALS AND PASTURES:
THE POLITICS OF THE PASTORAL MAASAI

1 Why the 'neolithic revolution' occurred, and why it occurred in a variety of places during the same space of time, is not entirely clear. An account of some of the interpretations which have been offered may be found in Marvin Harris, *Cultural Materialism. The Struggle for a Science of Culture*, New York, Vintage Books, 1980, chapter 4. The continuing concern with the problems of pastoral societies in the modern age is reflected in the work of the Commission on

Nomadic Peoples, of the International Union of Anthropological and Ethnological Sciences, whose publication *Nomadic Peoples* may be obtained from the Department of Anthropology, McGill University, Montreal, Canada.

2 See, for a further elaboration and definition of pastoralism, Claude Lefébure, 'Introduction: the specificity of nomadic pastoral societies' and Walter Goldschmidt, 'A general model for pastoral social systems', both in Équipe Écologie et Anthropologie des Sociétés Pastorales, *Pastoral Production and Society*, Cambridge University Press, 1979. See also Lawrence Krader, 'Pastoral nomadism in Eurasia: as evolution and as history', *Proceedings of the Eighth Congress of Anthropological and Ethnological Sciences* (1968), Tokyo and Kyoto, 1969; Philip C. Salzman, 'Political organization among nomadic peoples', *Proceedings of the American Philosophical Society*, 3 (2), April 1967; Brian Spooner, 'Towards a generative model of nomadism', *Anthropological Quarterly*, 44 (3), July 1971; Brian Spooner, 'The cultural ecology of pastoral nomads', *Current Topics in Anthropology*, 8, Reading, Mass., Addison-Wesley, 1974; and W. Irons and N. Dyson-Hudson (eds), *Perspectives on Nomadism*, Leiden, Brill, 1972.

3 Theodore Monod, 'Introduction', in T. Monod (ed.), *Pastoralism in Tropical Africa*, London, Oxford University Press, 1975, 106.

4 Lawrence Krader, 'Pastoralism', in *International Encyclopaedia of the Social Sciences*, New York, Macmillan and The Free Press, 1968, vol. 11, *passim*.

5 Douglas L. Johnson, *The Nature of Nomadism: a Comparative Study of Pastoral Migrations in Southwestern Asia and Northern Africa*, University of Chicago, Department of Geography Research Paper 118, 1969, 2-3.

6 It has been suggested that the degree of centralization of political authority and the extent of social stratification in the pastoral societies of Central and East Asia have been closely related to the degree of population concentration on the one hand, and the closeness of relations with settled agricultural peoples on the other. See L. Krader, 'The origin of the state among the nomads of Asia', in Équipe Écologie et Anthropologie des Sociétés Pastorales, *Pastoral Production*, and also his 'The ecology of Central Asian pastoralism', *Southwestern Journal of Anthropology*, 11 (4), 1955, and 'Principles and structures in the organization of the Asiatic steppe-pastoralists', *Southwestern Journal of Anthropology*, 11 (2), 1955. Also E. D. Phillips, *The Royal Hordes: Nomad Peoples of the Steppes*, London, Thames & Hudson, 1965.

7 See E. E. Evans-Pritchard, *The Nuer*, Oxford University Press, 1971 edn, chapter 1 and *passim*; and Paul Spencer, *The Samburu*, Los Angeles, University of California Press, 1965, chapter 1 and *passim*. This affection for their stock is found too amongst the Somali of the Horn of Africa who also sing to, and about, their camels, and praise them. See I. M. Lewis, *A Pastoral Democracy*, Oxford University Press, 1961, especially chapter 3.

8 D. B. Grigg, *The Agricultural Systems of the World*, London, Oxford University Press, 1974, chapter 7, and Lawrence Krader, *Peoples of Central Asia*, The Hague, Mouton, 1966, chapter 4. However it should be noted that the retreat and decline of the pastoral societies has not taken place without their putting up a fight.

9 This account of the Maasai rests heavily on the fascinating fieldwork done

amongst them by Alan H. Jacobs, and the various written materials deriving from it. I refer especially to his *The Pastoral Maasai of Kenya. A Report of Anthropological Field Research*, London, Overseas Development Ministry, 1963; 'The traditional political organization of the Pastoral Maasai', D. Phil. thesis, University of Oxford, 1965; and his 'Maasai pastoralism in historical perspective', in T. Monod (ed.), *Pastoralism in Tropical Africa*, cited in note 3. See also Daryll Forde, *Habitat, Economy and Society*, London, Methuen, 1934, chapter 14.

10   *Report of the East Africa Royal Commission, 1953-55* (Chairman: Sir Hugh Dow), London, HMSO, 1955, 252-67, cited in Jacobs, 'The traditional political organization of the Pastoral Maasai', 132.

11   I. L. Mason and J. P. Maule, *The Indigenous Livestock of Eastern and Southern Africa*, Farnham Royal, Buckinghamshire, Commonwealth Agricultural Bureaux, 1960; W. J. A. Payne, 'The origin of domestic cattle in Africa', *Empire Journal of Experimental Agriculture*, 32 (126), 1964; G. Williamson and W. J. A. Payne (eds), *Animal Husbandry in the Tropics*, London, Longman, 1959; and David W. Phillipson, *The Later Prehistory of Eastern and Southern Africa*, London, Heinemann, 1977, especially chapter 4.

12   Kang-Jey Ho *et al.*, 'The Maasai of East Africa: some unique biological characteristics', *Archives of Pathology*, 91, May 1971, 387.

13   Cited in Jacobs, 'The traditional political organization of the Pastoral Maasai', 22.

14   Theoretically, each age-set should follow the one above it through the various grades from Junior Warriors to Senior Elders, and beyond. In practice it is more complicated than this and sometimes there may be a few age-sets in one age-grade. Friction may arise between such sets over rights and duties.

15   Jacobs, 'The traditional political organization of the Pastoral Maasai', 391.

16   ibid., 26-7.

17   P. H. Gulliver, *The Family Herds: a Study of Two Pastoral Peoples in East Africa, the Jie and the Turkana*, London, Routledge & Kegan Paul, 1955; and Alan H. Jacobs, 'African pastoralists: some general remarks', *Anthropological Quarterly*, 38, 1965, 144-54.

18   On this, see Charles Lane, 'Pastures, paupers and paddocks: a new approach for development with pastoralists', M.Sc. thesis, Agricultural Extension and Rural Development Centre, University of Reading, August 1980; and Claude Lefébure, 'Introduction' cited in note 2.

19   Randall Baker, *Sociological Factors in the Commercialization of Cattle in Africa*, Discussion Paper 61, School of Development Studies, University of East Anglia, January 1980, 8.

20   Randall Baker, 'Nomadism in Africa', in Williamson and Payne (eds), op. cit., 727-9; and Lane, op. cit., chapters 3 and 4.

21   Jacobs, 'Maasai pastoralism in historical perspective', 416-18.

CHAPTER 5
FROM VILLAGE TO WORLD BANK:
POLITICS IN DEPARTMENTS AND INSTITUTIONS

1   This was the case in and around the village of Alona, studied by John Peristiany.

See his 'Introduction to a Cyprus highland village', in J. G. Peristiany (ed.), *Contributions to Mediterranean Sociology*, Paris, Mouton, 1968. Also his 'Honour and shame in a Cyprus highland village', in J. G. Peristiany (ed.), *Honour and Shame. The Values of Mediterranean Society*, London, Weidenfeld & Nicolson, 1965. Other fascinating material on Cypriot village affairs may be found in Peter Loizos, *The Greek Gift: Politics in a Cypriot Village*, Oxford, Blackwell, 1975, and his 'Politics and patronage in a Cypriot village, 1920-1970', in E. Gellner and J. Waterbury (eds), *Patrons and Clients in Mediterranean Societies*, London, Duckworth, 1971. A useful survey of the development of the economy of Cyprus may be found in A. J. Mayer and S. Vassiliou, *The Economy of Cyprus*, Cambridge, Mass., Harvard University Press, 1962.

2   D. Christodoulou, *The Evolution of the Rural Land Use Patterns in Cyprus* (Monograph 2 of the World Land Use Survey), London, Geographical Publications, 1959, 83-90; N. C. Lantis, *Rural Indebtedness and Agricultural Cooperation in Cyprus*, Limassol, 1944; Robin Jenkins, *The Road to Alto*, London, Pluto Press, 1979, *passim*.

3   Peter Loizos, 'Changes in property transfer among Greek Cypriot villages', *Man*, 10, 512 and *passim*. This is a fascinating article.

4   The notion of 'livelihood' is a helpful one in the discussion of less commercialized societies. It means 'that quantum of goods, services and facilities needed to maintain the life of an individual or family'. In many communities it is not possible to exchange this for money, or to express its value in money terms. See Andrew Pearse, *Seeds of Plenty, Seeds of Want: Social and Economic Implications of the Green Revolution*, Oxford, Clarendon Press, 1980, 17. The fortunes of a Panamanian village in these respects are traced with great care by Stephen Gudemans in his *The Demise of a Rural Economy*, London, Routledge & Kegan Paul, 1978.

5   A fine account of certain aspects of such changes in societies as a result of increasing contacts and wider relations may be found in the now classic study undertaken on the basis of fieldwork in Central Africa in the 1930s by Godfrey and Monica Wilson, written up in their *The Analysis of Social Change*, Cambridge University Press, 1945. This book still merits careful reading.

6   A useful and systematic account of the institutional arrangements and government (but not the politics) of British universities is contained in G. C. Moodie and Rowland Eustace, *Power and Authority in British Universities*, London, Allen & Unwin, 1974. For a more local account of one political issue in a university, see Max Beloff, 'The politics of Oxford politics', *Political Studies*, 23 (2-3), June-September 1975. See also Adrian Leftwich, 'The politics of case study: problems of innovation in university education', *Higher Education Review*, Spring 1981.

7   Students or staff interested in this sort of work might find it useful to try to think about and analyse their own departments in these kinds of terms. It can be great fun and very fruitful indeed. During the summer term of 1981 a small group of first-year students did this in a short (too short) four-week preliminary investigation of the 'politics of the Politics Department' in the University of York. The results were fascinating, as were the reactions of the department to the exercise. See Hugo Brown, David Evans, Sally Taylor and Lesley Turner,

Redefining Politics - the politics of the Politics Department, Department of Politics, University of York, 1981, mimeo.

8 The standard history of the World Bank is in E. S. Mason and R. E. Asher, *The World Bank since Bretton Woods*, Washington, DC, Brookings Institute, 1973. See also Aart van de Laar, *The World Bank and the Poor*, The Hague, Martinus Nijhoff, 1980, which takes a critical look at some aspects of Bank organization and operations. There are shorter, more critical accounts in Teresa Hayter, *Aid as Imperialism*, Harmondsworth, Penguin, 1971; Susan George, *How the Other Half Dies: the Real Reasons for World Hunger*, Harmondsworth, Penguin, 1976; and F. M. Lappé and J. Collins, *Food First: beyond the Myth of Scarcity*, London, Souvenir Press, 1980. See also R. W. Oliver, *International Economic Cooperation and the World Bank*, London, Macmillan, 1975. (After completing the manuscript a new book on the World Bank was published. It is Cheryl Payer, *The World Bank. A Critical Analysis*, New York, Monthly Review Press, 1982.)

9 See International Bank for Reconstruction and Development, *First Annual Meeting of the Board of Governors, Proceedings and Related Documents*, Washington, DC, IBRD, 1946, especially 5-16, and also Mason and Asher, op. cit., chapters 2, 6 and 7.

10 The term 'development' is used in inverted commas here because the notion is very complicated and also a disputed one. The scope of the Bank's operations may be grasped by reading its *Annual Reports*. See also the World Bank, *World Development Report*, published annually since 1978, and its many other publications. They provide one of the most valuable sources of information on a wide range of issues, from international debt tables to health issues in the Third World.

11 World Bank, *Annual Report, 1980*, Washington, DC, The World Bank, 1980, 66.

12 Warren C. Baum, 'The World Bank project cycle', *Finance and Development*, December 1978; and Mason and Asher, op. cit., chapter 8.

13 Davide Morawetz, *Twenty-Five Years of Economic Development, 1950 to 1975*, Washington, DC, The World Bank, 1977, 41.

14 World Bank, *Annual Report, 1980*, 182-4.

15 The World Bank recognizes the importance of these matters. See its Sector Policy Papers, *Rural Development*, February 1975, and *Land Reform*, May 1975, both published by the Bank in Washington, DC.

16 Hayter, op. cit., see Appendix on 'The birth and death of an ODI study'. See also Helen Pace, 'The secrecy at work in poverty politics', *The Guardian*, London, 14 January 1981, and the reply to this article by Mark Cherniavsky of the World Bank, in *The Guardian*, London, 20 January 1981.

17 For further information on this, see the reports in *The New York Times*, 13 August 1981; and *Newsweek*, 14 September 1981.

18 Quoted in *Newsweek*, op. cit., 41.

19 ibid.

20 *The Guardian*, London, 20 February 1982.

21 *Sunday Times*, London, 7 March 1982.

22 Catharine Watson, 'Bank's terms', *The Guardian*, London, 6 August 1982.

23 Cherniavsky, op. cit.

CHAPTER 6
THE POLITICS OF DESPAIR, DUSTBOWLS,
DISEASE AND DAVASTATION

1 Marvin Harris, *Cows, Pigs, Wars and Witches*, London, Fontana, 1977, 8.
2 There is a dense literature on the methodology and philosophy of the social sciences. The following books are useful introductions to aspects of this. Peter Winch, *The Idea of a Social Science*, London, Routledge & Kegan Paul, 1958; Gordon Leff, *History and Social Theory*, London, Merlin, 1969: Hugh Stretton, *The Political Sciences: General Principles of Selection in Social Science and History*, London, Routledge & Kegan Paul, 1969; Alan Ryan, *The Philosophy of the Social Sciences*, London, Macmillan, 1970; Alan Ryan (ed.), *The Philosophy of Social Explanation*, Oxford University Press, 1973; and E. H. Carr, *What is History?*, Harmondsworth, Penguin, 1964.
3 For an interesting account of the nature of disciplines and changes in their central frameworks, or 'paradigms', see Thomas Kuhn, *The Structure of Scientific Revolutions*, University of Chicago Press, 1970. While this book is mainly concerned with the natural sciences, its implications are far-reaching for other disciplines.
4 A good account of this process of selection may be found in Hugh Stretton, op. cit.
5 Although I do not refer to Geography in this book, it is important to note that many modern geographers have moved in an interdisciplinary direction with fascinating results.
6 See Gerald Studdert-Kennedy, *Evidence and Explanation in Social Science*, London, Routledge & Kegan Paul, 1975, especially chapters 1, 7, 8 and 9.
7 This much I agree with Gordon Leff, though not much more. See Leff, op. cit., 2.
8 Studdert-Kennedy, op. cit., 3. He is quite clear that interdisciplinarity is much more than this.
9 An indication of the usefulness of interdisciplinary perspectives in the analysis of such societies and their histories can be found in such diverse accounts as the following: E. O. J. Westphal, 'The linguistic perhistory of Southern Africa: Bush, Kwadi, Hottentot, and Bantu linguistic relationship', *Africa*, 33 (3), July 1963; John E. Yellen and Henry Harpenden, 'Hunter-gatherer populations and archaeological inference', *World Archaeology*, 4 (2), 1972; J. E. Yellen, 'Long-term hunter-gatherer adaptation to desert environments: a bio-geographical perspective', *World Archaeology*, 8 (3), 1967; Christopher Ehret, 'Linguistic evidence and its correlation with archaeology', *World Archaeology*, 8 (1), June 1976; Jeremy Keenan, 'The concept of the mode of production in hunter-gatherer societies', *African Studies*, 36 (1); T. Jenkins, A. Zoutendyk and A. G. Steinberg, 'Gammaglobulin groups (Gm and Inv) of various Southern African populations', *American Journal of Physical Anthropology*, 32 (2), 1970; P. V. Tobias, 'Recent human biological studies in Southern Africa, with special reference to Negroes and Khoisans', *Transactions of the Royal Society of South Africa*, 40 (part 3), 1972; R. Singer and J. S. Weiner, 'Biological aspects of some indigenous African populations', *Southwestern Journal of Anthropology*, 19 (2), 1963; C. Meillassoux, 'On the mode of production of the hunting band', in Pierre

Alexandre (ed.), *French perspectives in African studies*, Oxford University Press, 1973.

10   See for instance Lewis Binford, 'The nature of archaeology', a series of three talks printed in *The Listener*, London, 9, 16 and 23 April 1981, especially 'Let the present serve the past'.

11   Monica Wilson, 'Cooperation and conflict: the Eastern Cape frontier', in M. Wilson and L. M. Thompson (eds), *The Oxford History of South Africa*, Oxford University Press, 1969, I; and A. C. Jordan, 'Towards an African literature: the Tale of Nonqwase', *Africa South*, 3 (4). In the words of an observer quoted by Jordan: 'The sun did not set, no dead persons came back to life, and not one of the things that had been predicted came to pass.'

12   Interesting examples of these can be found in Vittorio Lanternari, *The Religions of the Oppressed*, New York, Mentor, 1963; Bryan Wilson, *Magic and the Millennium: a Sociological Study of Religious Movements of Protest among Tribal and Third World Peoples*, London, Heinemann, 1973; and in Norman Cohn, *The Pursuit of the Millennium*, London, Heinemann, 1957. Cohn is concerned to explore and explain how traditional beliefs about a future Golden Age become the 'ideologies of popular movements' in 'certain situations of mass disorientation and anxiety'. See Cohn, op. cit., v.

13   This account of the Dust Bowl draws heavily on the superb book on the subject by Donald Worster. His *Dust Bowl: The Southern Plains in the 1930s*, New York and London, Oxford University Press, 1979, makes compelling reading.

14   Worster, op. cit., 13-16.

15   ibid., 29.

16   John Steinbeck, *The Grapes of Wrath*, Harmondsworth, Penguin, 1963 (first published in the United States in 1939) provides a moving fictional account of the migration to California.

17   On the Indian reaction, or part of it, to their defeat see Alexander B. Adams, *Sitting Bull: an Epic of the Plains*, London, New English Library, 1975; and also Peter d'A. Jones, *An Economic History of the United States since 1783*, London, Routledge & Kegan Paul, 1956, especially chapter 8 for an account of the Indian Wars.

18   Jones, op. cit., chapter 8.

19   Worster, op. cit., 94, and *passim*.

20   ibid., chapter 5. For an overview of the continuing changes in US agriculture, see R. Burbach and P. Flynn, *Agribusiness in the Americas*, New York, Monthly Review and North American Congress on Latin America, 1980, chapter 1.

21   Worster, op. cit., 97.

22   G. Breuer, *Air in Danger. Ecological Perspectives on the Atmosphere*, Cambridge University Press, 1980, 15.

23   Rachel Carson, *The Silent Spring*, London, Hamish Hamilton, 1963. This was one of the first post-war books, by a biologist, to alert people to the ecological dangers of industrial and other forms of pollution.

24   Breuer, op. cit., 1-13, and *passim*.

25   Paul Harrison, *Inside the Third World*, Harmondsworth, Penguin, 1979, 131-4.

26   ibid., 126-7.

27   See, for instance, the accounts of this in Barry Commoner, *The Closing Circle*.

Confronting the Environmental Crisis, London, Cape, 1972. On the 1952 'smog' see P. Hall, H. Land, R. Parker and A. Webb, *Change, Choice and Conflict in Social Policy*, London, Heinemann, 1975, chapter 13 and their references, 515-16; also M. A. Crenson, *The Un-politics of Air Pollution*, Baltimore, Md, and London, Johns Hopkins University Press, 1972, 6-7.

28 Barry Commoner, 'Reflections: the Solar Transition, II', *The New Yorker*, 30 April 1979; and Political Ecology Research Group, *Public Participation and Energy Policy*, Oxford, PERG, 1978.

29 M. K. Barakatt, 'Pellagra', in G. H. Beaton and J. M. Bengoa (eds), *Nutrition in Preventive Medicine*, Geneva, World Health Organization, 1976; Daphne A. Roe, *A Plague of Corn. The Social History of Pellagra*, Ithaca, NY, Cornell University Press, 1973; and Elizabeth W. Etheridge, *The Butterfly Caste. A Social History of Pellagra in the South*, Westport, Conn., Greenwood, 1972. I have relied heavily on these accounts and am grateful to Ms J. L. Mead for drawing my attention to this literature and for explaining some of the technical issues.

30 Roe, op. cit., 107.

31 ibid., 19.

32 Department of Health and Social Security, *Prevention and Health. Everybody's Business*, London, HMSO, 1979; and Lesley Doyal with Imogen Pennell, *The Political Economy of Health*, London, Pluto Press, 1979.

33 World Bank, *Health*, Washington, DC, The World Bank, Sector Policy Paper, February 1980; and Doyal, op. cit., chapter 3.

34 H. Brenner, *Estimating the Social Costs of National Economic Policy. Implication for Mental and Physical Health, and Criminal Aggression. Volume I: Employment*, Study prepared for the use of the Joint Economic Committee of the US Congress, 26 October 1976, Washington, DC, US Government Printing Office, 1976; and his 'Mortality and national economy: a review of the experience of England and Wales, 1936-1976', *The Lancet*, London, 15 September 1979. See too the editorial, 'Does unemployment kill?', *The Lancet*, London, 31 March 1979; and Wally Gordon, 'The need for funds for health research', letter in *New York State Journal of Medicine*, October 1979.

35 Department of Health and Social Security, *Inequalities in Health. Report of a Research and Working Group* ('The Black Report'), London, DHSS, 1980; also Doyal, op. cit., 57-96 and *passim*.

36 For some of the detail on these famines see the references and account by F. M. Lappé and J. Collins in their *Food First: Beyond the Myth of Scarcity*, London, Souvenir Press, 1980, chapters 7 and 8. See also Amartya Sen, 'Starvation and exchange entitlements: a general approach and its application to the great Bengal famine', *Cambridge Journal of Economics*, 1, 1977, 33-59, and also his *Poverty and Famines: an Essay on Entitlement and Deprivation*, Oxford University Press, 1981. Also Harrison, op. cit. chapter 15, and William W. Murdoch, *The Poverty of Nations*, Baltimore, Md, and London, Johns Hopkins University Press, 1980, especially 293-306.

37 There is a rich literature on modern political and social movements. For an unusual account of a religious movement, with very important social implications, which arose out of war and subsequent uncertainties and conflicts, see Gerald Studdert-Kennedy, *Democracy and the Dog-Collar*, London, Macmillan, 1982.

Edward Thompson vividly describes some of the religious movements (and the prophets and prophetesses associated with them) which emerged in the late eighteenth and early nineteenth centuries in England, some of which he characterizes as embodying the 'chiliasm of despair'. See E. P. Thompson, *The Making of the English Working Class*, Harmondsworth, Penguin, 1968, especially chapter 11 on 'The transforming power of the Cross'.

CHAPTER 7
THE POLITICS OF EUROPEAN EXPANSION,
CONQUEST AND CONTROL

1   Peter Worsley, *The Third World*, London, Weidenfeld & Nicolson, 1967, 1.
2   For a superb survey of all these empires and states which pre-dated European empires, see J. M. Roberts, *History of the World*, Harmondsworth, Penguin, 1980, Books 2, 3 and 4.
3   K. M. Panikkar, *Asia and Western Dominance*, London, Allen & Unwin, 1953, part I; C. R. Boxer, *The Portuguese Seaborne Empire*, Harmondsworth, Penguin, 1973, chapter 2; Roberts, op. cit., Book 4, chapters 6 and 7.
4   Adam Smith, *Wealth of Nations* (1776), London, Routledge & Sons, 1892, Book IV, 488. A similar view about these events and 'Europe's assault on the World' can be found in Roberts, op. cit., who states that 'the change in world history after 1500 is quite without precedent', 600. See also G. Barraclough, *An Introduction to Contemporary History*, Harmondsworth, Penguin, 1967, 10, 64 and 92.
5   Worsley, op. cit., 2-3.
6   Smith, op. cit., 488.
7   K. Marx and F. Engels: 'The Communist Manifesto', in Marx and Engels, *Selected Works*, Moscow, Foreign Languages Publishing House, 1958, I, 35.
8   Karl Marx and F. Engels, *The German Ideology*, London, Lawrence & Wishart, 1965, 75-6.
9   The best introductory accounts of this may be found in A. G. Keller, *Colonization*, New York, Ginn, 1908; J. H. Parry, *The Spanish Seaborne Empire*, London, Hutchinson, 1966; Boxer, op. cit; C. R. Boxer, *The Dutch Seaborne Empire*, Harmondsworth, Penguin, 1973; J. H. Parry, *The Age of Reconnaisance*, London, Weidenfeld & Nicolson, 1963.
10 Boxer, *The Portuguese Seaborne Empire*, 15-38; Denys Hay, *Europe in the Fourteenth and Fifteenth Centuries*, London, Longman, 1966; N. R. Bennett, 'Christian and Negro slavery in eighteenth century North Africa', *Journal of African History*, 1 (1), 1960; N. Levtzion, 'The early states of the Western Sudan to 1500', in J. F. A. Ajayi and M. Crowder (eds), *History of West Africa*, London, Longman, 1971, I; Edgar Prestage, 'The search for the searoute to India, 1415-1460', in A. P. Newton (ed.), *Travel and Travellers in the Middle Ages*, London, Kegan Paul, 1930; Eileen Power, 'The opening of the land routes to Cathay', in Newton (ed.) op. cit.
11 F. M. Rogers, *The Quest for Eastern Christians*, Minneapolis, University of Minnesota Press, 1962; Sir D. Ross, 'Prester John and the Empire of Ethiopia', in Newton (ed.), op. cit.
12 Malcolm Letts, *Sir John Mandeville. The Man and his Book*, London, The

Batchworth Press, 1949; Ross, op. cit.

13　Parry, *The Spanish Seaborne Empire*, 44-5.
14　Boxer, *the Portuguese Seaborne Empire*, 20-1.
15　ibid., 51-2.
16　B. Vlekke, *Nusantara. A History of Indonesia*, The Hague, W. van de Hoeve, 1959; J. S. Furnivall, *Netherlands India*, London, Cambridge University Press, 1944.
17　Joshua Rowntree, *The Imperial Drug Trade*, London, Methuen, 1905, 277-90; and also Panikkar, op. cit., 95 ff. Rowntree's account shows how reluctant British governments were to condemn or control the trade.
18　*Niles' National Register*, 22 January 1842, 327-8, cited in H. Magdoff, *The Age of Imperialism*, New York, Monthly Review, 1969, 174.
19　On Japan, see Paul Akamatsu, *Meiji 1868*, London, Allen & Unwin, 1972; and J. Livingstone *et al.* (eds), *The Japan Reader*, Harmondsworth, Penguin, 1976, I.
20　Eric Williams, *Capitalism and Slavery*, London, André Deutsch, 1964; Herbert S. Klein, *The Middle Passage*, Princeton, NJ, Princeton University Press, 1978; Philip D. Curtin, *The Atlantic Slave Trade*, Madison, University of Wisconsin Press, 1969.
21　R. Oliver and A. Atmore, *Africa since 1800*, Cambridge University Press, 1967; Lord Hailey, *An African Survey*, Oxford University Press, 1956, 143.
22　W. H. Prescott, *History of the Conquest of Mexico and History of the Conquest of Peru* (1843 and 1847), New York, Modern Library, n.d., 130.
23　Roberts, op. cit., 612; R. T. Davies, *The Golden Century of Spain 1501-1621*, London, Macmillan, 1937, 299-300; Peter d'A. Jones, *Since Columbus*, London, Heinemann, 1975.
24　Parry, op. cit., chapter 11.
25　ibid., 213-20.
26　Keller, op. cit., 271. On the relationship of livestock to human population, see C. Gibson, *Spain in America*, New York, Harper, 1966, 153. On depopulation and forced labour in Peru, see John Hemming, *The Conquest of the Incas*, London, Macmillan, 1970.
27　S. J. Stein and B. H. Stein, *The Colonial Heritage of Latin America*, Oxford University Press, 1970; Frank Tannenbaum, *Slave and Citizen*, New York, Knopf, 1946; Marvin Harris, *Patterns of Race in the Americas*, New York, Walker, 1964.
28　Williams, op. cit.
29　A. G. Frank, *Capitalism and Underdevelopment in Latin America*, Harmondsworth, Penguin, 1971, especially sections 3 and 4; A. O. Hirschman, *Journeys toward Progress*, New York, Anchor Books, 1965, chapter 1.
30　Boxer, *The Portuguese Seaborne Empire*, 87, 105, 156 and 167-8; Christopher Hill, *Reformation to Industrial Revolution*, Harmondsworth, Penguin, 1969, 230.
31　E. J. Hobsbawm, *Industry and Empire*, Harmondsworth, Penguin, 1968, 50.
32　On slavery in the US South, see K. M. Stampp, *The Peculiar Institution*, New York, Knopf, 1956; S. M. Elkins, *Slavery: A Problem in American Institutional Life*, University of Chicago Press, 1959; E. D. Genovese, *The Political Economy of Slavery*, New York, Vintage Books, 1967; and his *The World the Slaveholders Made*, New York, Vintage Books, 1971.

33 For an interesting if complex interpretation of the American Civil War, see Barrington Moore Jr, *Social Origins of Dictatorship and Democracy*, Boston, Mass., Beacon Press, 1966, chapter 3.

34 Hobsbawm, op. cit., figure 33, p. 351; and Michael Barratt Brown, *After Imperialism*, London, Heinemann, 110.

35 A. M. Carr-Saunders, *World Population*, Oxford University Press, 1936, 42.

36 R. McNamara, *Address to the Massachusetts Institute of Technology*, Washington, DC, The World Bank, 1977, 4 and *passim*.

37 Fictional and brilliant sketches of characters of this kind may be found in the novels of Joseph Conrad, like *Almayer's Folly*, *Lord Jim*, and *Nostromo*.

38 For Brazil, see Gilbert Freyre, *The Masters and the Slaves*, New York, Knopf, 1946; and on plantation economy and society see George Beckford, *Persistent Poverty*, Oxford University Press, 1972. For Kenya, see M. P. K. Sorrenson, *Origins of European Settlement in Kenya*, Nairobi, Oxford University Press, 1968, and Colin Leys, *Underdevelopment in Kenya*, London, Heinemann, 1975.

39 Marvin Harris, *Patterns of Race in the Americas*; E. Franklin Frazier, *Race and Culture Contacts in the Modern World*, New York, Knopf, 1957.

40 On the *encomienda*, *repartimiento* and *mita* see Keller, op. cit., Parry, op. cit. and Hemming, op. cit., chapters 18 and 20. On slavery in Angola, see Henry W. Nevinson, *A Modern Slavery*, New York, Schocken Books, 1968, first published in 1906. On the appalling conditions of forced labour in the Congo, see E. D. Morel, *Black Man's Burden*, New York, Monthly Review, 1969, especially chapter 9; Ruth Slade, *King Leopold's Congo*, Oxford University Press, 1962, 189; Roger Anstey, *King Leopold's Legacy*, Oxford University Press, 1966, 6; and W. R. Louis and Jean Stengers, *E. D. Morel's History of the Congo Reform Movement*, Oxford University Press, 1968.

41 There is a great variety of books on the nationalist movements in individual African countries, but some general introductions to this may be found in Thomas Hodgkin, *Nationalism in Colonial Africa*, London, Muller, 1956; R. Emerson and M. Kilson (eds), *The Political Awakening of Africa*, Englewood Cliffs, NJ, Prentice-Hall, 1968; P. C. Lloyd (ed.), *The New Elites of Tropical Africa*, Oxford University Press, 1966. A fine analysis of nationalism and decolonization in the Caribbean may be found in Trevor Munroe, *The Politics of Constitutional Decolonization*, Kingston, Jamaica, Institute of Social and Economic Research, 1972. On India, see K. M. Panikkar, op. cit., parts 5 and 6.

42 See Hannah Arendt, 'Race thinking before racism', *The Review of Politics*, IV (1), 1944; V. G. Kiernan, *The Lords of Human Kind*, Harmondsworth, Penguin, 1972; Anthony J. Barker, *The African Link*, London, Frank Cass, 1978. A good survey of the different types of race and colonial relations can be found in Philip Mason, *Patterns of Dominance*, Oxford University Press, 1972.

43 There is a substantial literature on South African history and politics. One of the best introductory accounts remains that of C. W. de Kiewiet, *A History of South Africa, Social and Economic*, Oxford University Press, 1960. See also Monica Wilson and L. M. Thompson (eds), *The Oxford History of South Africa*, 2 vols, Oxford University Press, 1969-71; T. R. H. Davenport, *South Africa. A Modern History*, London, Macmillan, 1977. On the history of South Africa, or parts of it, up to 1820, see R. Elphick and H. Giliomee (eds), *The Shaping of South African Society*, London, Longman, 1979. A first-rate account of the politics of the

nineteenth and twentieth centuries, following the discovery of diamonds and gold, is that of H. J. Simons and R. E. Simons, *Class and Colour in South Africa, 1850-1950*, Harmondsworth, Penguin, 1969. Much of the evidence and argument for the Cape in the present chapter is drawn from Adrian Leftwich, 'Colonialism and the constitution of Cape society under the Dutch East India Company', D. Phil. thesis, University of York, 1976.

44 Leftwich, op. cit., I, 282-3 and 272-3.

45 The suggestive term belongs to Martin Legassick, 'The Griqua, the Sotho-Tswana, and the missionaries, 1780-1840: the politics of a frontier zone', Ph. D. thesis, University of California, 1969, which explores similar relations of conflict in and beyond the Northern Cape region.

46 L. M. Thompson, 'The subjection of the African chiefdoms, 1870-1898', in Wilson and Thompson (eds), op. cit., II, 257.

47 Simons, op. cit., chapters 1-4.

48 Thompson, op. cit., 284; see also Davenport, op. cit., chapter 7. On the significance of the mineral revolution in South Africa, see for instance D. Hobart Houghton, *The South African Economy*, Cape Town, Oxford University Press, chapter 1.

49 R. B. Lee, *The !Kung San*, Cambridge University Press, 1979, chapter 14.

50 Joseph Conrad, *Nostromo* (1904), Harmondsworth, Penguin, 1963, 81.

51 There is a rich literature on the whole question of the transformation of Europe, especially England as the first industrial society, by historians and especially economic historians. See M. M. Postan, *Medieval Economy and Society*, Harmondsworth, Penguin, 1974; Christopher Hill, *Reformation to Industrial Revolution*, Harmondsworth, Penguin, 1969; D. G. North and R. P. Thomas, *The Rise of the Western World*, Cambridge University Press, 1973; Hobsbawm, op. cit.; B. A. Holderness, *Pre-Industrial England, 1500-1750*, London, Dent, 1976; Barrington Moore, op. cit.; Maurice Dobb, *Studies in the Development of Capitalism*, London, Routledge & Kegan Paul, 1946. On Europe more generally, see Carlo Cipolla (ed.), *The Fontana Economic History of Europe*, London, Fontana, 1973 and 1974, especially vols 2, 3 and 4.

52 See especially North and Thomas, op. cit., chapter 11; Moore, op. cit., chapter 1; and Hill, op. cit., part 3.

53 Kiernan, op. cit. The concern for individual rights and obligations is reflected in John Stuart Mill, *On Liberty* (1859), Harmondsworth, Penguin, 1974. Two valuable discussions of changing ideas are Asa Briggs, *Victorian People*, Harmondsworth, Penguin, 1965, and Raymond Williams, *Culture and Society 1780-1950*, Harmondsworth, Penguin, 1963. On attitudes to the Empire in a Salford slum see R. Roberts, *The Classic Slum*, Harmondsworth, Penguin, 1980, 140-4.

54 Hill, op. cit., 237.

55 Williams, op. cit., 52.

56 Material on the benefits which flowed to England is drawn from Hill, op. cit.; Williams, op. cit., 52; Barratt Brown, op. cit.; John Strachey, *The End of Empire*, London, Gollancz, 1959; Basil Davidson, *Black Mother*, London, Gollancz, 1961; Dobb, op. cit.; Ernest Mandel, *Marxist Economic Theory*, London, Merlin Press, 1968, II, chapter 13.

57 Albert Imlah, *Economic Elements in the Pax Britannica*, Cambridge, Mass.,

Harvard University Press, 1958, table 4; Hobsbawm, op. cit.; Michael Barratt Brown, *The Economics of Imperialism*, Harmondsworth, Penguin, 1974; D. K. Fieldhouse, *Economics and Empire 1830-1914*, London, Weidenfeld & Nicolson, 1973; Michael Barratt Brown, *Essays in Imperialism*, Nottingham, Spokesman Books, 1972.

58 Barratt Brown, *The Economics of Imperialism*; Hobsbawm, op. cit.; Fieldhouse, op. cit.

59 Barratt Brown, *The Economics of Imperialism*, 119; Davidson, op. cit.; Walter Rodney, *How Europe Underdeveloped Africa*, Dar Es Salaam, Tanzania Publishing House, 1972; Teresa Hayter, *The Creation of World Poverty*, London, Pluto Press, 1981; on Guinea, see R. W. Johnson, 'French imperialism in Guinea', in R. Owen and B. Sutcliffe (eds), *Studies in the Theory of Imperialism*, London, Longman, 1972; Michael Crowder, *Colonial West Africa*, London, Frank Cass, 1978, 244-8; E. A. Brett, *Colonialism and Underdevelopment in East Africa*, London, Heinemann, 1973.

60 On Sri Lankan irrigation in the ancient civilizations, see Rhoads Murphey, 'The ruin of ancient Ceylon', *Journal of Asian Studies*, XVI (2), February 1957; R. C. Brohier, *Ancient Irrigation Works in Ceylon*, Colombo, Ceylon Government Press, 1934; E. R. Leach, 'Hydraulic society in Ceylon', *Past and Present*, 15, 1959, 2-26.

61 Hill, op. cit., 237; Panikkar, op. cit.; Strachey, op. cit.; Barratt Brown, *After Imperialism*, 60 and 174.

62 Karl Marx, 'The future results of British rule in India', in Shlomo Avineri (ed.), *Karl Marx on Colonialism and Modernization*, New York, Anchor Books, 1969.

63 Raymond Vernon, *Sovereignty at Bay*, Harmondsworth, Penguin, 1971; R. J. Barnet and R. E. Müller, *Global Reach. The Power of the Multinational Corporations*, New York, Simon & Schuster, 1974.

64 Barnet and Müller, op. cit., 15.

65 *North-South. A Programme for Survival* (The Brandt Report), London, Pan, 1980, 187.

66 Barnet and Müller, op. cit., 26; see also J. K. Galbraith, 'A frenzy of mergers', *Washington Post*, 12 August 1981.

67 On 'vertical integration' in the plantation economies, see Beckford, op. cit., 128-30.

68 P. E. Sigmund, *Multinationals in Latin America*, Madison, University of Wisconsin Press, 1980, chapter 5.

69 Paul Harrison, *Inside the Third World*, Harmondsworth, Penguin, 1979, 346-52.

70 A. G. Frank, *Crisis in the Third World*, London, Heinemann, 1981, chapter 6; and Latin America Bureau, *Unity is Strength*, London, 1980.

71 Harrison, op. cit., 350; Vernon, op. cit., 171.

72 Frank, op. cit., 170.

73 Hayter, op. cit., 96-108; Frank, op. cit., chapter 5. On the Mexican *maquiladoras* see P. Baird and E. McCaughan, *Beyond the Border*, New York, North American Congress on Latin America, 1979, especially chapter 4. *Maquiladoras* are workshops and small factories in Mexico (just over the border from the USA) where low wage rates enable American companies to make handsome profits on goods subsequently sold in the US market.

74 Hans Singer and J. Ansari, *Rich and Poor Countries*, London, Allen & Unwin, 1977, 43.
75 L. H. Gann and P. Duignan, *The Burden of Empire*, London, Pall Mall, 1968, 382 and chapter 22.
76 Paul Samuelson, *Economics*, New York, McGraw Hill, 11th edn, 1980, 2.

CHAPTER 8
SCARCITY, INEQUALITY AND IMBALANCE:
POLITICS IN THIRD WORLD SOCIETIES

1 Karl Marx, 'The Eighteenth Brumaire of Louis Bonaparte', in Karl Marx and Frederick Engels, *Selected Works*, Moscow, Foreign Languages Publishing House, 1958, I, 247.
2 L. M. Thompson, 'Cooperation and conflict: the Zulu Kingdom and Natal', in Monica Wilson and L. M. Thompson (eds), *The Oxford History of South Africa*, Oxford University Press, 1969, I, 315. See also D. R. Morris, *The Washing of the Spears*, London, Sphere Books, 1965; J. D. Omer-Cooper, *The Zulu Aftermath*, London, Longman, 1966; and E. A. Ritter, *Shaka Zulu*, London, Panther, 1969.
3 D. B. Davis, *The Problem of Slavery in Western Culture*, Ithaca, NY, Cornell University Press, 1966; George MacMunn, *Slavery Through the Ages*, London, Nicholson & Watson, 1938.
4 Louis Dumont, *Homo Hierarchicus*, London, Paladin, 1972.
5 John Beattie, *Bunyoro*, New York, Holt, Rinehart & Winston, 1960.
6 Ester Boserup, *Women's Role in Economic Development*, London, Allen & Unwin, 1970; Barbara Rogers, *The Domestication of Women*, London, Tavistock, 1980, especially chapter 6.
7 World Bank, *World Tables*, Baltimore, Md, and London, Johns Hopkins University Press, 1980, Comparative Economic Data, table II, pp. 430-3.
8 ibid, 436-41.
9 Paul Harrison, *Inside The Third World*, Harmondsworth, Penguin, 1979, chapter 1 and maps, pp. 454-5.
10 World Bank, *World Tables*, 435-8.
11 W. W. Murdoch, *The Poverty of Nations*, Baltimore, Md, and London, Johns Hopkins University Press, 1980, chapter 5.
12 F. M. Lappé and J. Collins, *World Hunger, Ten Myths*, San Francisco, Calif., Institute for Food and Development Policy, 1980, 8.
13 ibid, 8; and Murdoch, op. cit., 156.
14 F. M. Lappé *et al.*, *Aid as Obstacle*, San Francisco, Calif., Institute for Food and Development Policy, 1980, 31; The Economist, *The World in Figures*, London, Macmillan, 1978, 105; Murdoch, op. cit., 99.
15 F. M. Lappé and J. Collins, *Food First: Beyond the Myth of Scarcity*, London, Souvenir Press, 1980, 21; Murdoch, op. cit., 2, 98 and 130; *Entering the Twenty First Century, The Global 2000 Report to the President*, Harmondsworth, Penguin, 1982, Major Findings and Conclusions.
16 M. F. Lofchie, 'Political and economic origins of African hunger', *Journal of Modern African Studies*, 13 (4), 554.

17   Hans Singer and J. Ansari, *Rich and Poor Countries*, London, Allen & Unwin, 1977, 74.

18   A. S. Banks *et al.* (eds), *Economic Handbook of the World, 1981*, New York, McGraw Hill, 1981, *passim*.

19   Lofchie, op. cit., 558.

20   Paul Bairoch, *The Economic Development of the Third World since 1900*, London, Methuen, 1975, chapter 2.

21   Murdoch, op. cit., 162-3; R Burbach and P. Flynn, *Agribusiness in the Americas*, New York, Monthly Review, 1980.

22   Banks, *et al.* (eds) op. cit., *passim*.

23   Data from the United Nations Conference on Trade and Development (UNCTAD), *Handbook of International Trade and Development Statistics, 1976*, and *Supplements, 1977, 1979* and *1980*, New York, United Nations, 1976, 1977, 1979 and 1980, tables 2.8; see also *North-South: The Report of the Independent Commission on International Development Issues under the Chairmanship of Willy Brandt*, London, Pan, 1980, 144-6; Harrison, op. cit., 336-42; and George Beckford, *Persistent Poverty*, New York, Oxford University Press, 1972.

24   Bairoch, op. cit., chapter 6; *North-South*, 147; Harrison, op. cit., 342-9.

25   UNCTAD, op. cit., tables 2.5 and 2.6.

26   Michael Manley, *The Politics of Affirmation*, London, Third World Foundation, 1979, 9; and information on Mozambique from an official of the President's staff.

27   World Bank, *World Development Report 1981*, Washington, DC, The World Bank, 1981, table 5-2, p. 57; also A. G. Frank, *Crisis in the Third World*, London, Heinemann, 1981, chapter 4.

28   A. S. Banks, *et al.*, op. cit., *passim*.

29   *World Development Report, 1981*, table 13, pp. 158-9; Inter-American Development Bank, *Economic and Social Progress in Latin American, 1980-1 Report*, Washington, DC, 1981. These amounts also fluctuate from year to year, reflecting either reduced payments or better export earnings, or both. In the case of India, the figure in 1970 was 20.9 per cent; in 1977 it was 10.5 per cent, and in 1979 it was 9.5 per cent. Sri Lanka's debt service ratio went from 10.3 per cent in 1970 to 14.6 per cent in 1977, to 6.5 per cent in 1979.

30   Michael Lipton, *Why Poor People Stay Poor*, London, Temple Smith, 1977, 13.

31   Figures on land and landlessness for Latin America and Asia come from M. J. Esman, *Landlessness and Near-Landlessness in Developing Countries*, Ithaca, NY, Cornell University Development Committee, 1978; International Labour Office, *Poverty and Landlessness in Rural Asia*, Geneva, ILO, 1977; Harrison, op. cit., 80-116; Claire Whittemore, *Land for People*, Oxford, Oxfam, 1981; I. Singh, *Small Farmers and the Landless in South Asia*, Washington, DC, The World Bank, 1979.

32   Colin Leys, *Underdevelopment in Kenya*, London, Heinemann, 1975; Lord Hailey, *An African Survey, Revised 1956*, Oxford University Press, 1957; R. Palmer and N. Parsons (eds), *The Roots of Rural Poverty in Central and Southern Africa*, London, Heinemann, 1977; Murdoch, op. cit., 216-23.

33   World Bank, *World Economic and Social Indicators, 1978*, Washington, DC, World Bank, table XI; see also *World Development Report, 1981*, and *World Tables, 1980* for other versions of this.

34 Rehman Sobhan, 'Politics of food and famine in Bangladesh', *Economic and Political Weekly*, 14, 1 December 1979; Amartya Sen, *Poverty and Famines*, Oxford University Press, 1981; D. F. McHenry and K. Bird, 'Food bungle in Bangladesh', *Foreign Policy*, 27, Summer 1977; M. D. Morris, 'What is a famine?', *Economic and Political Weekly*, IX (44), 2 November 1974; Gail Omvedt, 'South Asia and the politics of food', *Economic and Political Weekly*, IX (49), 7 November 1974. In 1981 an official of the US government declared: 'Food aid has always been one of the most political things we've got.' See 'Thought for food', *New York Times*, 2 August 1981.

35 On this diversity in Africa, see Leo Kuper and M. G. Smith (eds), *Pluralism in Africa*, Berkeley, University of California Press, 1971, especially chapter 4; and John Barnes, *Politics in a Changing Society*, Manchester University Press, 1967, on the Ngoni. On Latin America, see S. J. Stein and B. H. Stein, *The Colonial Heritage of Latin America*, New York, Oxford University Press, 1970.

36 See, for instance, M. B. Leigh, *The Rising Moon: Political Change in Sarawak*, Sydney University Press, 1974; and R. S. Milne and K. J. Ratnam, *Malaysia - New States in a New Nation*, London, Frank Cass, 1974. The inclusion of Singapore in Malaysia at the same time was short-lived. It withdrew in 1965.

37 Catherine Hoskyns, *The Congo since Independence*, Oxford University Press, 1965; and Crawford Young, *Politics in the Congo*, Princeton University Press, 1965.

38 P. C. Lloyd, *Classes, Crises and Coups*, London, MacGibbon & Kee, 1971, especially chapter 8; John de St Jorre, *The Nigerian Civil War*, London, Hodder & Stoughton, 1972.

39 Cited in F. Forsyth, *The Biafra Story*, Harmondsworth, Penguin, 1969, 46.

40 For a useful introduction see T. Shanin (ed.), *Peasants and Peasant Society*, Harmondsworth, Penguin, 1971.

41 See Norman Long, *An Introduction to the Sociology of Rural Development*, London, Tavistock, 1977, chapter 3; and Andrew Pearse, *Seeds of Plenty, Seeds of Want*, London, Oxford University Press, 1980, chapter x.

42 A good introduction to some of the issues may be found in Peter Lloyd, *Third World Proletariat?*, London, Allen & Unwin, 1982, especially chapter 2.

43 See, for instance, Hamza Alavi, 'The state in post-colonial societies: Pakistan and Bangladesh', *New Left Review*, 74, July-August 1972; Issa Shivji, *Class Struggles in Tanzania*, London, Heinemann, 1976; A. G. Frank, *Lumpenbourgeoisie and Lumpenproletariat, Dependency, Class and Politics in Latin America*, New York, Monthly Review, 1972; on the control of resources by these groups in Africa and the emergence of 'indigenous capitalist classes', see for instance Nicola Swainson, 'The Kenyan bourgeoisie', and Paul Kennedy, 'Indigenous capitalism in Ghana', both in *Review of African Political Economy*, 8, January-April 1977.

44 See James Jupp, 'Modernization and pluralism: Ceylon and Malaysia', in Adrian Leftwich (ed.), *South Africa. Economic Growth and Political Change*, London, Allison & Busby, 1974; and Richard Sandbrook, *Proletarians and African Capitalism*, Cambridge University Press, 1975.

45 See Eric Wolf, *Peasant Wars of the Twentieth Century*, London, Faber, 1969; and John Dunn, *Modern Revolutions*, Cambridge University Press, 1972.

46 Donald R. Snodgrass, *Ceylon. An Export Economy in Transition*, Homewood, Ill., Richard D. Irwin, 1966, 156; and also Harrison, op. cit., 82-5.

47 S. Ganewatta, *Socio-economic Factors in Rural Indebtedness*, Colombo, Agrarian Research and Training Institute, 1974, 21; Harrison, op. cit., 83; B. Hartmann and J. Boyce, *Needless Hunger*, San Francisco, Calif., Institute for Food and Development Policy, 1979, 18.

48 Esman, op. cit., 25; Hartmann and Boyce, op. cit.

49 See Kathleen Gough and H. P. Sharma (eds), *Imperialism and Revolution in South Asia*, New York, Monthly Review, 1973; Harrison, op. cit., 102-4; and Leela Visaria, 'The Harijan's worsening plight', *Economic and Political Weekly*, IX (5), 2 February 1974; and 'Massacre at Devbaath', *Economic and Political Weekly*, IX (39), 28 September 1974.

50 Eduardo Lachica, *The Huks. Philippine Agrarian Society in Revolt*, New York, Praeger, 1971; Fred Halliday, 'The Ceylonese insurrection', in Robin Blackburn (ed.), *Explosion in a Sub-continent*, Harmondsworth, Penguin, 1975; James Jupp, *Sri Lanka. Third World Democracy*, London, Frank Cass, 1978, especially chapter 10.

51 G. B. Keerawella, 'The Janatha Vimukthi Peramuna and the 1971 uprising', *Ceylon Studies Seminar, 1979*, Series no. 1, University of Peradeniya, Sri Lanka, Serial Number 78.

52 Richard Gott, *Rural Guerrillas in Latin America*, Harmondsworth, Penguin, 1973; E. J. Hobsbawm, 'Guerrillas in Latin America', in *Socialist Register 1970*, London, Merlin, 1970.

53 Robert Moss, *Urban Guerrillas*, London, Temple Smith, 1972; Alain Labrousse, *The Tupamaros*, Harmondsworth, Penguin, 1973.

54 For instance, see Kerstin Leitner, 'Kenyan Agricultural Workers', *Review of African Political Economy*, 6, May-August 1976.

55 Alan Angell, *Politics and the Labour Movement in Chile*, New York, Oxford University Press, 1972.

56 See Josh De Wind, 'From peasants to miners: the background to strikes in the mines of Peru', in Robin Cohen *et al.* (eds), *Peasants and Proletarians: The Struggles of Third World Workers*, London, Hutchinson, 1979.

57 Joan Davies, *African Trade Unions*, Harmondsworth, Penguin, 1966.

58 See Charles van Onselen, *Chibaro: African Mine Labour in Southern Rhodesia, 1900-1933*, London, Pluto Press, 1976; A. L. Epstein, *Politics in an Urban African Community*, Manchester University Press, 1958; R. H. Bates, *Unions, Parties and Political Development. A Study of Mineworkers in Zambia*, New Haven, Conn., Yale University Press, 1971; R. Sandbrook and R. Cohen (eds), *The Development of an African Working Class*, London, Longman, 1975.

59 See R. Cohen *et al.* (eds), op. cit., *passim*; Jim Silver, 'Ghana's mining industry', *Review of African Political Economy*, 12, May-August 1978; Dafe Otobo, 'The Nigerian General Strike of 1981', *Review of African Political Economy*, 22, October-December 1981; 'The fall out', article on the Indian railway strike, *Economic and Political Weekly*, IX (23), 8 June 1974.

60 *The Guardian*, London, 28 January 1981.

61 Stockholm International Peace Research Institute (SIPRI), *World Armament and Disarmament, 1982*, London, Taylor & Francis, 1982, xxiv and Appendix 5-B, 140-5.

62 Ruth Leger Sivard, *World Military and Social Expenditure, 1981*, Leesburg, Va, World Priorities, 1981, 8.

63 World Bank, *World Tables*, Economic Data Sheets, 272-369; see also M. Kidron and R. Segal, *The State of the World Atlas*, London, Pan, 1981, 7-12.

64 *International Herald Tribune*, 1 June 1982; Frank, op. cit., especially chapters 7 and 8; Kidron and Segal, op. cit., table 28.

65 Sivard, op. cit., 7; and R. L. Sivard, *World Military and Social Expenditure, 1982, passim*.

66 *World Development Report, 1981*, table 24. Chilean 'defence' expenditure rose from 6.1 per cent of government spending to 12 per cent; and International Institute of Strategic Studies, *The Military Balance*, London, International Institute of Strategic Studies, 1972-3 and 1981-2.

67 On the 'doctrine of National Security', see Penny Lernoux, *Cry of the People*, Harmondsworth, Penguin, 1982. On police and military training, see Centre for Research on Criminal Justice, *The Iron Fist and the Velvet Glove*, Berkeley, Centre for Research on Criminal Justice, 1975; and Frank, op. cit., 281-2.

68 I am very grateful to David Skidmore for much help with this section and for guiding me to appropriate literature. Some of this includes M. Mamalakis and C. Reynolds, *Essays on the Chilean Economy*, Homewood, Ill., Richard D. Irwin, 1965; I. Roxborough *et al.*, *Chile: The State and Revolution*, London, Macmillan, 1977; Brian Loveman, *Struggle in the Countryside: Politics and Rural Labour in Chile, 1919-1973*, Bloomington, University of Indiana Press, 1976; David Skidmore, 'The Chilean experience of change: the primacy of the political', in Adrian Leftwich, op. cit; World Bank, *Chile: an Economy in Transition*, Washington, DC, The World Bank, 1980; Ralph Miliband, 'The coup in Chile', in *Socialist Register 1973*, London, Merlin, 1973; F. B. Pike, *Chile and the United States, 1880-1962*, University of Notre Dame Press, 1963; Brian Loveman, *Chile: the Legacy of Hispanic Capitalism*, New York, Oxford University Press, 1979; M. Cavarozzi and J. Petras, 'Chile', in R. Chilcote and M. Edelstein (eds), *Latin America: the Struggle with Dependency and Beyond*, New York, Wiley, 1974.

69 World Bank, *World Economic and Social Indicators*, Washington, DC, The World Bank, April 1978.

70 P. O'Brien (ed.), *Allende's Chile*, New York, Praeger, 1976, chapter 9; J. Petras and M. Morley, *How Allende Fell*, Nottingham, Spokesman Books, 1974; P. E. Sigmund, *The Overthrow of Allende and the Politics of Chile, 1964-76*, University of Pittsburgh Press, 1977; Arturo Valenzuela, *The Breakdown of Democratic Regimes: Chile*, Baltimore, Md, and London, Johns Hopkins University Press, 1978.

71 Amnesty International, *Chile*, London, Amnesty International Publications, 1974.

72 See Rex Mortimer, 'The downfall of Indonesian Communism', in *Socialist Register 1969*, London, Merlin, 1969.

73 Amnesty International, *Report, 1981*, London, Amnesty International Publications, 1981.

74 A good introduction to China's development may be found in Sartaj Aziz, *Rural Development. Learning from China*, London, Macmillan, 1978; and Benedict Stavis, *People's Communes and Rural Development in China*, Ithaca, NY, Cornell University Rural Development Committee, 1974; and also his *Making Green Revolution: the Politics of Agricultural Development in China*, Ithaca,

NY, Cornell University Rural Development Committee, 1974; Neville Maxwell (ed.), *China's Road to Development*, Oxford, Pergamon Press, 2nd edn, 1979. R. H. Tawney's *Land and Labour in China*, London, Allen & Unwin, 1932, still makes good reading.

75 Tawney, op. cit., 77. He also draws attention to the problem of debt, see 58-60.
76 *World Development Report 1981*, tables 1 and 22; 'The 1982 Census results, *Beijing Review*, vol. 25, no. 45, 8 Nov. 1982, p. 20.
77 A. R. Khan, 'The distribution of income in rural China', in International Labour Organization, op. cit., chapter 12.
78 Keith Griffin, *Land Concentration and Rural Poverty*, London, Macmillan, 1981; see chapter 7 on Taiwan.
79 World Bank, *Land Reform. Sector Policy Paper*, Washington, DC, The World Bank, 1975; H. Chenery *et al.*, *Redistribution with Growth*, Oxford University Press, 1974, part 3; F. M. Lappé and J. Collins, *Food First; Beyond the Myth of Scarcity*, London, Souvenir Press, 1980; World Bank, *World Tables*, 374-5; Lipton, op. cit., *passim*; Griffin, op. cit., 272-3.
80 Frank, op. cit., especially chapters 5, 6 and 7.
81 Dudley Seers, 'Cuba' in Chenery *et al.*, op. cit.; John Griffiths and Peter Griffiths (eds), *Cuba: The Second Decade*, London, Writers and Readers Cooperative, 1979; Jorge I. Dominguez, 'Cuba in the 1980s', *Problems of Communism*, March-April 1981; Dunn, op. cit., chapter 8; James O'Connor, *The Origins of Socialism in Cuba*, Ithaca, NY, Cornell University Press, 1970; Wolf, op. cit., chapter 6. On Cuban debt, see *Wall Street Journal*, 1 September 1982.
82 Lipton, op. cit., chapter 1 and table 1.1.

CHAPTERS 9 AND 10
EQUAL RIGHTS, UNEQUAL OPPORTUNITIES:
POLITICS IN INDUSTRIAL SOCIETIES, THE CASE OF BRITAIN

1 The questions of 'objectivity' in social science is a central one, whether the society concerned is one's own or another. There is a bristling literature on the question, stretching back to the classics. See for instance, Max Weber, *The Methodology of the Social Sciences*, Chicago, The Free Press, 1949, and also such works as Peter Winch, *The Idea of a Social Science*, London, Routledge & Kegan Paul, 1958; W. G. Runciman, *Social Science and Political Theory*, Cambridge University Press, 1965; Lucien Goldman, *The Human Sciences and Philosophy*, London, Cape, 1969, and E. H. Carr, *What is History?*, Harmondsworth, Penguin, 1964.
2 See *The Government Reply to the Fifth Report from the Home Affairs Committee, 1980-81, Racial Disadvantage*, London, HMSO, 1982.
3 There is a vast literature on British politics. Amongst the most popular of the college texts are R. M. Punnett, *British Government and Politics*, London, Heinemann, 1970; Graeme C. Moodie, *The Government of Great Britain*, London, Methuen, 1965; Richard Rose, *Politics in England*, London, Faber, 2nd edn, 1980; J. Blondel, *Voters, Parties and Leaders*, Harmondsworth, Penguin, 1965; Samuel H. Beer, *Modern British Politics*, London, Faber, 1969; Richard Rose, *The Problem of Party Government*, London, Macmillan, 1974; and J. P.

Mackintosh, *The Government and Politics of Britain*, London, Hutchinson, 1982.

4   One author has recently argued that a major crisis of industrial 'democratic' societies is the confrontation 'between democratic distributions of power and capitalist distributions of goods' (Hugh Stretton, *Capitalism, Socialism and the Environment*, Cambridge University Press, 1976, 1). This expresses the point in a useful but limited way. The point I make here is that power is *not* distributed democratically, nor is its use democratic, in either the private or public spheres. Indeed, the private sphere - of production and employment - which is the dominant sphere, is substantially bereft of any democratic principles or procedures, as I have argued before, because private ownership is incompatible with democratic control and management.

5   Phyllis Deane and W. A. Cole, *British Economic Growth, 1688-1959*, Cambridge University Press, 1969, 155-6.

6   Central Statistical Office, *Facts in Focus*, Harmondsworth, Penguin, in association with HMSO, 1980, table 156, p. 187; and HMSO, *Britain 1982*, London, HMSO, 178.

7   J. F. Wright, *Britain in the Age of Economic Management*, Oxford University Press, 1979, 27; *Britain 1982*, table 29, p. 288.

8   World Bank, *World Development Report*, Washington, DC, The World Bank, 1981, table 20, pp. 172-3.

9   L. J. Williams, *Britain and the World Economy, 1919-1970*, London, Fontana, 1971, 10.

10 R. Mordue and J. Parrett, 'UK self-sufficiency in food, 1970-8', in *Economic Trends*, no. 312, October 1979, London, Central Statistical Office, 151-5; see also *Britain 1982*, 253.

11 Barclays Bank, *Finance for Farmers and Growers, 1980-81*, 50. Also, *Food from Our Own Resources*, Cmnd 6020, London, HMSO, 1975.

12 *Annual Statement of the Overseas Trade of the UK* (1975), London, HMSO, 1978, vol IV, Country Figures of Imports and Exports, table II.

13 The formal categories here include (a) crude inedible materials, not fuels, (b) minerals, fuels and lubricants and (c) chemicals. ibid., table I.

14 ibid., table II. Machinery, cars etc. and manufactured goods accounted for nearly 40 per cent of imports in 1975.

15 ibid., Exports, table IV; see also M. Kidron and R. Segal, *The State of the World Atlas*, London, Pan, 1981, table 10; and Sam Aaronovitch *et al.*, *The Political Economy of British Capitalism*, London, McGraw-Hill, 1981, 145.

16 Confederation of British Industry, *The Will to Win*, London, CBI, 1981; The Trades Union Congress, *The Reconstruction of Britain*, London, TUC, 1981.

17 A useful way of distinguishing *wealth* and *income* is that the former is a *stock*, the latter is a flow over time. 'The term "distribution of wealth" refers to the distribution of physical and financial assets, whereas the "distribution of income" refers to receipts accruing from the ownership of assets (and from other sources such as earnings) in a given period.' See A. B. Atkinson, *Unequal Shares, Wealth in Britain*, Harmondsworth, Penguin, 1974, p. 5 and chapter 1, *passim*.

18 Doreen Massey and Alejandro Catalano, *Capital and Land. Land Ownership by Capital in Great Britain*, London, Edward Arnold, 1978, 4; James Bellini, *Rule*

Britannia, London, Cape, 1981, 115 and *passim*.

19 *Report of the Commission of Inquiry into the Acquisition and Occupancy of Agricultural Land* (The Northfield Report), London, HMSO, 1979, Cmnd 7595, 109; and The Royal Commission on the Distribution of Income and Wealth (The Diamond Commission), *Report No. 7*, Cmnd 7595, London, HMSO, 1979, 152.

20 Massey, op. cit., 6; Bellini; op. cit., 113.

21 The Northfield Report, 30.

22 The Diamond Commission, *Report No. 7*, table 6.13, p. 150.

23 Massey, op. cit., table 3.6, pp. 59-60. In recent years the financial institutions (like insurance companies and pension funds) have turned to investment in land, which is a good hedge against inflation.

24 Counter Information Services, *The Wealthy*, London, CIS, n.d., 15.

25 Central Statistical Office, op. cit., table 45, p. 63; see also Ivan Reid, *Social Class Differences in Britain*, London, Grant McIntyre, 1981, 192; Peter Townsend, *Poverty in the United Kingdom*, Harmondsworth, Penguin, 1979, 514-16. It is important to remember that although a majority of people 'own' their houses or flats, less than 20 per cent own them outright, since most are on a mortgage which has not been paid off.

26 The Diamond Commission, *Report No. 7*, table 6.14, p. 151.

27 Massey, op. cit., 10-11.

28 ibid., 12.

29 John McEwen, *Who Owns Scotland*, Edinburgh, Polygon Books, rev. edn, 1980, 109 and *passim*; The Diamond Commission, *Report No. 7*, 152.

30 The Northfield Report, 32.

31 Massey, op. cit., 6; Bellini, op. cit., 116-17.

32 The Diamond Commission, *Report No. 7*, 84-7. Liabilities (loans, HP arrangements and payable accounts) have been deducted from the gross figure to give the net figure.

33 ibid., 88-91.

34 ibid., 149-51.

35 ibid., 95, and Townsend, op. cit., 146. See also John Westergaard and H. Resler, *Class in a Capitalist Society*, Harmondsworth, Penguin, 1976, 110-11; A. B. Atkinson, *The Economics of Inequality*, Oxford University Press, 1974, 134; Trevor Noble, *Modern Britain, Structure and Change*, London, Batsford, 1975, 172-5.

36 Noble, op. cit., 305 ff.; Atkinson, *Unequal Shares*, 42.

37 Westergaard and Resler, op. cit., and P. Stanworth and A. Giddens (eds), *Elites and Power in British Society*, Cambridge University Press, 1974.

38 Atkinson, *Unequal Shares*, 38-43; Westergaard and Resler, op. cit., 117; Counter Information Services, op. cit., 11; Atkinson, *The Economics of Inequality*, 135.

39 P. E. Hart, M. A. Utton and G. Walshe, *Mergers and Concentration in British Industry*, Cambridge University Press, 1973; 2-3; G. Locksley, 'The UK economy, 1960-1979, a generation of decline', *Politics*, vol. 1, no. 2, November 1971; and S. J. Prais, *The Evolution of Giant Firms in Britain*, Cambridge University Press, 1976; Wright, op. cit., 66-7; *Britain 1982*, 183; *Social Trends, 12*, London, HMSO, table 4.9, p. 67.

40 Prais, op. cit., 10; *Britain 1982*, table 15, p. 200.

41 Prais, op. cit., table 1.3, p. 10; Wright, op. cit., 66-7; *Report of Registrar of Friendly Societies, 1980*, London, HMSO, 1981, 36; *Britain 1982*, 224.

42 Prais, op. cit., 164; and *Britain 1982*, 183-4.

43 Department of Industry, 'The importance of the top 100 manufacturing companies', *Economic Trends*, no. 274, London, HMSO, August 1976, 85 and *passim*; *Britain 1982*, 187.

44 See The Diamond Commission, *Report No. 7*, 157; Townsend, op. cit., chapter 4; A. B. Atkinson, *The Economics of Inequality*, chapter 4.

45 Atkinson, op. cit., 51.

46 The Diamond Commission, *Report No. 7*, table 1.7, p. 157.

47 Guy Routh, Dorothy Wedderburn and B. Wootton, *The Roots of Pay Inequalities*, London, The Low Pay Unit, 1980, 6 and *passim*; see also The Royal Commission on the Distribution of Income and Wealth (The Diamond Commission), *Report No. 8*, Cmnd 7679, London, HMSO, 1979, chapter 14.

48 A. B. Atkinson, *The Economics of Inequality*, 17, 23 and 74-8; also Bellini, op. cit., 72-4; Townsend, op. cit., 133-42.

49 D. Wedderburn, 'Inequalities in pay', in Routh *et al.*, op. cit., 12-13; Atkinson, op. cit., 18-19; Townsend, op. cit., 136-41.

50 Pauline Gluklich and Mandy Snell, *Women: Work and Wages*, London, The Low Pay Unit, 1982, table 6, 4.

51 For some basic figures for the USA with regard to the distribution of both wealth and income see Paul Samuelson, *Economics*, New York, McGraw Hill, 11th edn, 1980, 79-84. For the European countries, see 'Social change in OECD Countries', *OECD Observer*, no. 10, November 1980.

52 A great deal has been written in the literature of political science on 'power'. Readers will find a useful introduction to some recent debates on the subject in Stephen Lukes, *Power: A Radical View*, London, Macmillan, 1976. See also his essay 'Power and structure' in his *Essays in Social Theory*, London, Macmillan, 1977.

53 J. K. Galbraith, *The New Industrial State*, Harmondsworth, Penguin, 1969, where he explores some aspects of the power of modern corporations today.

54 S. E. Finer, *Comparative Government*, Harmondsworth, Penguin, 1974, 176 and 178.

55 One of the classic explanations of an institutional and psychological kind of why this should be so for political parties and trade unions was given by Robert Michels in his *Political Parties*, New York, Dover Publications, 1959 edn, first published in English in 1915. A useful recent introduction to some modern aspects of the issue may be found in Peter Bachrach, *The Theory of Democratic Elitism*, University of London Press, 1969.

56 For a good introduction to all this, see the essays by W. L. Guttsman, 'The British political élite and the class structure' and C. J. Hewitt, 'Elites and the distribution of power in British society', in Stanworth and Giddens, op. cit.; Noble, op. cit., chapter 9; and Westergaard and Resler, op. cit., part 3; and Jean Blondel, *Voters, Parties and Leaders*, Harmondsworth, Penguin, 1965.

57 *Sunday Times*, London, 14 March 1982, 56-7.

58 On quangos, see Anthony Barker (ed.), *Quangos in Britain*, London, Macmillan, 1982, especially the chapters by Richard Wilding on 'A triangular affair: quangos, ministers and MPs', and Anne Davies, 'Patronage and quasi-

government: some proposals for reform', especially 171-2. Also, Philip Holland, *The Governance of Quangos*, London, Adam Smith Institute, 1981. On the problem of classifying government and quasi-government bodies, see Christopher Hood and Andrew Dunsire, *Bureaumetrics. The Quantitiative Comparison of British Central Government Agencies*, London, Gower, 1981, especially chapters 3 and 8. A good example of the informal but highly political system of appointments is given by David Donnison in his account of how he came to be appointed Chairman of the Supplementary Benefits Commission, in his book *The Politics of Poverty*, Oxford, Martin Robertson, 1982, chapter 3. The book also gives, in passing, some very interesting insights into the way in which senior civil servants can, on occasions, seek and ensure that the workings of their departments are not opened up to wider participation (or scrutiny) and how they can ensure that access to information and arguments going on inside a government body like the Supplementary Benefits Commission is restricted.

59 Stanworth and Giddens (eds), op. cit.; Westergaard and Resler, op. cit., part 3; Noble, op. cit.; Anthony Sampson, *The Anatomy of Britain Today*, London, Hodder & Stoughton, 1965, *passim*; Reid, op. cit., chapter 8.

60 Ralph Miliband, *The State in Capitalist Society*, London, Weidenfeld & Nicholson, 1969.

61 An amusing account of this may be found in Sampson, op. cit., chapters 1 and 18.

62 *Whitakers Almanack 1982*, London, 1982.

63 For instance, see Norman Dennis, *People and Planning*, London, Faber, 1970; and his *Public Participation and Planner's Blight*, London, Faber, 1972; and Michael Fagence, *Citizen Participation in Planning*, Oxford, Pergamon Press, 1977.

64 Foreign and Commonwealth Office, *Report on the Supply of Petroleum and Petroleum Products to Rhodesia* (The Bingham Enquiry), London, HMSO, 1978; and see also Peter Kellner and Lord Crowther-Hunt, *The Civil Servants, an Inquiry into Britain's Ruling Class*, London, Macdonald, 1980, 277. South African Institute of Race Relations, *Survey of Race Relations, 1976*, 269-72.

65 Attempts to get more information on the operations and expenditure of the Nationwide Building Society met with just such opposition from the Board in March 1982. See *The Guardian*, London, 27 March 1982.

66 See 'Yes, or then again no, Minister', *The Times*, London, 9 March 1982.

67 Ronald E. Wraith, 'United Kingdom' in Donald C. Rowat (ed.), *Administrative Secrecy in Developed Countries*, London, Macmillan, 1979, 188 and *passim*.

68 B. Donoughue, 'Between you and me, secrecy is here to stay', *The Times*, London, 25 February 1982.

69 James Michael, *The Politics of Secrecy*, Harmondsworth, Penguin, 1982, 18 and *passim*; and Rosemary Delbridge and Martin Smith, *Consuming Secrets; How Official Secrecy Affects Everyday Life in Britain*, London, Burnett Books, 1982, *passim*, and see Appendix A.

70 Maurice Frankel, *The Alkali Inspectorate, The Control of Industrial Pollution*, London, Social Audit, 1974; and Michael, op. cit., *passim*.

71 See *The Public Records Act, 1958* and *The Administration of Justice Act, 1970*, sections 31-3.

72 *Britain 1982*, 47.

73 Hugo Young, *The Crossman Affair*, London, Hamish Hamilton and Jonathan Cape, 1976.

74 This list was submitted to the Select Committee on Parliamentary Questions and is contained in Appendix 9 of its *Report*, London, HMSO, 1972, H. C., 393.

75 ibid., Appendix 9.

76 Michael, op. cit., 67; Kellner and Crowther-Hunt, op. cit., 277.

77 Glasgow University Media Group, *Bad News*, London, Routledge & Kegan Paul, 1976, and *More Bad News* (vol II), London, Routledge & Kegan Paul, 1980; and E. P. Thompson, 'The segregation of dissent', in his *Writing by Candlelight*, London, Merlin, 1980.

78 Bellini, op. cit., 217. A former assistant to the Director General of the BBC admitted quite openly on a Radio 4 programme that his office was regularly 'leant on' by members of the government and officials. Peter Hardiman Scott, on *Start The Week*, BBC Radio 4, 29 March 1982.

79 Bellini, op. cit., 217 and 229; Michael, op. cit., 12.

80 See especially *The 'D' Notice System*, Cmnd 3312, London, HMSO, 1967; and *The Report of the Committee of Privy Counsellors Appointed to Enquire into 'D' Notice Matters*, Cmnd 3309, London, HMSO, 1967.

81 Crispin Aubrey, *Who's Watching You?*, Harmondsworth, Penguin, 1981; and his article in *The New Statesman*, London, 1 February 1980; and Peter Laurie, *Beneath the City Streets*, London, Panther, rev. edn, 1979.

82 Reported on *Panorama*, BBC TV, 8 March 1982; and Jeremy Tunstall, *The Westminster Lobby Correspondents*, London, Routledge & Kegan Paul, 1970.

83 Kellner and Crowther-Hunt, op. cit., 275 and chapter 11 generally.

84 There is a substantial literature on 'class' in Britain and industrial societies more generally. Good and important accounts may be found in T. B. Bottomore, *Classes in Modern Society*, London, Allen & Unwin, 1965; R. Dahrendorf, *Class and Class Conflict in Industrial Society*, Palo Alto, Calif., Stanford University Press, 1959; W. G. Runciman, *Relative Deprivation and Social Justice*, London, Routledge & Kegan Paul, 1966; Anthony Giddens, *The Class Structure of the Advanced Industrial Societies*, London, Hutchinson, 1973; Nicos Poulantzas, *Classes in Contemporary Capitalism*, London, Verso, 1978.

85 E. P. Thompson, 'The peculiarities of the English', in Ralph Miliband and John Saville (eds), *Socialist Register 1965*, London, Merlin, 1966, 357.

86 These are taken from Ivan Reid, *Social Class Differences in Britain*, London, Grant McIntyre, 2nd edn, 1981, 40-1. This is a superb book which provides rich data. All students in the social sciences ought to have and digest this book. I rely on it heavily in this section. Much of his data comes from the *1971 Census* and other official surveys and reports.

87 Reid, op. cit., table 3.1, p. 71.

88 B. E. Coates and E. M. Rawstron, *Regional Variations in Britain*, London, Batsford, 1971, 289 and *passim*.

89 Coates and Rawstron, op. cit., figure 11.2, p. 285; Reid, op. cit., table 3.6, p. 79.

90 Reid, op. cit., table 3.9, p. 84.

91 Department of Employment, *New Earnings Survey, 1981*, London, HMSO, part D, tables 86 and 87.

92 The Diamond Commission, *Report No. 8*, tables 6.8 and 6.9; and Reid, op. cit., table 3.12, p. 92.

93 Reid, op. cit., 192.
94 *General Household Survey, 1979*, London, HMSO, 1980, table 3.12, p. 41.
95 Reid, op. cit., 199 and 265; and Central Statistical Office, *Social Trends 11*, London, HMSO, 1981, 167 and their *Regional Trends, 1981*, London, HMSO, 1981.
96 Reid, op. cit., 222-5; A. H. Halsey, *Change in British Society*, Oxford University Press, 1978, 126 and chapter 6, *passim*; Julian Le Grand, *The Strategy of Equality*, London, Allen & Unwin, 1982, 56-60.
97 *Britain 1982*, 136; Sampson, op. cit., *passim*; Reid, op. cit., 226; Westergaard and Resler, op. cit., 255.
98 *Whitaker's Almanack 1982*, 535-44. Girls' schools like Badminton, Benenden and Roedean have annual fees between £3200 and £3600. See also *The Observer*. London, 17 September 1981.
99 Reid, op. cit., 225-7; Le Grand, op. cit., 67.
100 Reid, op. cit., 239. A slightly different way of measuring this reveals that 50 per cent of university *entrants* in 1977 were from Social Classes I and II, while 24 per cent were from Social Class III, and 24 per cent from Social Classes IV and V together.
101 ibid., table 6.2, p. 207.
102 Lesley Doyal, *The Political Economy of Health*, London, Merlin, 1979, 85-6.
103 J. M. Tanner, *Foetus into Man*, London, Open Books, 1978, 146-53; and R. Davie, N. Butler and H. Goldstein, *From Birth to Seven*, London, Longman, 1972, chapter 8.
104 Reid, op. cit., 98-101, 165-7, and 212.
105 ibid., 71.
106 The Diamond Commissions, *Report No. 8*, table 6.4, pp. 74-5.
107 A. V. Glass (ed.), *Social Mobility in Britain*, London, Routledge & Kegan Paul, 1954; A. J. Harris and R. Clausen, *Labour Mobility in Britain, 1953-1963*, London, HMSO, 1967; J. H. Goldthorpe *et al.*, *Social Mobility and Class Structure in Modern Britain*, Oxford University Press, 1980. See also Westergaard and Resler, op. cit., part 4; and Halsey, op. cit.
108 All this data is from Reid, op. cit., chapters 5 and 7.
109 A classic is of course George Orwell's *The Road to Wigan Pier* (1937), Harmondsworth, Penguin, 1962. But see also the studies by Richard Hoggart, *The Uses of Literacy*, Harmondsworth, Penguin, 1958; Norman Dennis, F. M. Henriques and C. Slaughter, *Coal is Our Life*, London, Eyre & Spottiswoode, 1957; Peter Willmott and Michael Young, *Family and Kinship in East London*, Harmondsworth, Penguin, 1962; Ronald Frankenberg, *Communities in Britain*, Harmondsworth, Penguin, 1966; Josephine Klein, *Samples from English Culture*, 2 vols, London, Routledge & Kegan Paul, 1965.
110 Marx to Sorge, 19 October 1877, cited in M. Evans, *Karl Marx*, London, Allen & Unwin, 1975, 95; and F. Engels, *The Condition of the Working Class in England*, London, Panther, 1969 edn. This was written originally in 1844-5 but published in English in 1887.
111 Sir T. Beckett, CBE, in the Confederation of British Industry, *The Will to Win*, London, CBI, 1981, 4.
112 Lorna Marshall, *The !Kung of Nyae Nyae*, Cambridge, Mass., Harvard University Press, 1976, chapter 10 and p. 314.

113 One such study is being undertaken by Marion Kerr, in the Sociology Department of the University of York. It is funded by the Health Education Council and is on 'Attitudes to the feeding and nutrition of young children'. See also Christine Delphy, 'Sharing the same table: consumption and the family', in Chris Harris (ed.), *The Sociology of the Family*, Sociological Review Monograph, no. 28, June 1979, University of Keele.

114 Arthur Brittan, *The Privatized World*, London, Routledge & Kegan Paul, 1978, chapter 3.

115 A provocative discussion of this may be found in Alasdair MacIntyre, *Secularization and Moral Change*, Oxford University Press, 1967.

116 *Social Trends, 12*, table 11.7, p. 191, and table 11.11, p. 193.

117 See for instance, Marvin Harris, *Cannibals and Kings*, London, Fontana/Collins, 1978, chapter 7.

118 World Bank, *World Development Report, 1981*, Washington, DC, The World Bank, 1981, table 1, p. 135. The GNP *per capita* in dollars in 1979 for Britain was $6320, compared with $8160 for Finland, $8360 for Austria, $8810 for Japan, $9640 for Canada, $9950 for France, $10,320 for the Netherlands, $10,630 for the USA and $11,730 for West Germany, compared with $90 for Bangladesh, $160 for Burma, $200 for Malawi, $130 for Nicaragua, $1410 for Cuba, for instance.

119 Donnison, op. cit., 13; *Britain 1982*, 127.

120 Peter Townsend, *Poverty in the United Kingdom*, Harmondsworth, Penguin, 1979, 895.

121 Townsend, op. cit., 898 and 563; also David Piachaud, *Children and Poverty*, London, Child Poverty Action Group, 1981.

122 Donnison, op. cit., 5-6.

123 Townsend, op. cit., 893.

124 See A. B. Atkinson, *Unequal Shares*, part II, and his *The Economics of Inequality*, 155-9, 117-20; Cedric Sanford, 'The Wealth Tax debate' in Frank Field (ed.), op. cit.

125 On the low paid see Frank Field (ed.), *Low Pay*, London, Arrow Books, 1973, and the publications of the Low Pay Unit. 'Low Pay' is usually taken to be earnings which are less than two-thirds of the median for all adult men working full-time, and usually means the bottom 10 per cent of earners in that category. In the 1970s there were more women than men in the category. In 1974 some 1.2 million men and 3.5 million women were low paid. See Chris Trinder, 'The low paid', in Michael Young (ed.), *Poverty Report, 1975*, London, Temple Smith, 1975. Many low paid are found in hotel and catering jobs, in garages and agriculture, and in the manual levels of the public services.

126 *Britain 1982*, 287. This is the official figure. But there is also a lot of disguised unemployment and also unemployment which does not get recorded, often women who do not register as unemployed. So the 'real' figure for unemployment may be a lot higher.

127 Brian Showler and Adrian Sinfield, *The Workless State*, Oxford, Martin Robertson, 1981, 126-9.

128 *Social Trends, 12*, table 4.21, p. 73; and Bernard Crick (ed.), *Unemployment*, London, Methuen, 1981.

129 F. Ridley, 'Unemployed youth in Merseyside', in Crick, op. cit., 20-1.

130   *The Guardian*, London 11 March 1981 and 18 September 1981; and Central
      Statistical Office, *Economic Trends*, London, HMSO, September 1982, table 7.
131   Peter Draper, 'Unemployment can seriously damage your health', *The
      Guardian*, London, 16 November 1981. See the earlier references to this topic in
      chapter 6, note 34.
132   Le Grand, op. cit., p. 39 and chapter 3, *passim*; Department of Health and Social
      Security, *Prevention and Health: Everybody's Business*, London, HMSO,
      1976.
133   Department of Health and Social Security, *Inequalities in Health, Report of a
      Working Group* (The Black Report), London, DHSS, 1980, 191-5.
134   Le Grand, op. cit., 27-8; *Inequalities in Health*, 105-8.
135   Le Grand, op. cit., 35-6.
136   See Richard Kelly, 'The farm's fat cats versus the people', *The Guardian*,
      London, 17 September 1982.

CHAPTER 11
CONCLUSION: THE POVERTY OF POLITICS;
THE POSSIBILITIES OF POLITICS

1   There are some who would take this view further. They identify politics amongst
    some of the primates, notably chimpanzees. See Frans de Waal, *Chimpanzee
    Politics*, London, Cape, 1982.
2   Some indication of the general patterns and preoccupations of the discipline may
    be gained by looking at the various panels of topics which are discussed at the
    annual meetings of the Political Studies Association. Even in 1982, they remain
    primarily of the traditional kind - nationalism, parties, bureaucracy, rights, the
    state, cabinet and ministerial matters, law, legislative reform and so on. See the
    Political Studies Association *Newsletter*, 22, February 1982. Of course there are
    exceptions. For instance, the January 1981 issue of *Political Quarterly* was
    devoted to unemployment and raised some important issues. There is also an
    increasing number of monographs - sometimes emerging from within the
    discipline of Politics, but often not - on current problems in the politics of Britain
    and other societies. A new series, edited by Bernard Crick, on *Politics Today* is
    one such example. It seeks to introduce students to such matters as the politics of
    poverty, town planning, inner cities, transport, energy, law and order. It is still the
    case, however, that few books of this kind find their way on to course reading lists.
    It is also important to refer to the general areas of 'political economy' and
    'political sociology' which have produced important work far beyond the
    concerns of traditional institutional, political and social analysis. Scholars working
    in many corners of these fields have combined aspects of Economics, Politics and
    Sociology in their work - notably in the field of development studies, though the
    seepage of such approaches into mainstream Politics is slow.
        For a rather dismal but, I am afraid, representative account of the central
    concerns of 'mainstream' Politics, see Jean Blondel, *The Discipline of Politics*,
    London, Butterworth, 1981. Elsewhere, the 'post-mortem of a profession', as one
    reviewer called it, is surveyed in the interesting accounts offered by a number of
    political scientists of their view of the discipline over the last twenty-five years. See

Government and Opposition, 15 (3-4), 1981. It makes interesting but gloomy reading.

3 J. P. Nettl, 'Political studies in universities in Great Britain', a paper presented to the Political Studies Association, March 1966, mimeo.

4 John Rawls, *A Theory of Justice*, Oxford University Press, 1972; Robert Nozick, *Anarchy, State and Utopia*, Oxford, Blackwell, 1974.

5 I have discussed some aspects of these and other pedagogic questions at length elsewhere. See Adrian Leftwich, 'The politics of case study: problems of innovation in university teaching', *Higher Education Review*, 13 (2), Spring 1981: and 'Social science, social relevance and the politics of educational development', *International Journal of Educational Development*, I (3), January 1982.

Index

Adams, John Quincy, 125
administration, colonial, 130, 133, 137
advertising, 246
Africa, 123, 149, 159, 167, 173, 186, 210;
agricultural societies, 133, 161; foraging
societies, 38-9; imperialism, colonialism in,
24, 126, 131-3, 146-7, 148, 154; military
intervention in government, 189-90;
Portuguese penetration of, 123-4; *see also*
East, South *and* West Africa *and* Third
World
age-set system, 71-3, 225
agricultural societies, 14, 17, 28, 46-8,
78-82, 133, 160, 161, 165-9, 210;
commercial, 14, 80, 167-8; shifting
cultivation, 17, 160, 161, 165; subsistence,
14, 79, 168
agriculture, 17, 46-7, 140, 159; cash-
cropping, 80, 111, 147, 167-8; commercial,
14, 80, 105-6, 210; export, 167-9; shifting
cultivation ('slash and burn'), 17, 48, 161;
subsistence, 14, 79, 80, 168, 169, 210; in
Third World, 165-9
Algeria, 128, 163, 184
Alkali Inspectorate, 231
Allende, Salvador, 192-3
Angola, 124, 131, 193, 194, 199
apartheid, 134, 136, 138, 139
appointments system, 227-8
archaeology, 13, 100-1
Argentina, 131, 152, 167, 171, 172, 185,
186, 188
armaments, 187-8, 189, 208
Asia, 120, 148, 159, 184-5, 186, 210,
274n.6; agricultural societies, 133, 161;
European penetration of, 122, 124-6, 146,
147-8, 154; 'hydraulic civilizations', 147,
159; landlessness, 172-3; *see also* Third
World
Aztecs, 43-63, 118, 119, 148; clans, 50-1,
55; culture and ideology, 52, 57-60;
distributional systems, 45, 52, 55-6;
human sacrifice and cannibalism, 45,

58-60; power system, 18, 50, 52, 54-6;
productive system, 45, 50-1, 52-4; religion
and priesthood, 20, 51, 55, 57-9; slavery,
53; social organization, 45, 50, 52, 54-7

Bangladesh, 163, 164, 166, 167, 171, 172-3,
184, 188; 1974 famine, 174-5
Bengal, 111, 112, 144, 147-8
Biafra, 177-8
Bingham Commission, 229-30
Black Report (*Inequalities in Health*), 253
Boer War, 138
Bolivia, 18, 152, 169, 171, 172, 173, 185,
186
Brazil, 17, 39, 106-7, 127-8, 131, 171, 185,
188, 190; income distribution, 173;
industrialization, 153, 163; landlessness,
172, 173
Britain, 200-58; arms sales, 189, 208; class,
16, 227-8, 235-43, 253-5; colonialism and
empire, 130-1, 133, 143-6, 149, in Africa,
126, 133, 135, 137, 138, in North
America, 128, penetration of Asia, 124,
125, in Caribbean, 127, 144-5, control of
India, 124, 143, 144, 148; competition,
202, 244-7, 248; conflict, 142, 200, 205,
256-7; cooperation, 142, 203, 205, 247-8;
culture and ideology, 16, 143, 202, 242-8,
256; as a democracy, 205-6, 220-4, 227,
234, 256; education, 239-41; the Establishment, 20, 227-9, 252; government, 220-4,
229-34; hierarchies, 224-9; honours
system, 228-9; income, national, 146,
personal, 216-18, 224, 238-9; industrial
concentration, 215-16; industrial revolution, 140-6, 206-7; inequalities in, 18, 200,
201, 204-5, 206, 217-18, 235, 237,
248-50, 253-7; ill-health, 109-10, 253-5;
imports/exports, 207-8; institutions, 202,
205, 219-20, 224-8; land ownership, 141,
211-14; politics, 200, 203-6, 209, 211,
223; population, 164, 201, 237; poverty,
201, 248-51; power and decision-making,